O N E

This volume introduces a ton of characters. From now on, don't miss who does what!

—ONE

Manga creator ONE began *One-Punch Man* as a webcomic, which quickly went viral, garnering over 10 million hits. In addition to *One-Punch Man*, ONE writes and draws the series *Mob Psycho 100* and *Makai no Ossan*.

Y U S U K E M U R A T A

I'm going to animation training with my assistants.

—Yusuke Murata

A highly decorated and skilled artist best known for his work on *Eyeshield 21*, Yusuke Murata won the 122nd Hop Step Award (1995) for *Partner* and placed second in the 51st Akatsuka Award (1998) for *Samui Hanashi*.

ONE-PUNCH MAN | 06

ONE + YUSUKE MURATA

★ The stories, characters and incidents mentioned in this publication are ENTIRELY FICTIONAL.

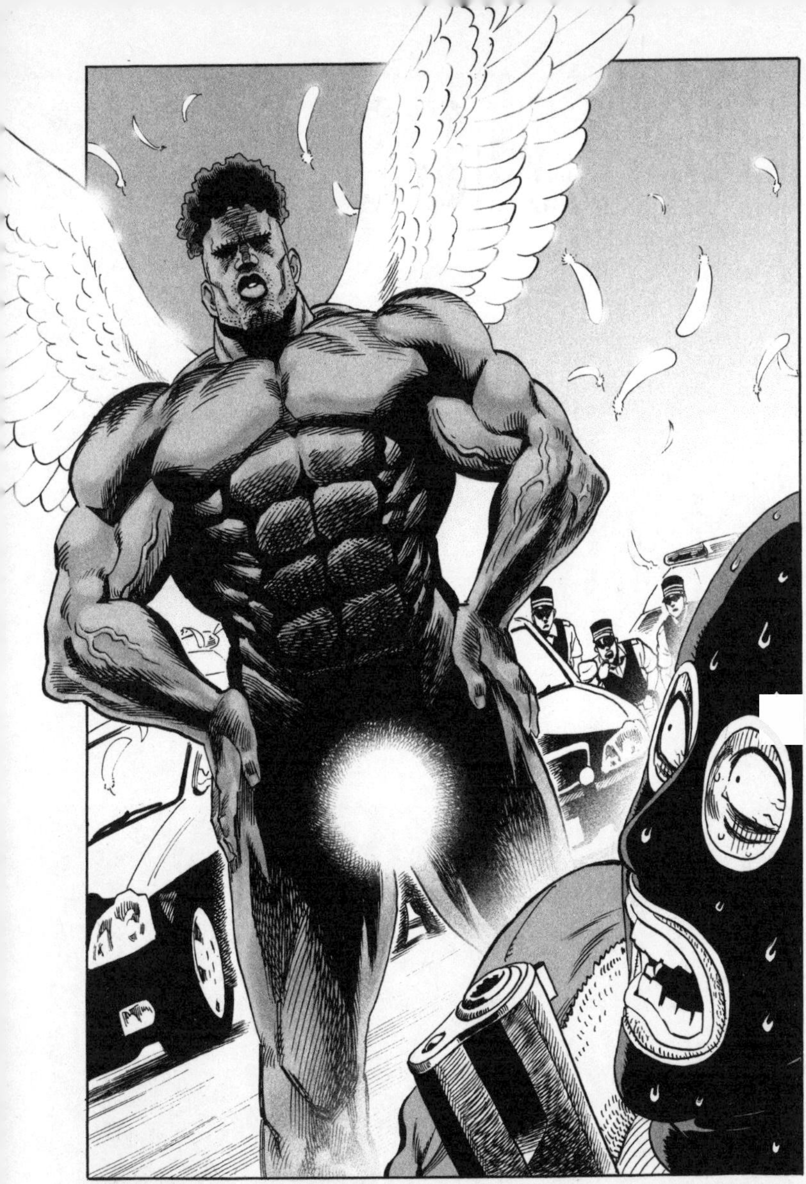

ONE-PUNCH MAN 06

STORY
O N E
ART
YUSUKE
MURATA

TORNADO

SAITAMA

GENOS

PURI-PURI PRISONER

BANG

ONE-PUNCHMAN 6 vol.

THE BIG PREDICTION

CONTENTS

ONE-PUNCH MAN VOLUME SIX

ONE-PUNCH MAN

ONE + YUSUKE MURATA

My name is Saitama. I am a hero. My hobby is heroic exploits. I got too strong. And that makes me sad. I can defeat any enemy with one blow. I lost my hair. And I lost all feeling. I want to feel the rush of battle. I would like to meet an incredibly strong enemy. And I would like to defeat it with one blow. That's because I am One-Punch Man.

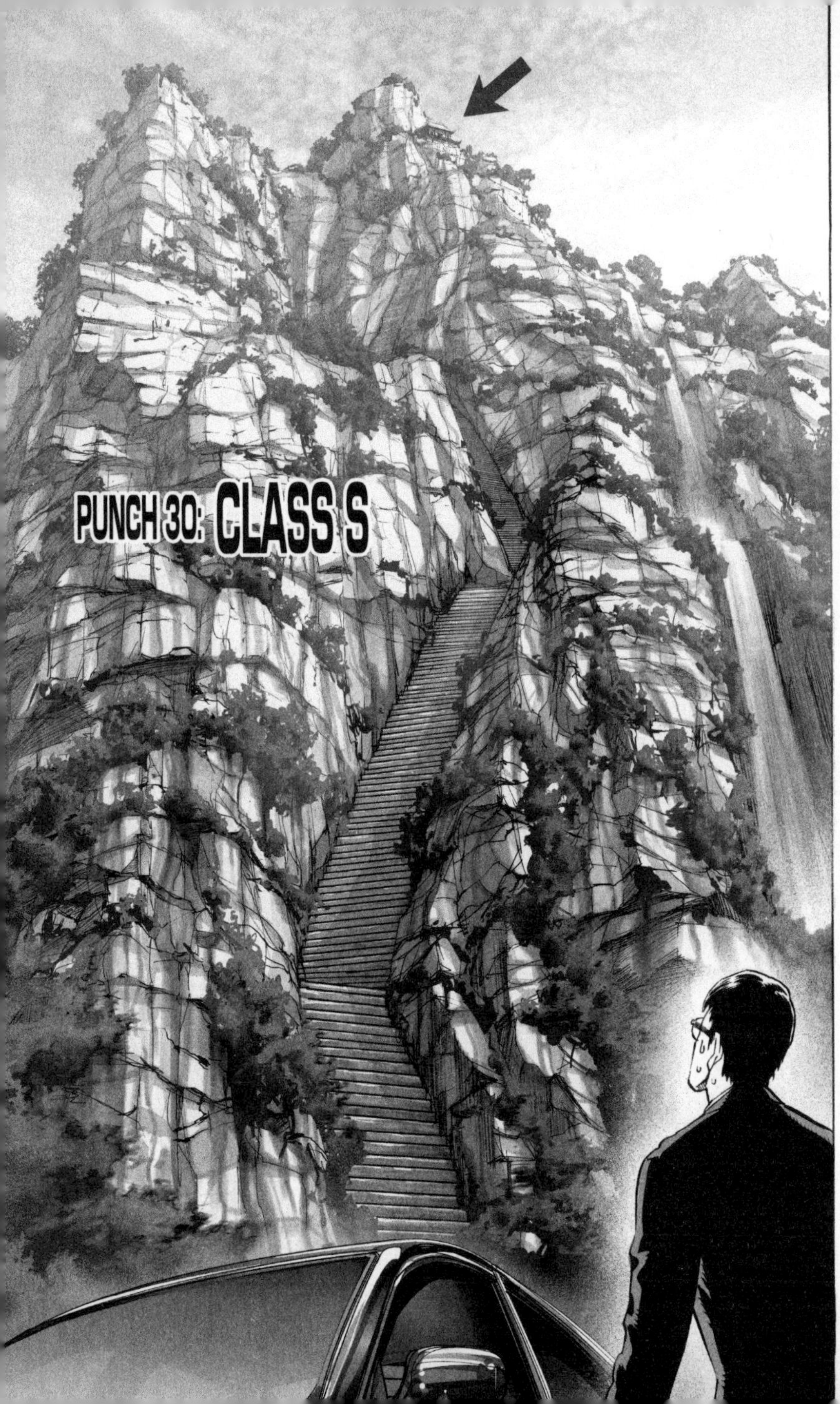
PUNCH 30: CLASS S

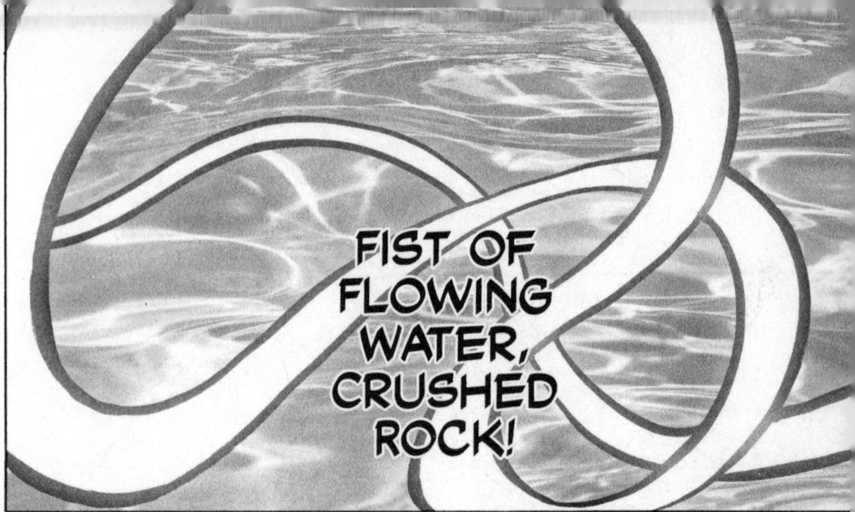
FIST OF FLOWING WATER, CRUSHED ROCK!
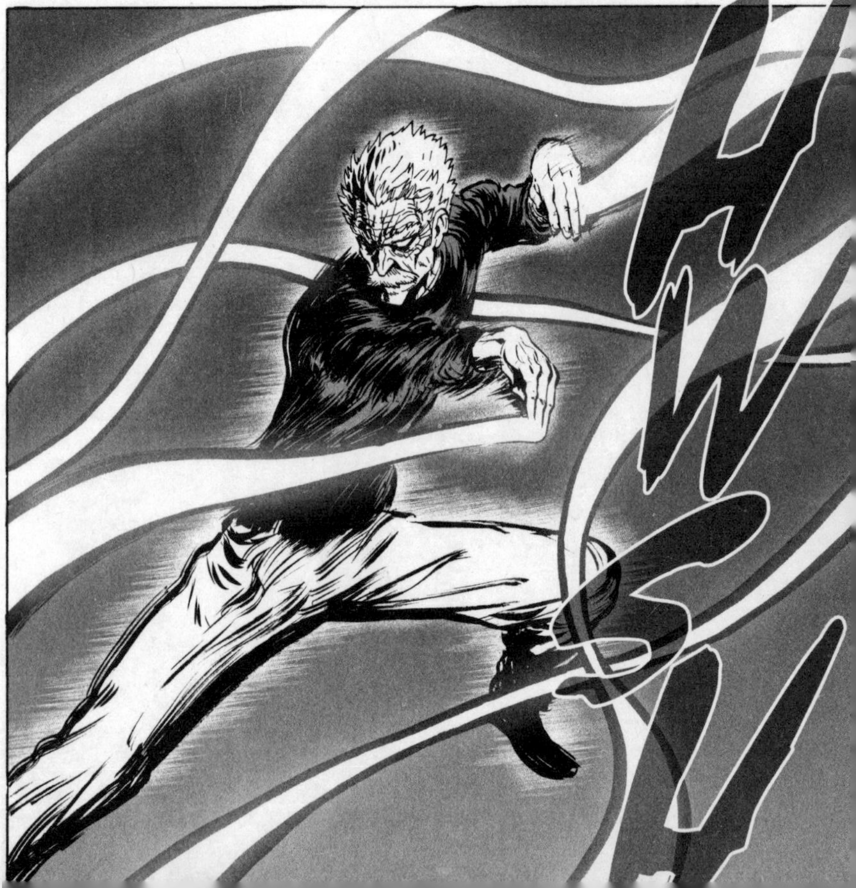

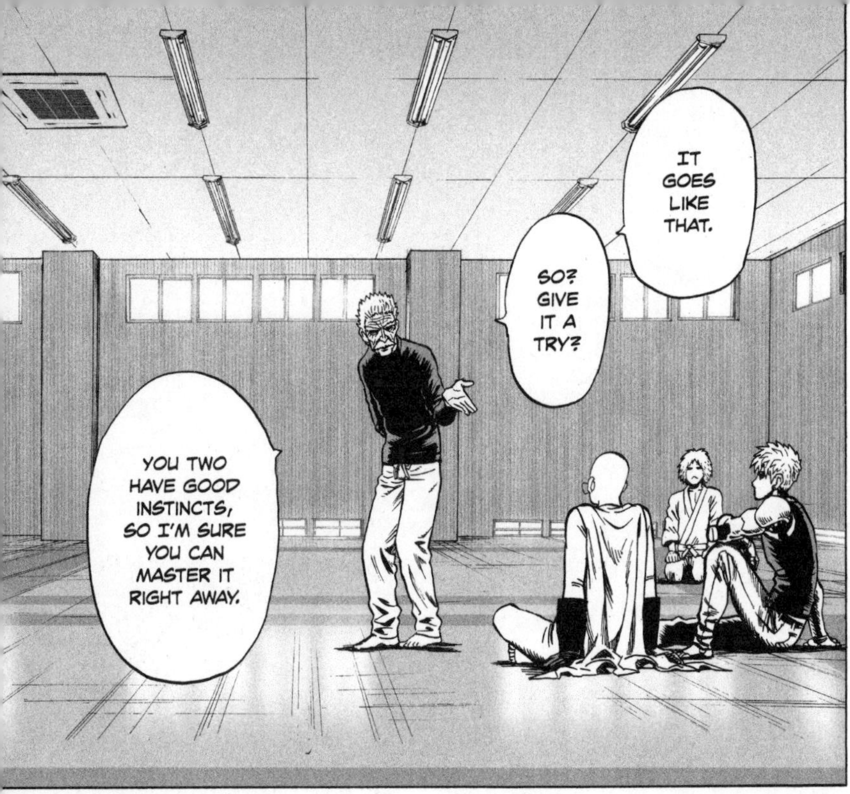
IT GOES LIKE THAT.
SO? GIVE IT A TRY?
YOU TWO HAVE GOOD INSTINCTS, SO I'M SURE YOU CAN MASTER IT RIGHT AWAY.

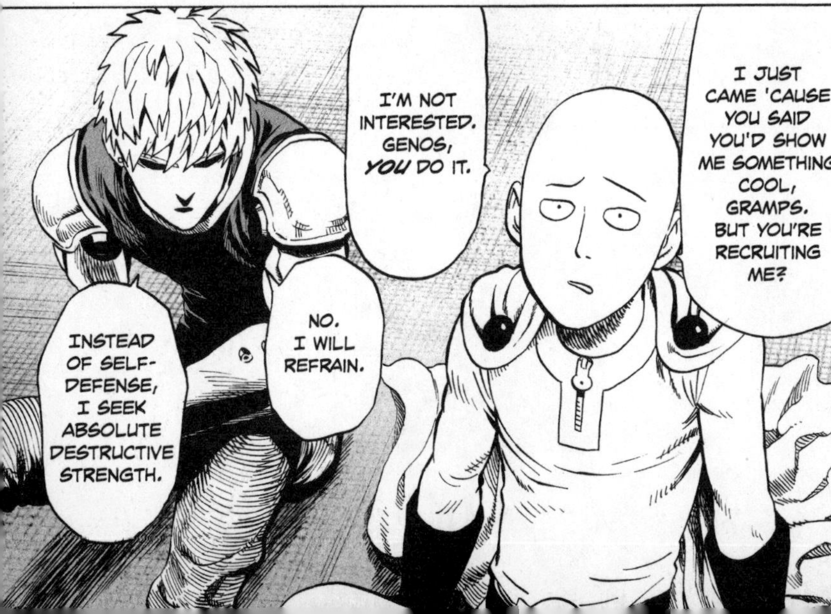
I JUST CAME 'CAUSE YOU SAID YOU'D SHOW ME SOMETHING COOL, GRAMPS. BUT YOU'RE RECRUITING ME?
I'M NOT INTERESTED. GENOS, *YOU* DO IT.
NO. I WILL REFRAIN.
INSTEAD OF SELF-DEFENSE, I SEEK ABSOLUTE DESTRUCTIVE STRENGTH.

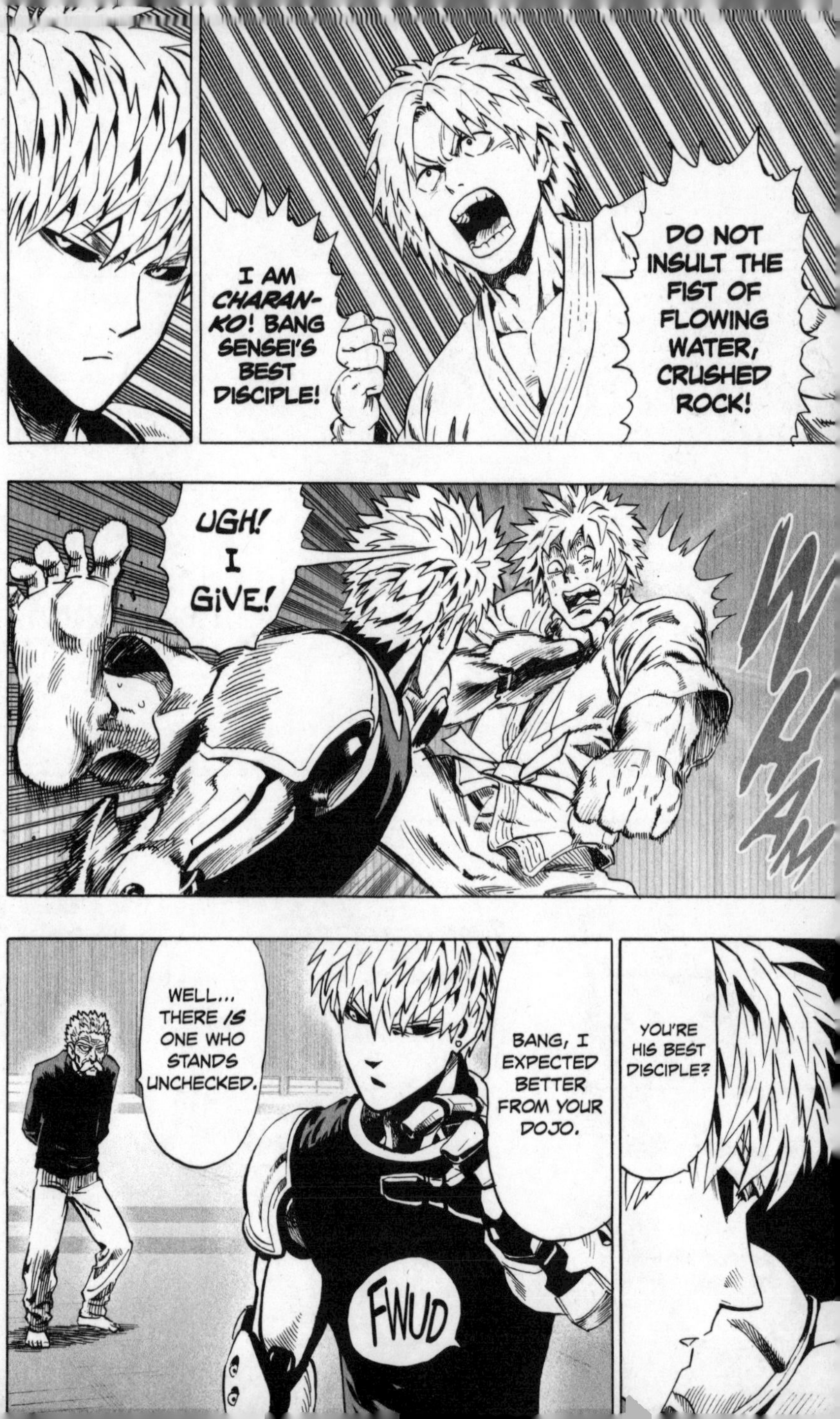
DO NOT INSULT THE FIST OF FLOWING WATER, CRUSHED ROCK!
I AM CHARANKO! BANG SENSEI'S BEST DISCIPLE!
WHAM
UGH! I GIVE!
YOU'RE HIS BEST DISCIPLE?
BANG, I EXPECTED BETTER FROM YOUR DOJO.
WELL... THERE IS ONE WHO STANDS UNCHECKED.
FWUD

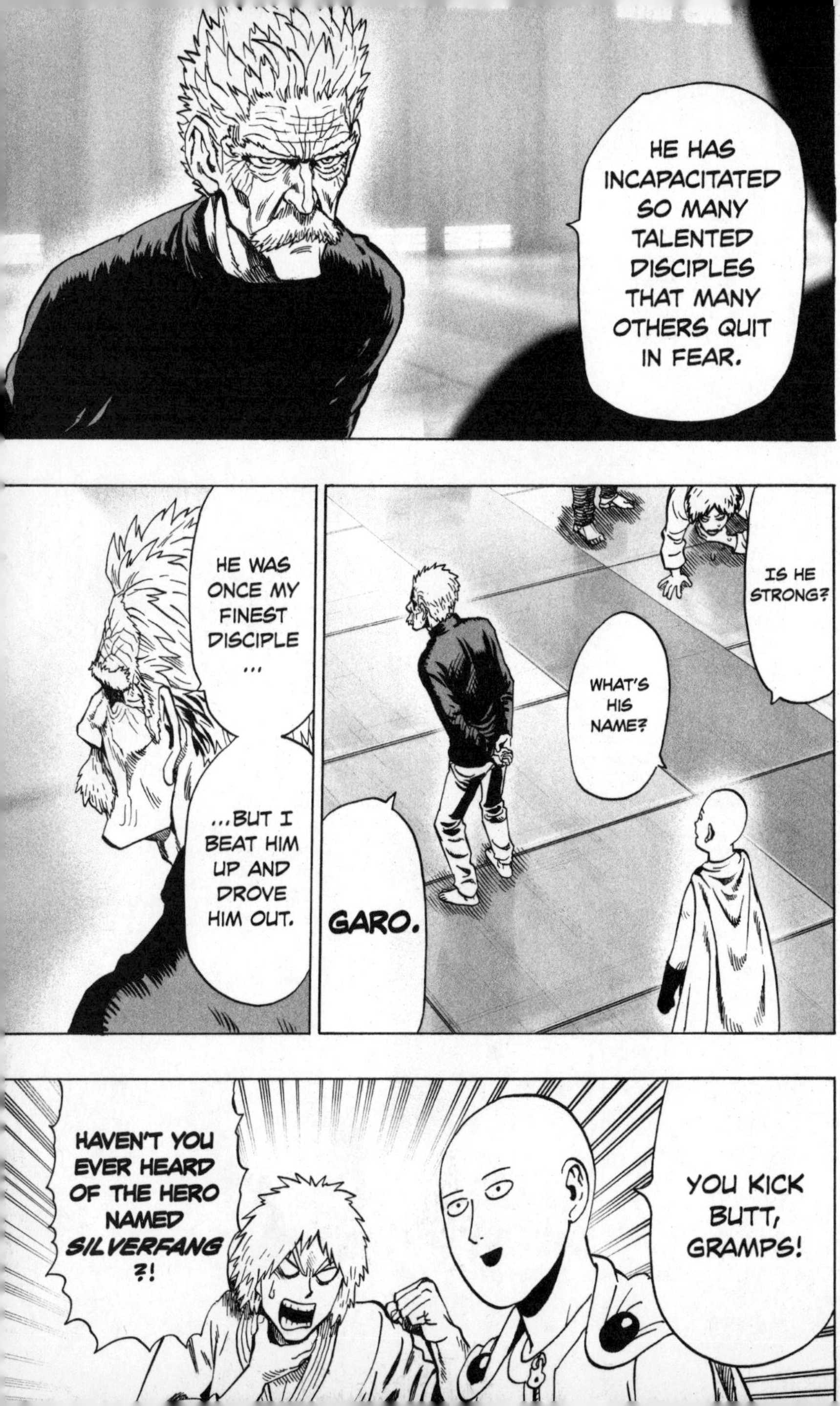
HE HAS INCAPACITATED SO MANY TALENTED DISCIPLES THAT MANY OTHERS QUIT IN FEAR.
IS HE STRONG?
WHAT'S HIS NAME?
GARO.
HE WAS ONCE MY FINEST DISCIPLE ...
...BUT I BEAT HIM UP AND DROVE HIM OUT.
YOU KICK BUTT, GRAMPS!
HAVEN'T YOU EVER HEARD OF THE HERO NAMED SILVERFANG ?!

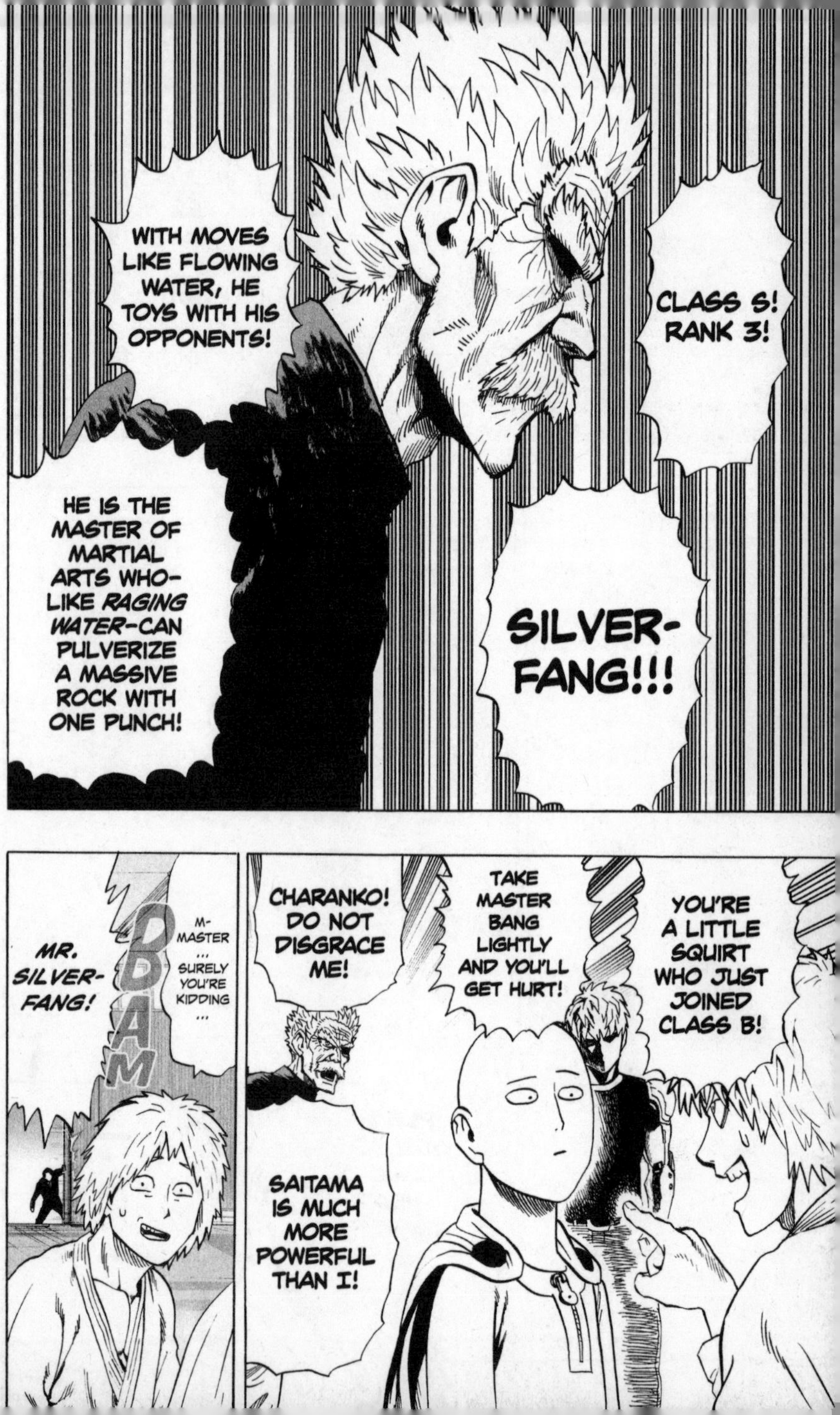
CLASS S! RANK 3!
WITH MOVES LIKE FLOWING WATER, HE TOYS WITH HIS OPPONENTS!
SILVER-FANG!!!
HE IS THE MASTER OF MARTIAL ARTS WHO–LIKE *RAGING WATER*–CAN PULVERIZE A MASSIVE ROCK WITH ONE PUNCH!
YOU'RE A LITTLE SQUIRT WHO JUST JOINED CLASS B!
TAKE MASTER BANG LIGHTLY AND YOU'LL GET HURT!
CHARANKO! DO NOT DISGRACE ME!
SAITAMA IS MUCH MORE POWERFUL THAN I!
M-MASTER ... SURELY YOU'RE KIDDING ...
BAM
MR. SILVER-FANG!

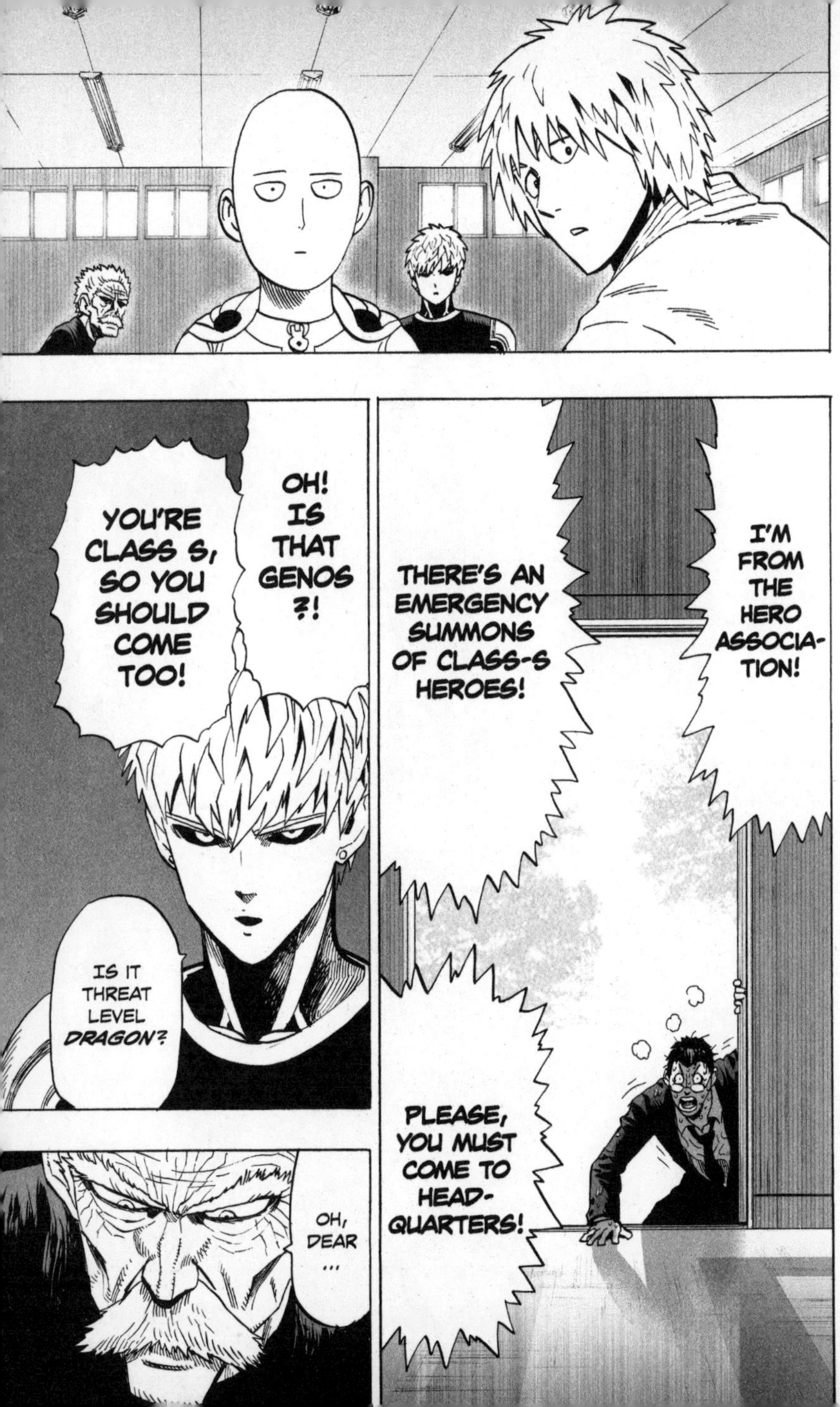
I'M FROM THE HERO ASSOCIATION!
THERE'S AN EMERGENCY SUMMONS OF CLASS-S HEROES!
PLEASE, YOU MUST COME TO HEADQUARTERS!
OH! IS THAT GENOS?!
YOU'RE CLASS S, SO YOU SHOULD COME TOO!
IS IT THREAT LEVEL *DRAGON*?
OH, DEAR ...

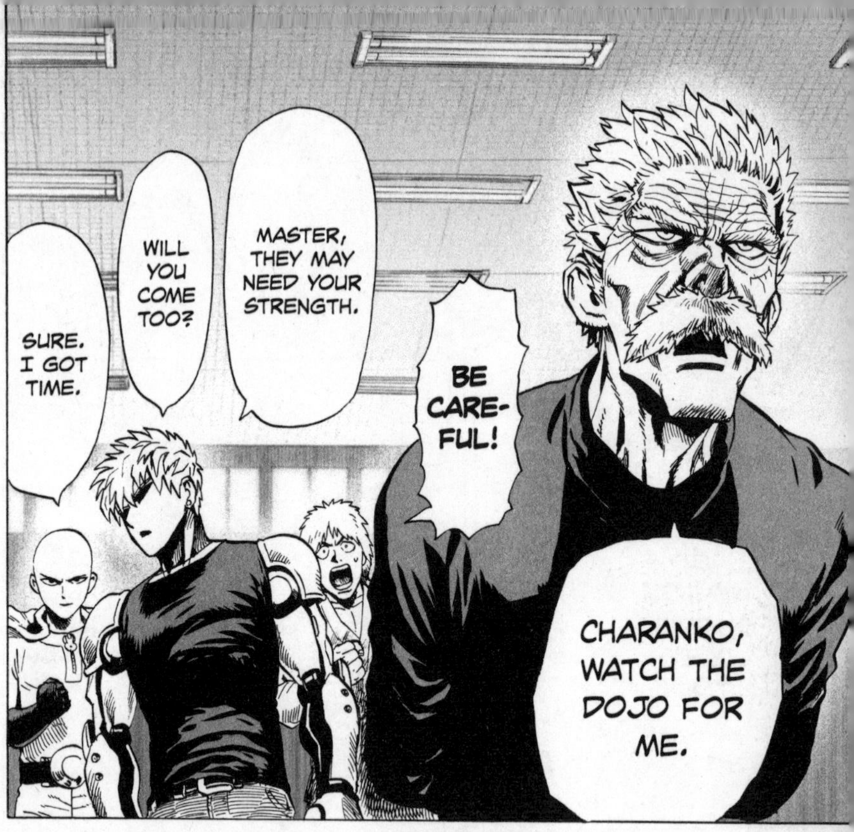
CHARANKO, WATCH THE DOJO FOR ME.
BE CAREFUL!
MASTER, THEY MAY NEED YOUR STRENGTH.
WILL YOU COME TOO?
SURE. I GOT TIME.

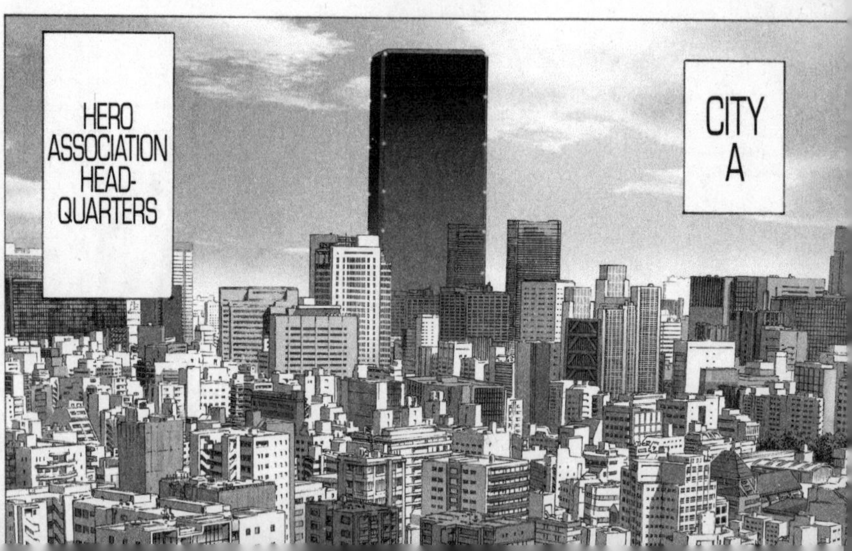
CITY A
HERO ASSOCIATION HEAD-QUARTERS

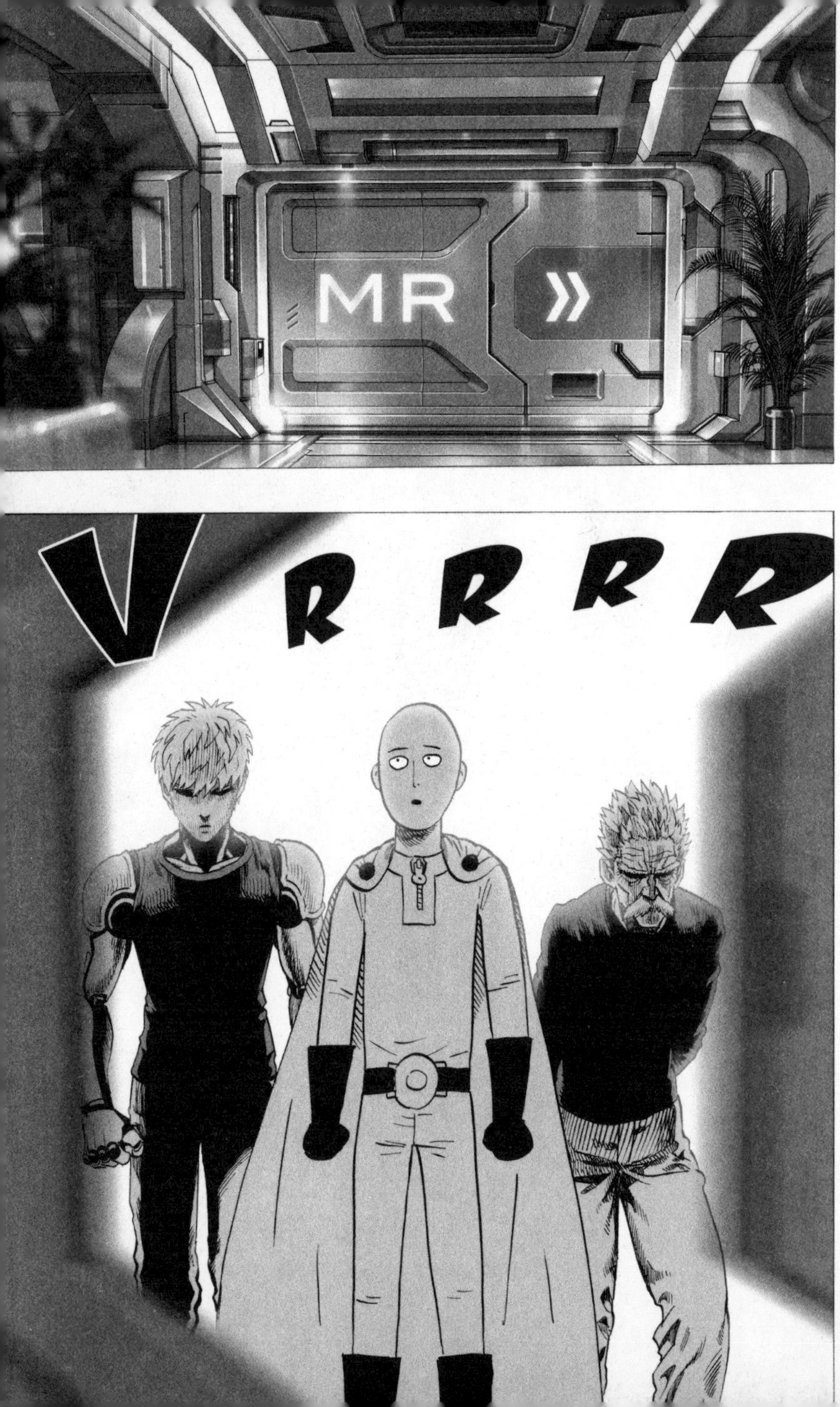
MR
VRRRR

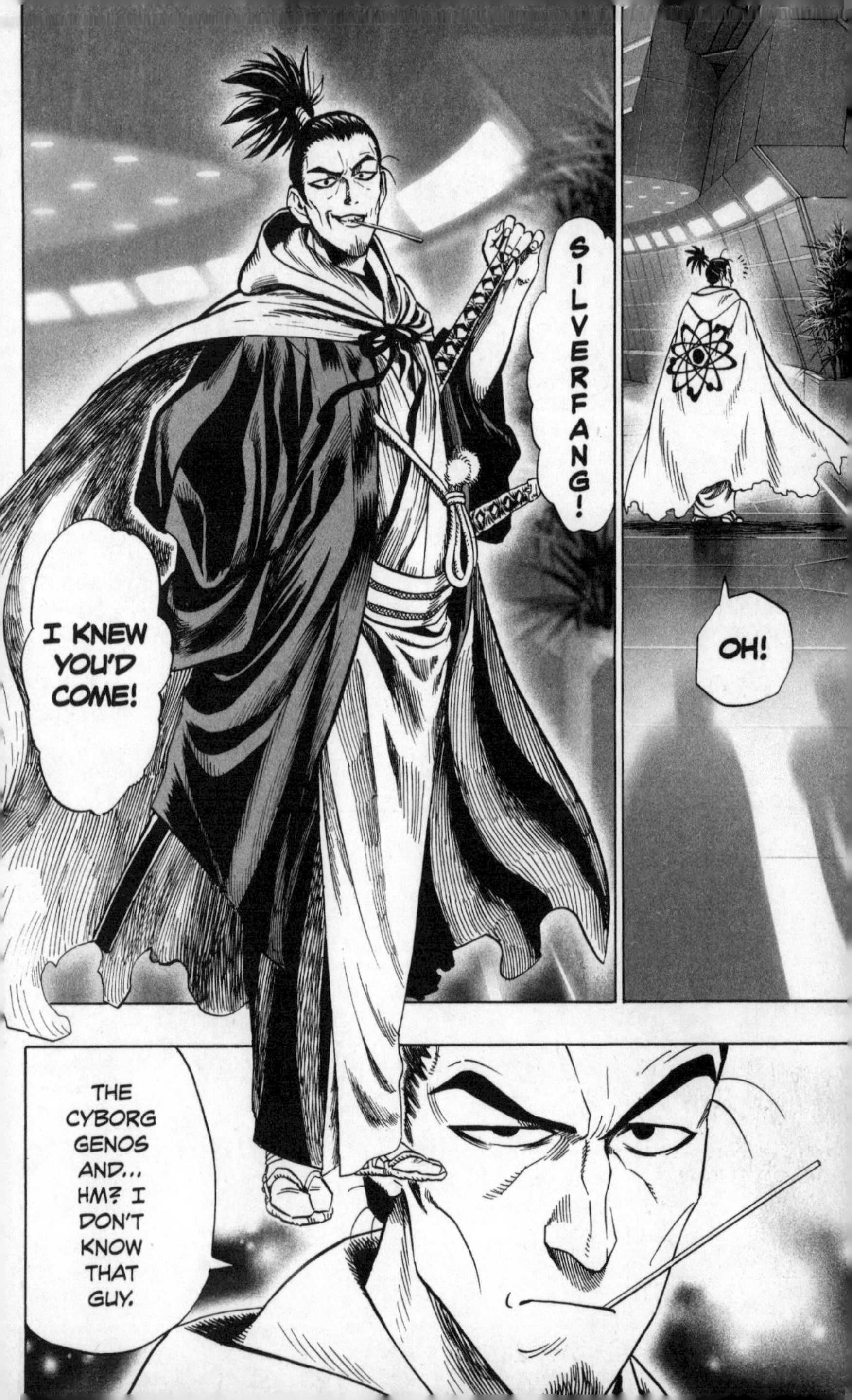
OH!
SILVERFANG!
I KNEW YOU'D COME!
THE CYBORG GENOS AND... HM? I DON'T KNOW THAT GUY.

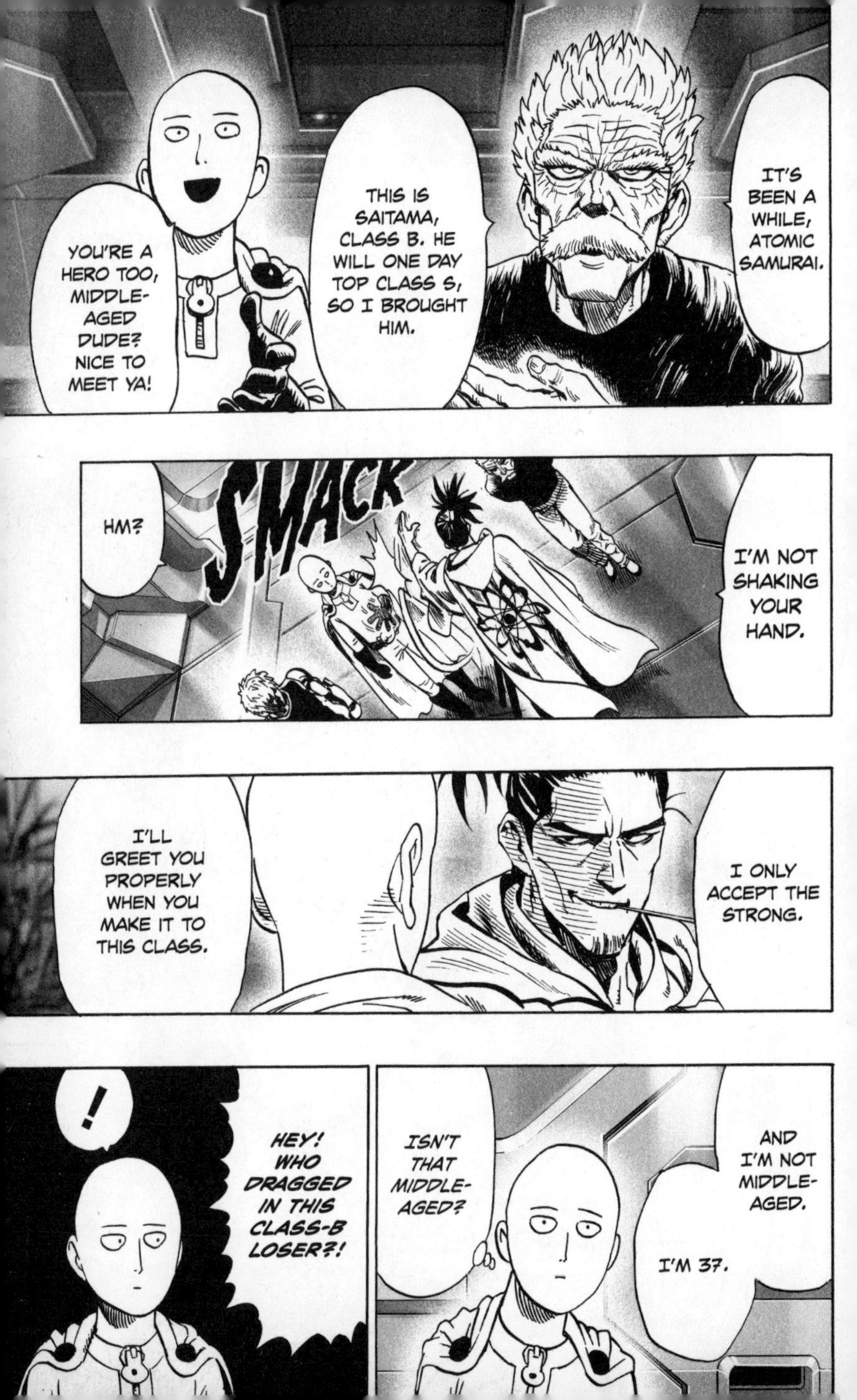
IT'S BEEN A WHILE, ATOMIC SAMURAI.
THIS IS SAITAMA, CLASS B. HE WILL ONE DAY TOP CLASS S, SO I BROUGHT HIM.
YOU'RE A HERO TOO, MIDDLE-AGED DUDE? NICE TO MEET YA!
I'M NOT SHAKING YOUR HAND.
SMACK
HM?
I ONLY ACCEPT THE STRONG.
I'LL GREET YOU PROPERLY WHEN YOU MAKE IT TO THIS CLASS.
AND I'M NOT MIDDLE-AGED.
I'M 37.
ISN'T THAT MIDDLE-AGED?
HEY! WHO DRAGGED IN THIS CLASS-B LOSER?!
!

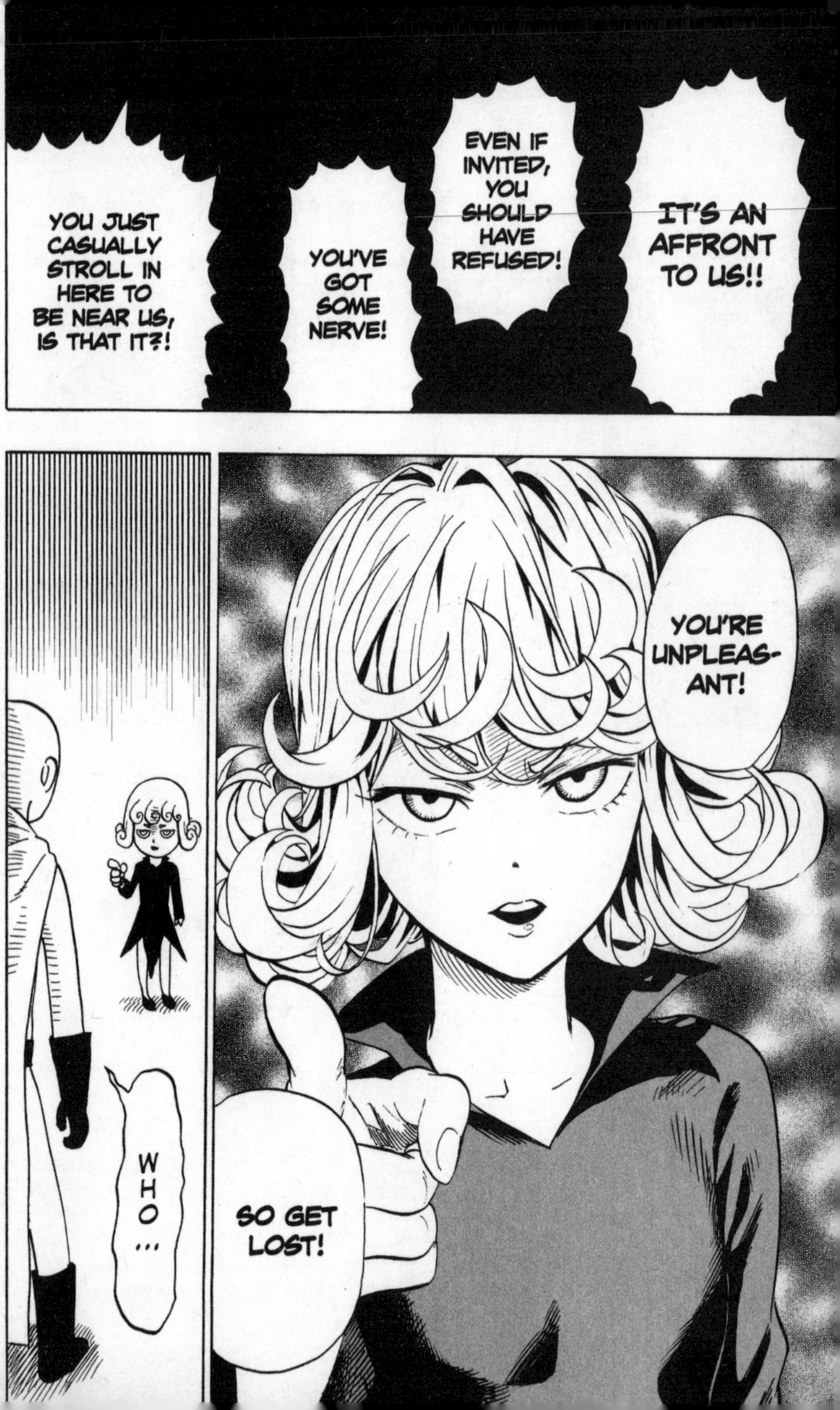
IT'S AN AFFRONT TO US!!
EVEN IF INVITED, YOU SHOULD HAVE REFUSED!
YOU'VE GOT SOME NERVE!
YOU JUST CASUALLY STROLL IN HERE TO BE NEAR US, IS THAT IT?!
YOU'RE UNPLEAS-ANT!
SO GET LOST!
WHO...

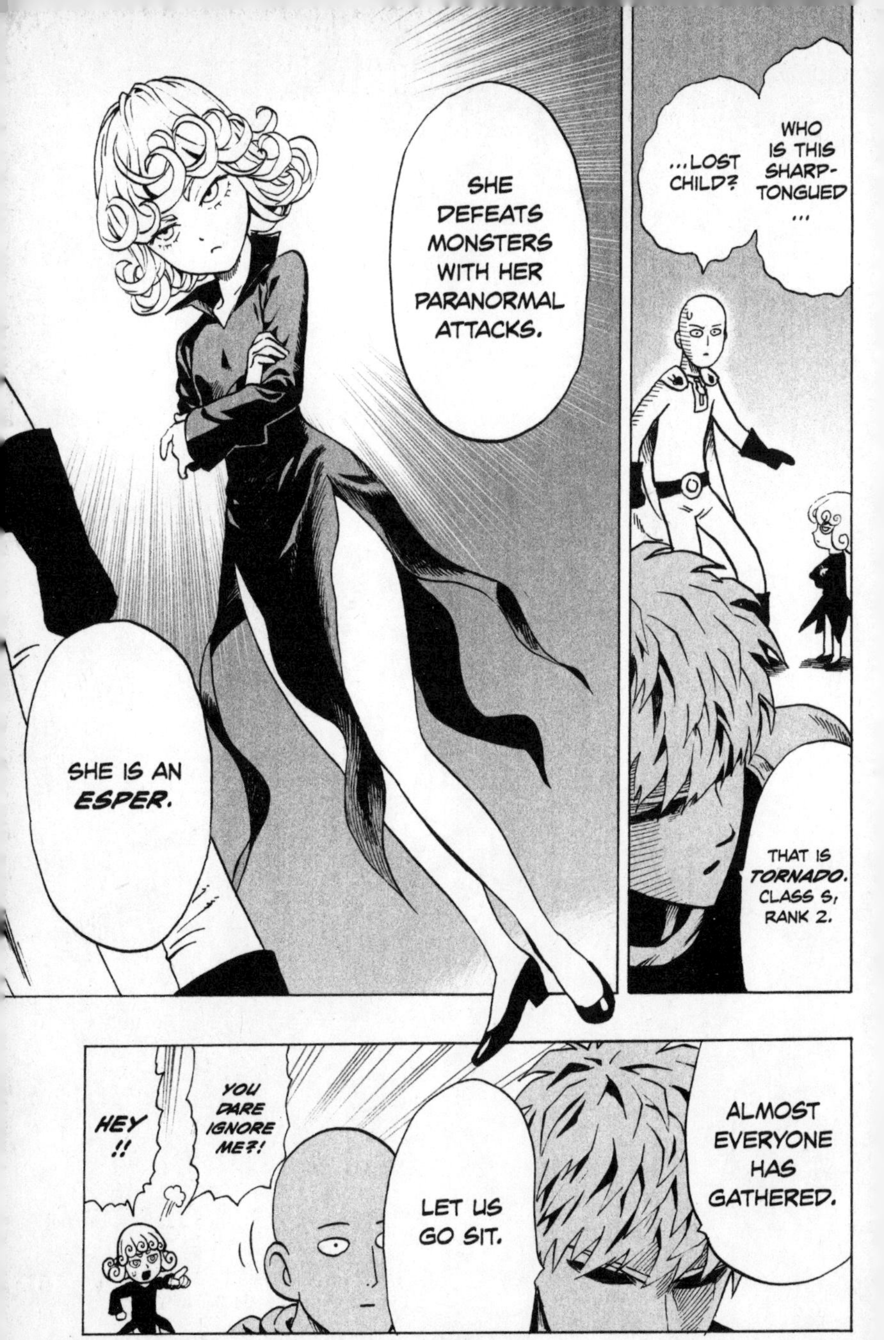
WHO IS THIS SHARP-TONGUED ...
...LOST CHILD?
THAT IS *TORNADO.* CLASS S, RANK 2.
SHE DEFEATS MONSTERS WITH HER PARANORMAL ATTACKS.
SHE IS AN *ESPER.*
ALMOST EVERYONE HAS GATHERED.
LET US GO SIT.
YOU DARE IGNORE ME?!
HEY !!

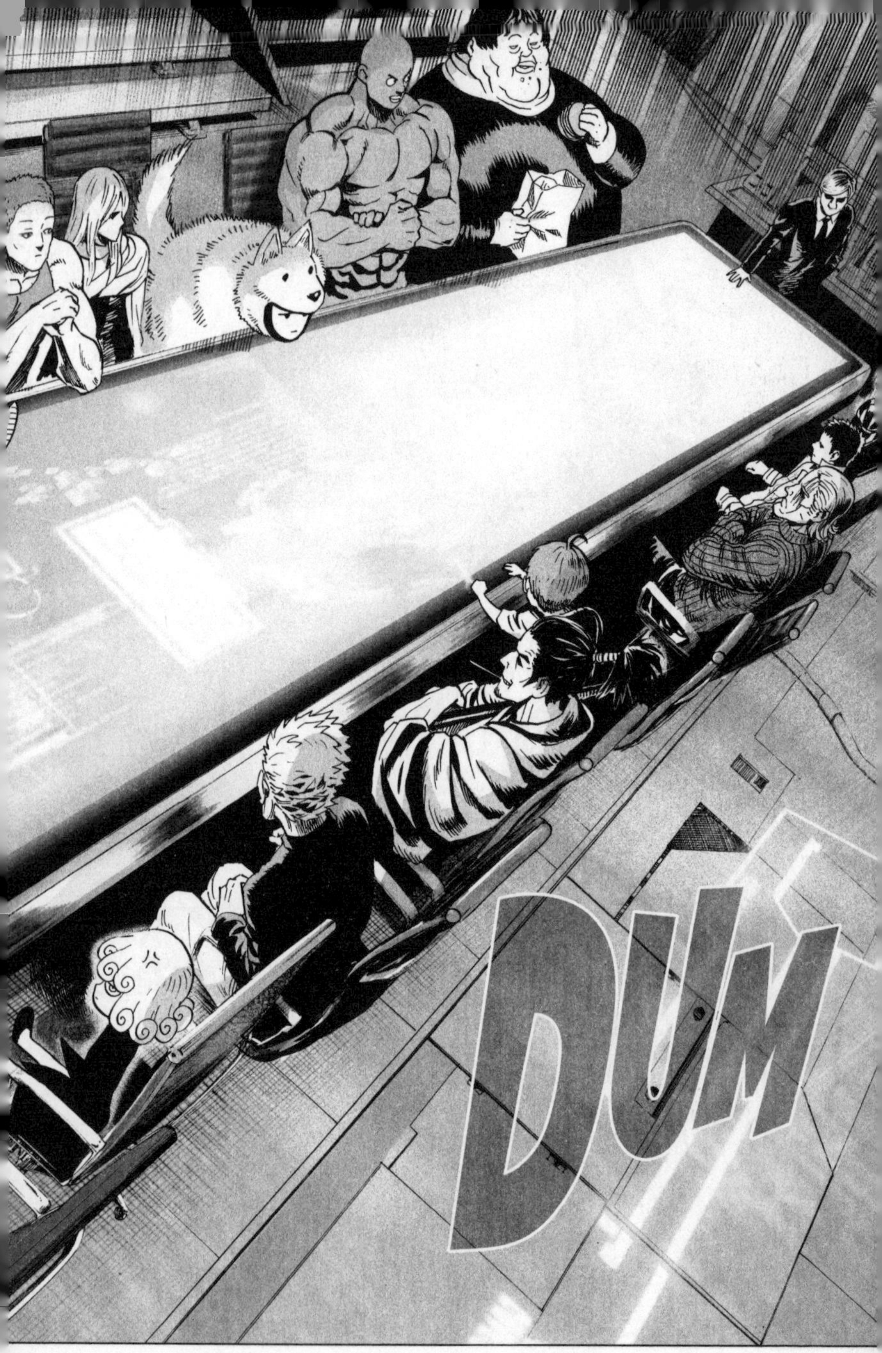
DUM

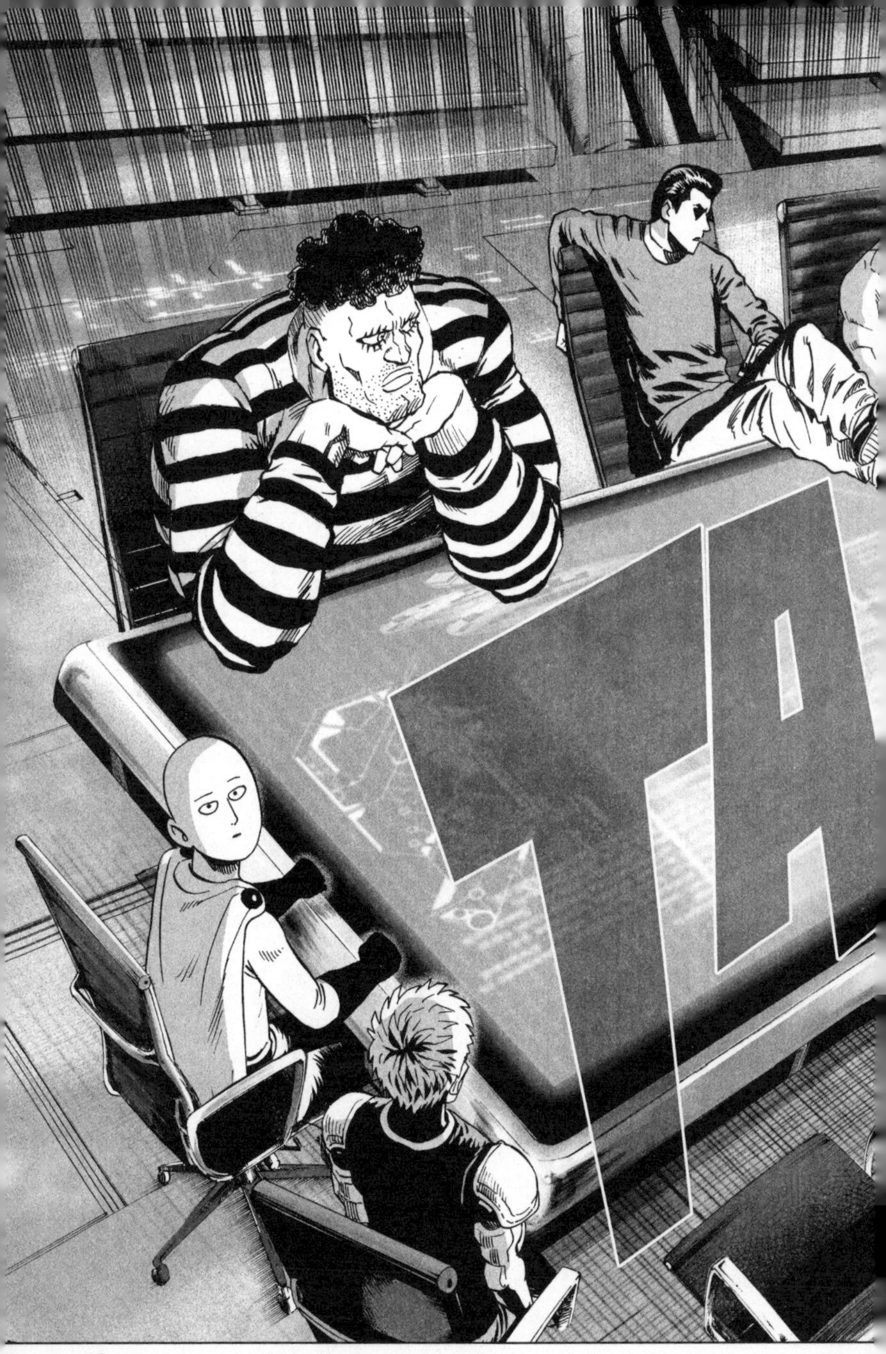

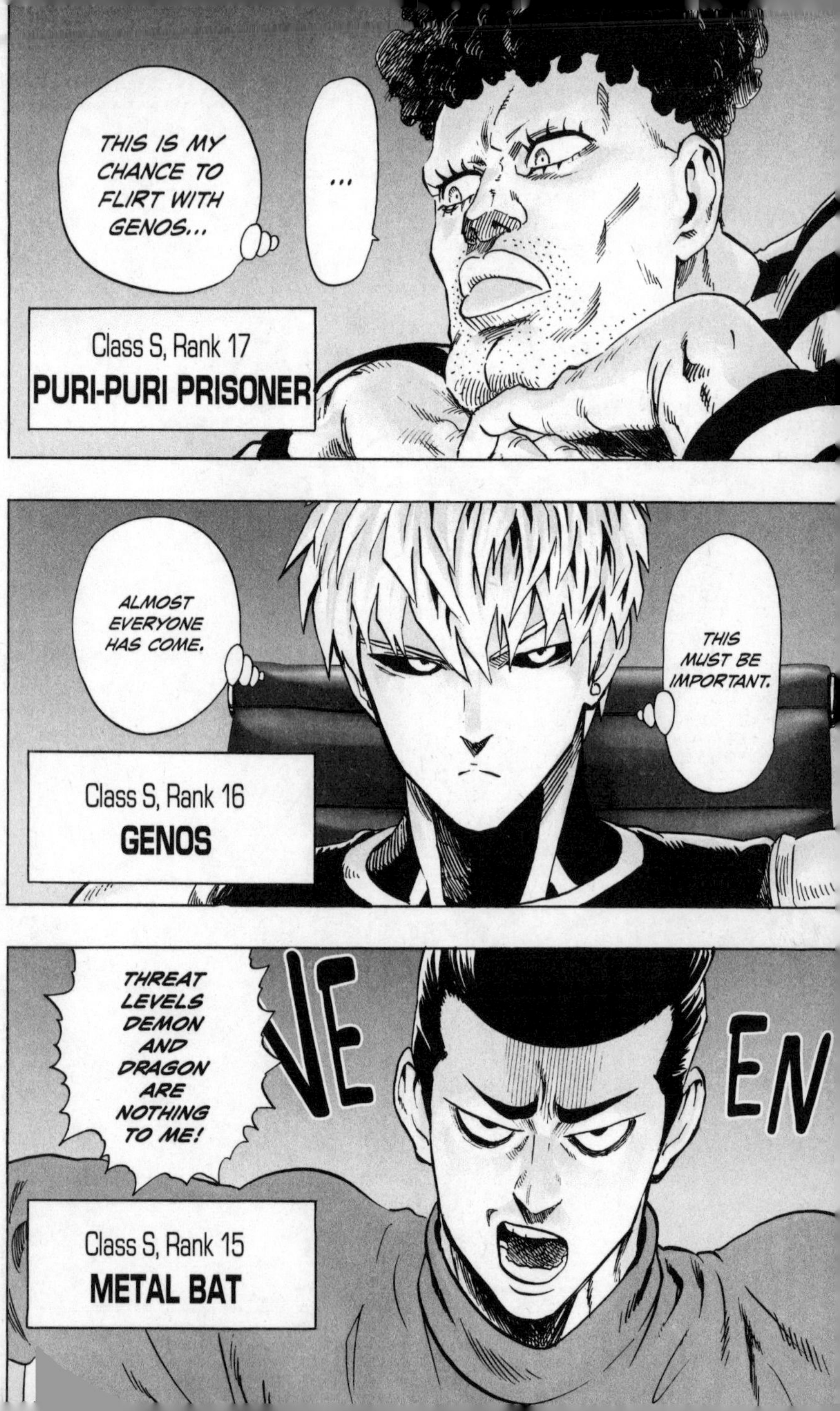
...
THIS IS MY CHANCE TO FLIRT WITH GENOS...
Class S, Rank 17
PURI-PURI PRISONER
ALMOST EVERYONE HAS COME.
THIS MUST BE IMPORTANT.
Class S, Rank 16
GENOS
VE EN
THREAT LEVELS DEMON AND DRAGON ARE NOTHING TO ME!
Class S, Rank 15
METAL BAT

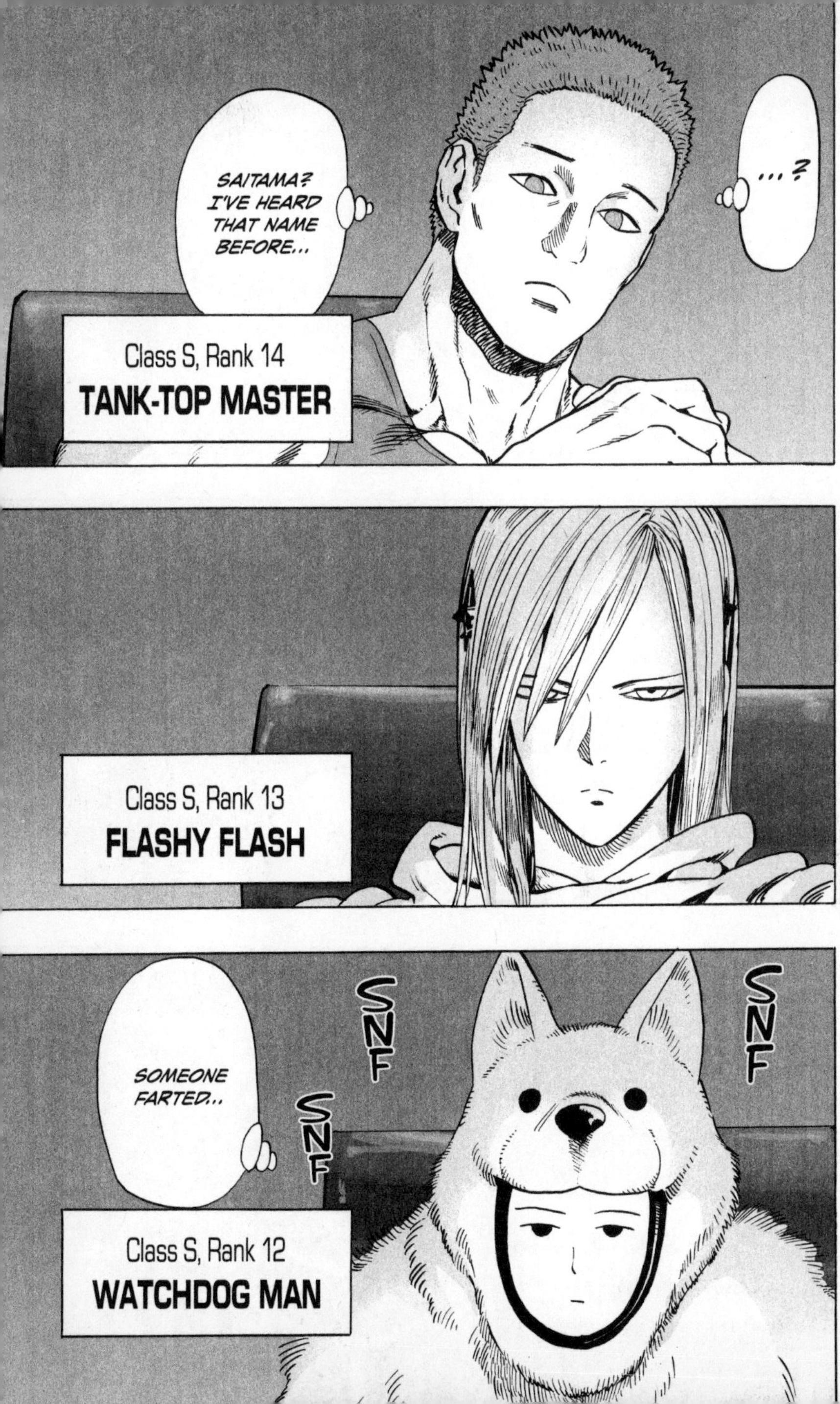
...?
SAITAMA? I'VE HEARD THAT NAME BEFORE...
Class S, Rank 14
TANK-TOP MASTER
Class S, Rank 13
FLASHY FLASH
SNF
SNF
SNF
SOMEONE FARTED...
Class S, Rank 12
WATCHDOG MAN

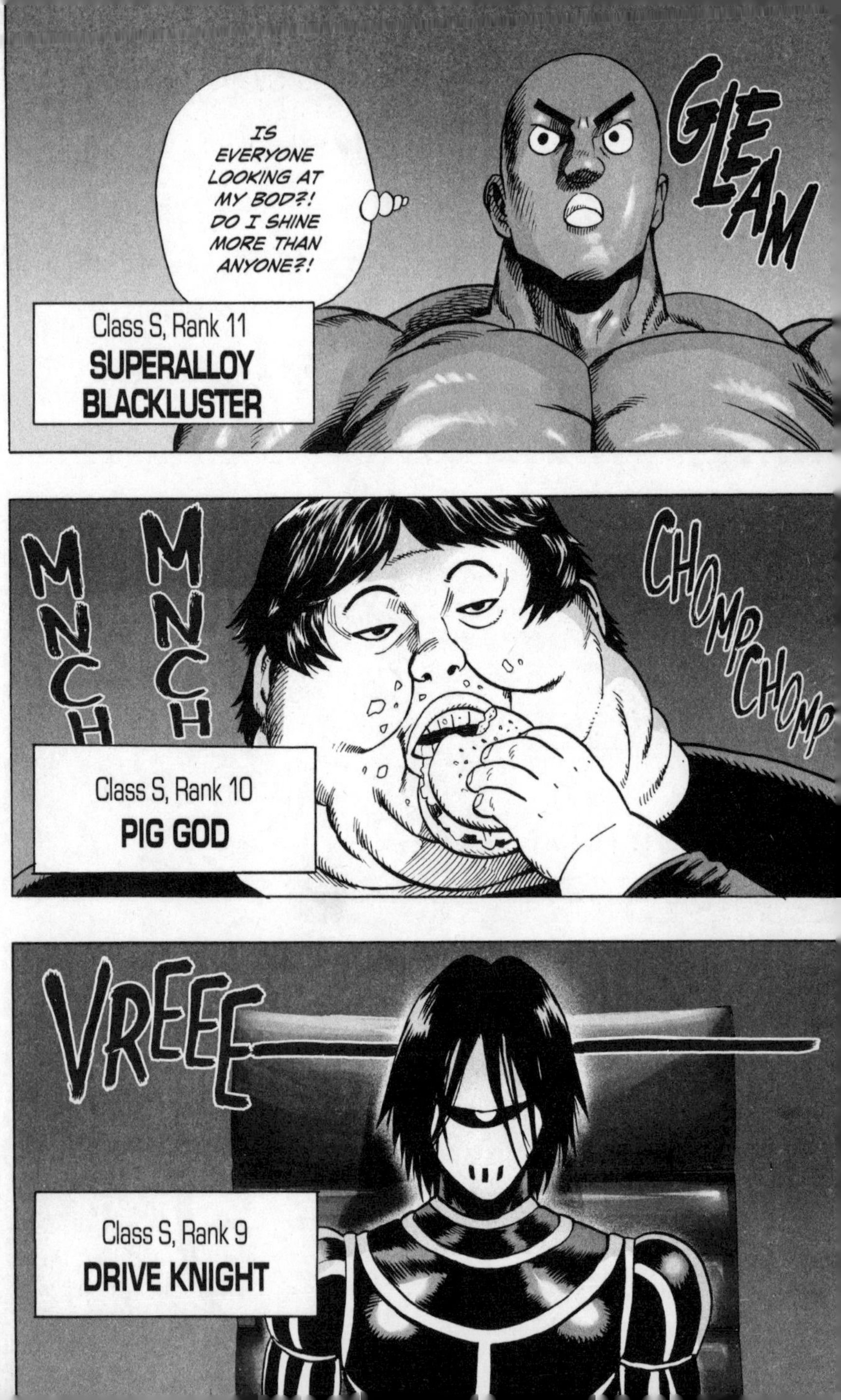
GLEAM
IS EVERYONE LOOKING AT MY BOD?! DO I SHINE MORE THAN ANYONE?!
Class S, Rank 11
SUPERALLOY BLACKLUSTER
CHOMP CHOMP
MNCH
MNCH
Class S, Rank 10
PIG GOD
VREEE
Class S, Rank 9
DRIVE KNIGHT

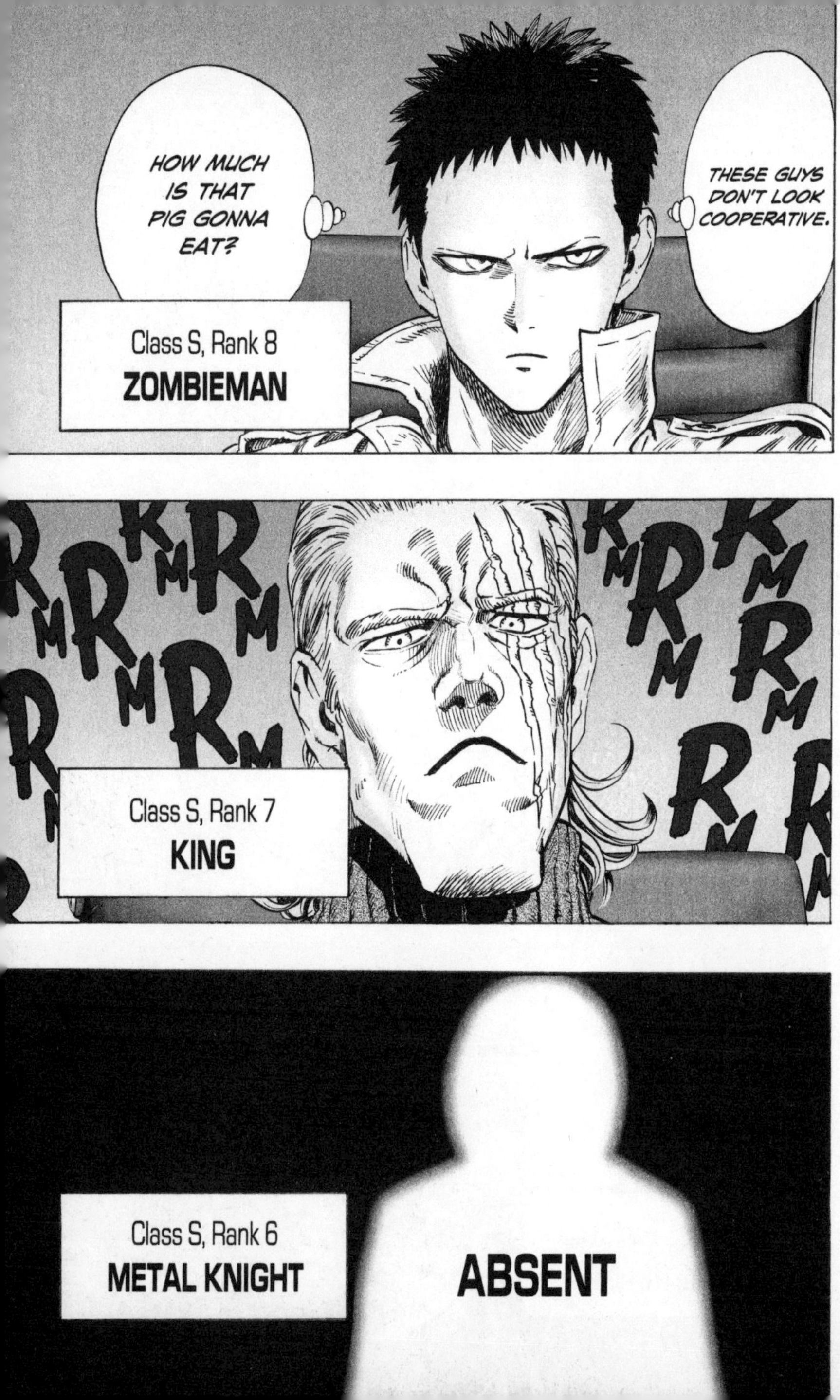
THESE GUYS DON'T LOOK COOPERATIVE.
HOW MUCH IS THAT PIG GONNA EAT?
Class S, Rank 8
ZOMBIEMAN
Class S, Rank 7
KING
ABSENT
Class S, Rank 6
METAL KNIGHT

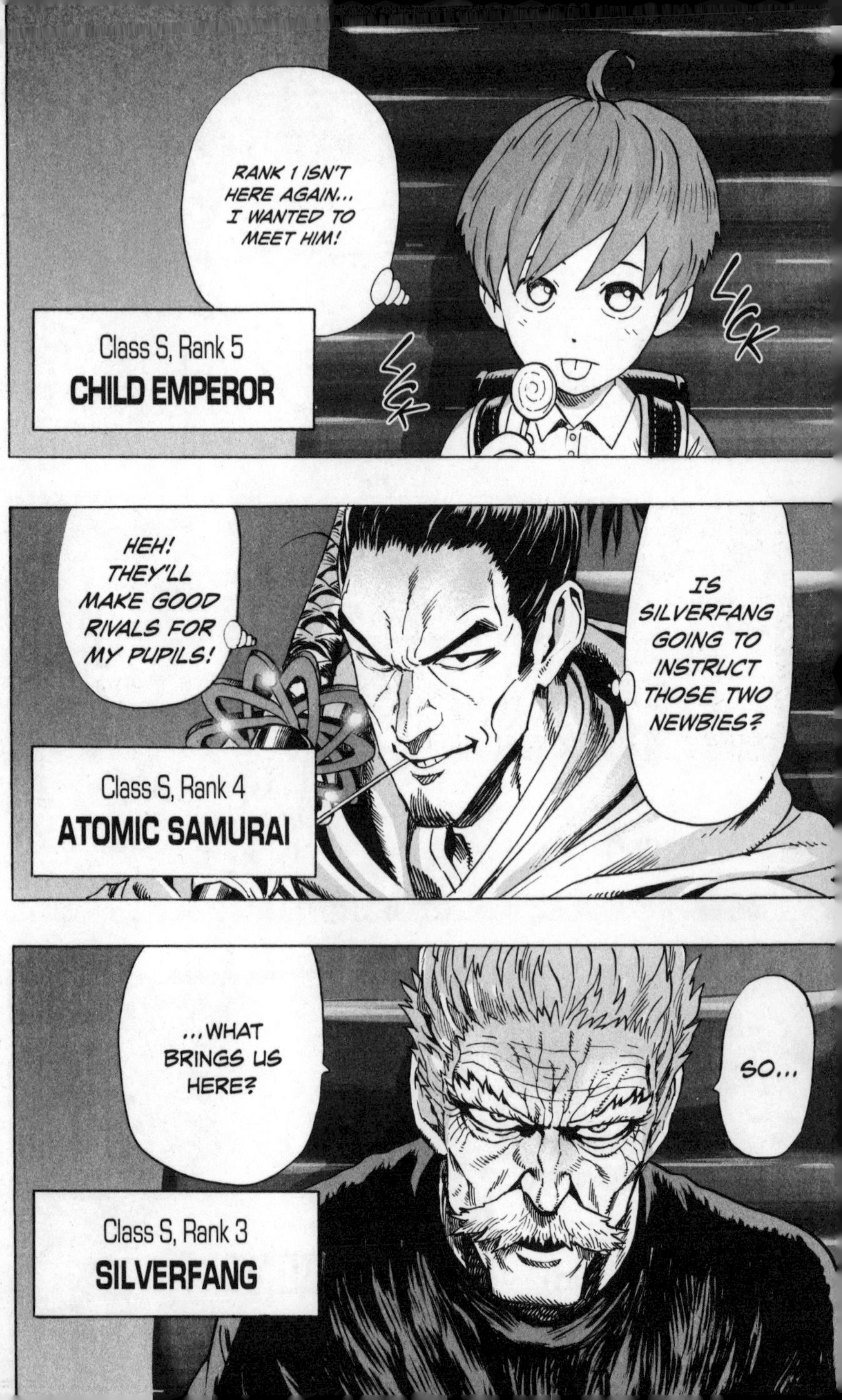
LICK
RANK 1 ISN'T HERE AGAIN... I WANTED TO MEET HIM!
LICK
Class S, Rank 5
CHILD EMPEROR
IS SILVERFANG GOING TO INSTRUCT THOSE TWO NEWBIES?
HEH! THEY'LL MAKE GOOD RIVALS FOR MY PUPILS!
Class S, Rank 4
ATOMIC SAMURAI
SO...
...WHAT BRINGS US HERE?
Class S, Rank 3
SILVERFANG

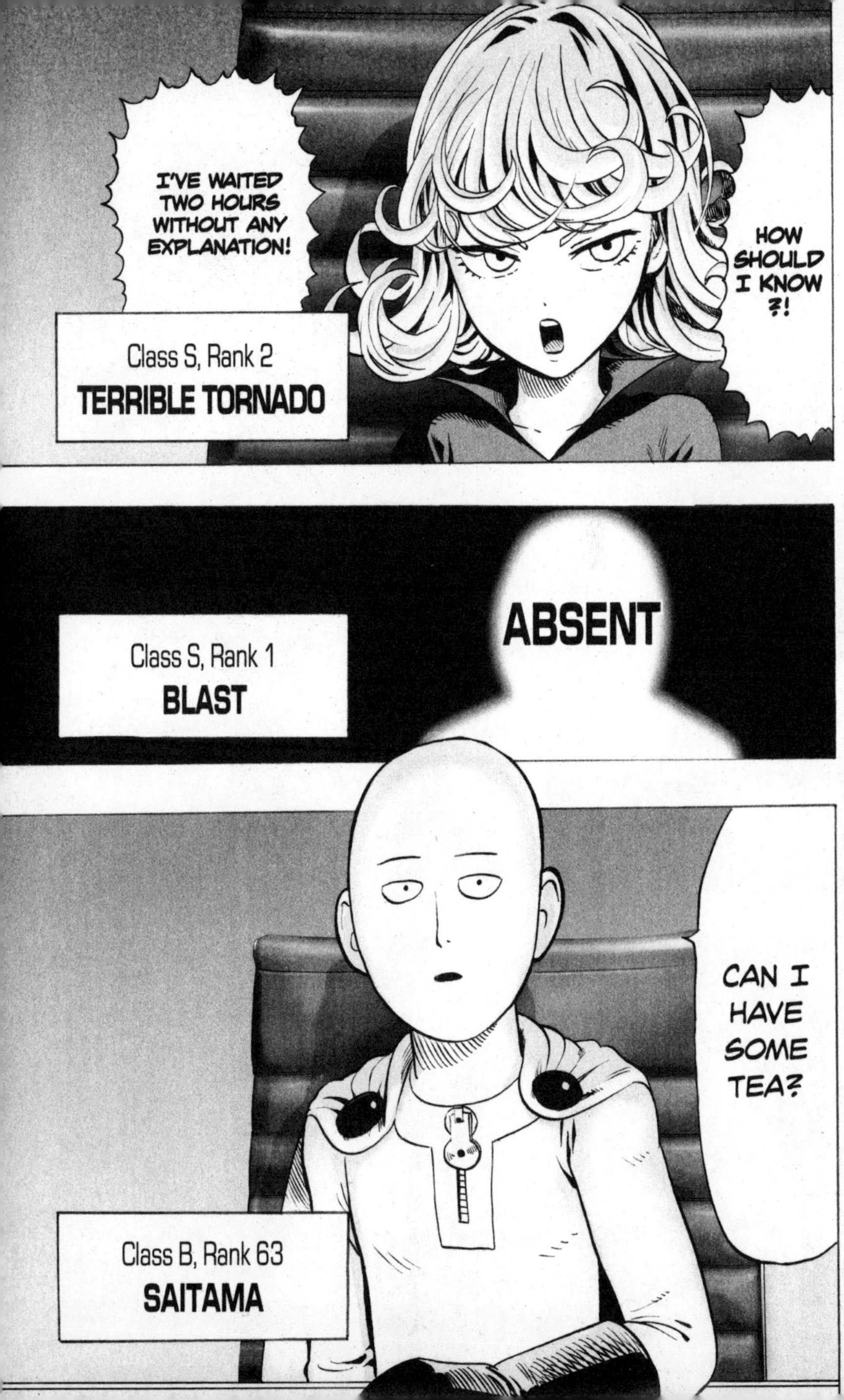
HOW SHOULD I KNOW ?!
I'VE WAITED TWO HOURS WITHOUT ANY EXPLANATION!
Class S, Rank 2
TERRIBLE TORNADO
ABSENT
Class S, Rank 1
BLAST
CAN I HAVE SOME TEA?
Class B, Rank 63
SAITAMA

BONUS

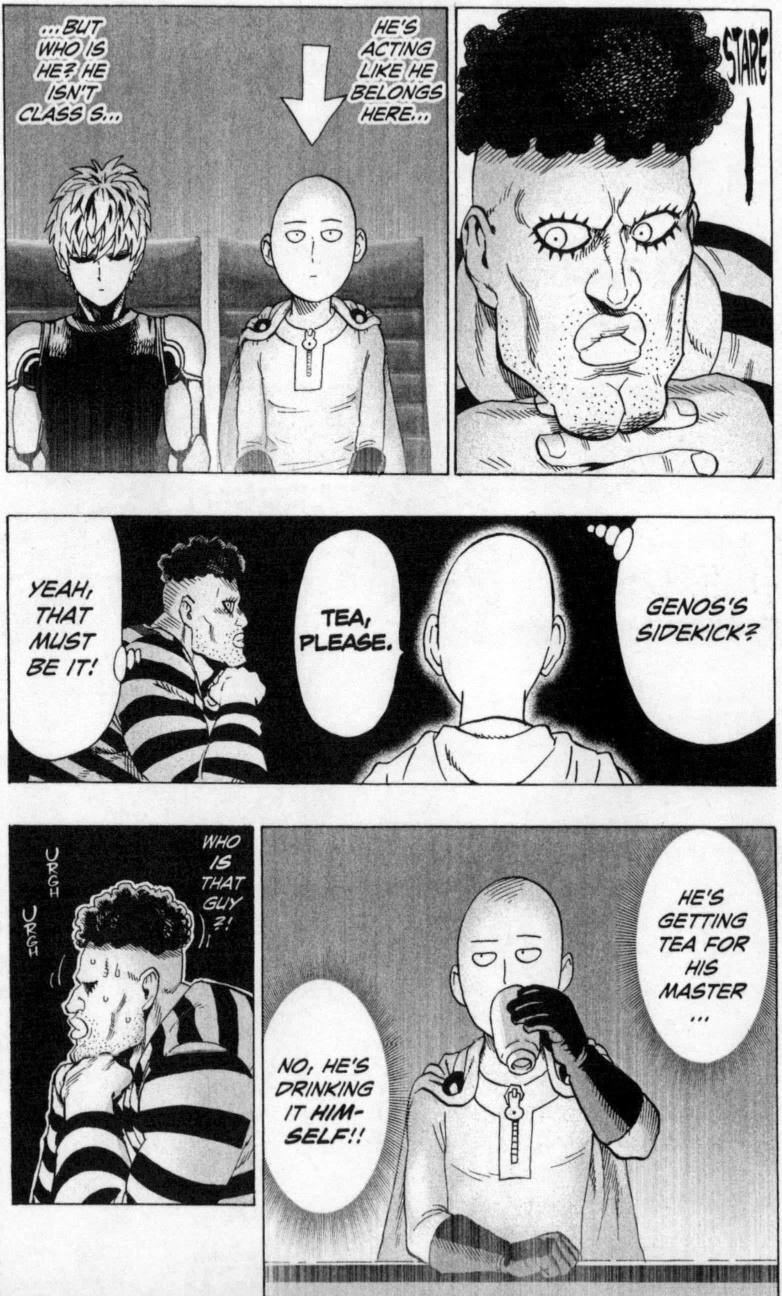
STARE
HE'S ACTING LIKE HE BELONGS HERE...
...BUT WHO IS HE? HE ISN'T CLASS S...
GENOS'S SIDEKICK?
TEA, PLEASE.
YEAH, THAT MUST BE IT!
HE'S GETTING TEA FOR HIS MASTER ...
NO, HE'S DRINKING IT HIMSELF!!
WHO IS THAT GUY ?!
URGH
URGH

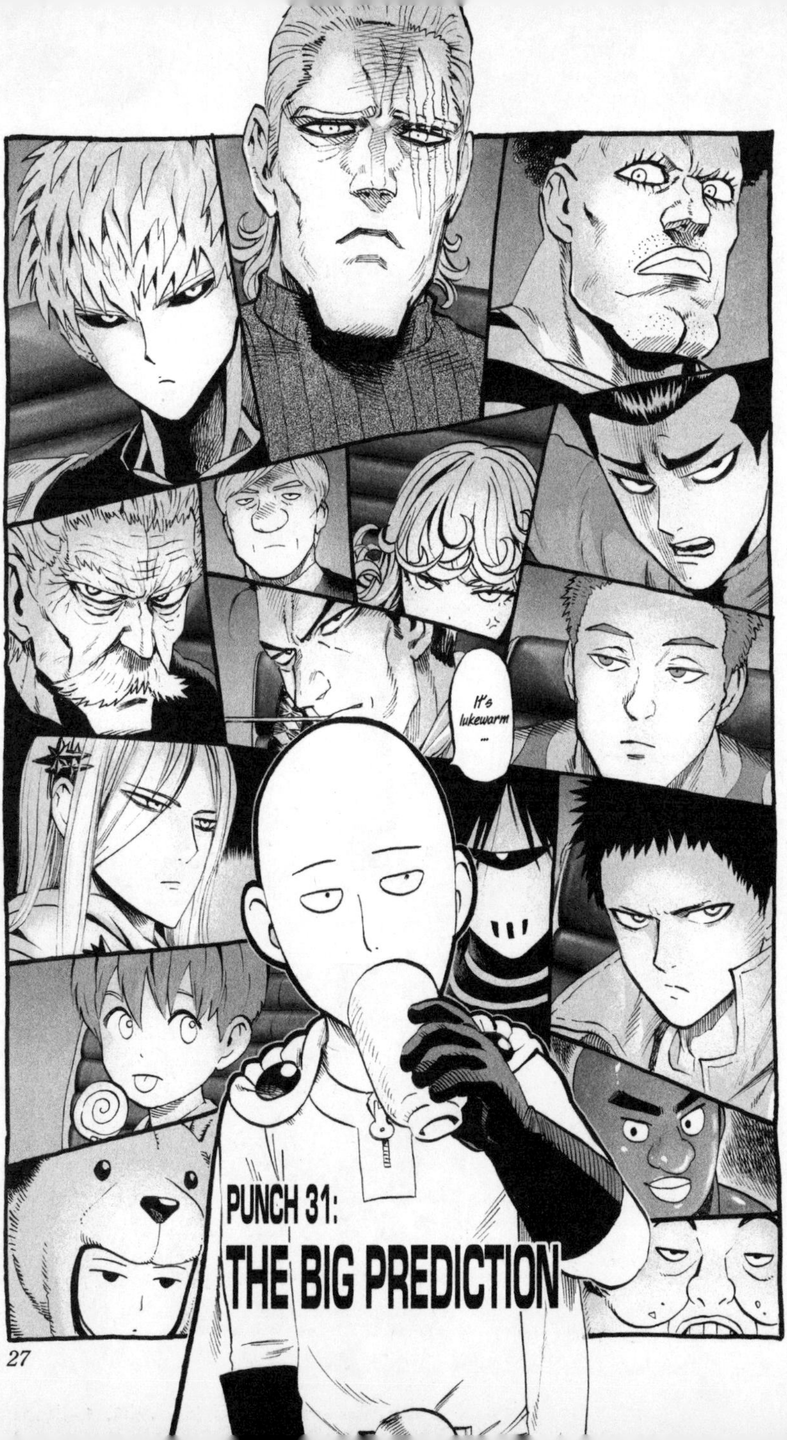
It's lukewarm ...
PUNCH 31:
THE BIG PREDICTION

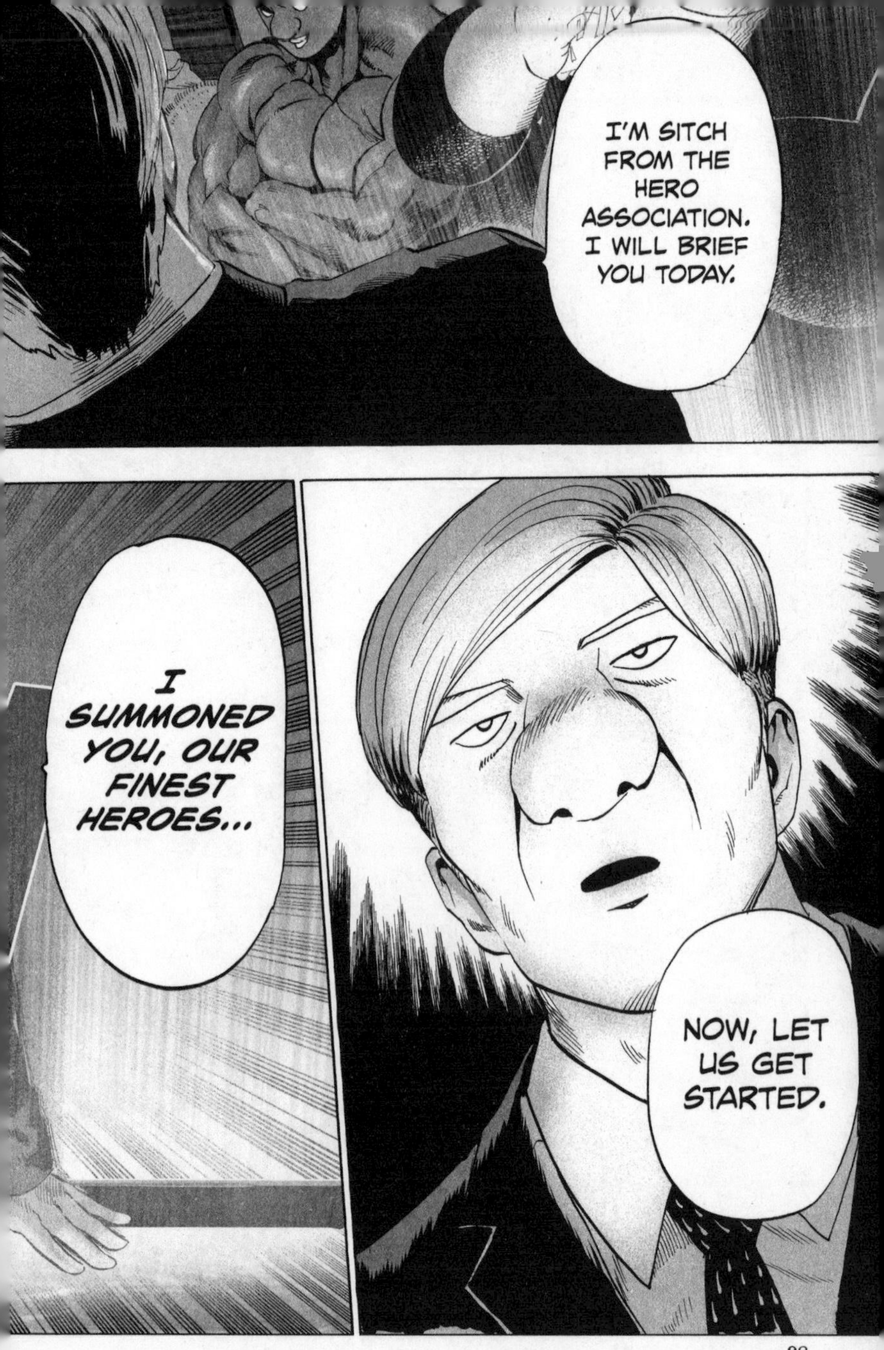
I'M SITCH FROM THE HERO ASSOCIATION. I WILL BRIEF YOU TODAY.
NOW, LET US GET STARTED.
I SUMMONED YOU, OUR FINEST HEROES...

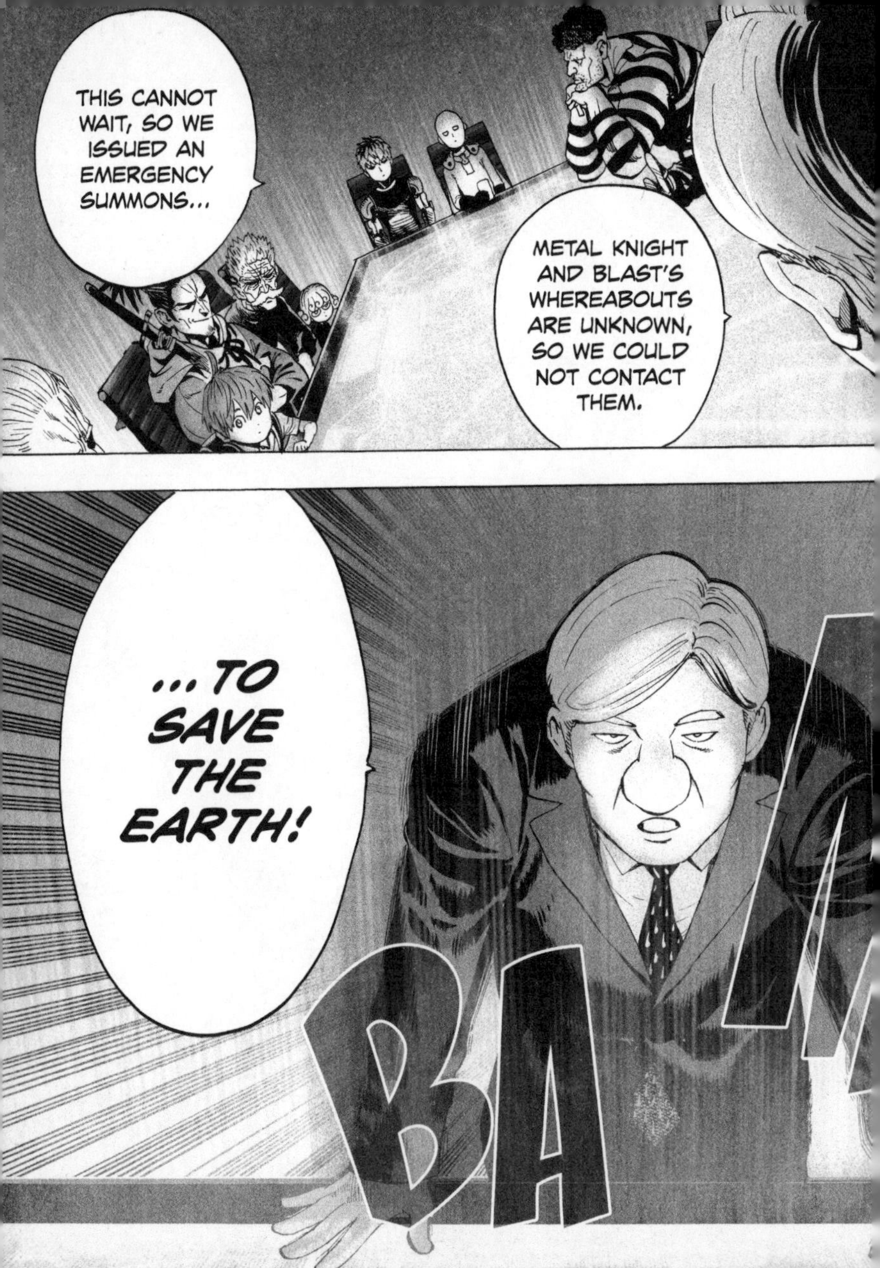
METAL KNIGHT AND BLAST'S WHEREABOUTS ARE UNKNOWN, SO WE COULD NOT CONTACT THEM.
THIS CANNOT WAIT, SO WE ISSUED AN EMERGENCY SUMMONS...
...TO SAVE THE EARTH!
BA

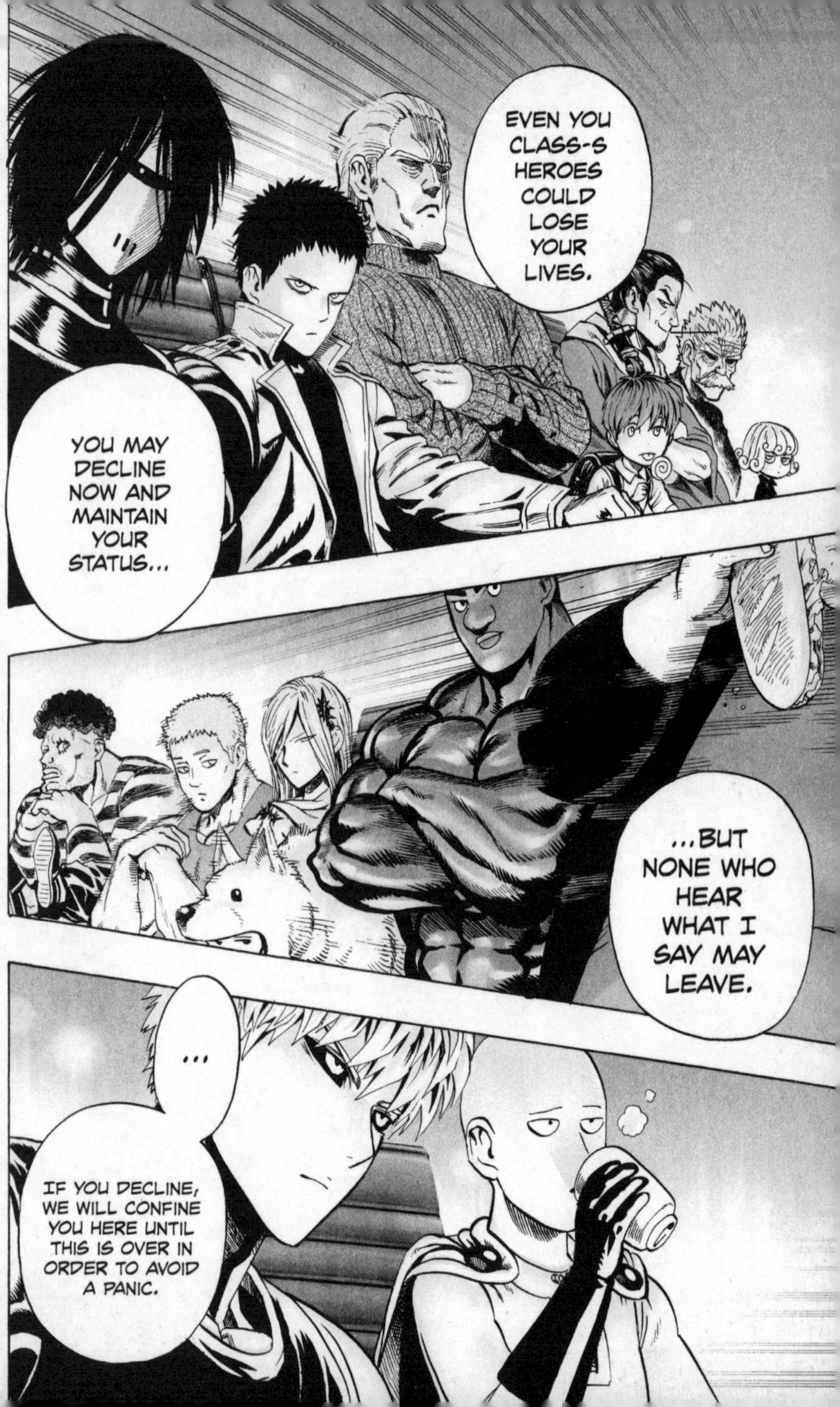
EVEN YOU CLASS-S HEROES COULD LOSE YOUR LIVES.
YOU MAY DECLINE NOW AND MAINTAIN YOUR STATUS...
...BUT NONE WHO HEAR WHAT I SAY MAY LEAVE.
...
IF YOU DECLINE, WE WILL CONFINE YOU HERE UNTIL THIS IS OVER IN ORDER TO AVOID A PANIC.

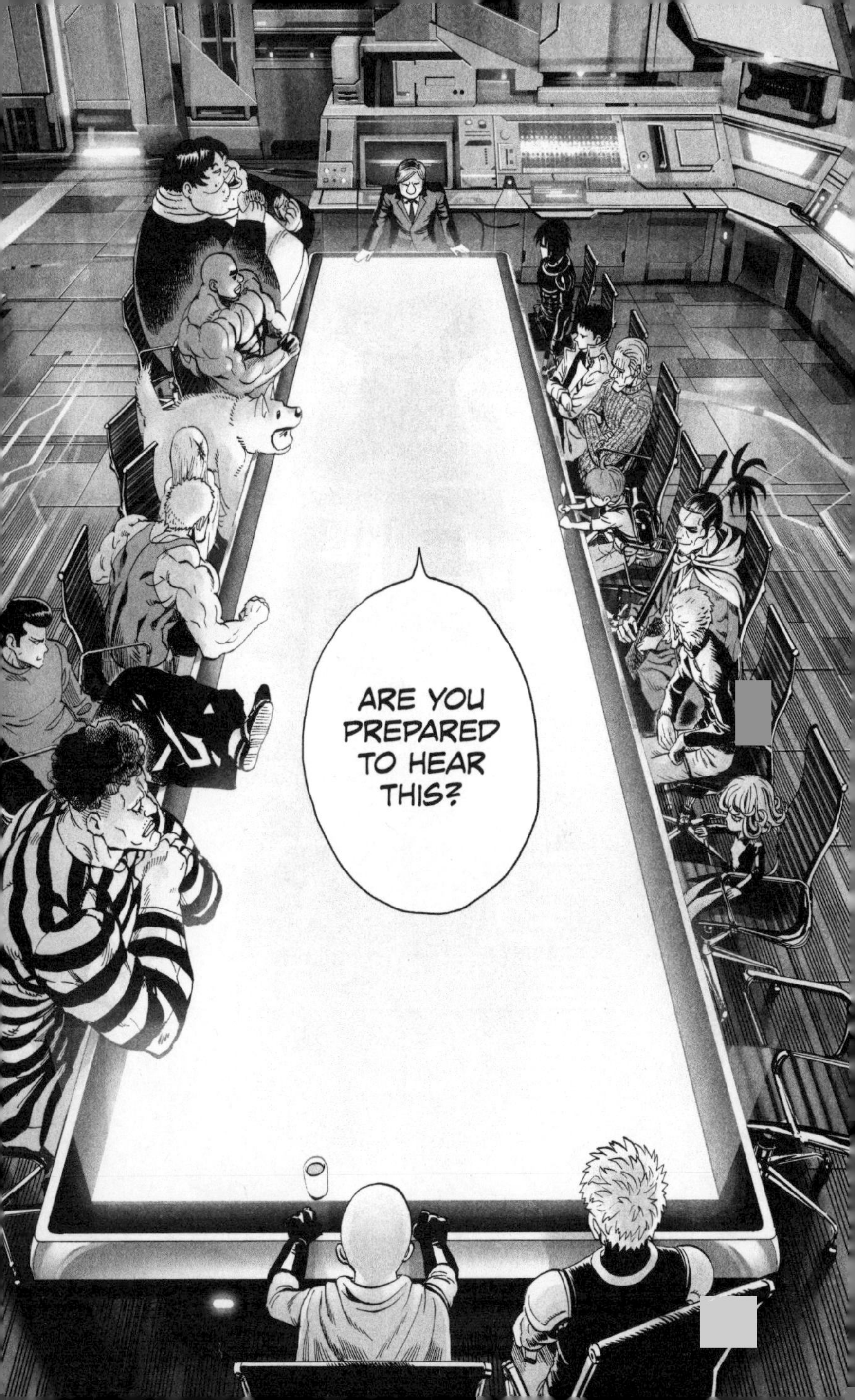
ARE YOU PREPARED TO HEAR THIS?

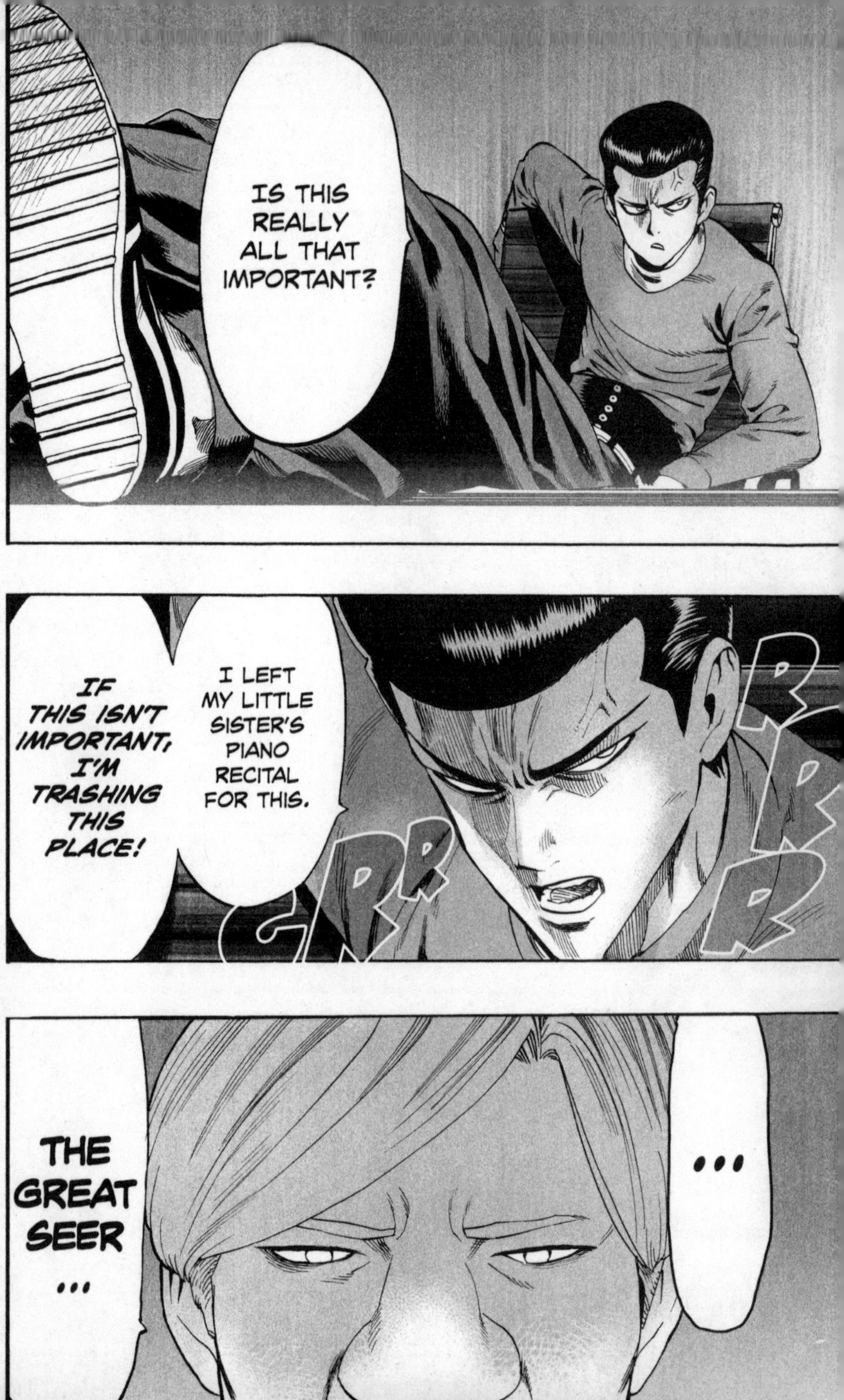
IS THIS REALLY ALL THAT IMPORTANT?
I LEFT MY LITTLE SISTER'S PIANO RECITAL FOR THIS.
IF THIS ISN'T IMPORTANT, I'M TRASHING THIS PLACE!
...
THE GREAT SEER ...

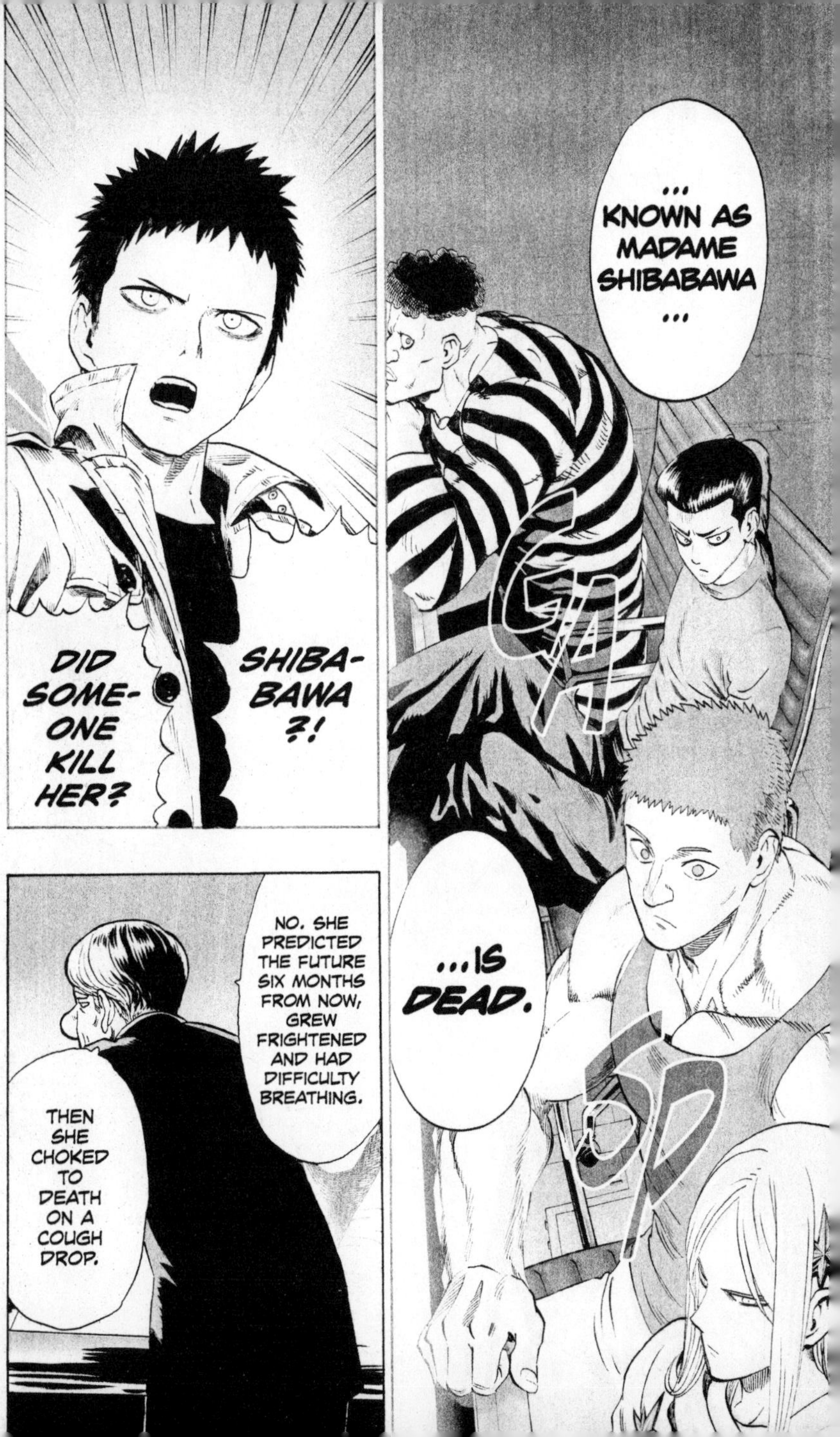
... KNOWN AS MADAME SHIBABAWA ...
GA
...IS DEAD.
SHIBA-BAWA?!
DID SOME-ONE KILL HER?
NO. SHE PREDICTED THE FUTURE SIX MONTHS FROM NOW, GREW FRIGHTENED AND HAD DIFFICULTY BREATHING.
THEN SHE CHOKED TO DEATH ON A COUGH DROP.

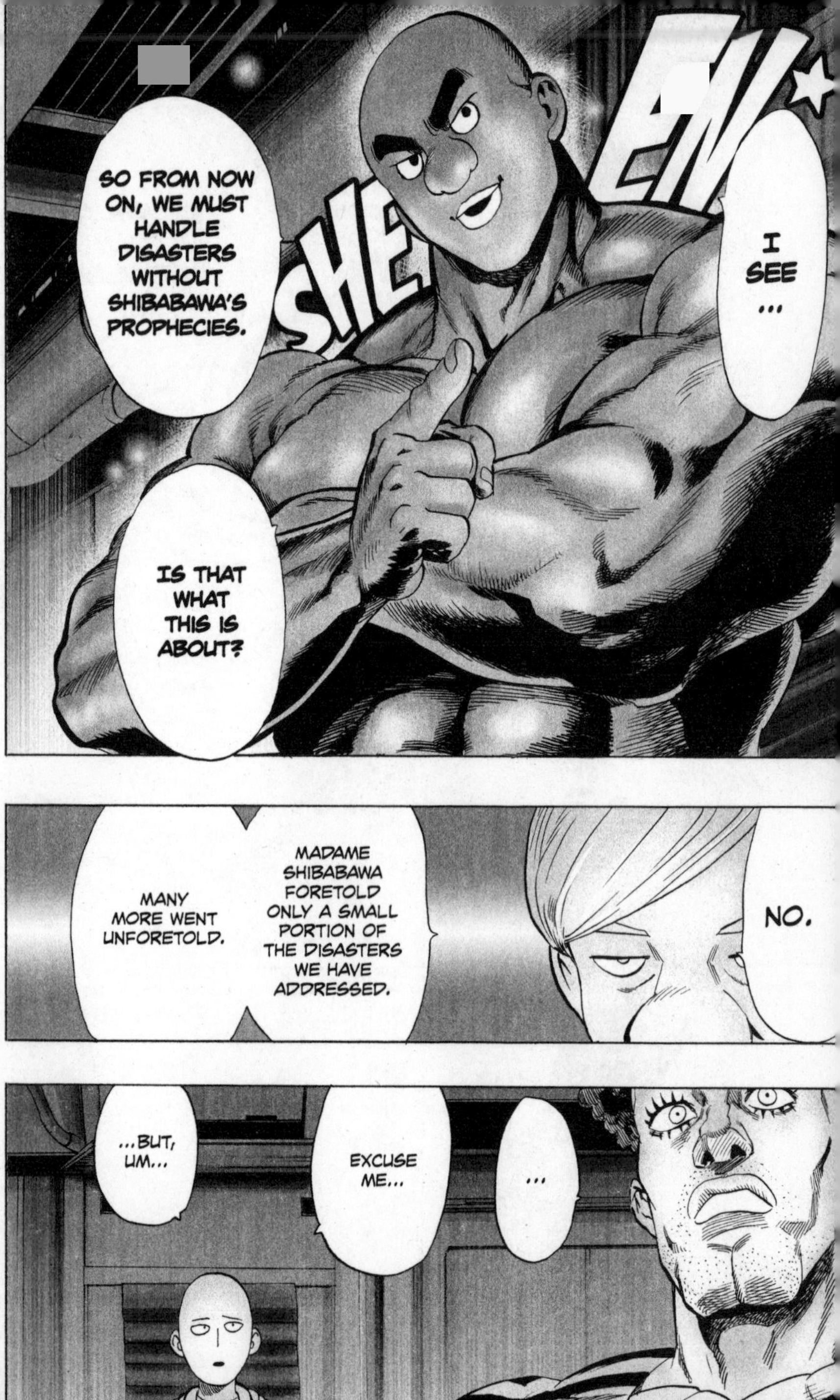
I SEE ...
SHE
EN☆
SO FROM NOW ON, WE MUST HANDLE DISASTERS WITHOUT SHIBABAWA'S PROPHECIES.
IS THAT WHAT THIS IS ABOUT?
NO.
MADAME SHIBABAWA FORETOLD ONLY A SMALL PORTION OF THE DISASTERS WE HAVE ADDRESSED.
MANY MORE WENT UNFORETOLD.
...
EXCUSE ME...
...BUT, UM...

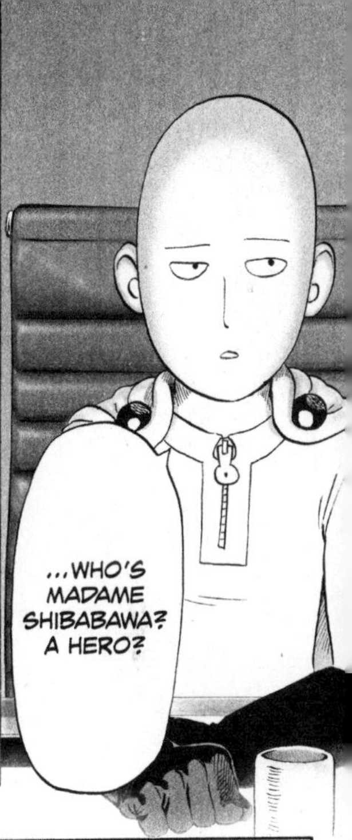
...WHO'S MADAME SHIBABAWA? A HERO?

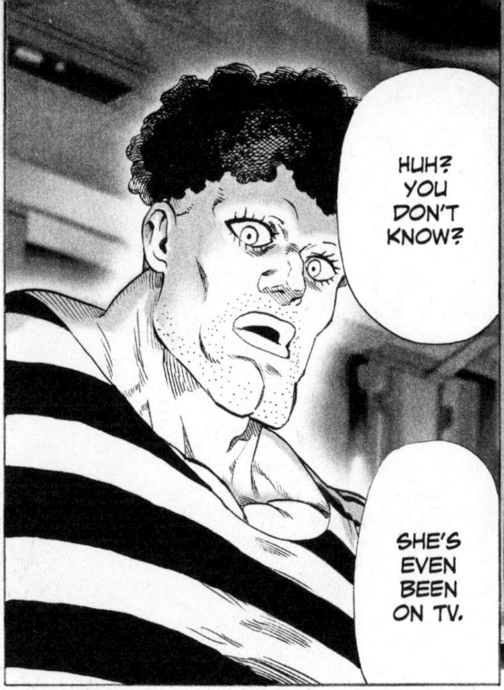
HUH? YOU DON'T KNOW?
SHE'S EVEN BEEN ON TV.

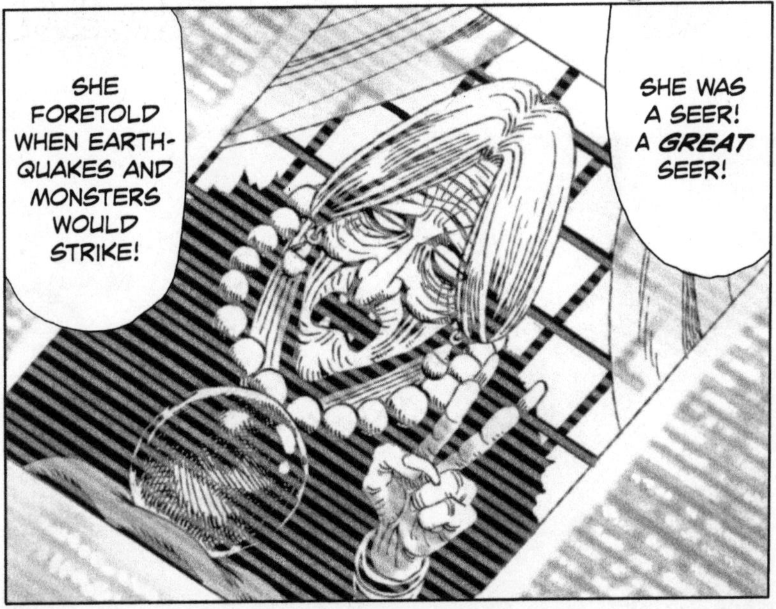
SHE WAS A SEER! A *GREAT* SEER!
SHE FORETOLD WHEN EARTH-QUAKES AND MONSTERS WOULD STRIKE!

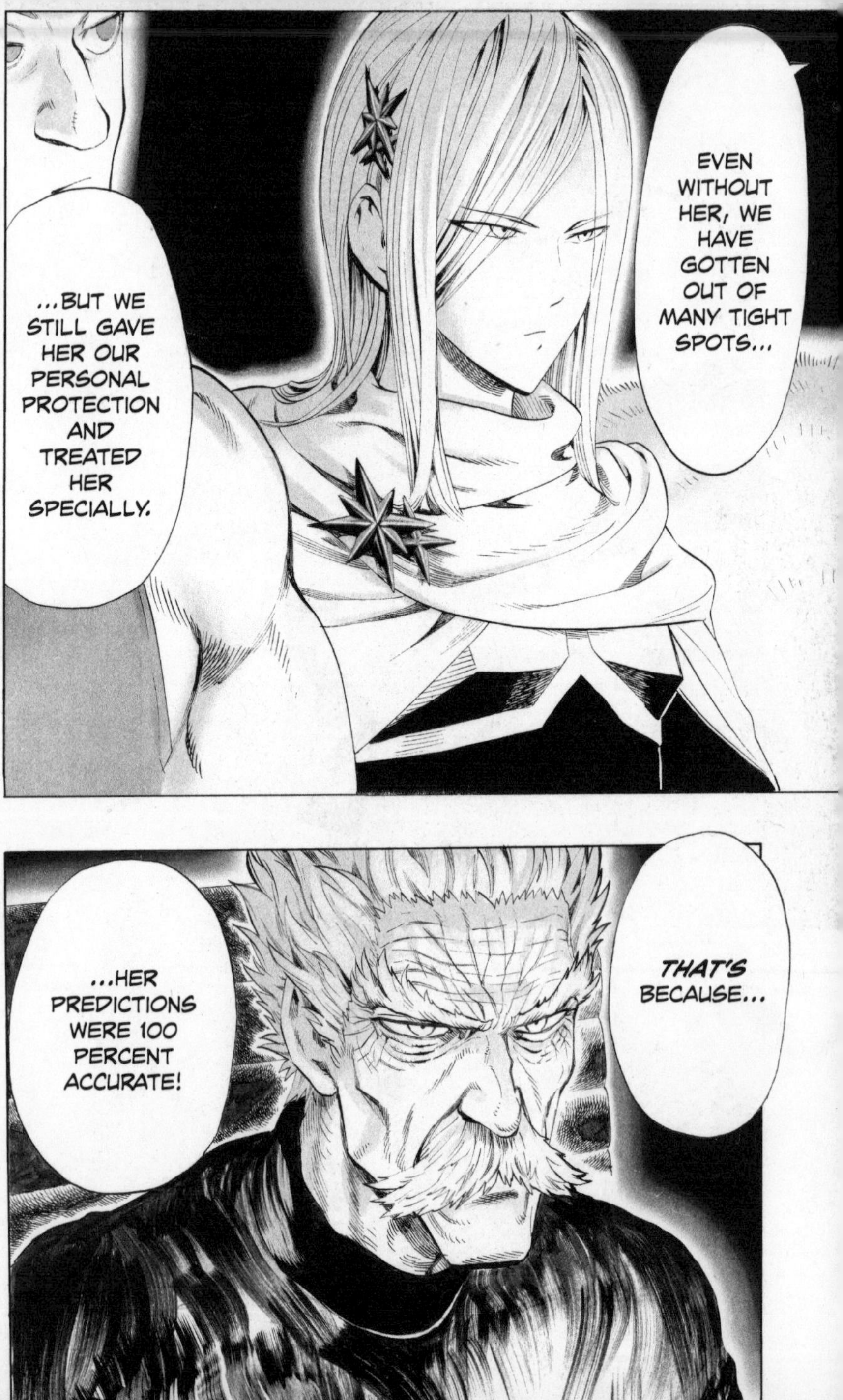
EVEN WITHOUT HER, WE HAVE GOTTEN OUT OF MANY TIGHT SPOTS...
...BUT WE STILL GAVE HER OUR PERSONAL PROTECTION AND TREATED HER SPECIALLY.
THAT'S BECAUSE...
...HER PREDICTIONS WERE 100 PERCENT ACCURATE!

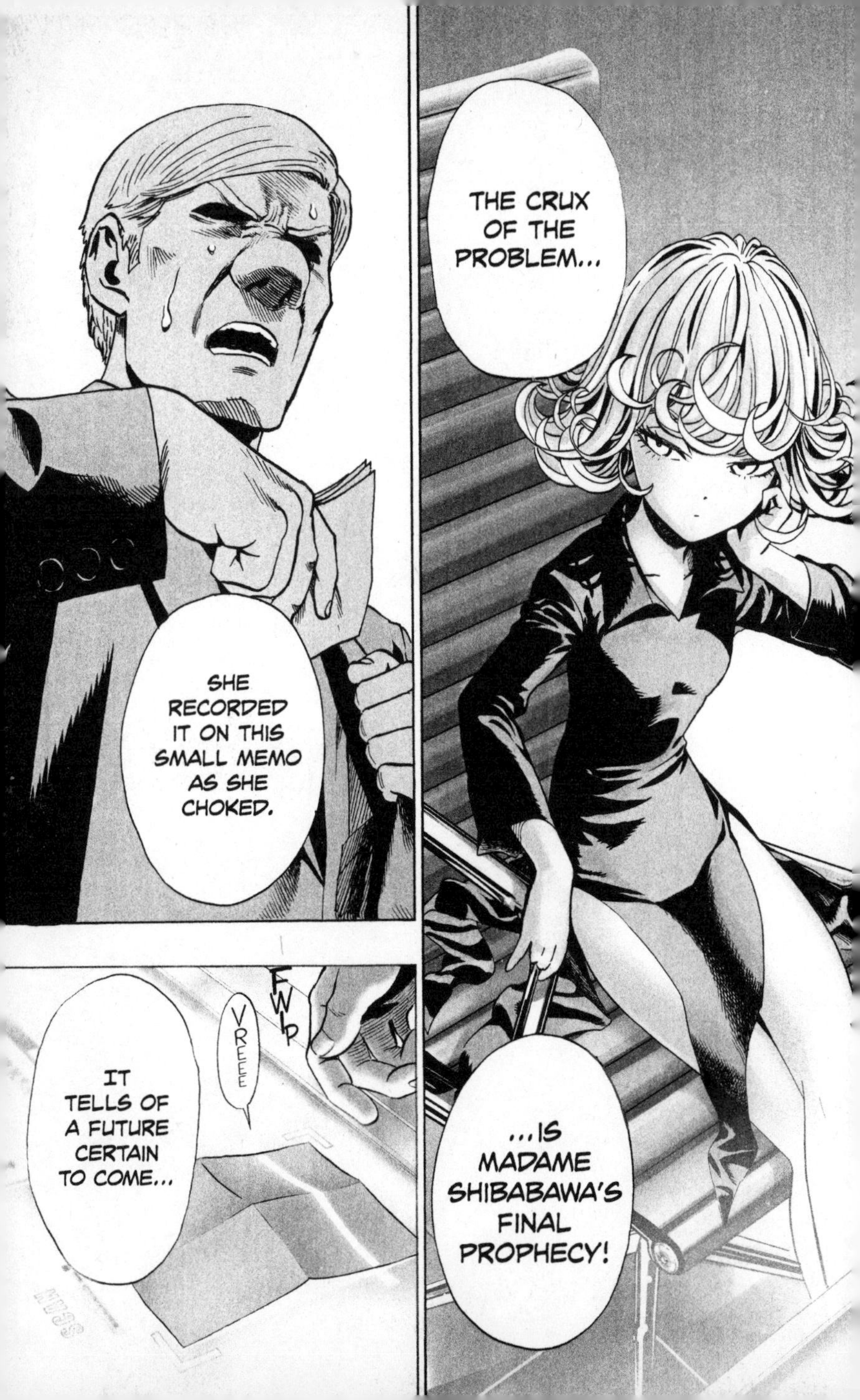
THE CRUX OF THE PROBLEM...
...IS MADAME SHIBABAWA'S FINAL PROPHECY!
SHE RECORDED IT ON THIS SMALL MEMO AS SHE CHOKED.
FWIP
VREEE
IT TELLS OF A FUTURE CERTAIN TO COME...

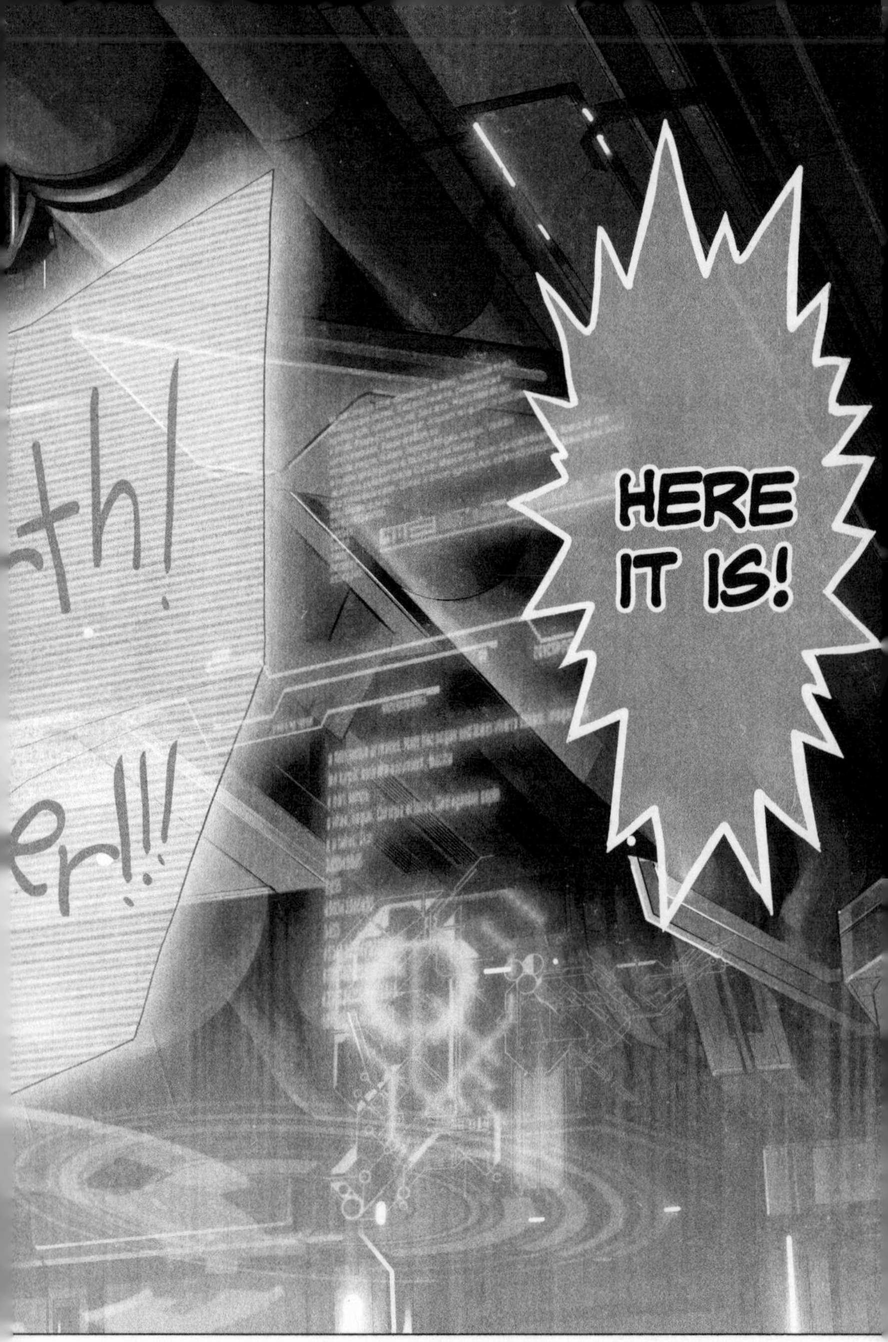
HERE IT IS!

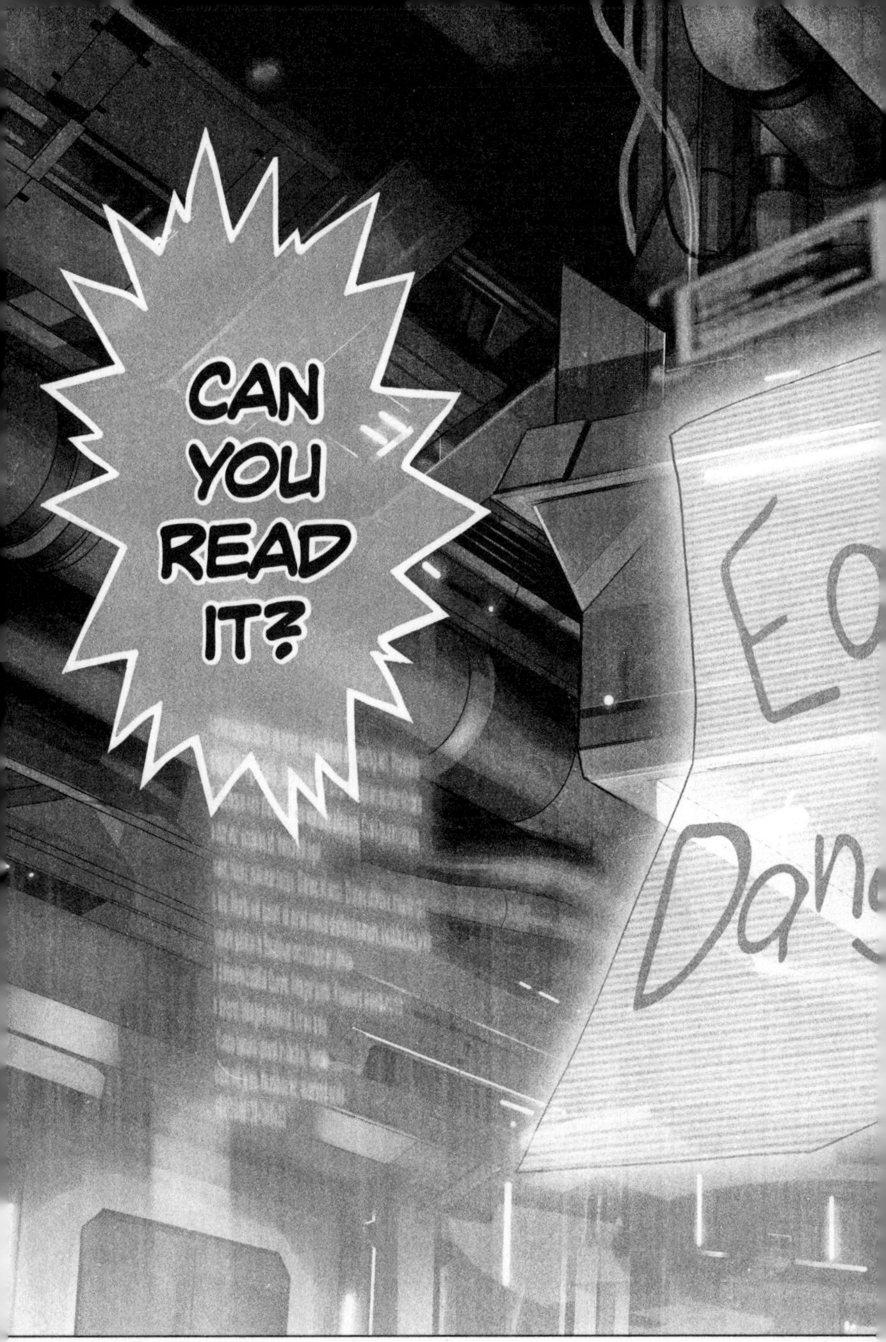
CAN YOU READ IT?

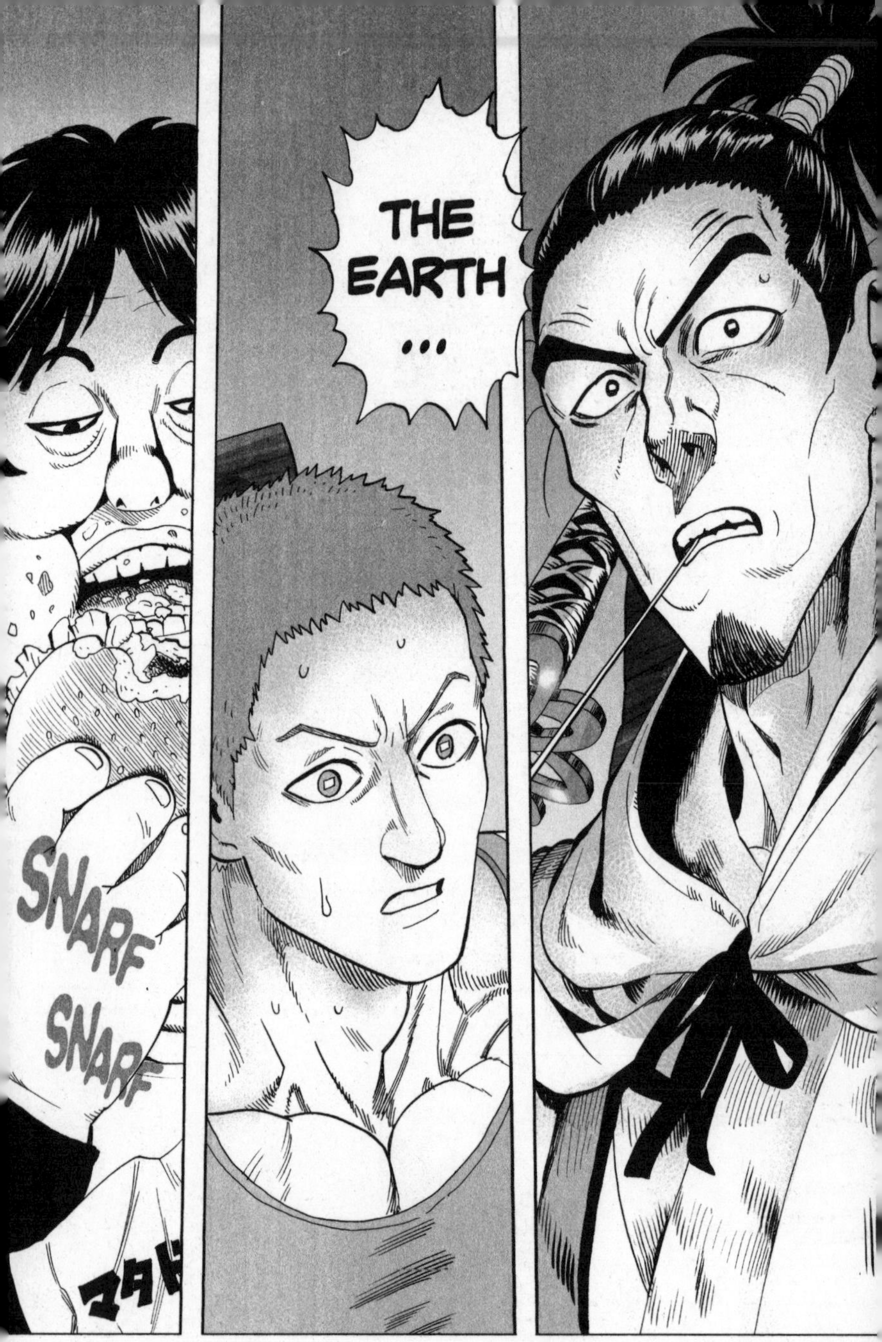
THE EARTH ...
SNARF
SNARF

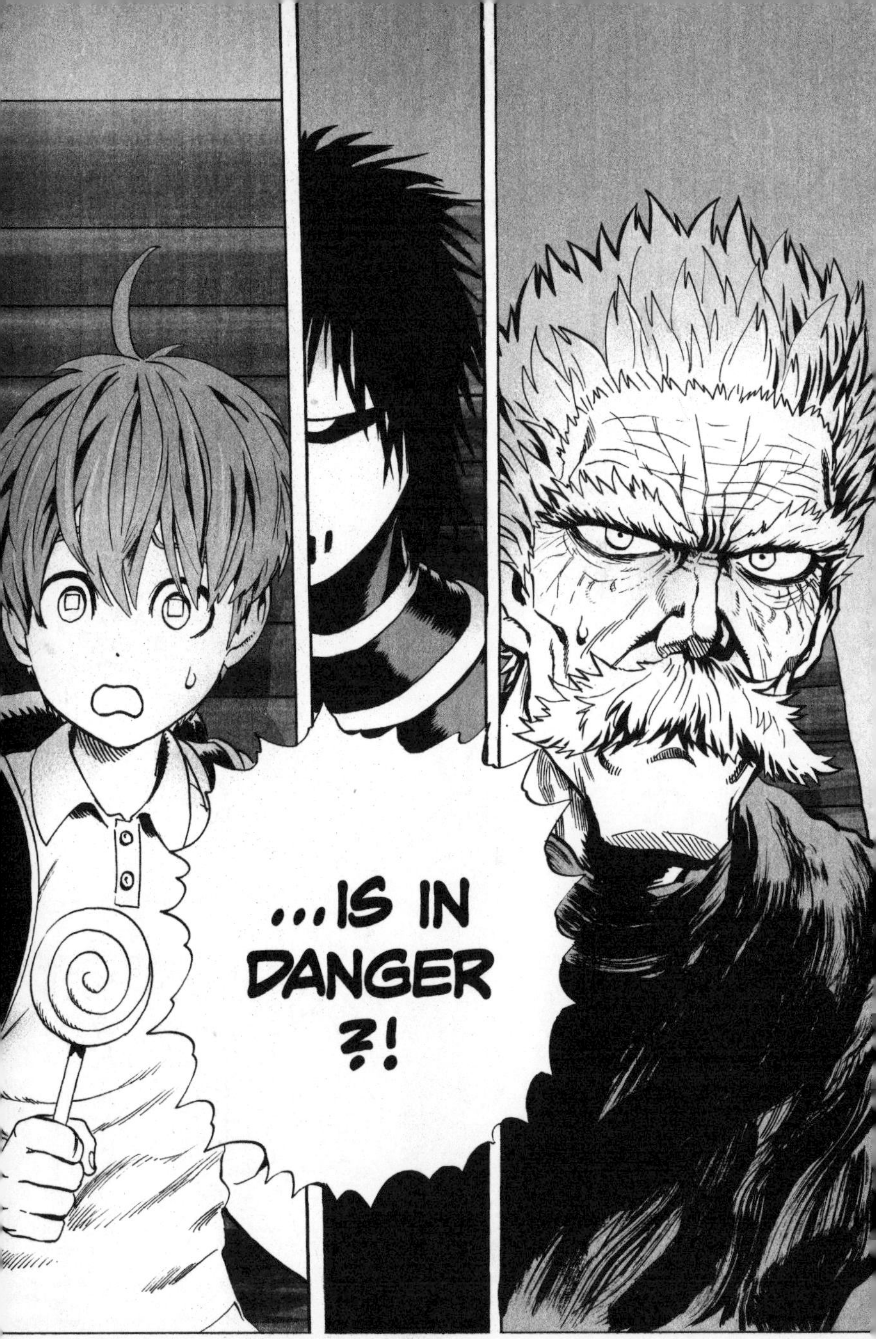
...IS IN DANGER ?!

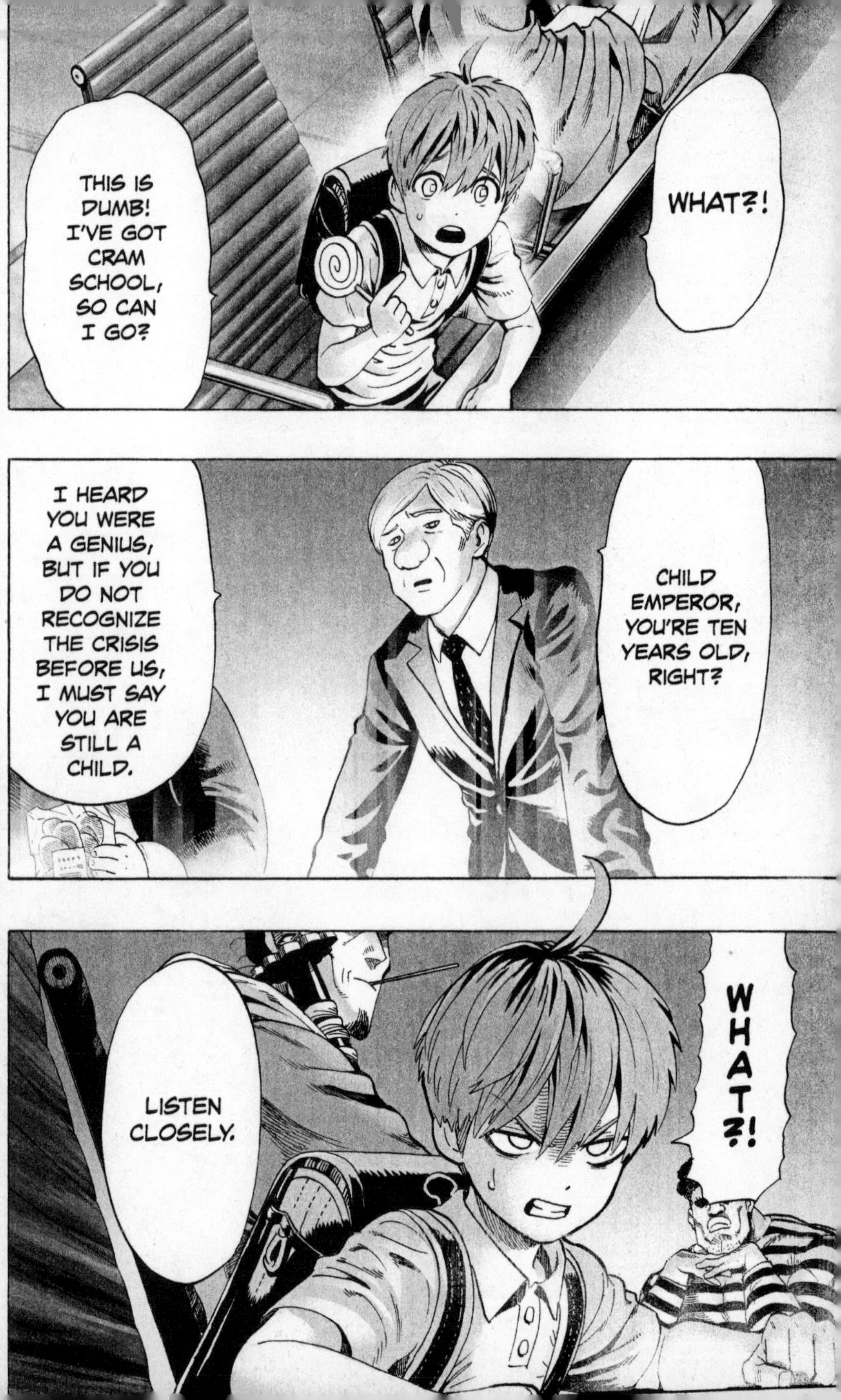
WHAT?!
THIS IS DUMB! I'VE GOT CRAM SCHOOL, SO CAN I GO?
CHILD EMPEROR, YOU'RE TEN YEARS OLD, RIGHT?
I HEARD YOU WERE A GENIUS, BUT IF YOU DO NOT RECOGNIZE THE CRISIS BEFORE US, I MUST SAY YOU ARE STILL A CHILD.
WHAT?!
LISTEN CLOSELY.

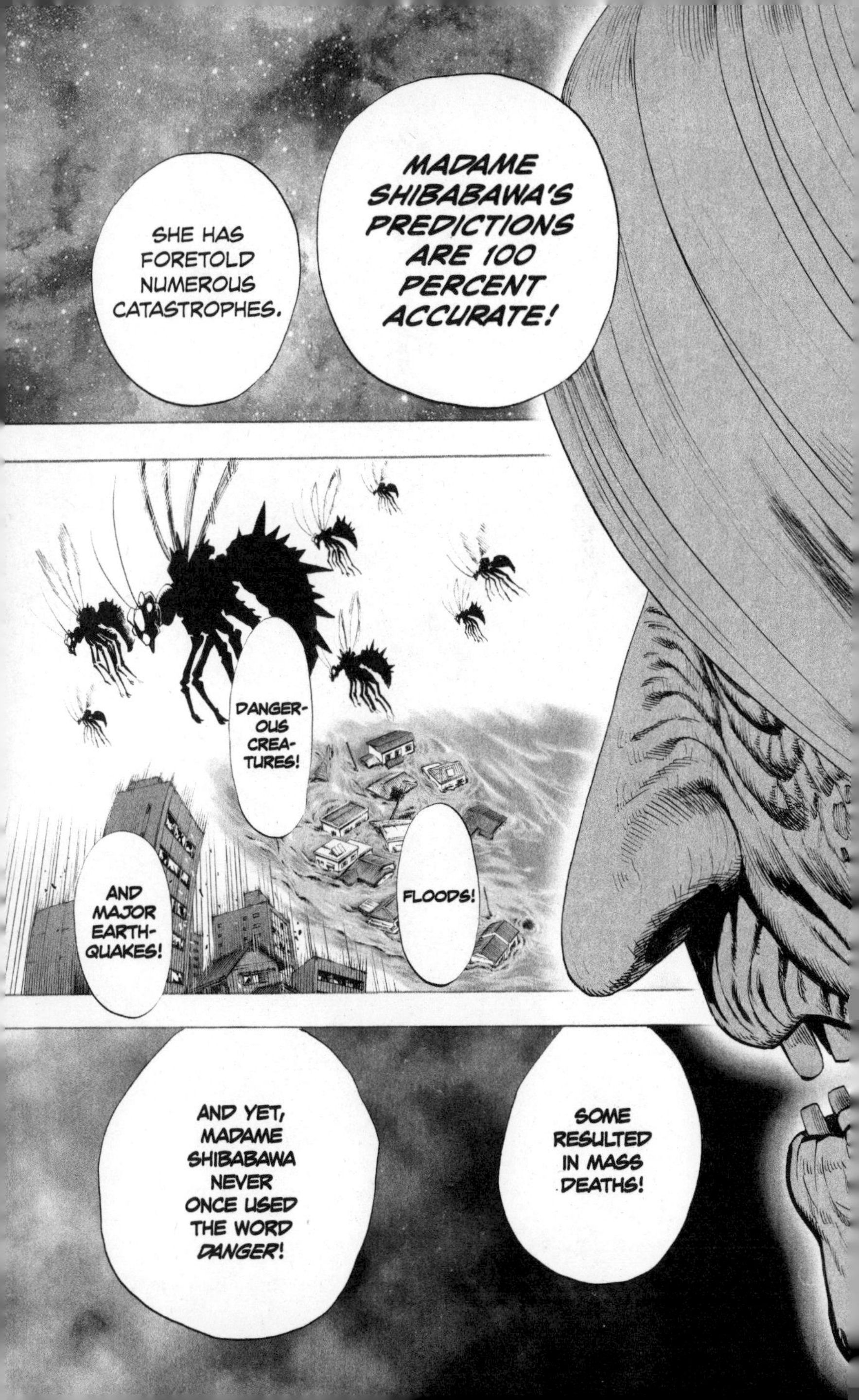
MADAME SHIBABAWA'S PREDICTIONS ARE 100 PERCENT ACCURATE!
SHE HAS FORETOLD NUMEROUS CATASTROPHES.
DANGER-OUS CREA-TURES!
FLOODS!
AND MAJOR EARTH-QUAKES!
SOME RESULTED IN MASS DEATHS!
AND YET, MADAME SHIBABAWA NEVER ONCE USED THE WORD *DANGER*!

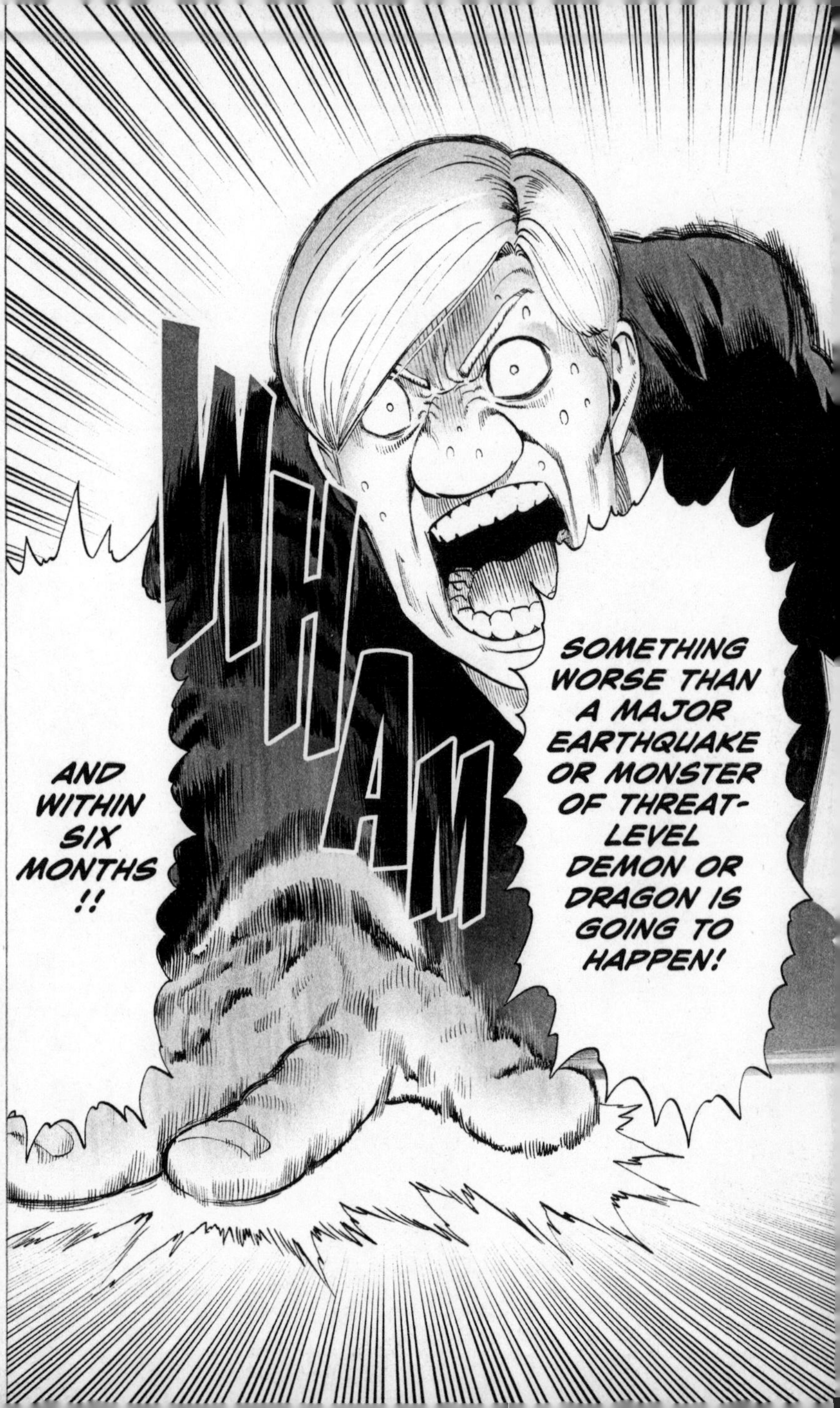
SOMETHING WORSE THAN A MAJOR EARTHQUAKE OR MONSTER OF THREAT-LEVEL DEMON OR DRAGON IS GOING TO HAPPEN!
WHAM
AND WITHIN SIX MONTHS !!

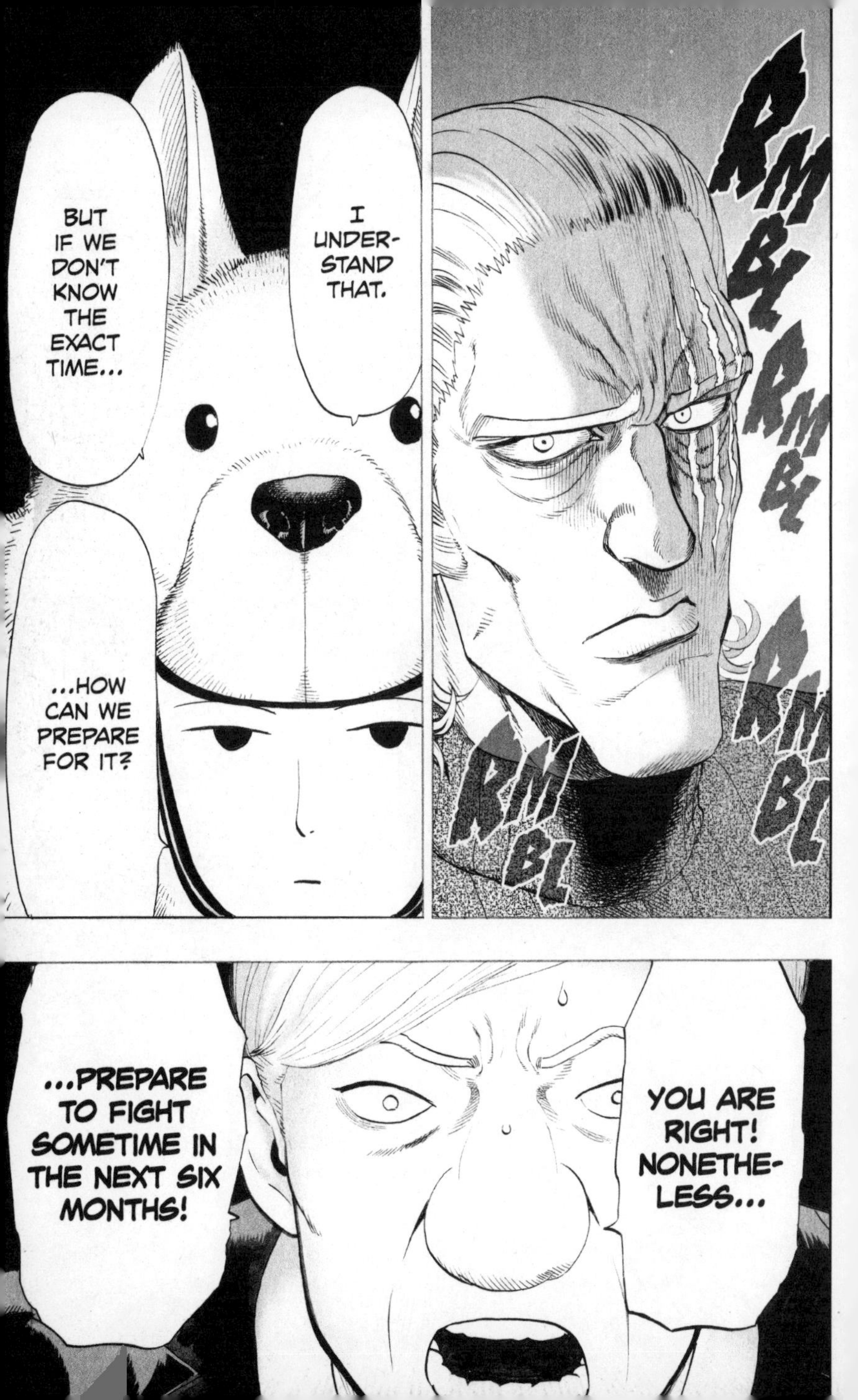
RMBL RMBL
RMBL
RMBL
I UNDERSTAND THAT.
BUT IF WE DON'T KNOW THE EXACT TIME...
...HOW CAN WE PREPARE FOR IT?
YOU ARE RIGHT! NONETHELESS...
...PREPARE TO FIGHT SOMETIME IN THE NEXT SIX MONTHS!

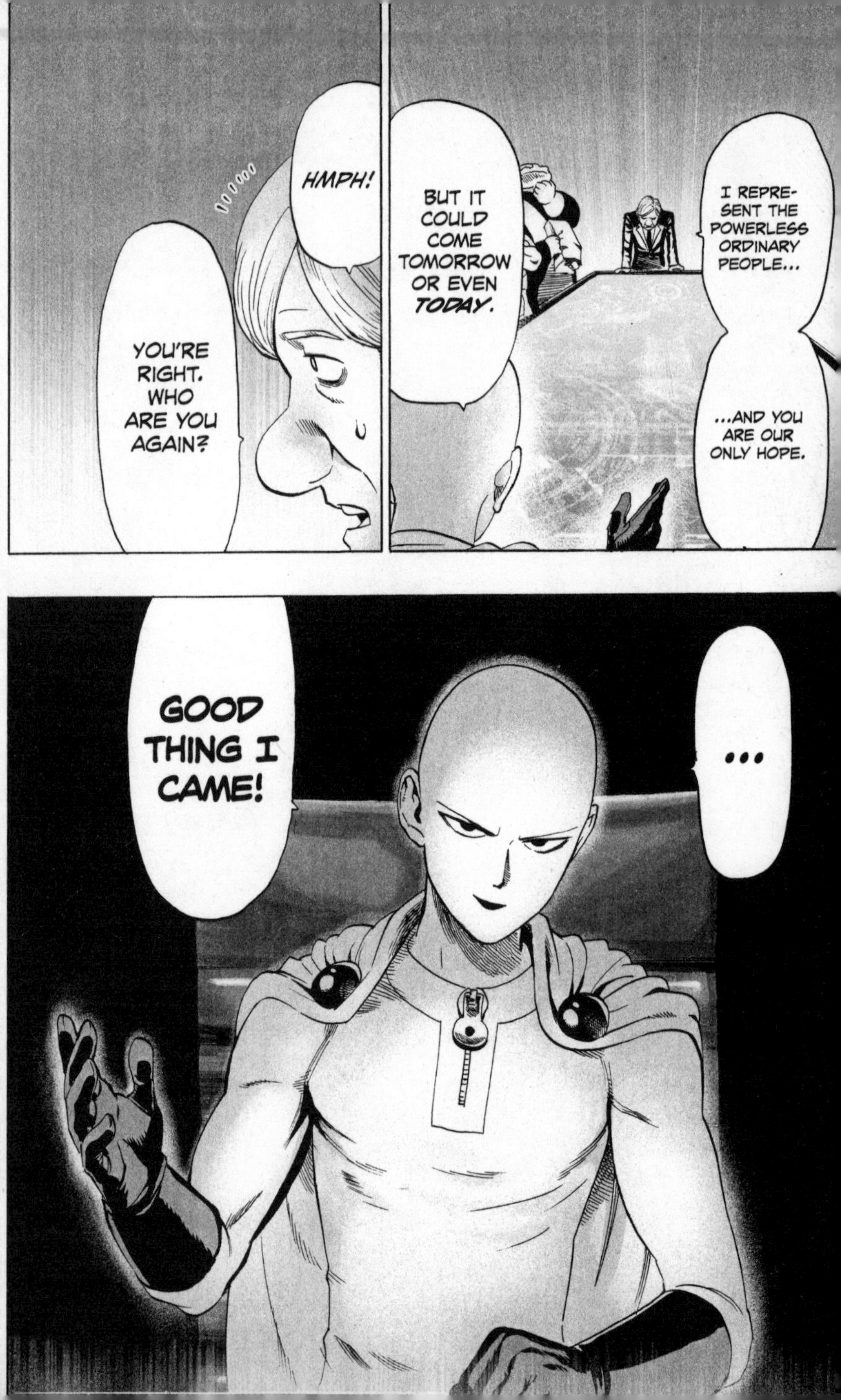
I REPRESENT THE POWERLESS ORDINARY PEOPLE...
...AND YOU ARE OUR ONLY HOPE.
BUT IT COULD COME TOMORROW OR EVEN *TODAY*.
HMPH!
YOU'RE RIGHT. WHO ARE YOU AGAIN?
...
GOOD THING I CAME!

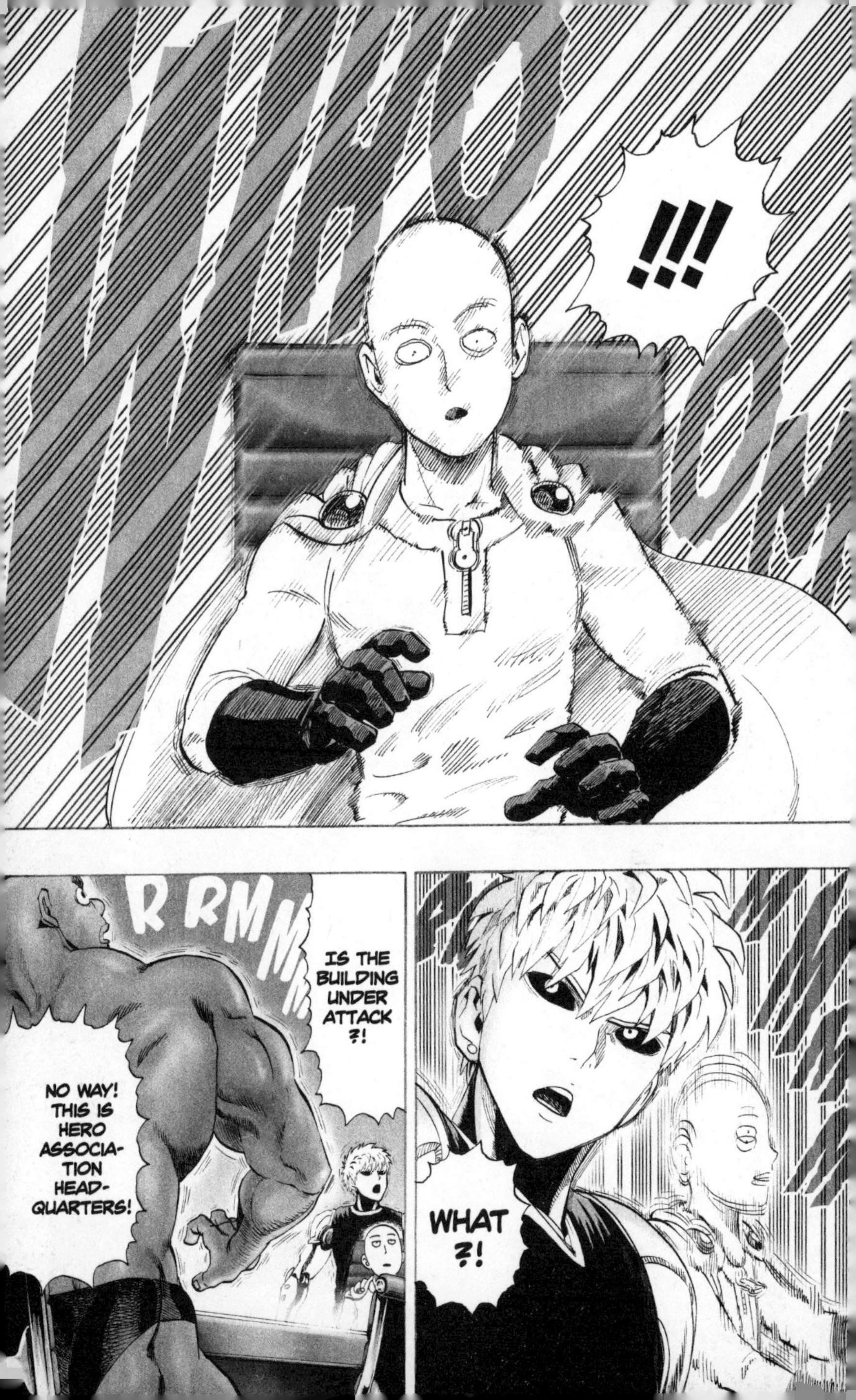
!!!
WHAT ?!
IS THE BUILDING UNDER ATTACK ?!
RRMMM
NO WAY! THIS IS HERO ASSOCIATION HEADQUARTERS!

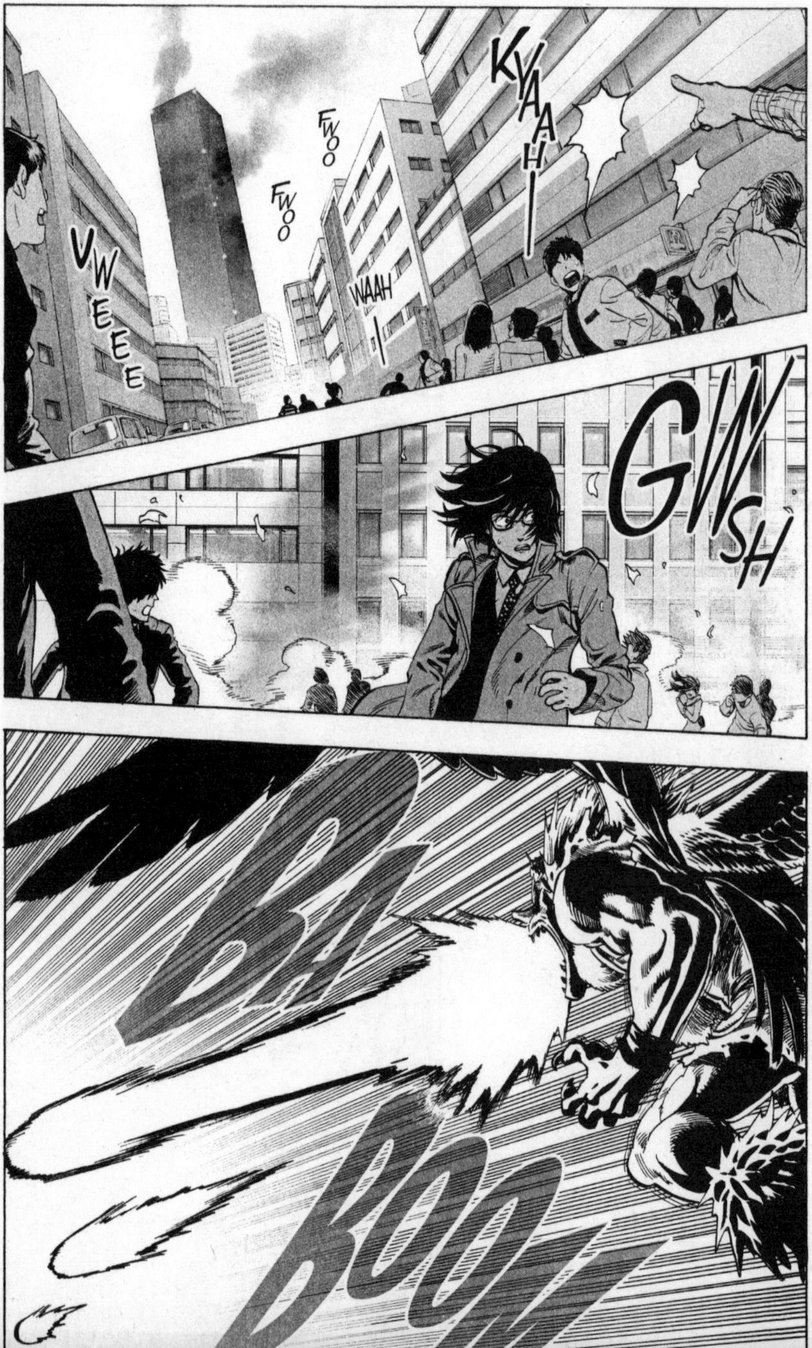
KYAAAH!
FWOO
FWOO
WAAH!
VWEEEE
GWSH

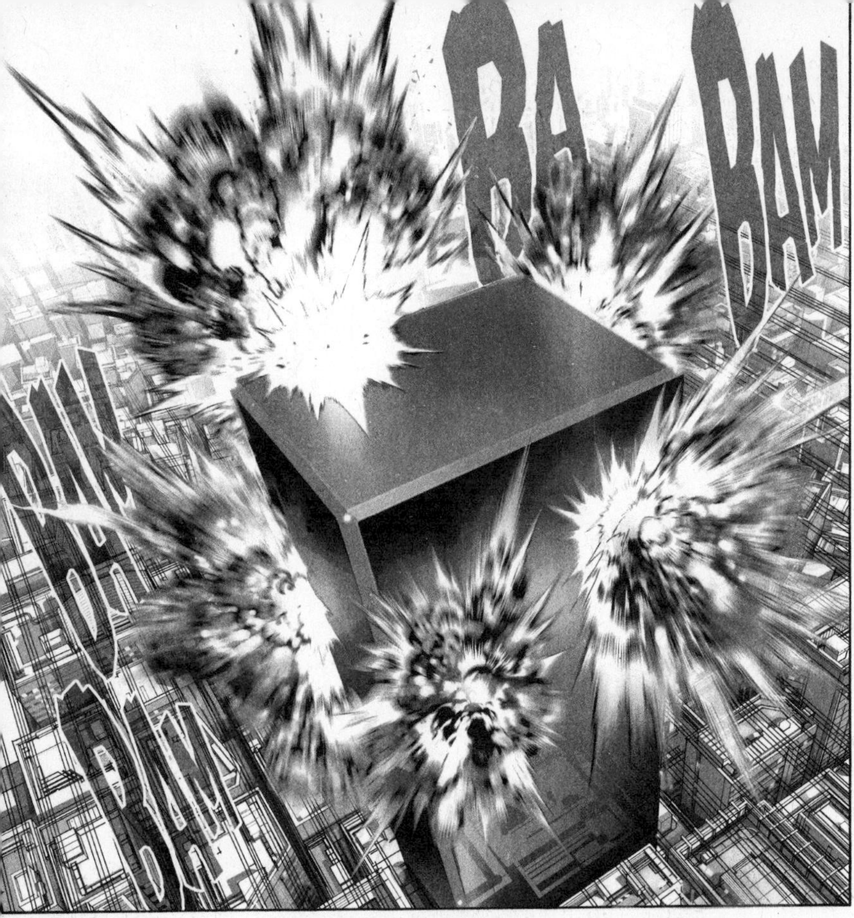
BA BAM

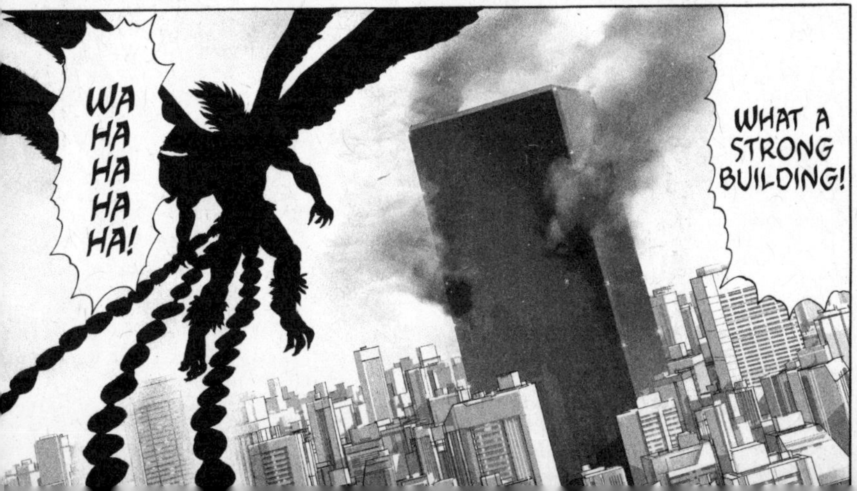
WHAT A STRONG BUILDING!
WA HA HA HA HA!

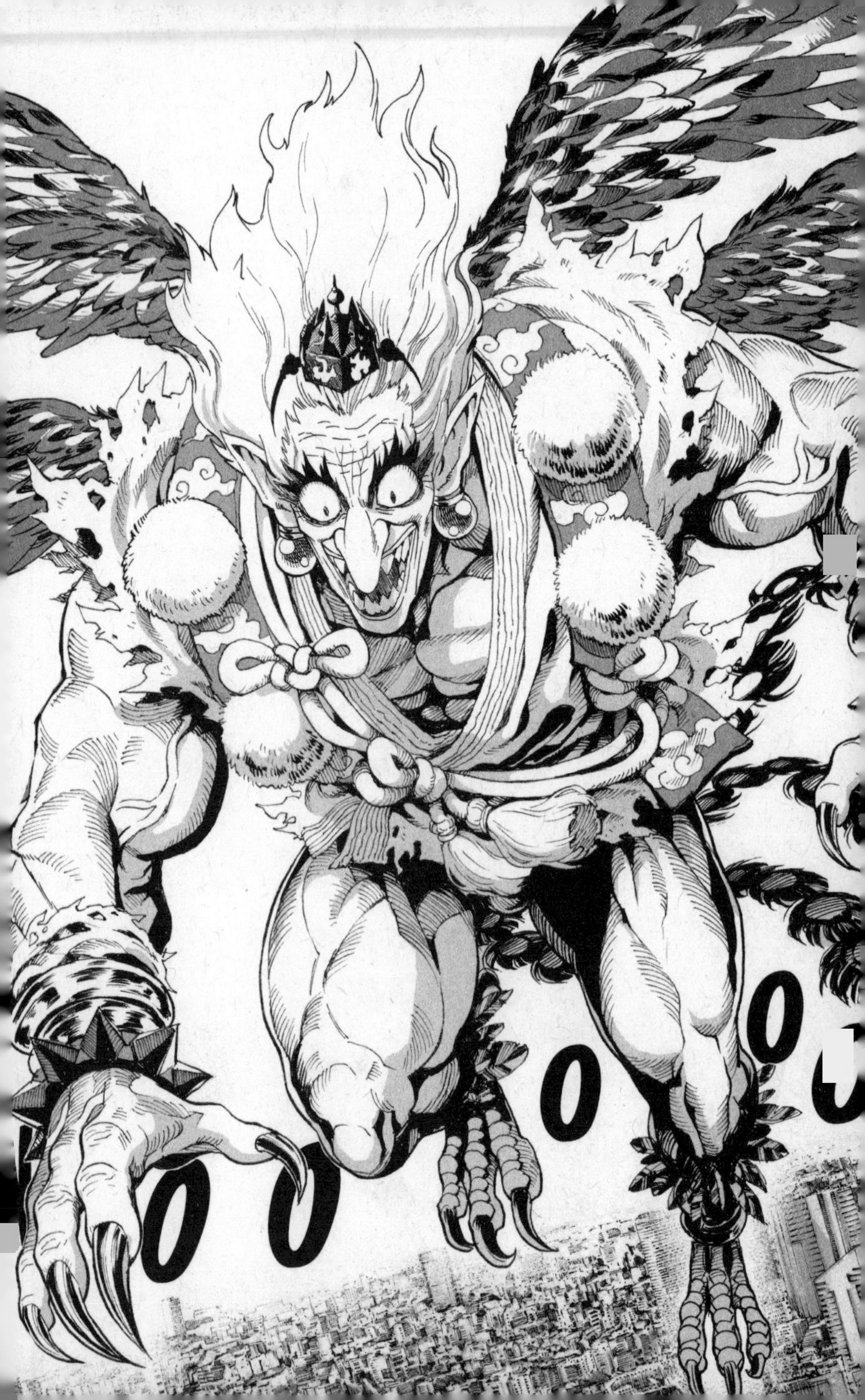

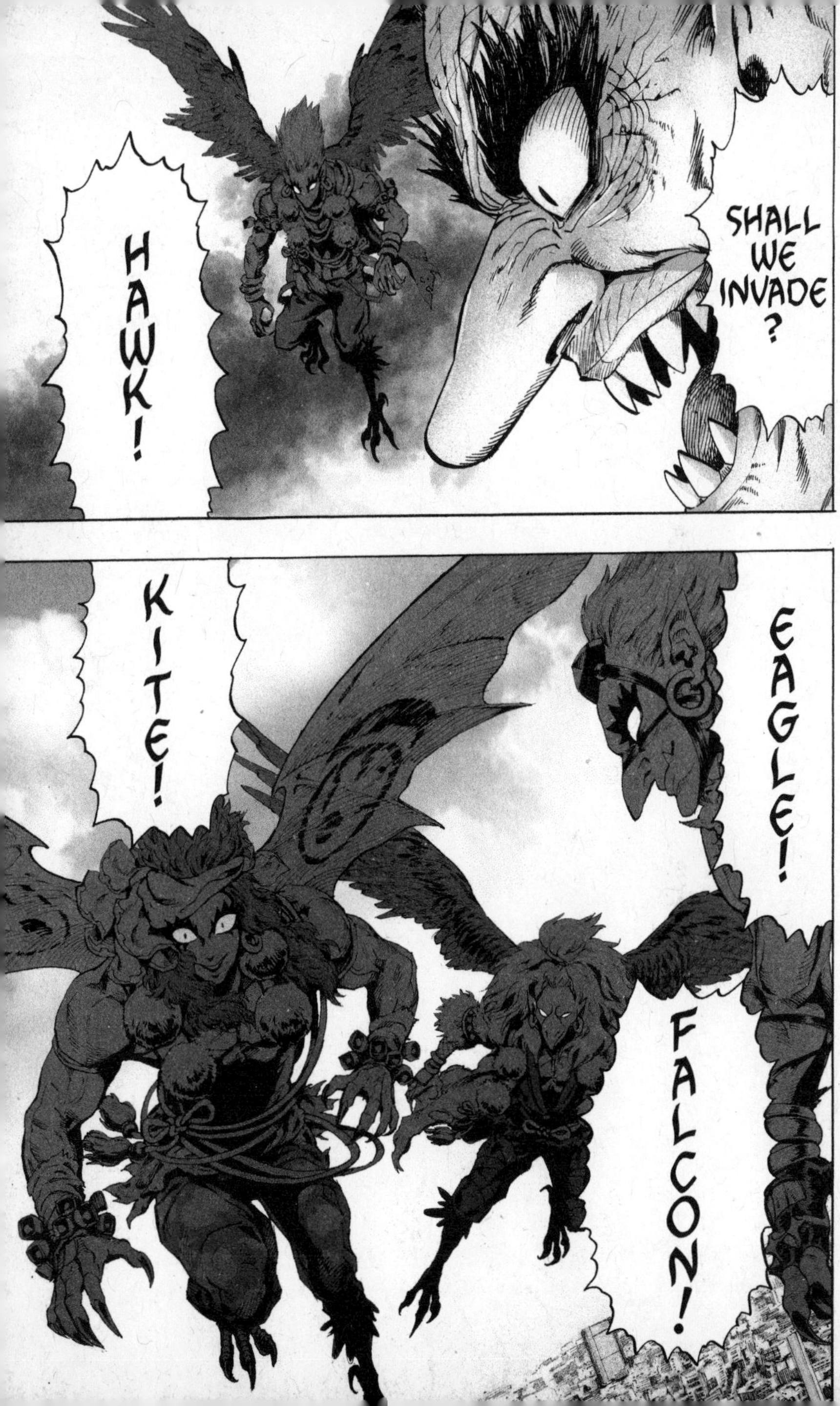
SHALL WE INVADE?
HAWK!
EAGLE!
KITE!
FALCON!

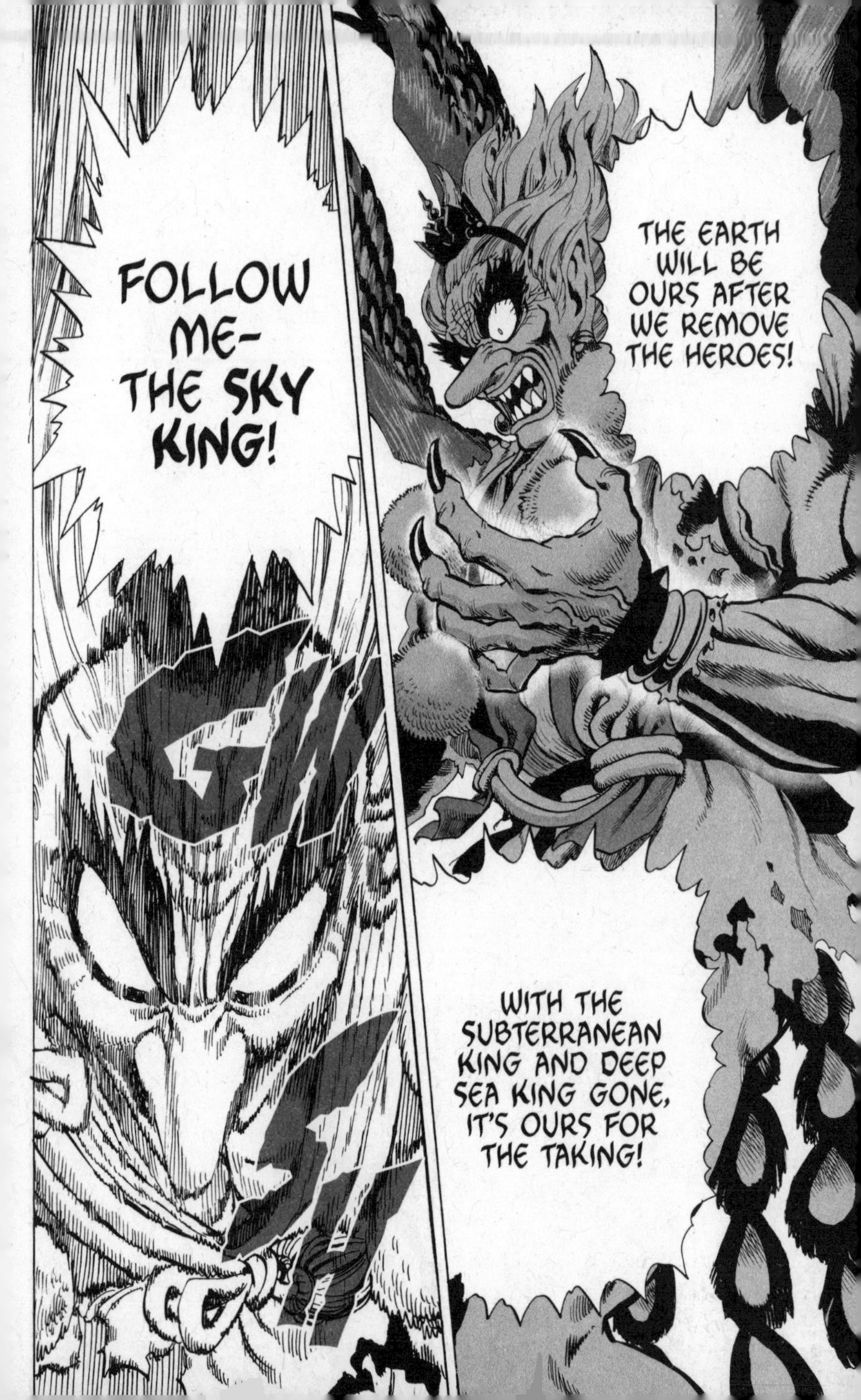
THE EARTH WILL BE OURS AFTER WE REMOVE THE HEROES!
WITH THE SUBTERRANEAN KING AND DEEP SEA KING GONE, IT'S OURS FOR THE TAKING!
FOLLOW ME- THE SKY KING!

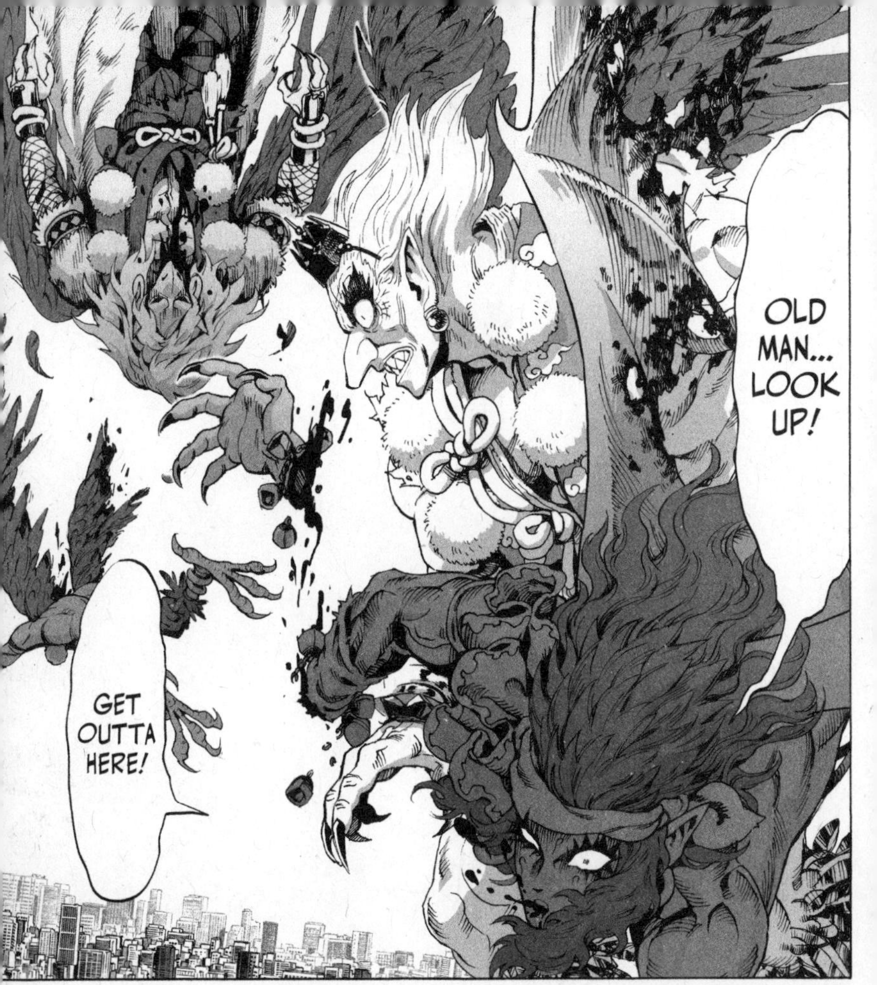
OLD MAN... LOOK UP!
GET OUTTA HERE!
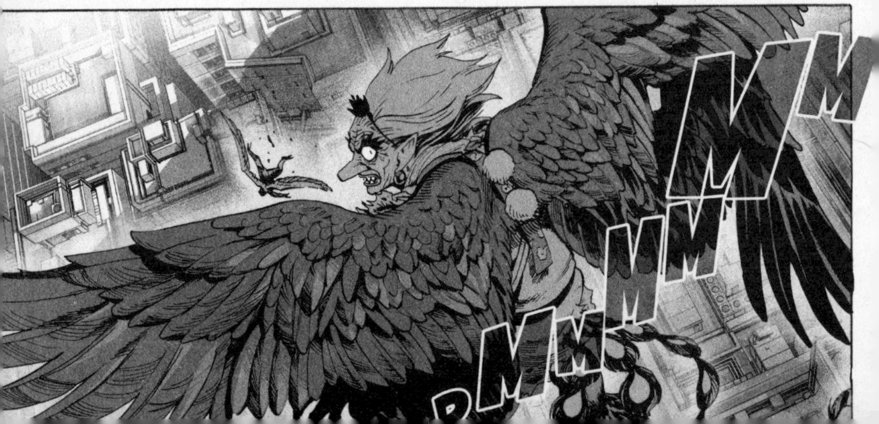

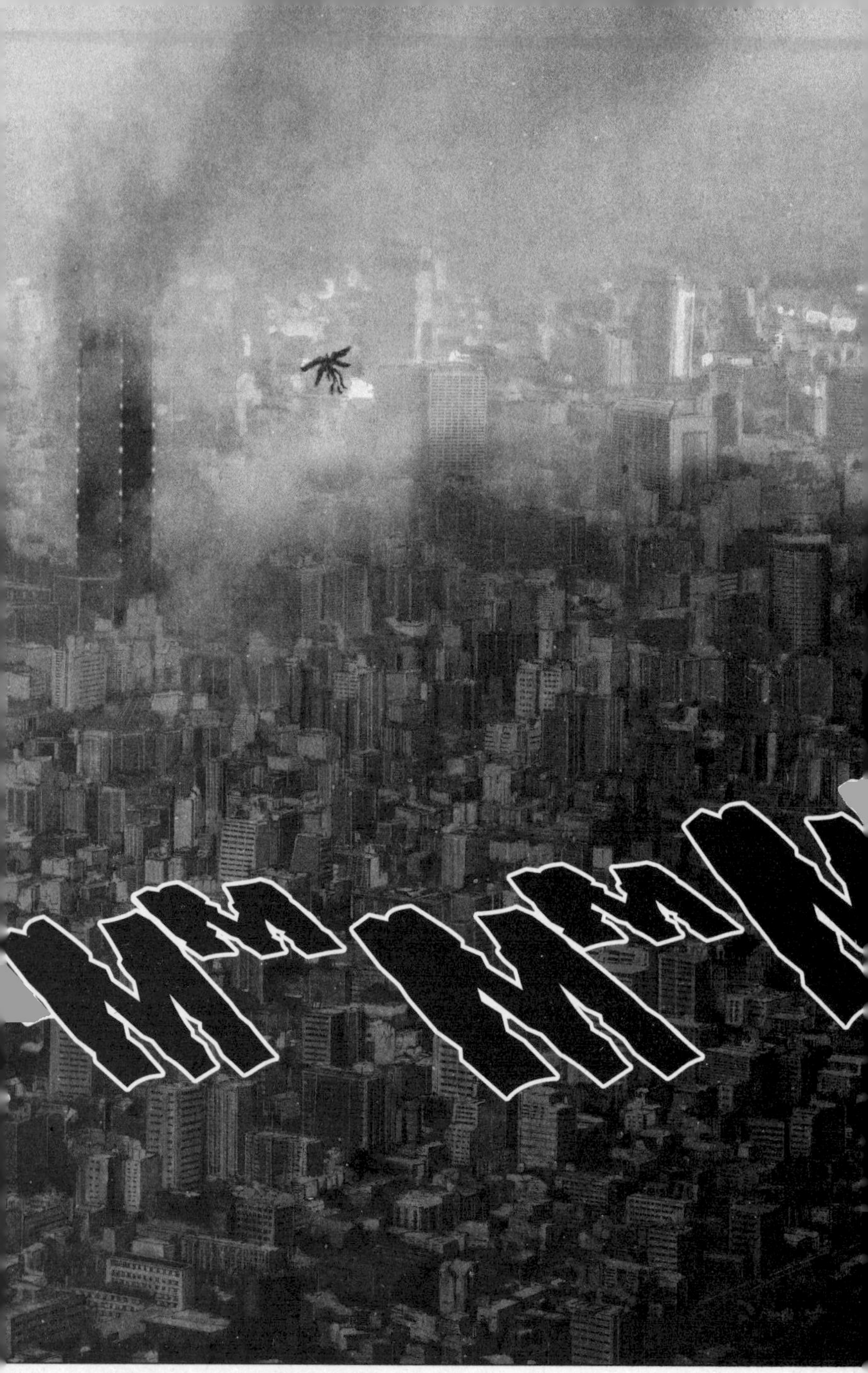

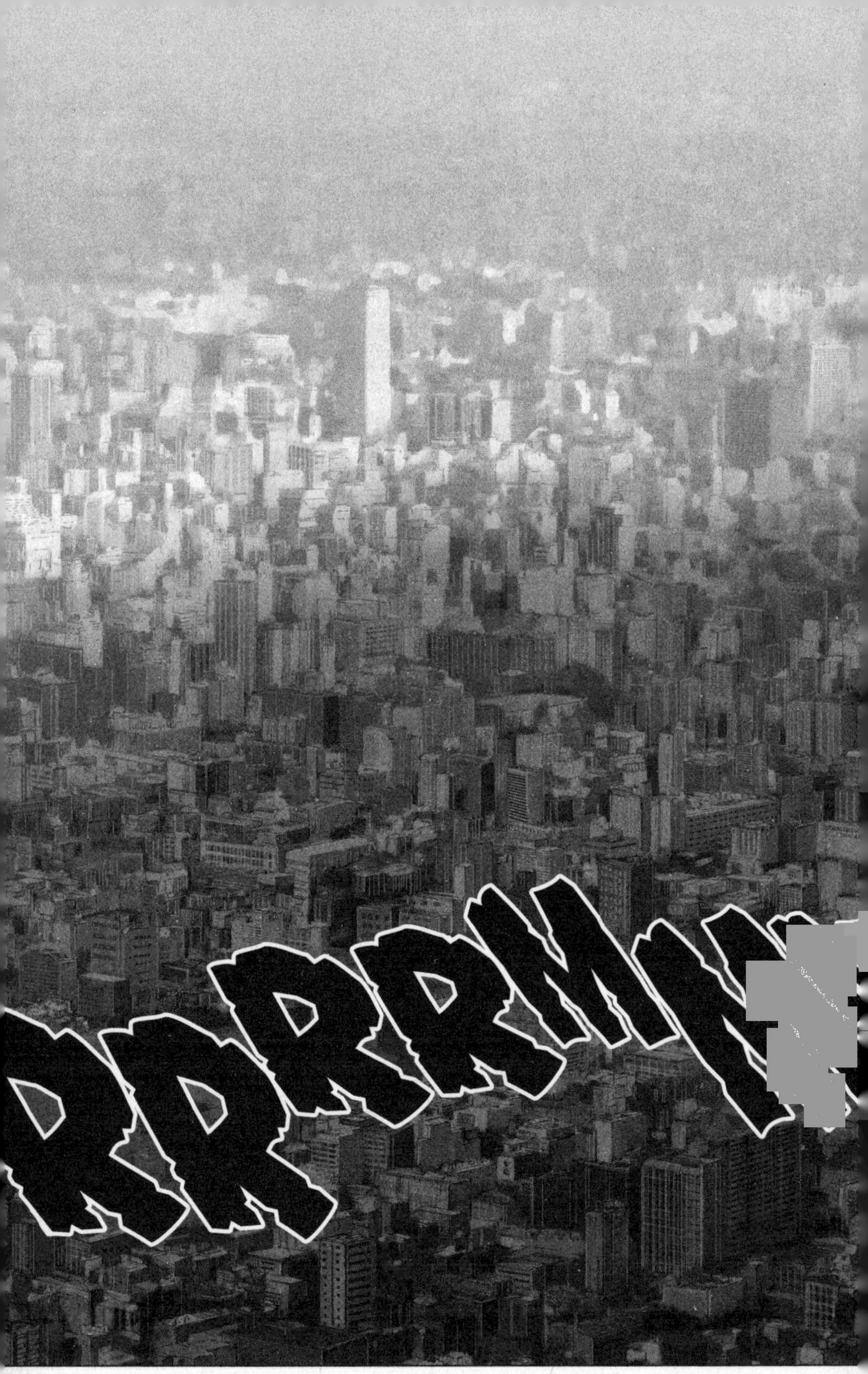
RRRRMM

BONUS

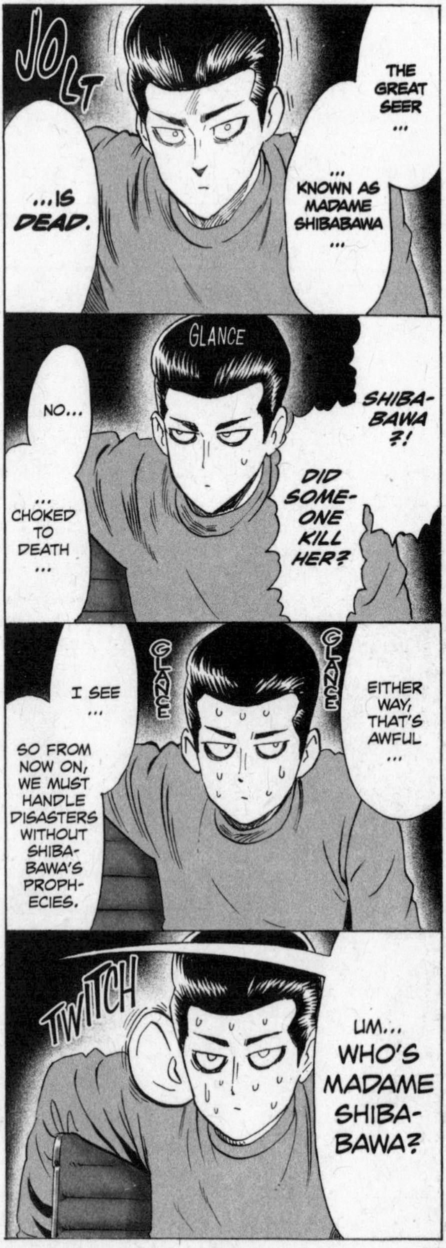

THE GREAT SEER ...
... KNOWN AS MADAME SHIBABAWA ...
JOLT
...IS DEAD.
GLANCE
SHIBA-BAWA?!
DID SOME-ONE KILL HER?
NO...
... CHOKED TO DEATH ...
EITHER WAY, THAT'S AWFUL ...
GLANCE
GLANCE
I SEE ...
SO FROM NOW ON, WE MUST HANDLE DISASTERS WITHOUT SHIBA-BAWA'S PROPH-ECIES.
UM... WHO'S MADAME SHIBA-BAWA?
TWITCH

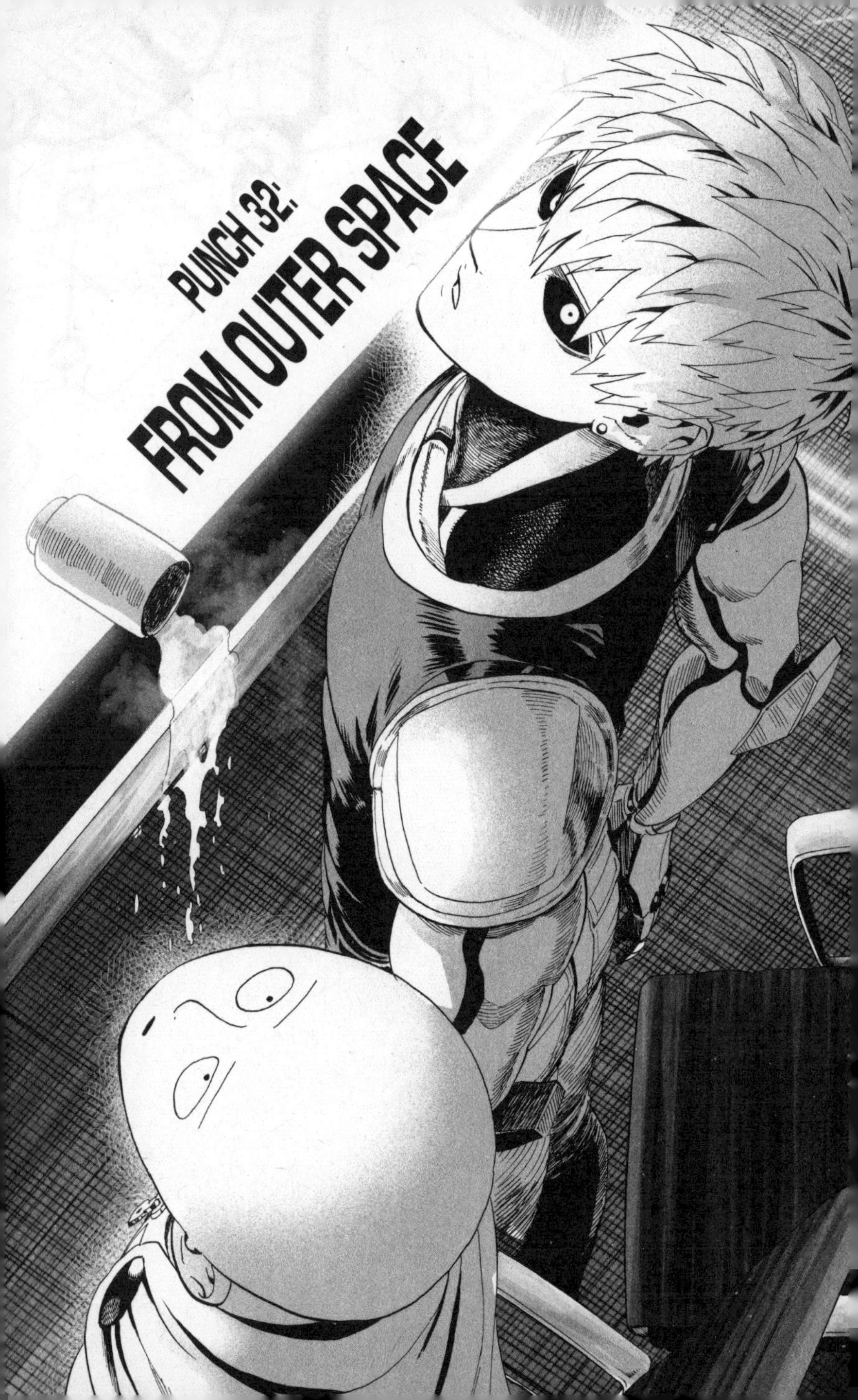
PUNCH 32:
FROM OUTER SPACE

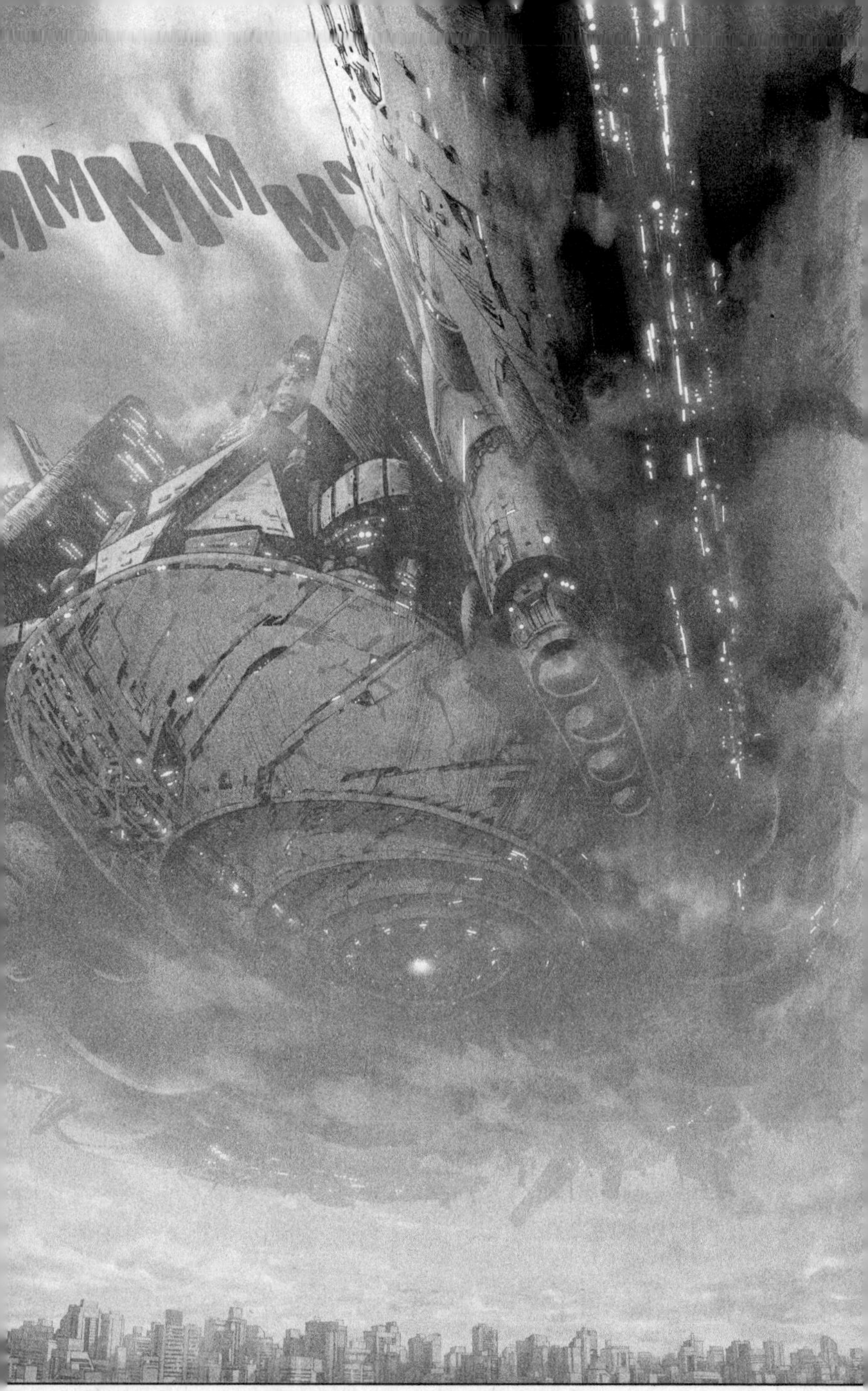
MMMMM-MM

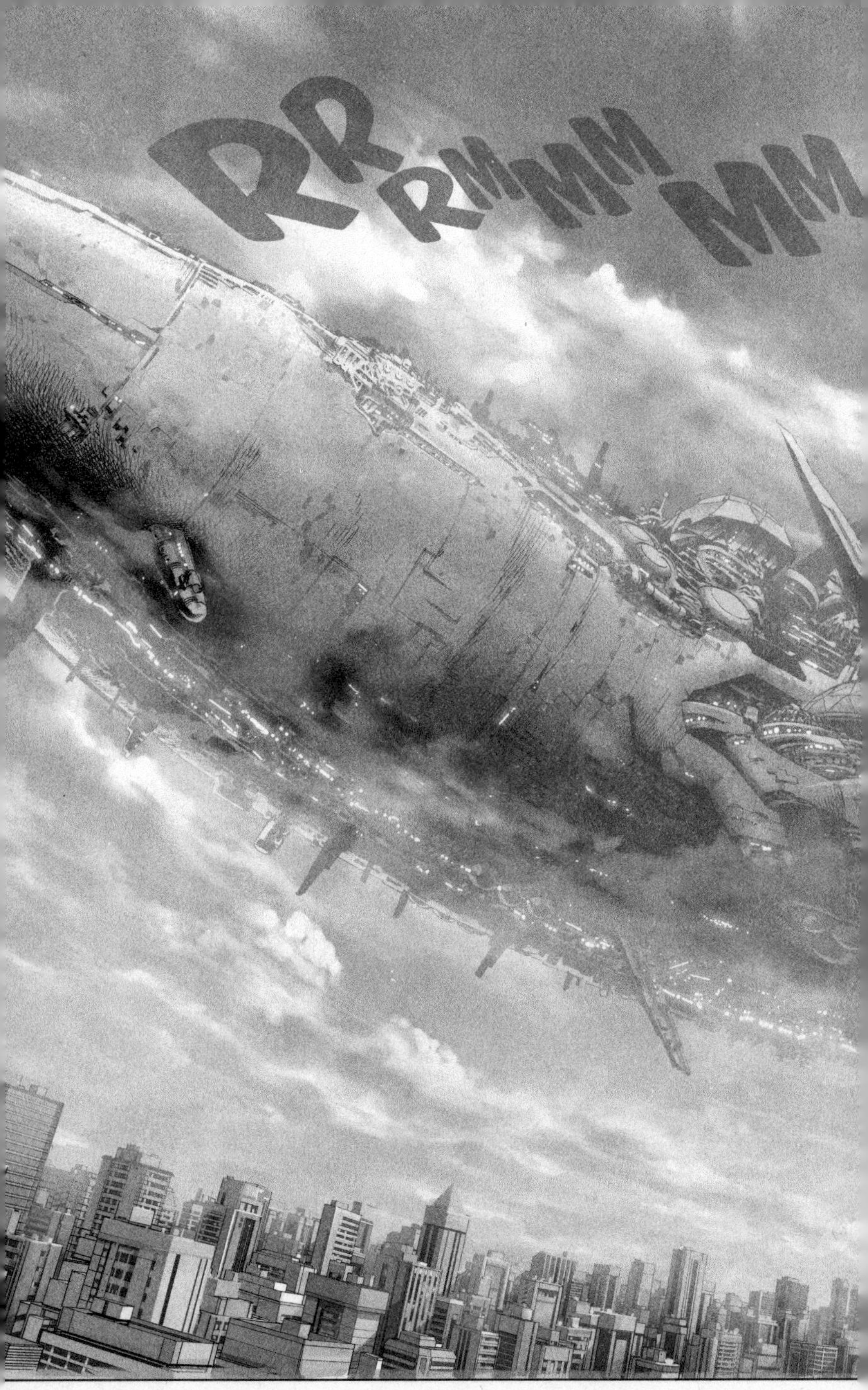
RRRMMMMMM

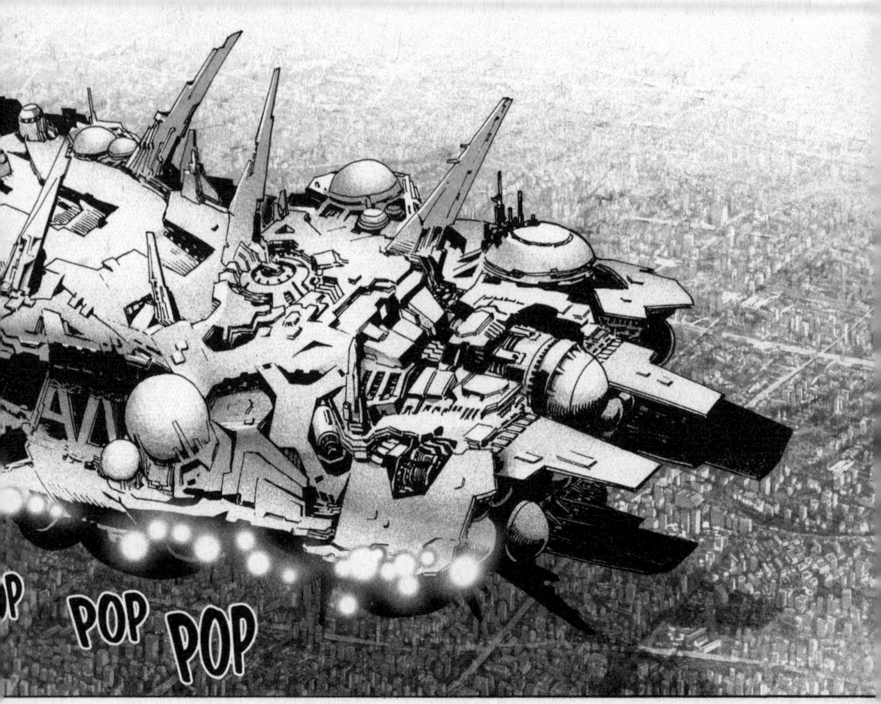
POP
POP

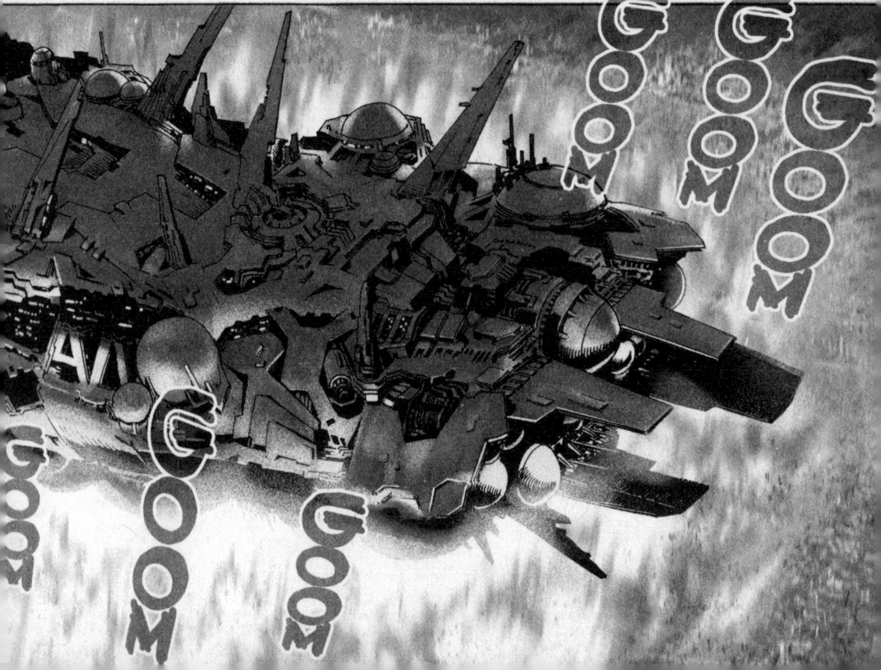
GOOOM
GOOOM
GOOOM
GOOOM
GOOOM

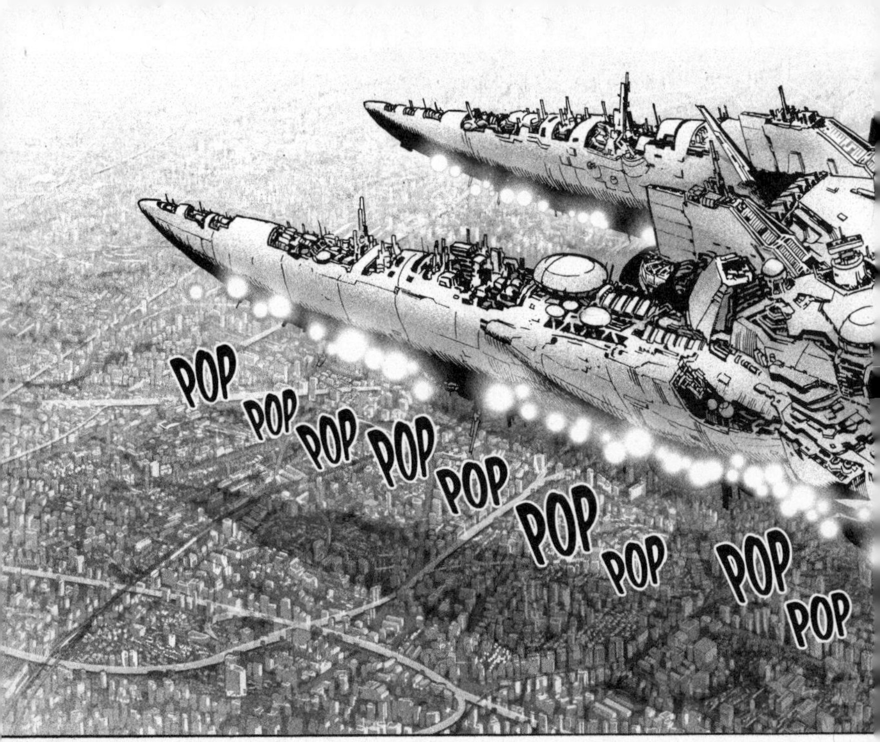
POP
POP
POP
POP
POP
POP
POP
POP
POP
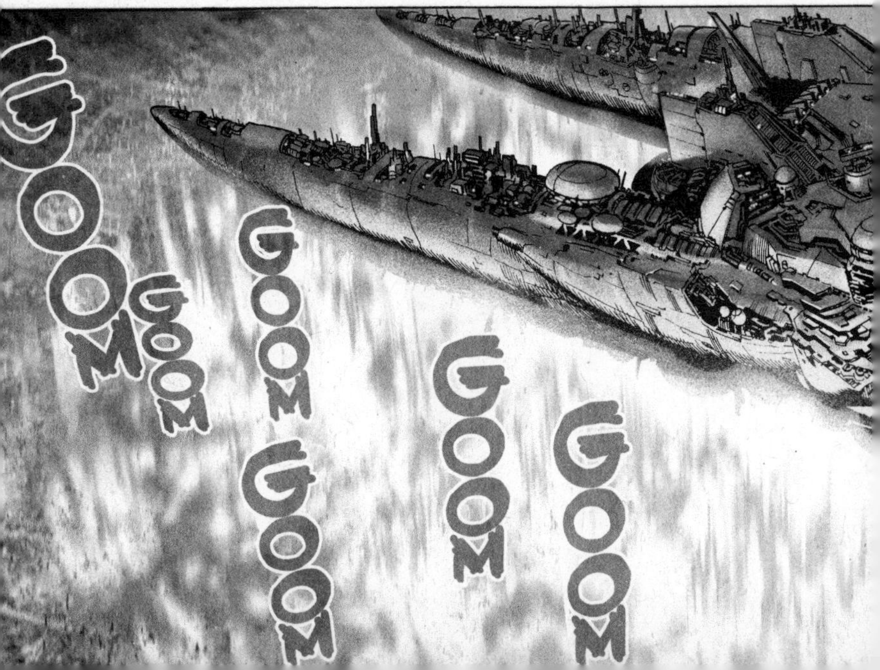
GOOM
GOOM
GOOM
GOOM
GOOM
GOOM

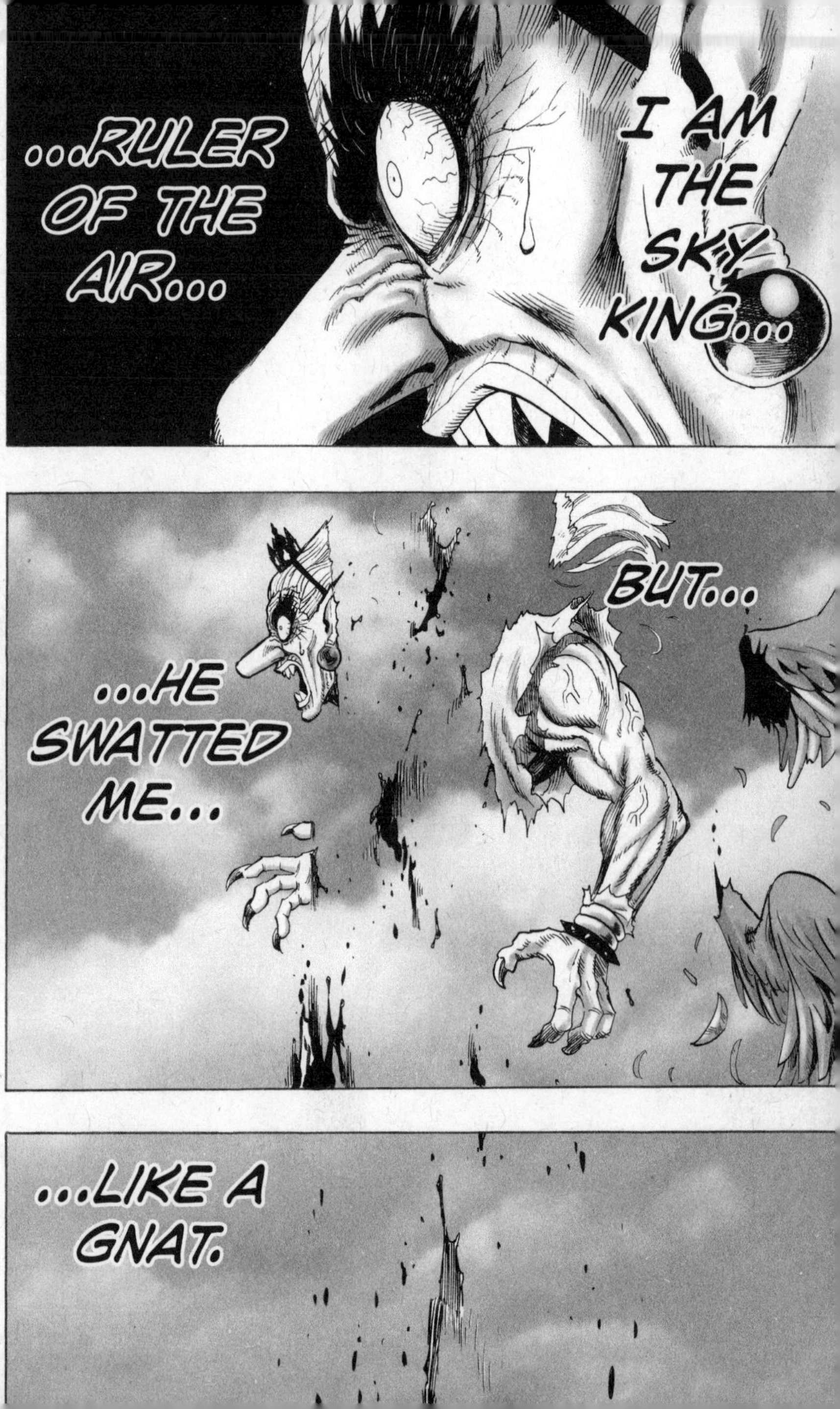
I AM THE SKY KING...
...RULER OF THE AIR...
BUT...
...HE SWATTED ME...
...LIKE A GNAT.

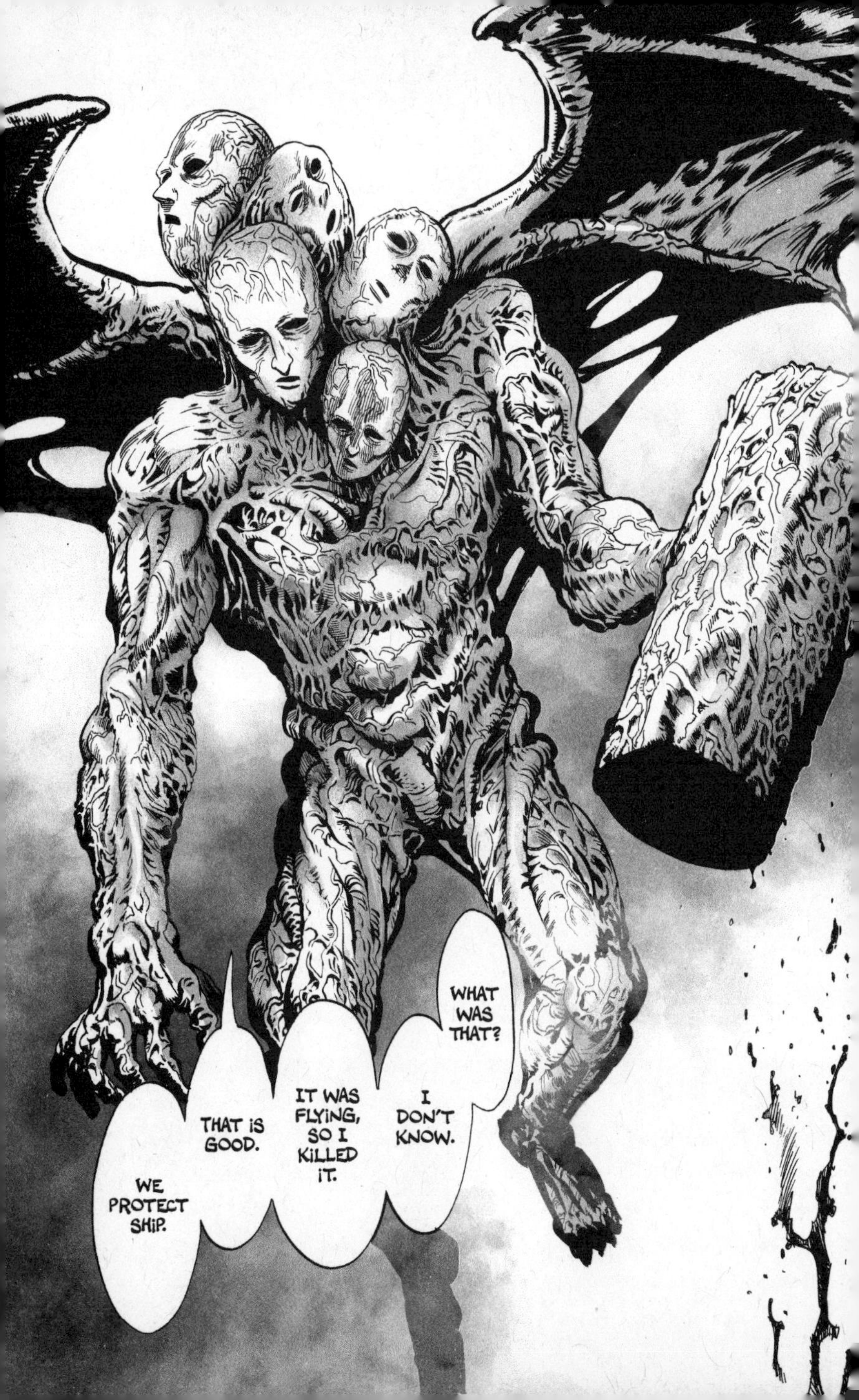
WHAT WAS THAT?
I DON'T KNOW.
IT WAS FLYING, SO I KILLED IT.
THAT IS GOOD.
WE PROTECT SHIP.

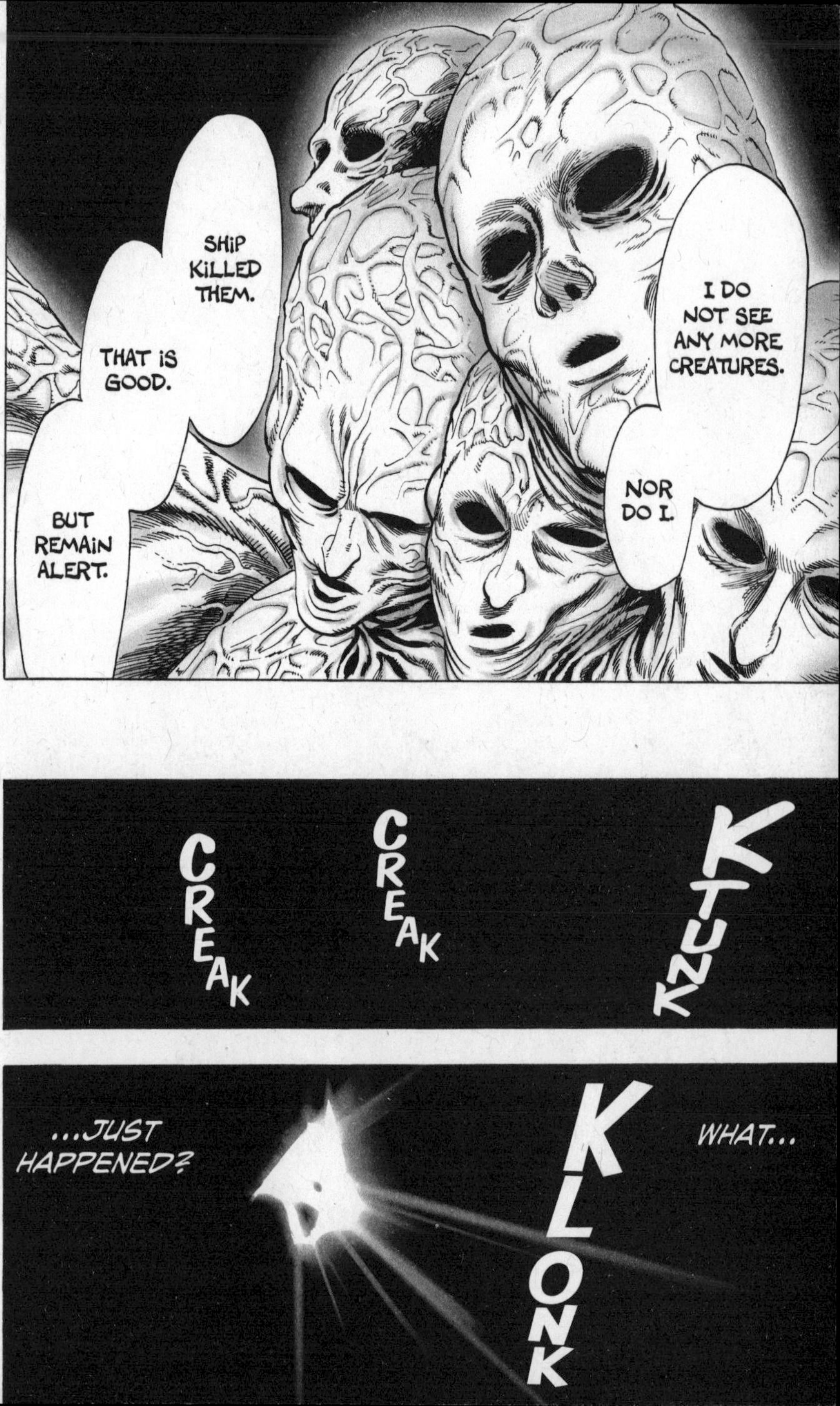
I DO NOT SEE ANY MORE CREATURES.
NOR DO I.
SHIP KILLED THEM.
THAT IS GOOD.
BUT REMAIN ALERT.
KTUNK
CREAK
CREAK
KLONK
WHAT...
...JUST HAPPENED?

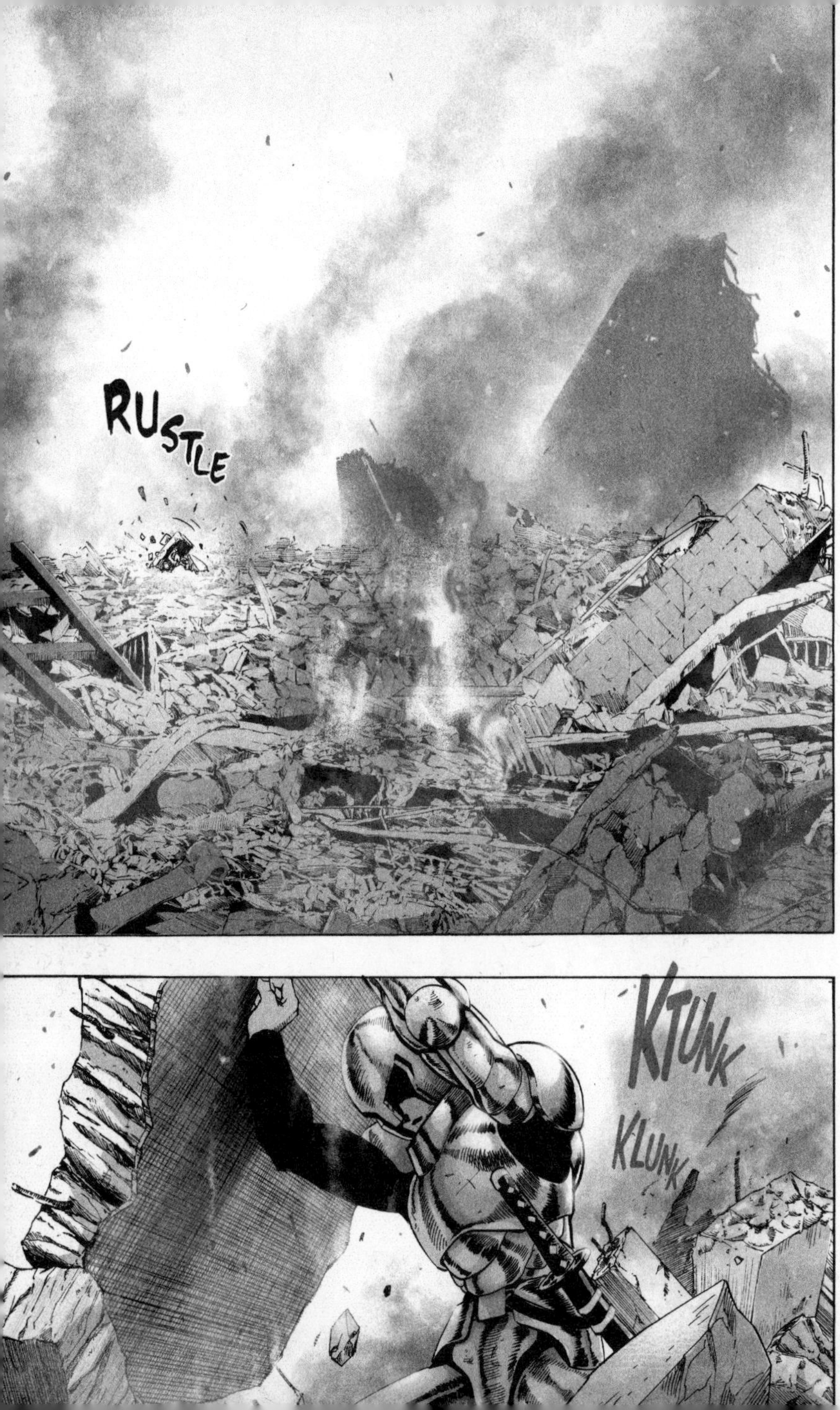
RUSTLE
KTUNK
KLUNK

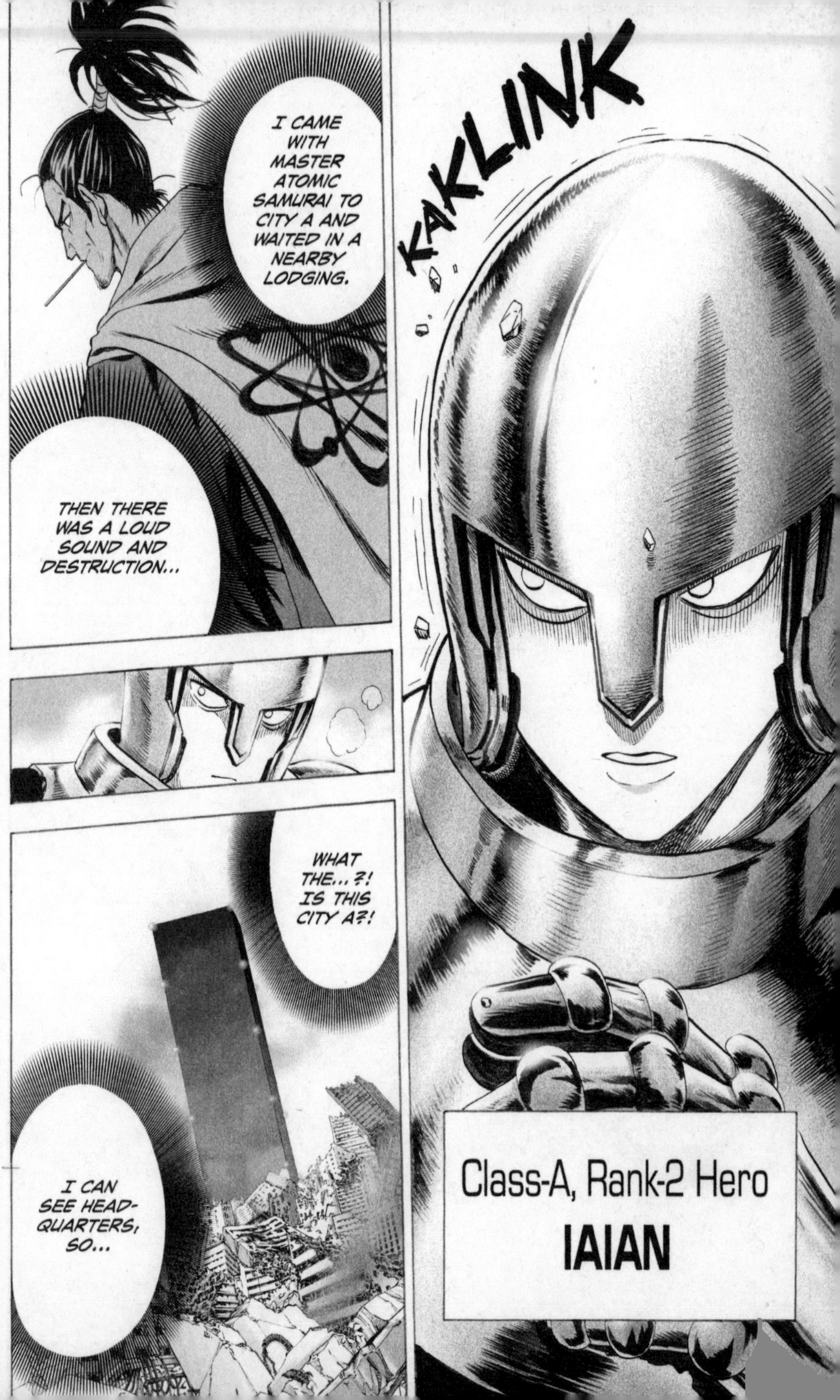
KAKLINK
Class-A, Rank-2 Hero
IAIAN
I CAME WITH MASTER ATOMIC SAMURAI TO CITY A AND WAITED IN A NEARBY LODGING.
THEN THERE WAS A LOUD SOUND AND DESTRUCTION...
WHAT THE...?! IS THIS CITY A?!
I CAN SEE HEAD-QUARTERS, SO...

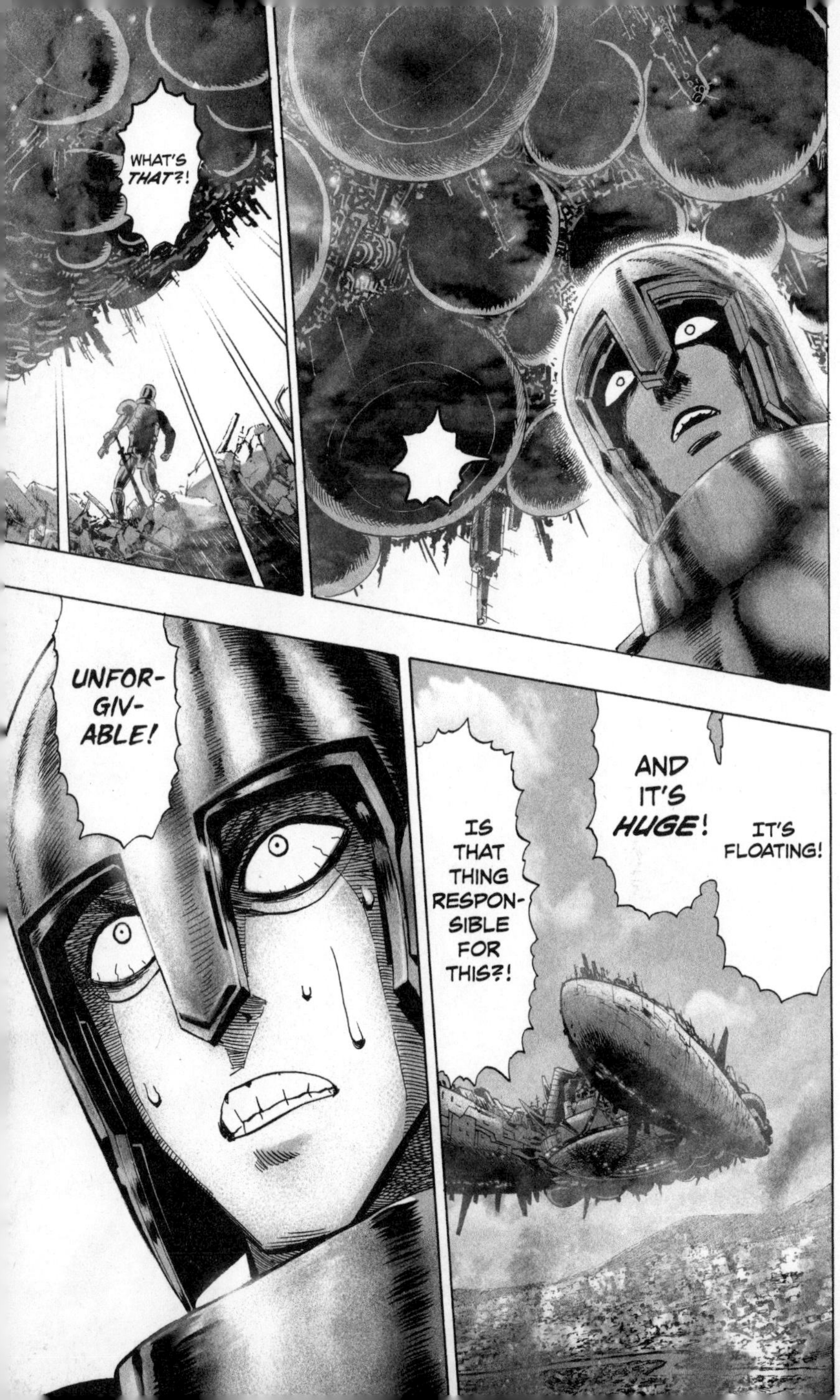
WHAT'S THAT?!
IT'S FLOATING!
AND IT'S HUGE!
IS THAT THING RESPONSIBLE FOR THIS?!
UNFORGIVABLE!

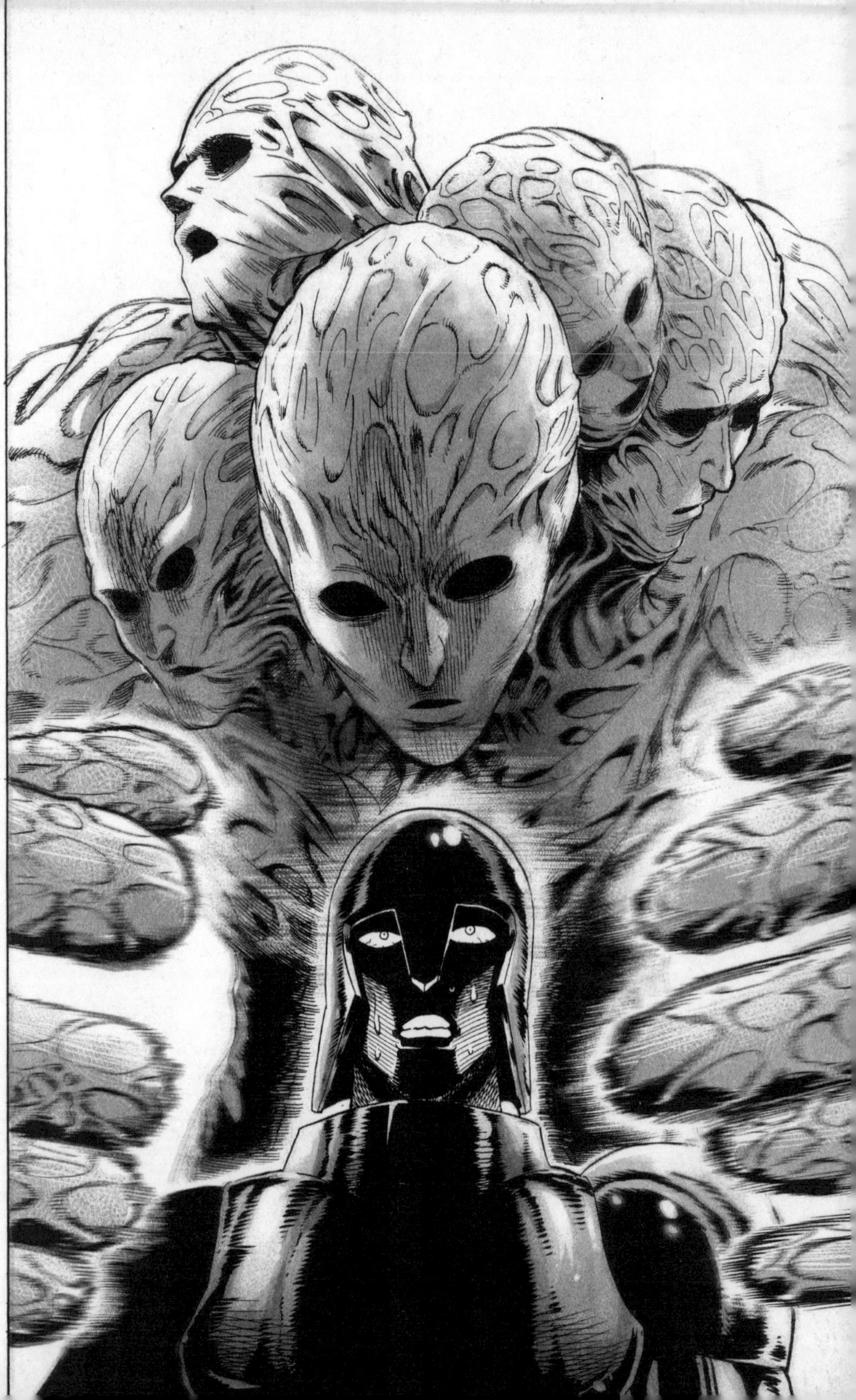

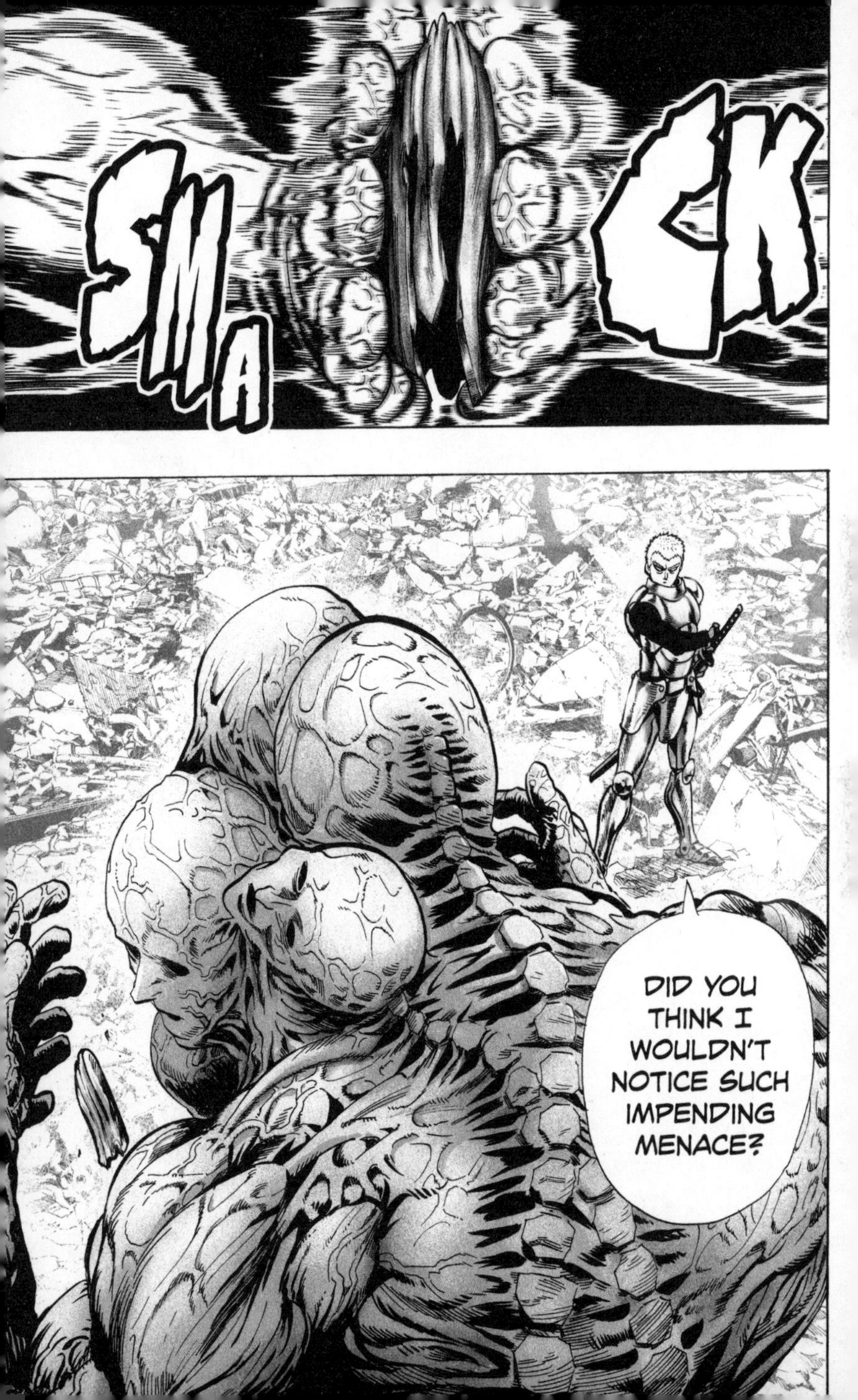
SMACK
DID YOU THINK I WOULDN'T NOTICE SUCH IMPENDING MENACE?

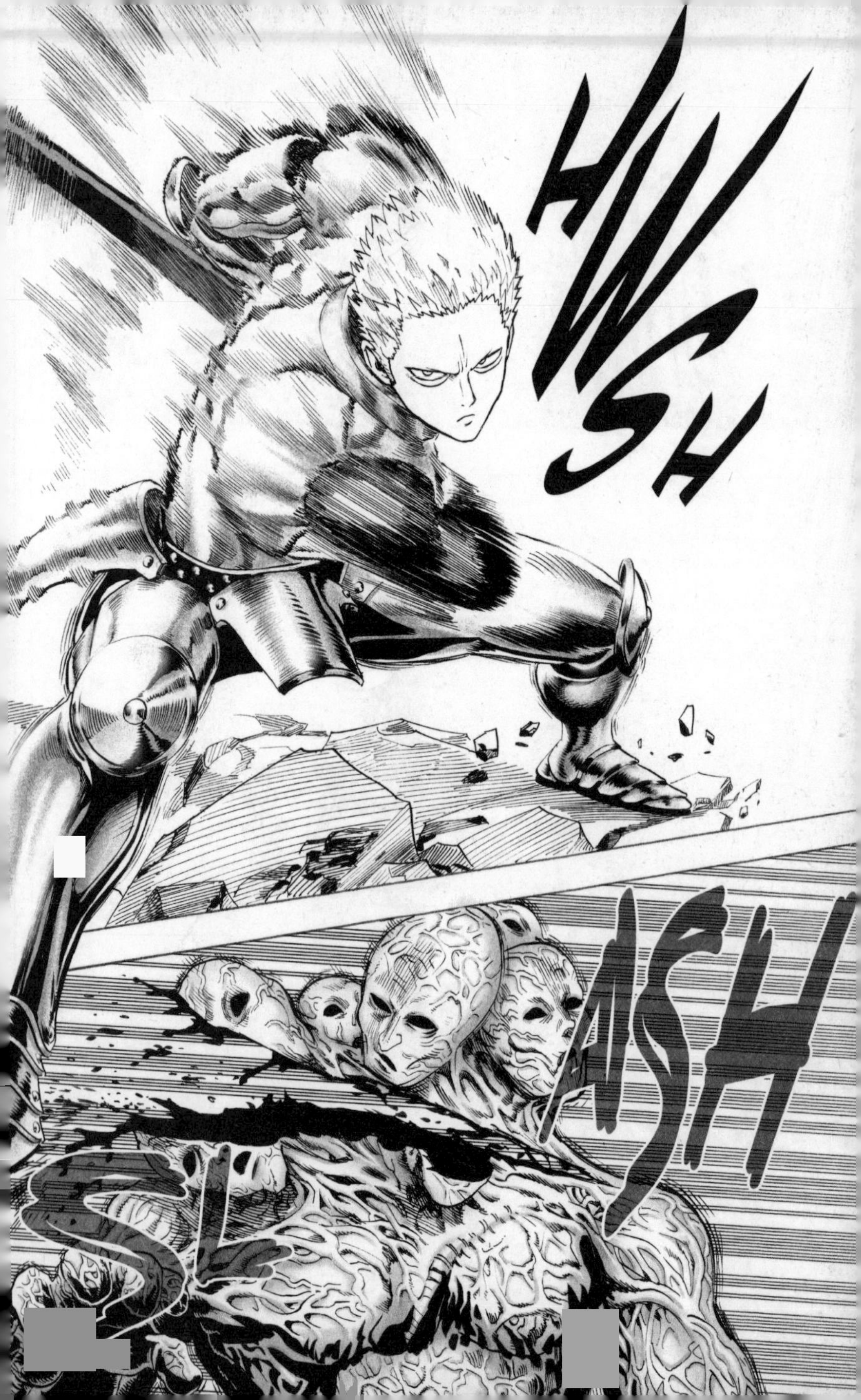
HWSH
SLASH

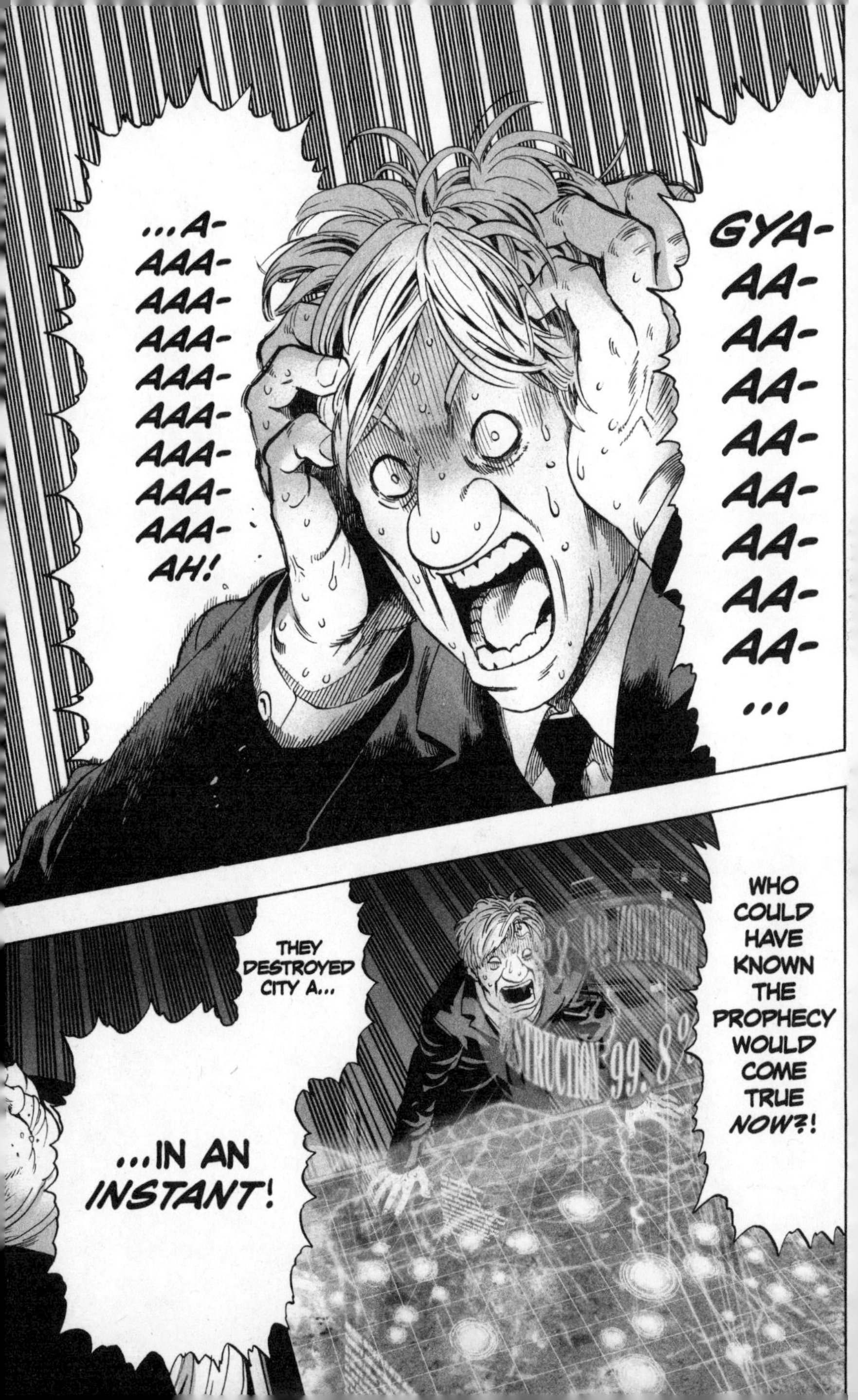
GYA-AA-AA-AA-AA-AA-AA-AA-AA-...
...A-AAA-AAA-AAA-AAA-AAA-AAA-AAA-AAA-AH!
WHO COULD HAVE KNOWN THE PROPHECY WOULD COME TRUE NOW?!
THEY DESTROYED CITY A...
...IN AN INSTANT!
STRUCTION 99.8%

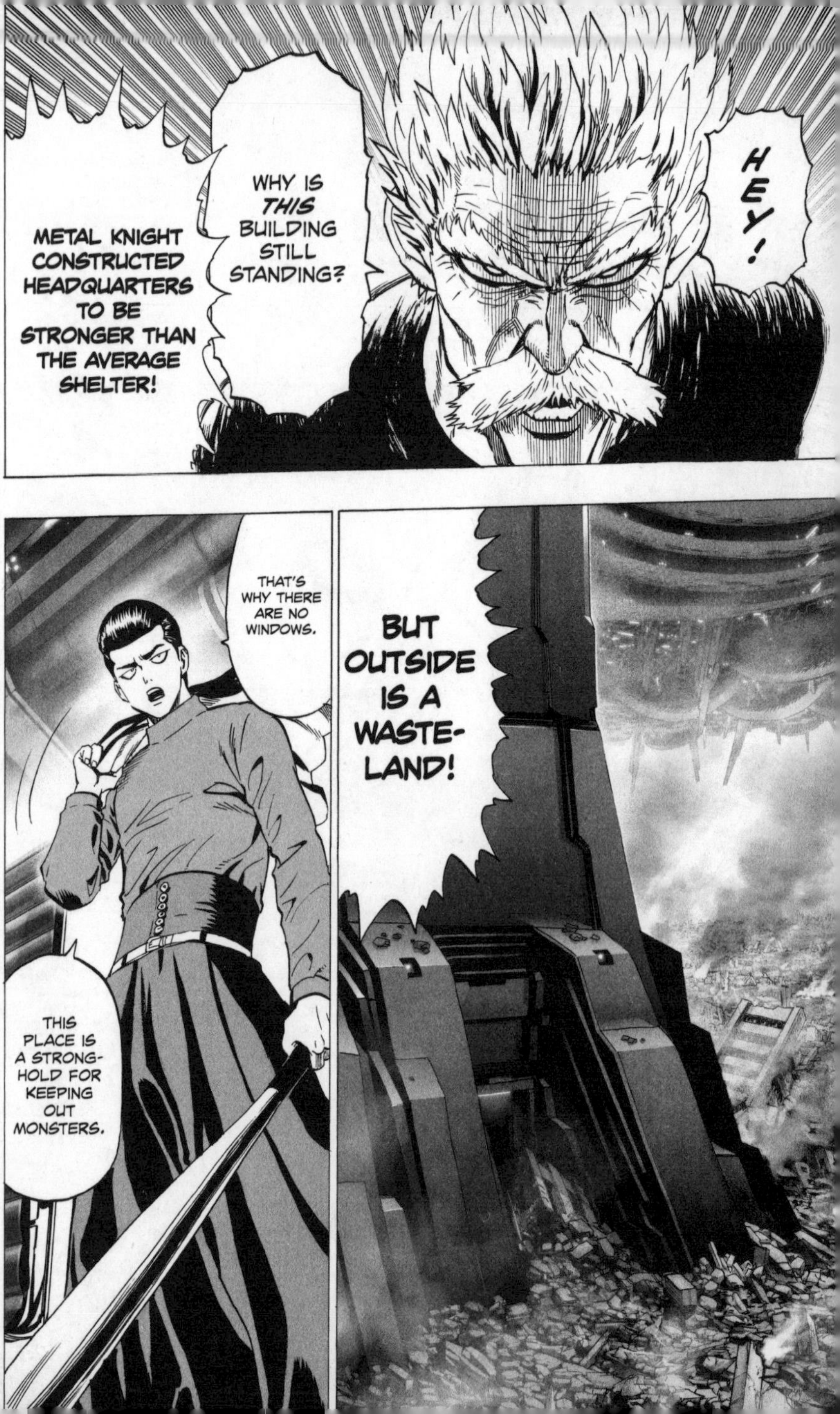
HEY!
WHY IS THIS BUILDING STILL STANDING?
METAL KNIGHT CONSTRUCTED HEADQUARTERS TO BE STRONGER THAN THE AVERAGE SHELTER!
BUT OUTSIDE IS A WASTE-LAND!
THAT'S WHY THERE ARE NO WINDOWS.
THIS PLACE IS A STRONG-HOLD FOR KEEPING OUT MONSTERS.

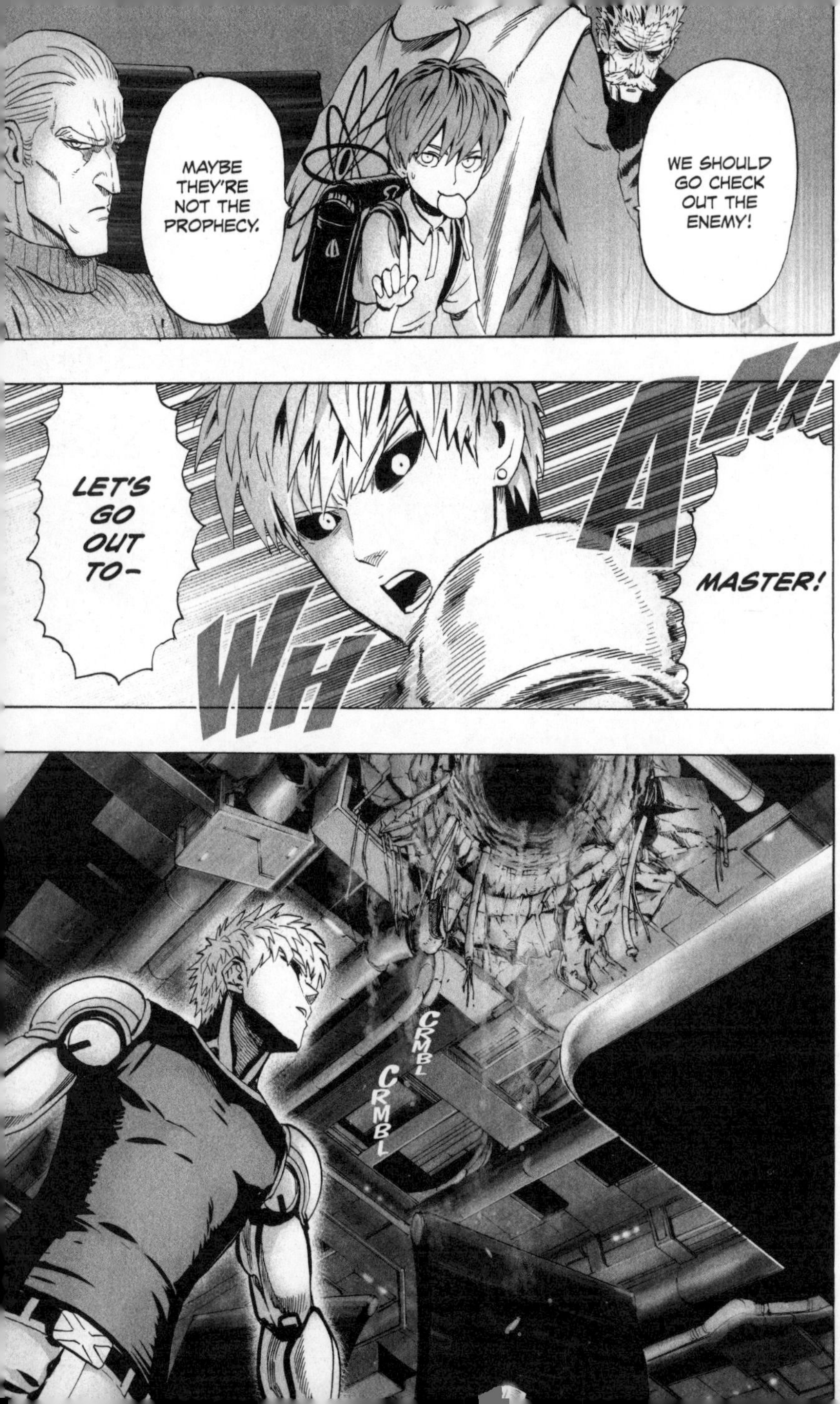
WE SHOULD GO CHECK OUT THE ENEMY!
MAYBE THEY'RE NOT THE PROPHECY.
MASTER!
WHAM
LET'S GO OUT TO-
CRMBL
CRMBL

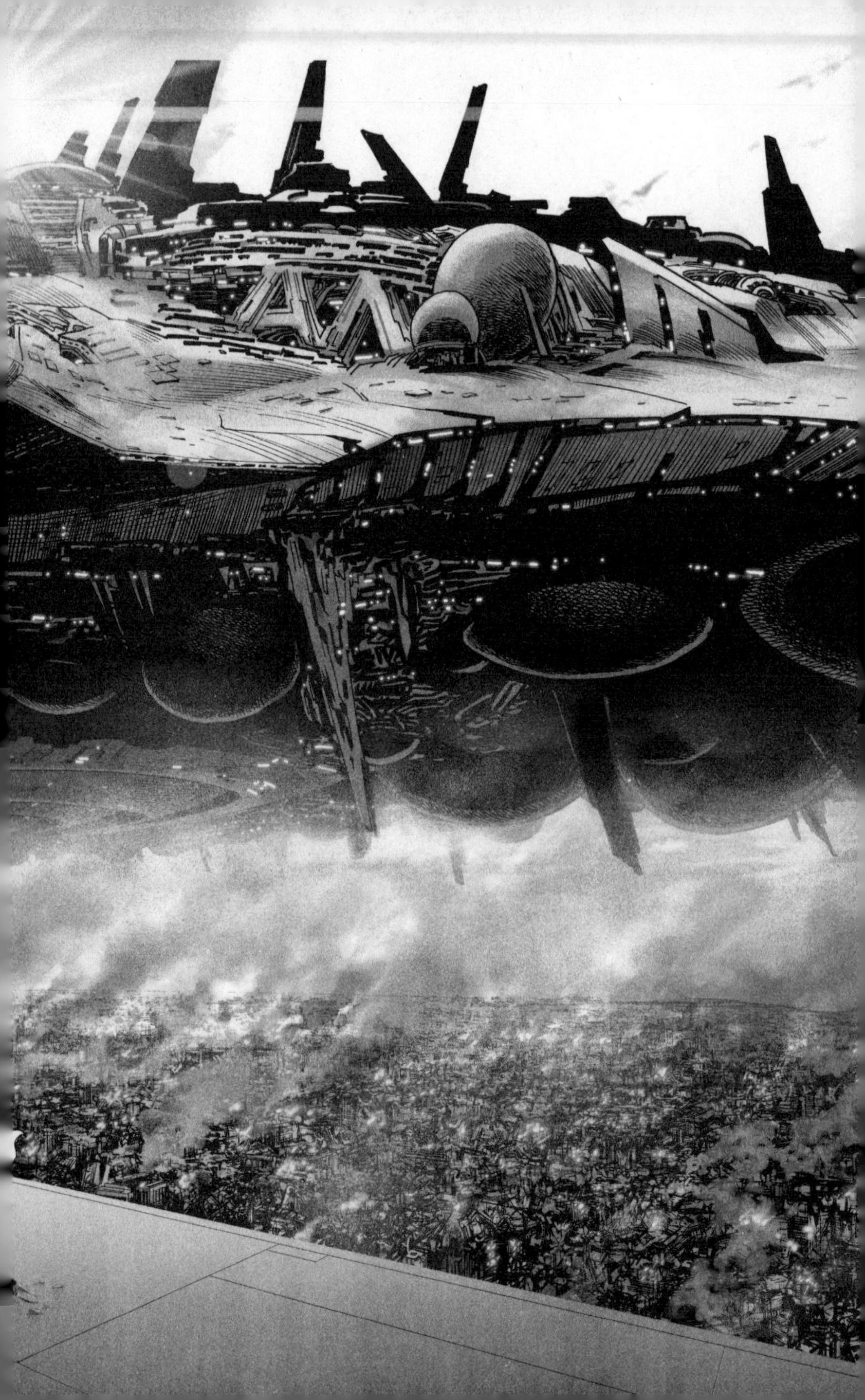

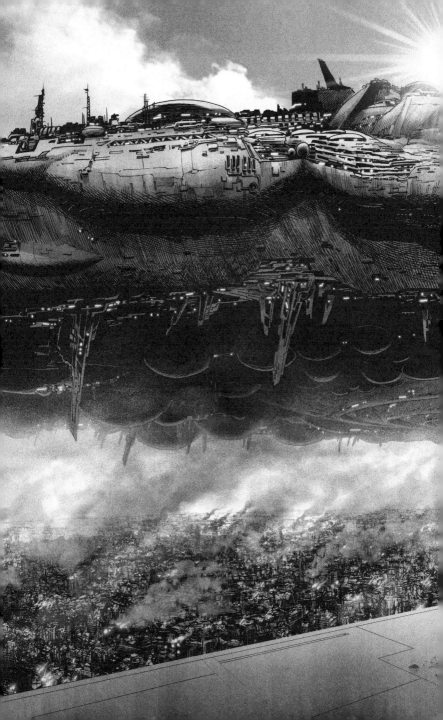

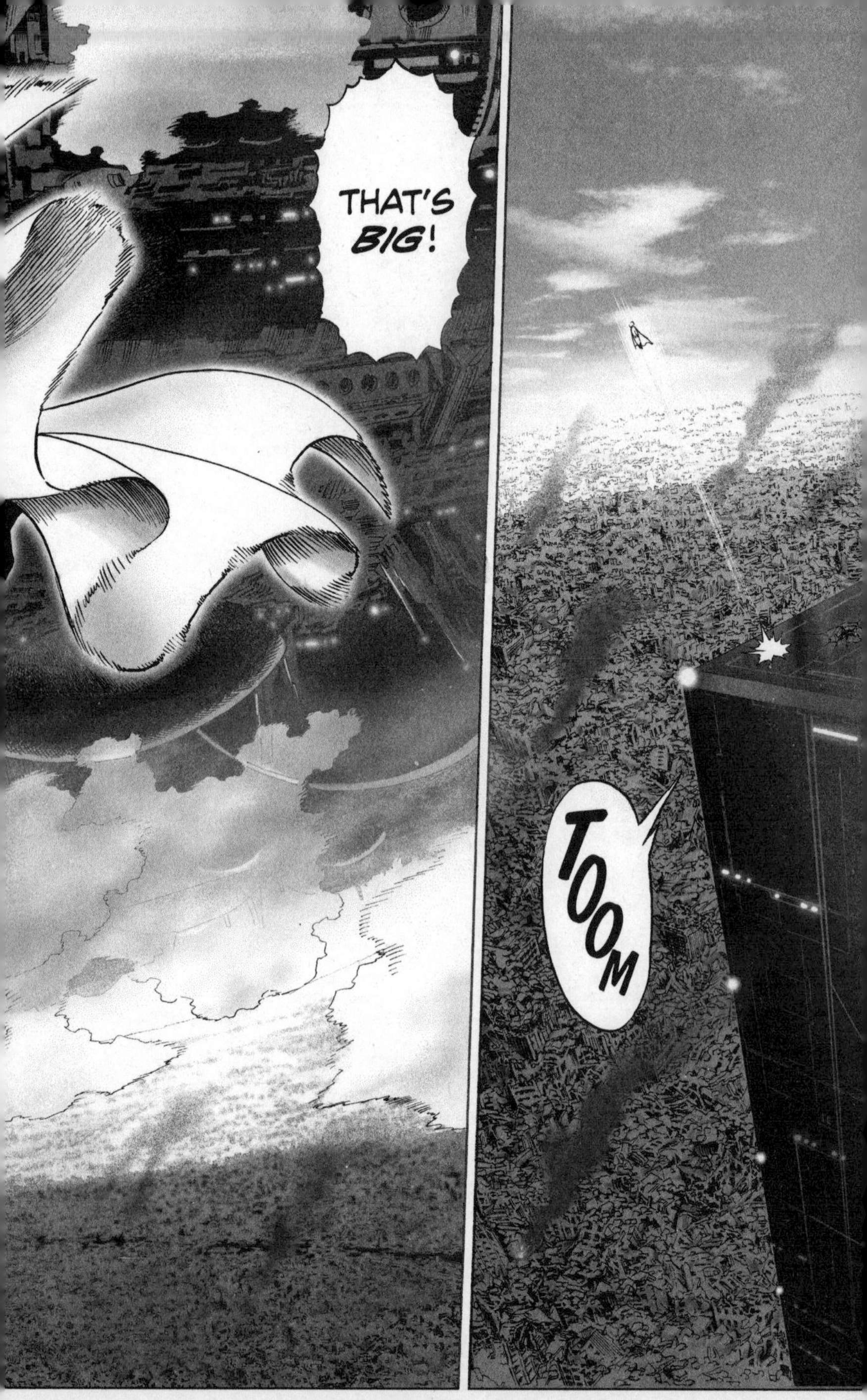
TOOM
THAT'S *BIG*!

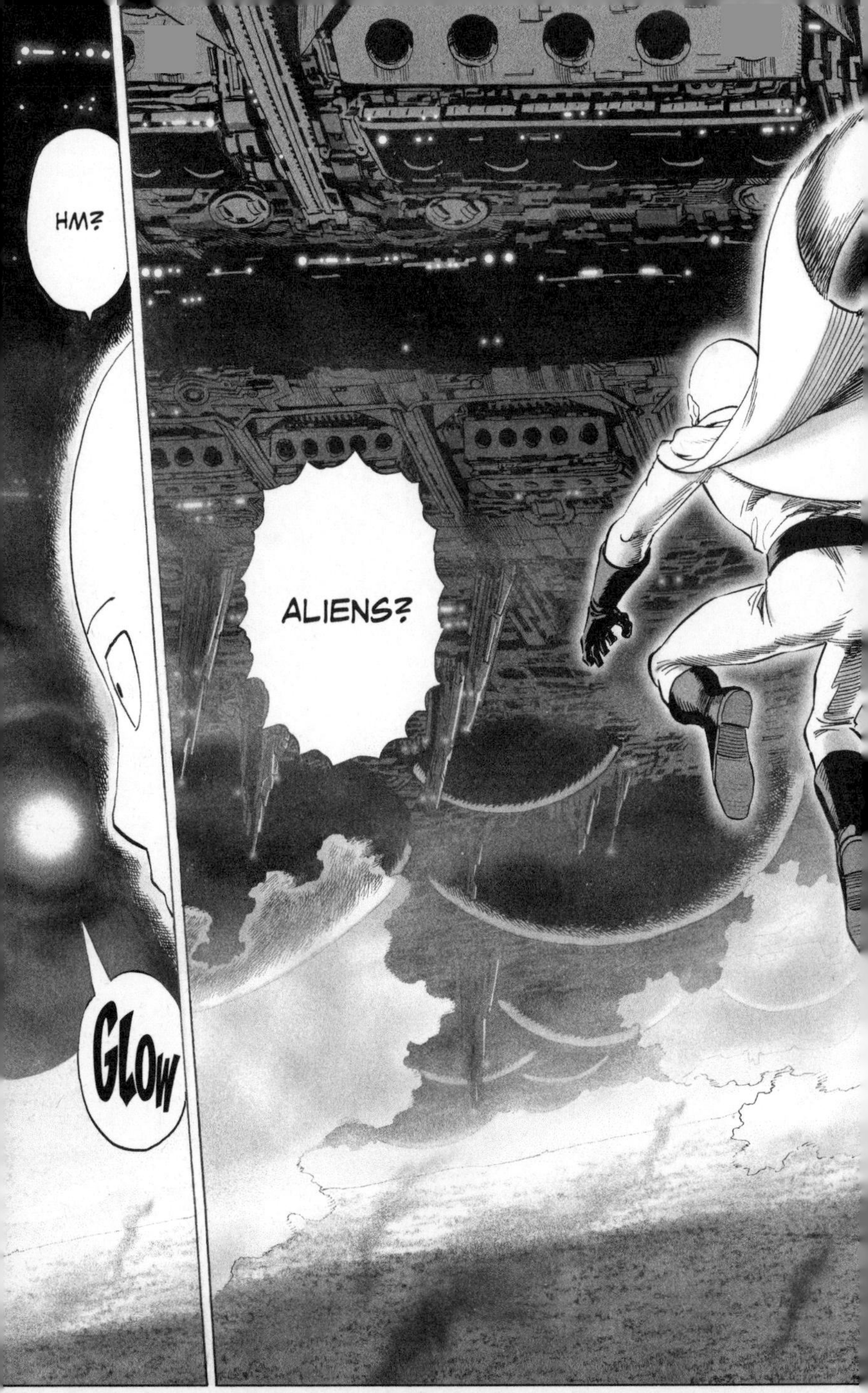
ALIENS?
HM?
GLOW

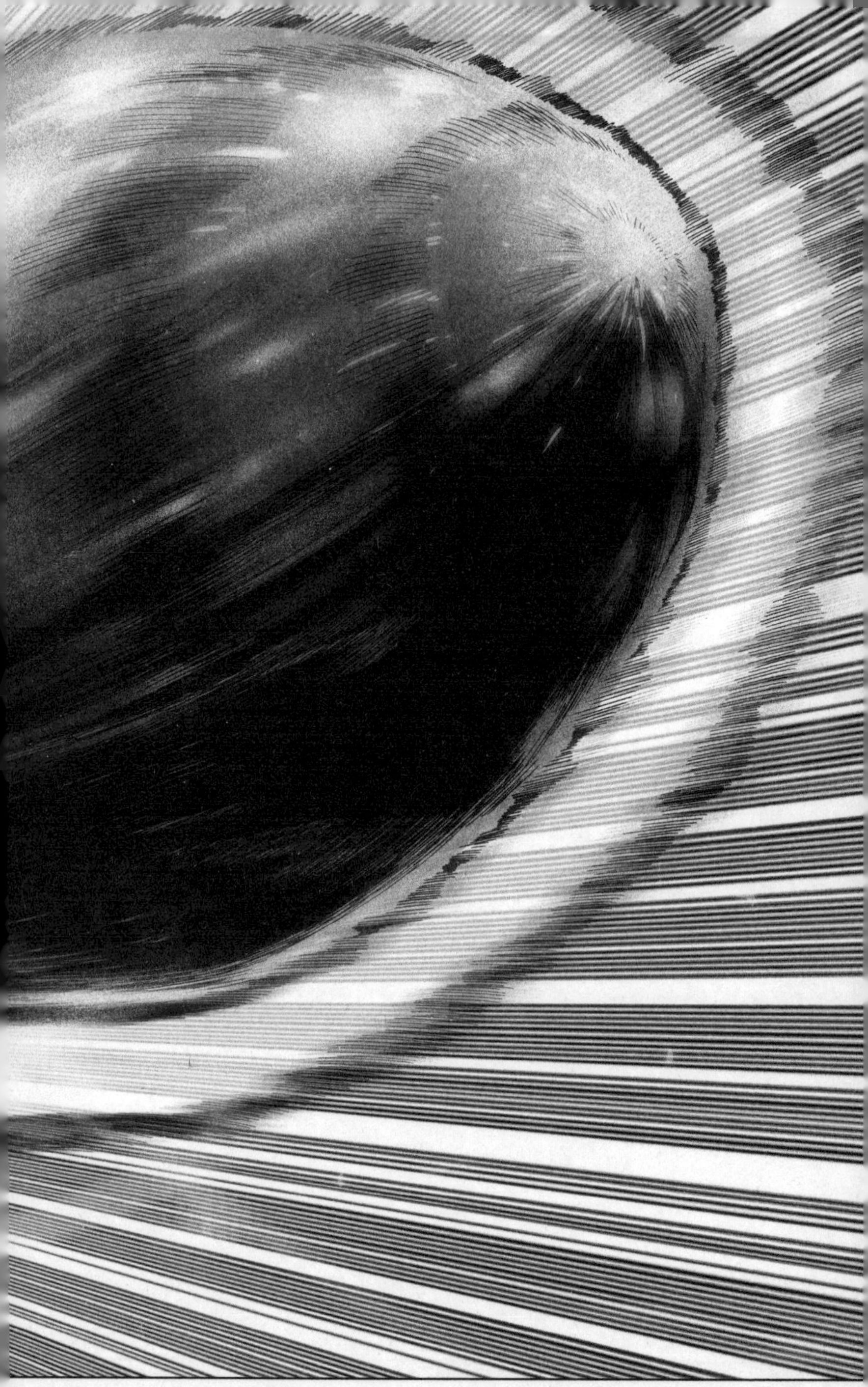

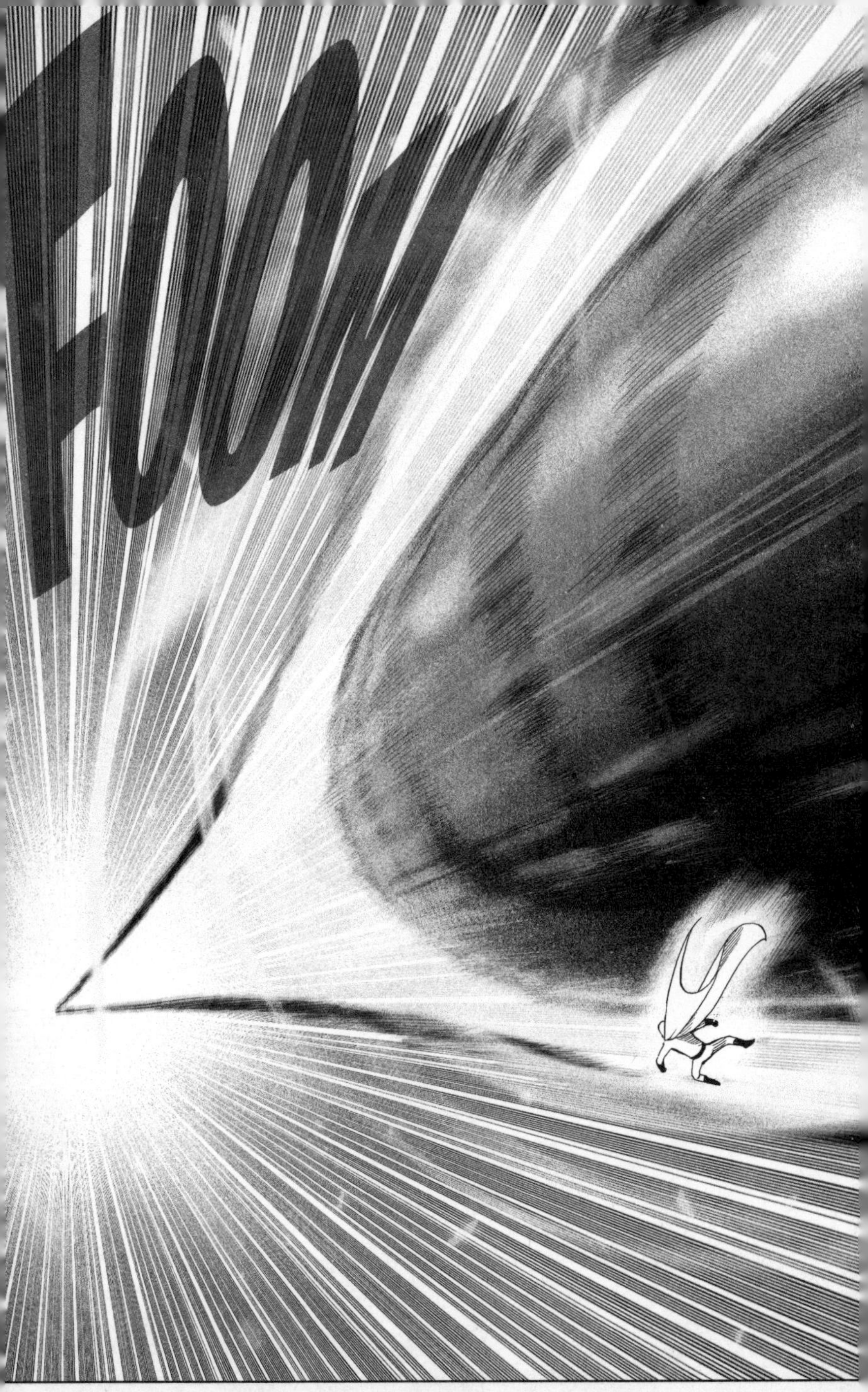
FOOM

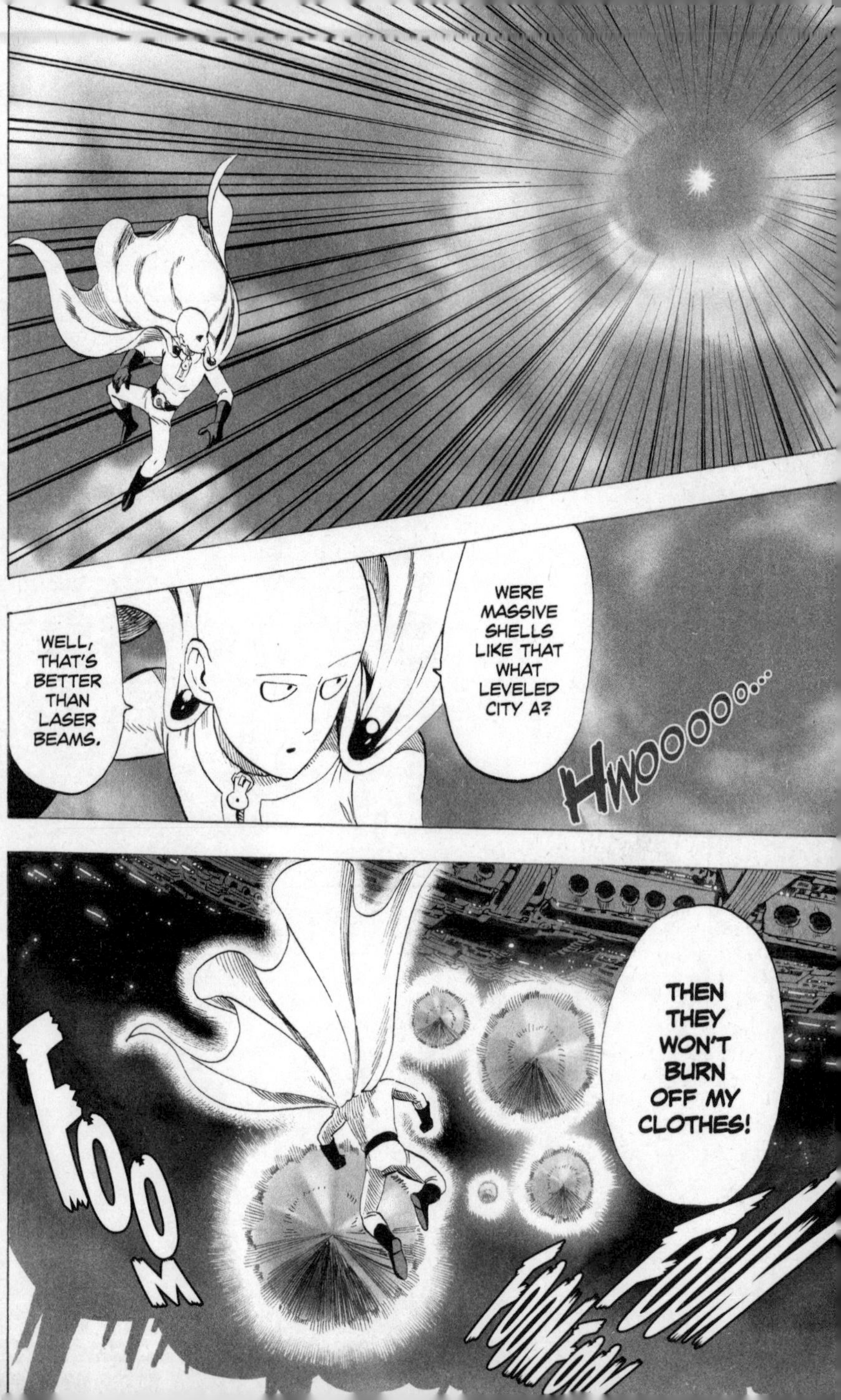
WERE MASSIVE SHELLS LIKE THAT WHAT LEVELED CITY A?
HWOOOOO...
WELL, THAT'S BETTER THAN LASER BEAMS.
THEN THEY WON'T BURN OFF MY CLOTHES!
FOOM FOOM FOOM
FOOOM

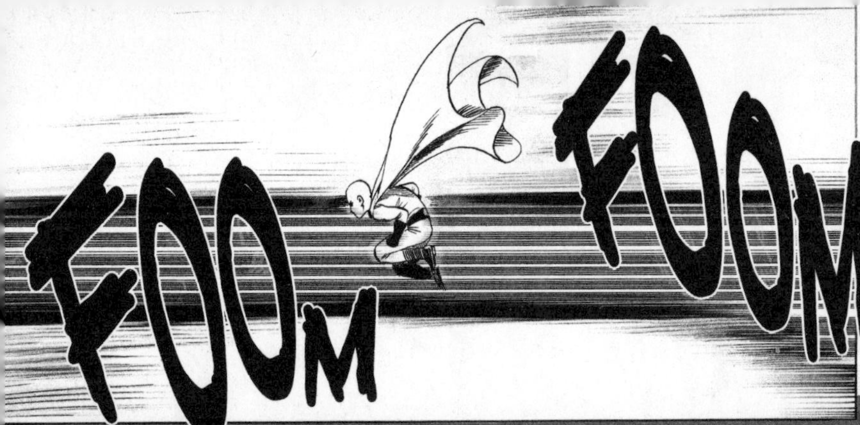
FOOM
FOOM
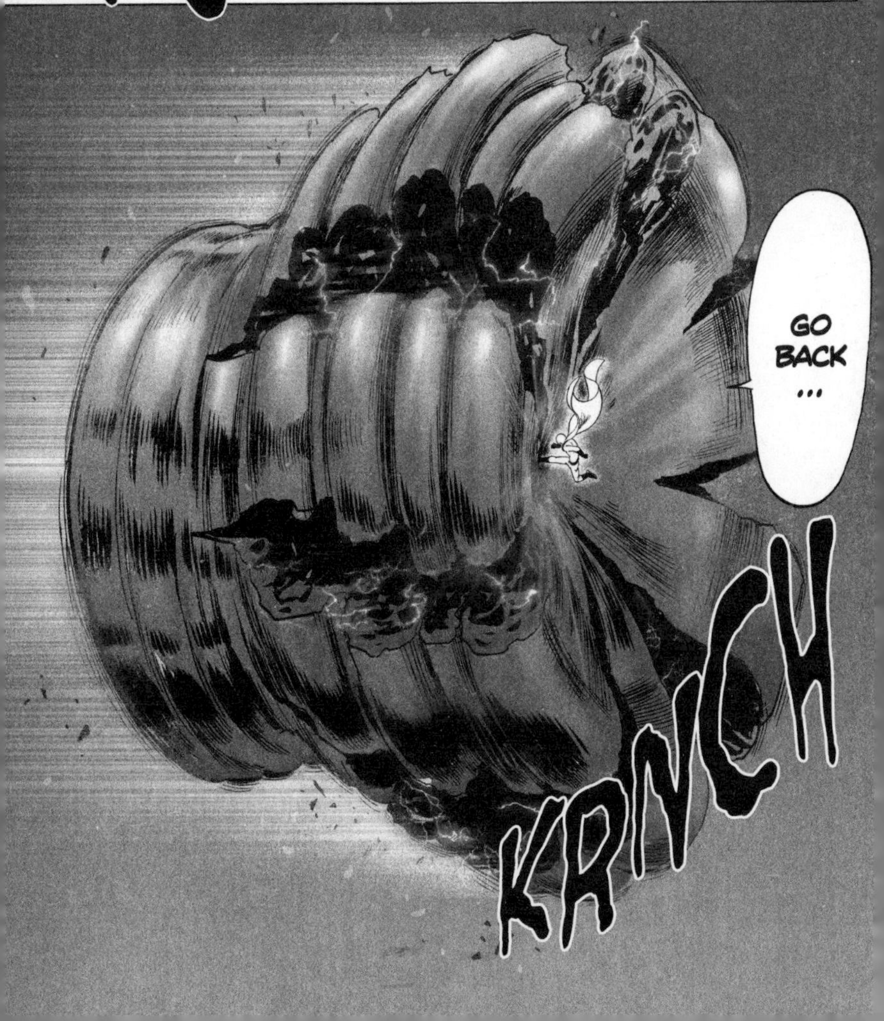
GO BACK ...
KRNCH

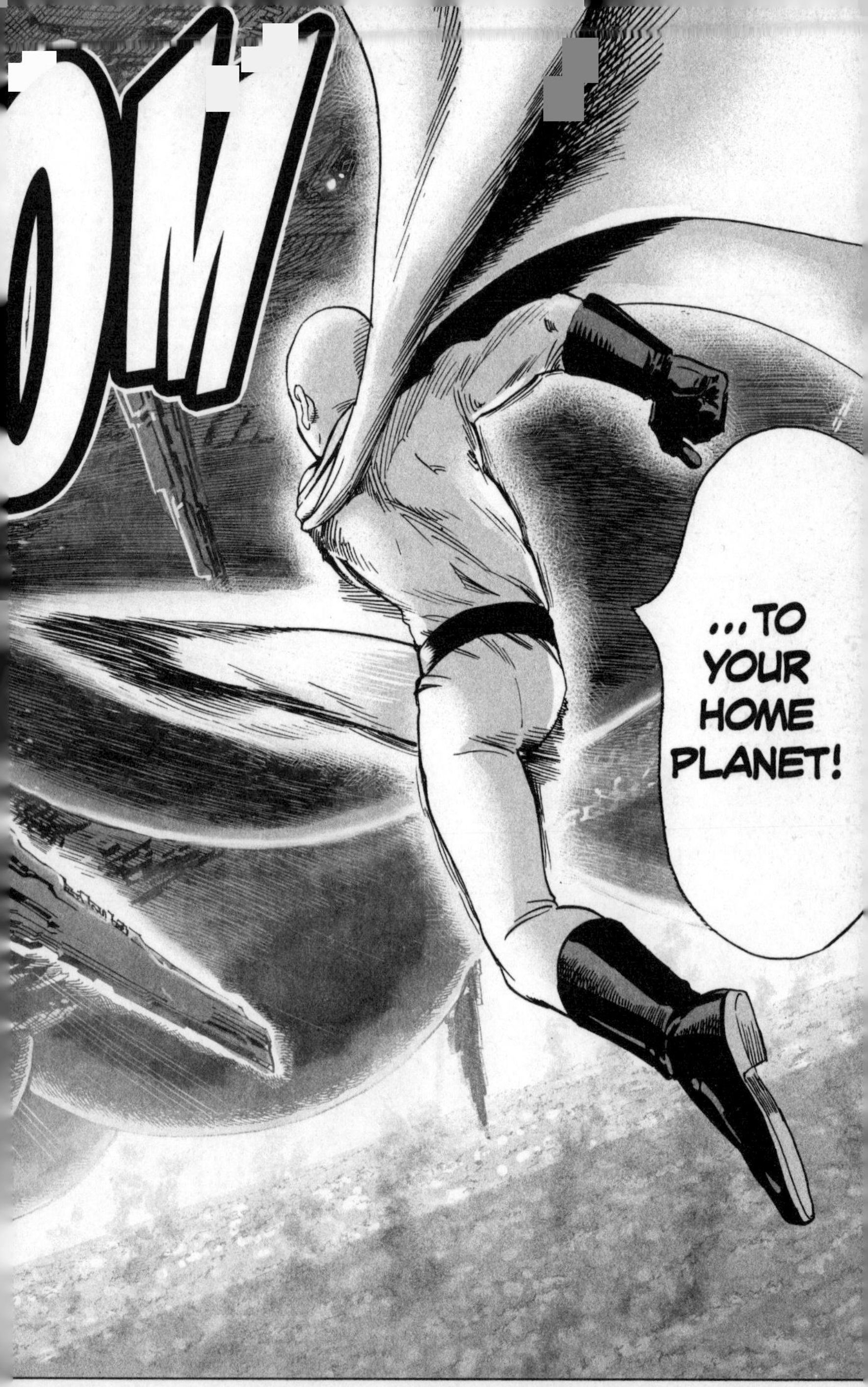
...TO YOUR HOME PLANET!

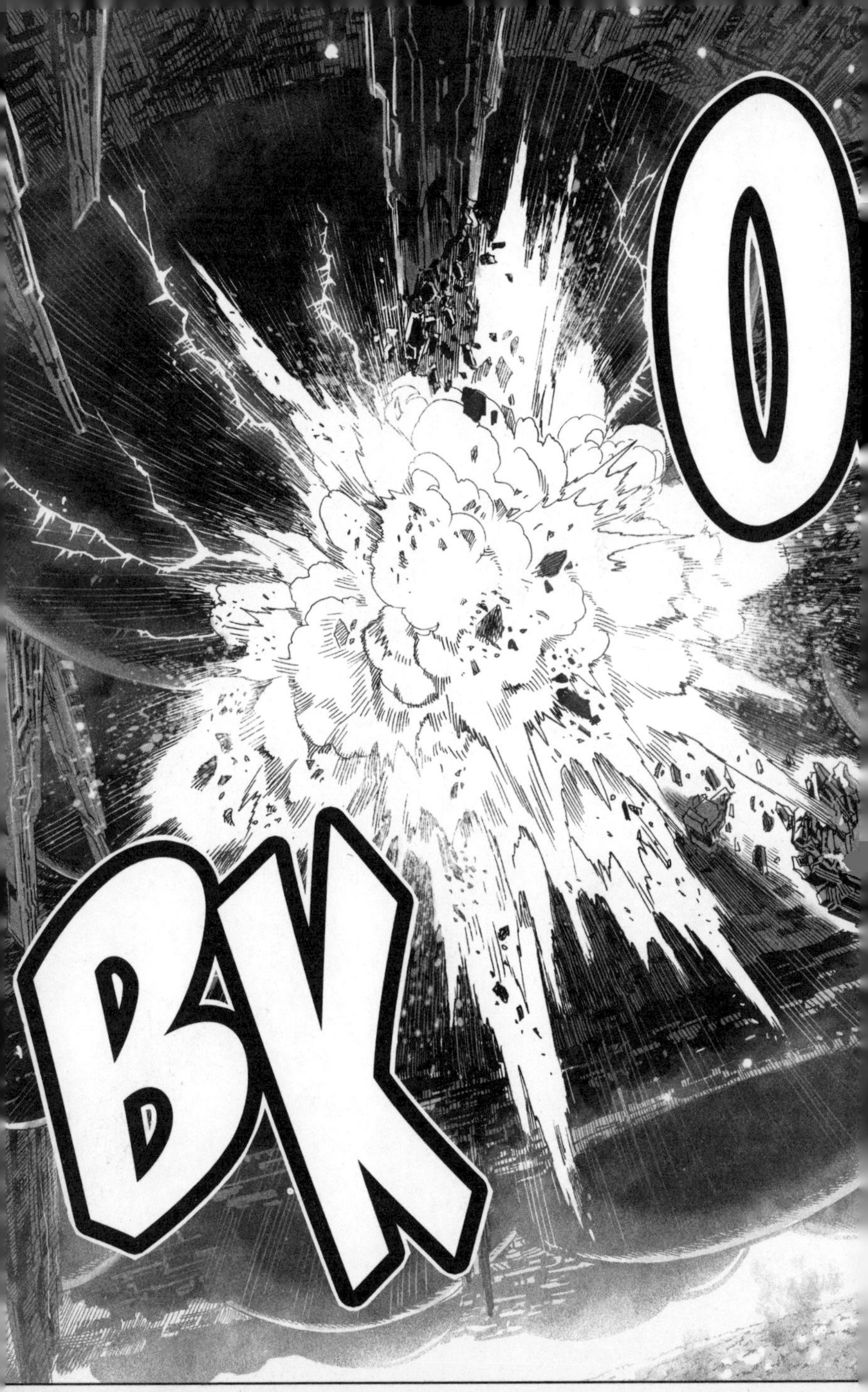
BKO

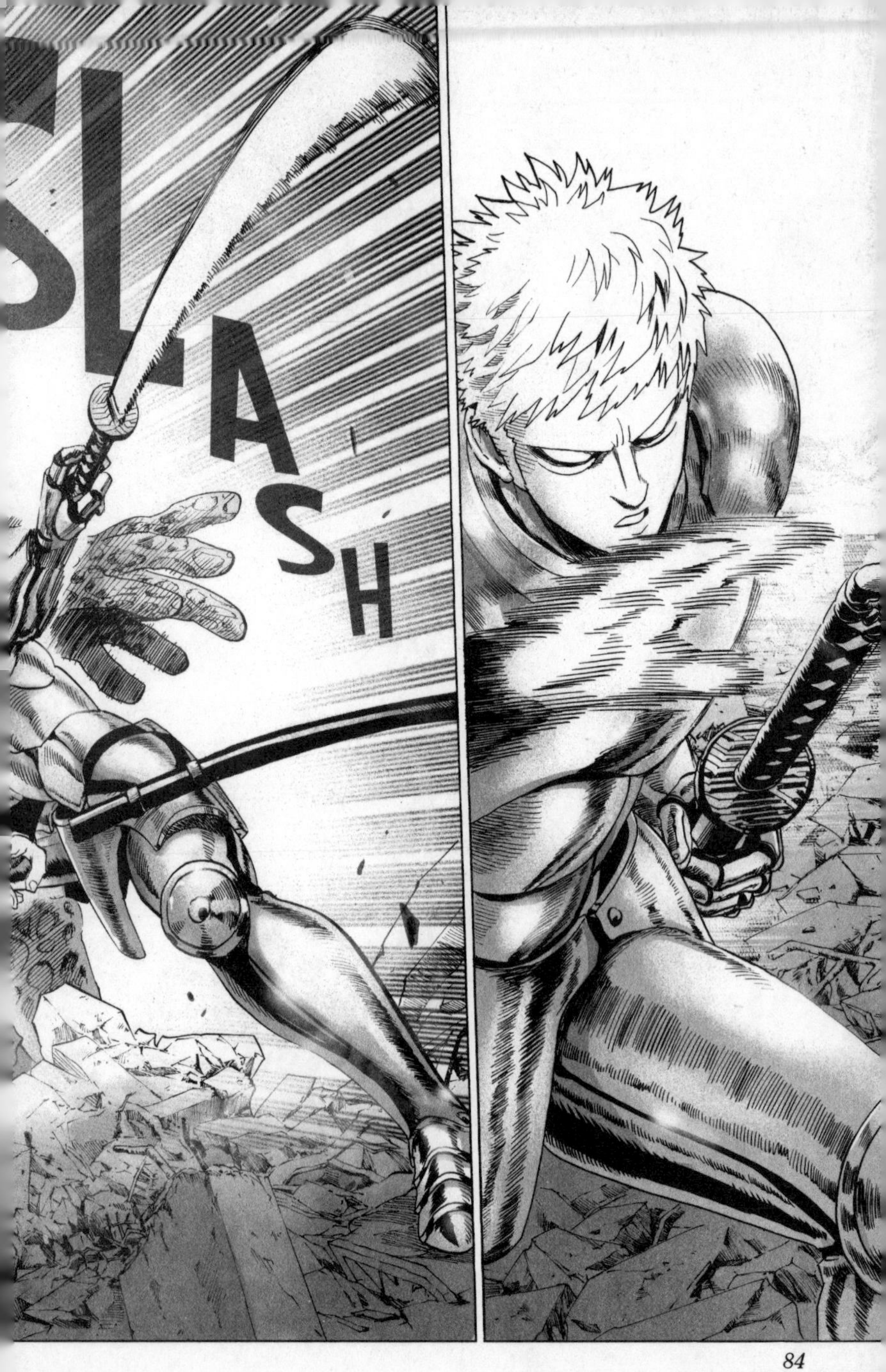
SLASH

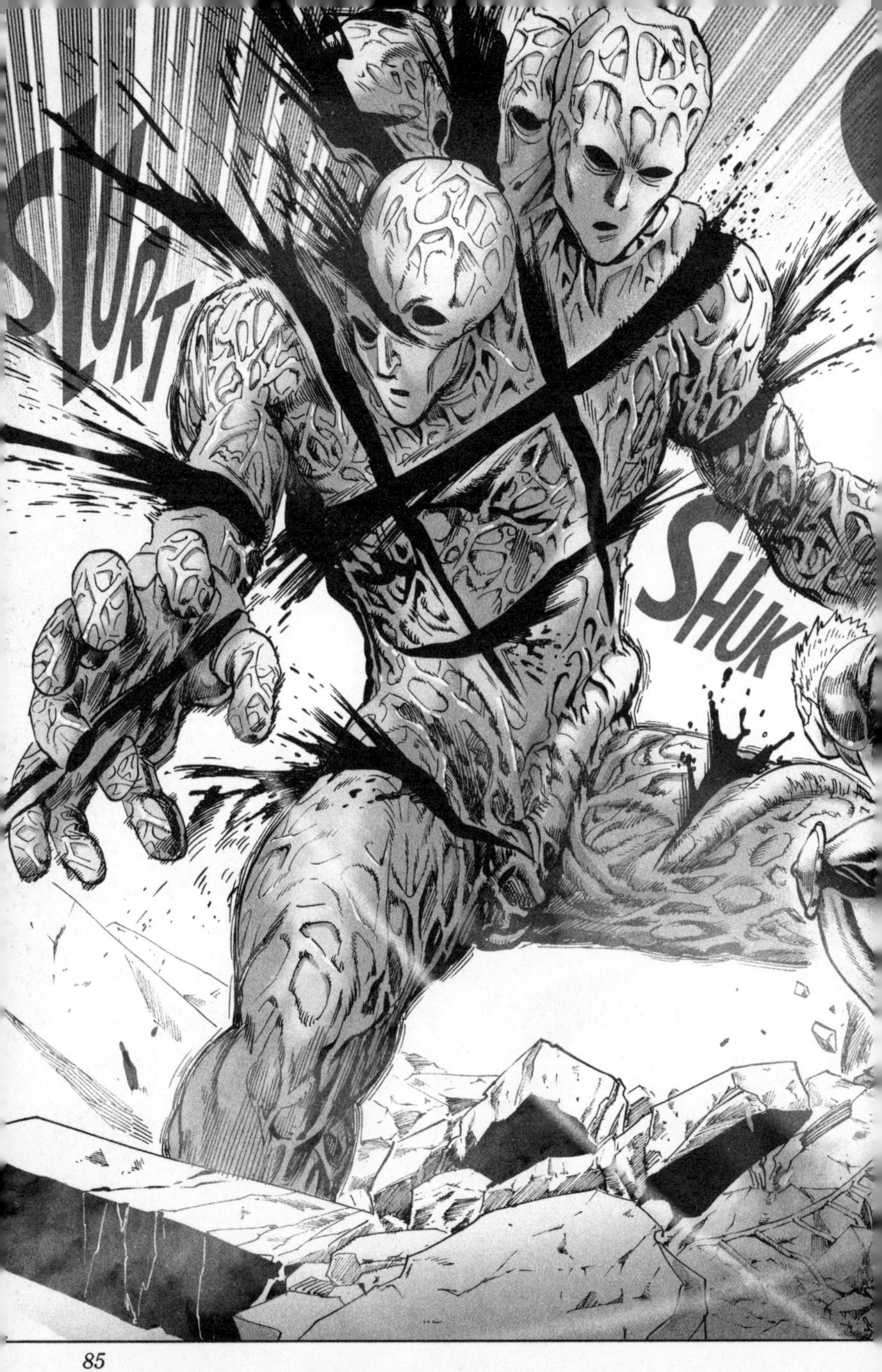
SLURT
SHUK

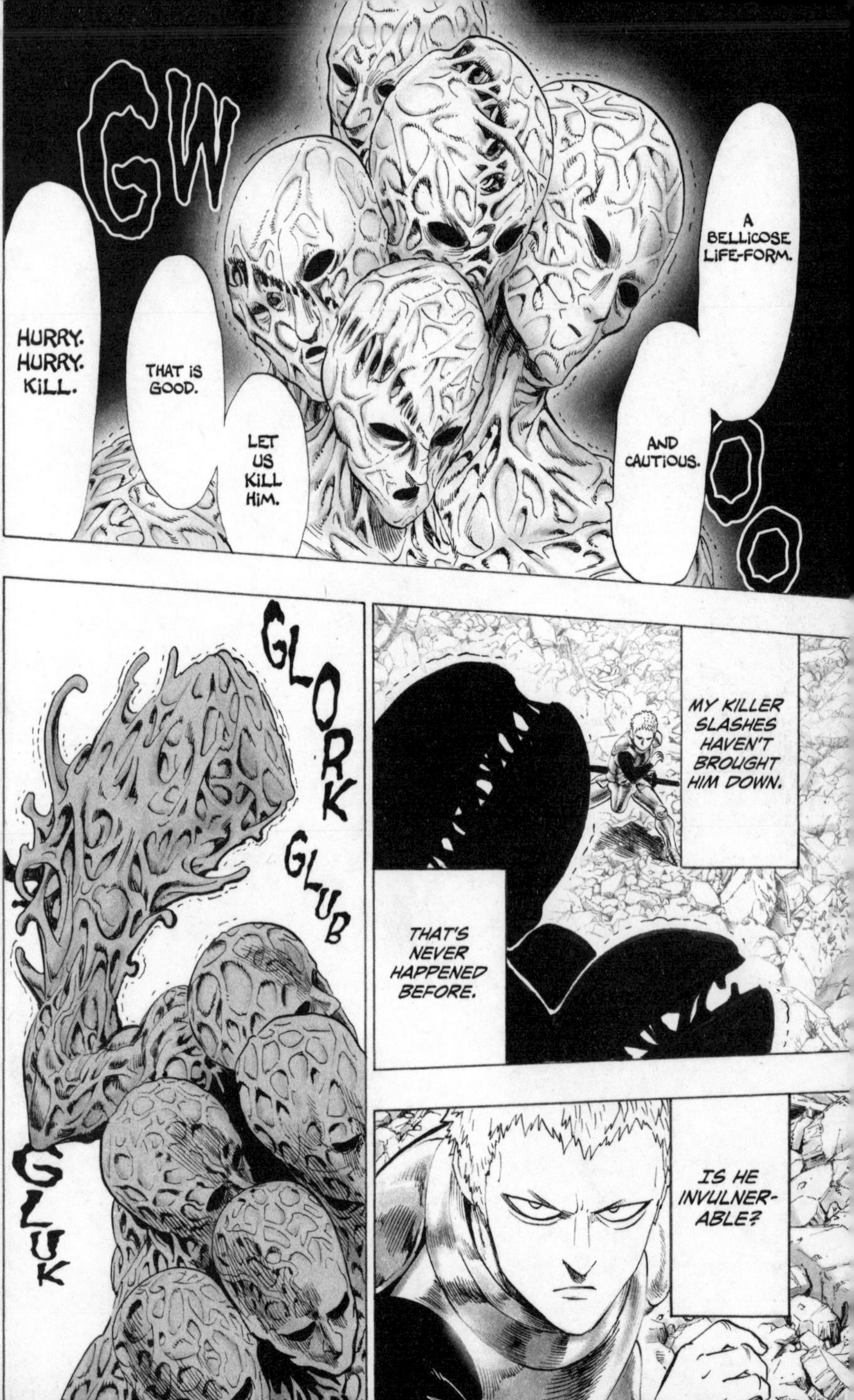
A BELLICOSE LIFE-FORM.
AND CAUTIOUS.
GWOOO
LET US KILL HIM.
THAT IS GOOD.
HURRY. HURRY. KILL.
MY KILLER SLASHES HAVEN'T BROUGHT HIM DOWN.
THAT'S NEVER HAPPENED BEFORE.
IS HE INVULNERABLE?
GLORK
GLUB
GLUK

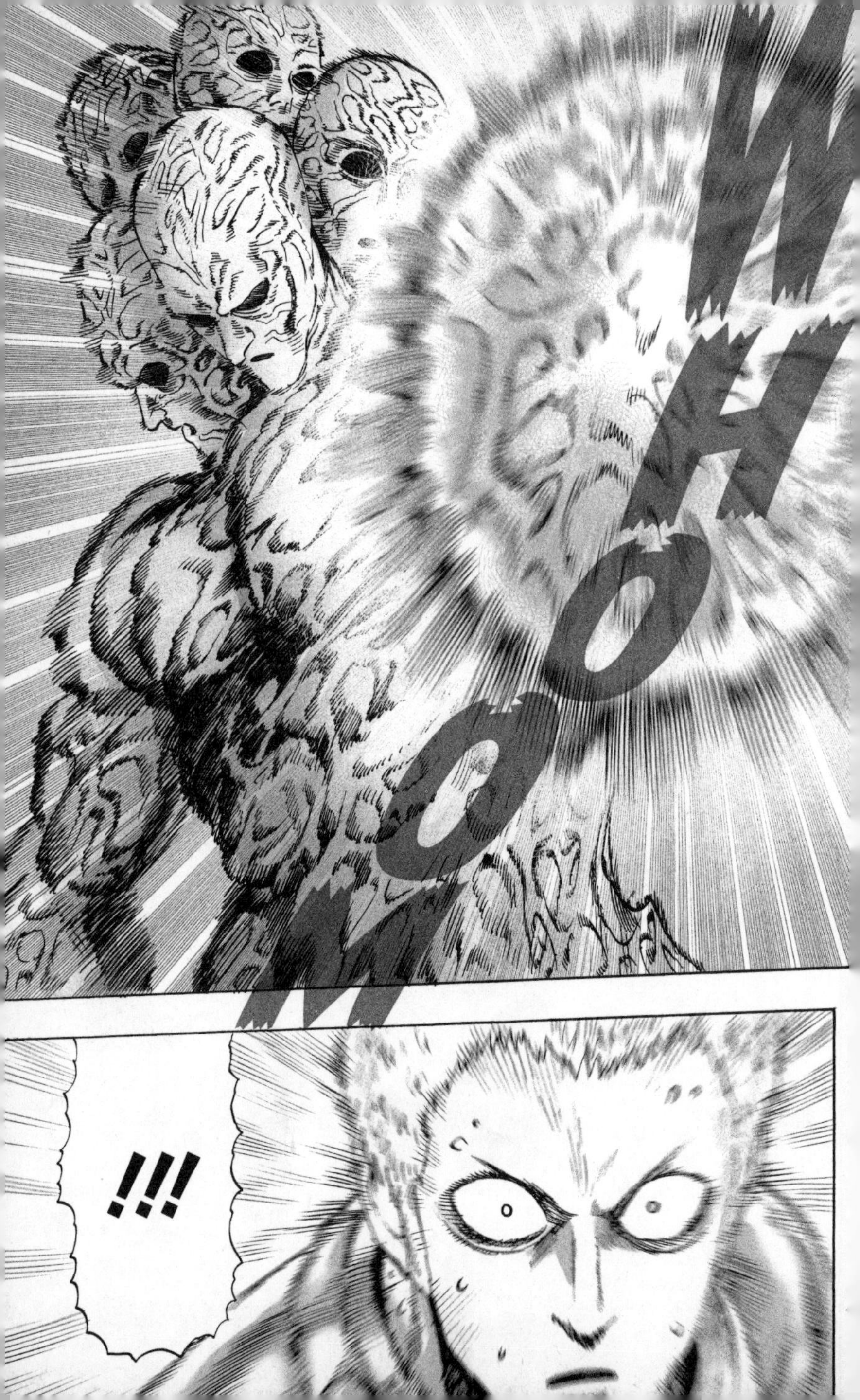
WHOOM
!!!

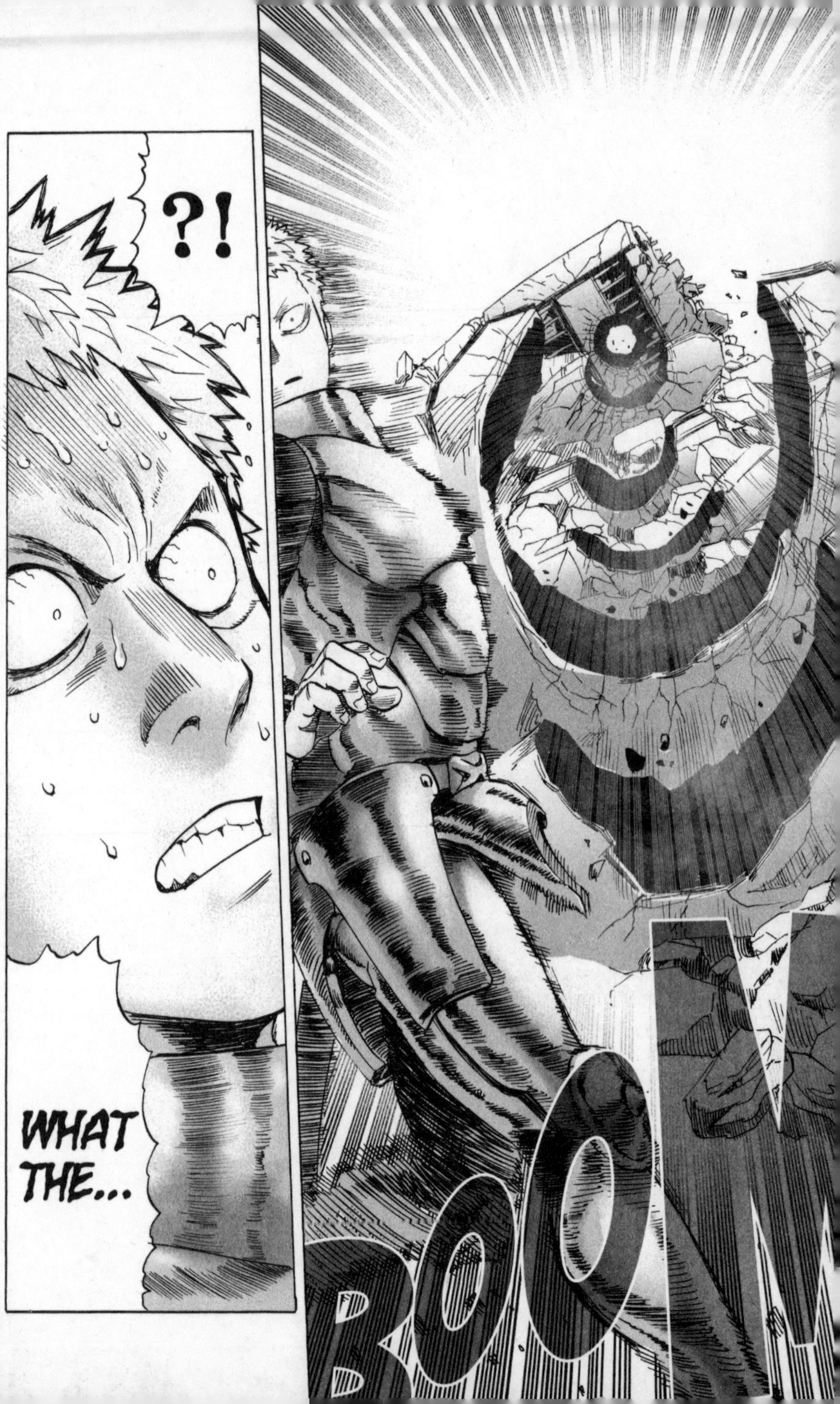
BOOM
?!
WHAT THE...

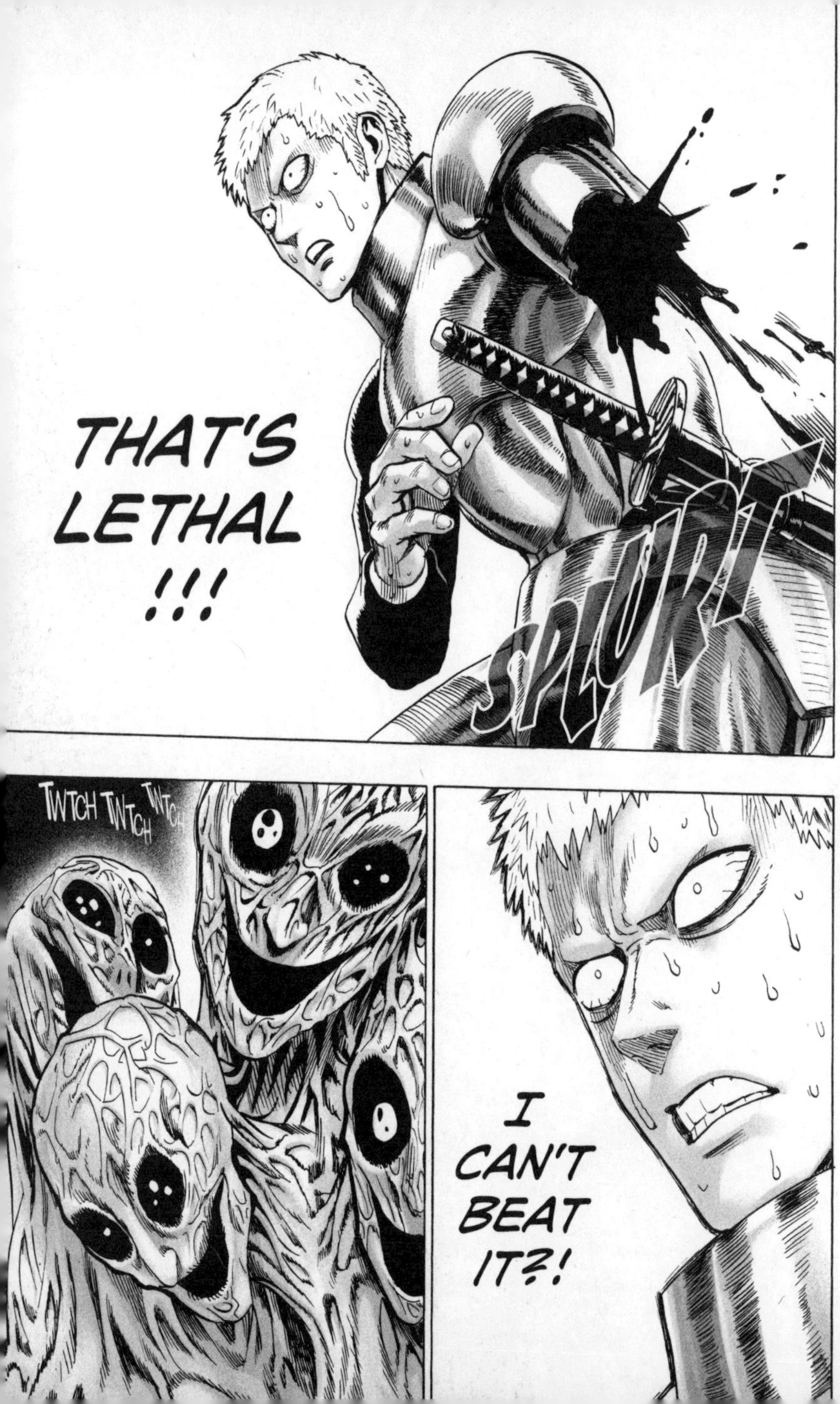
THAT'S LETHAL !!!
SPLURT
I CAN'T BEAT IT?!
TWITCH TWITCH TWITCH

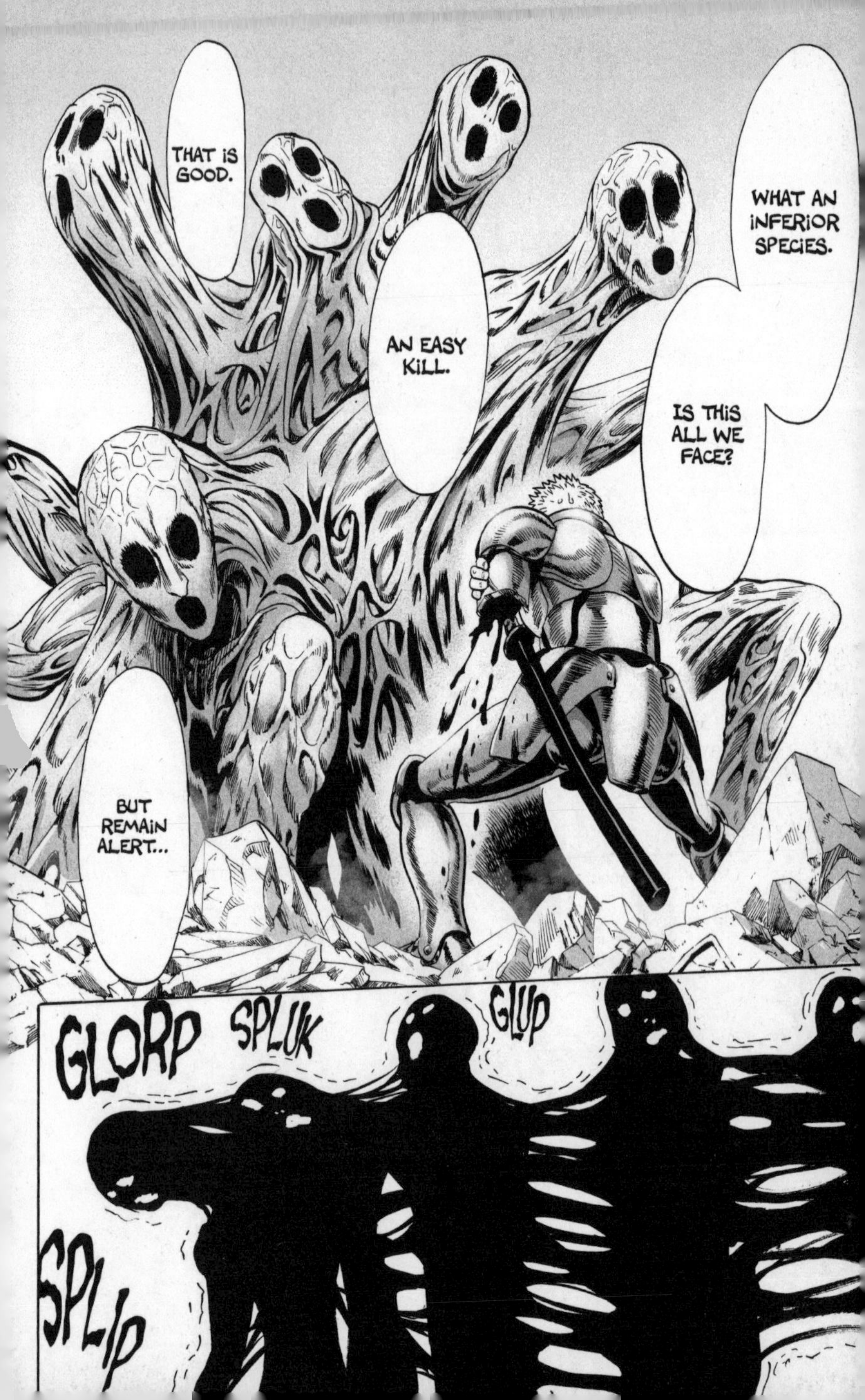
WHAT AN INFERIOR SPECIES.
IS THIS ALL WE FACE?
AN EASY KILL.
THAT IS GOOD.
BUT REMAIN ALERT...
GLUP
SPLUK
GLORP
SPLIP

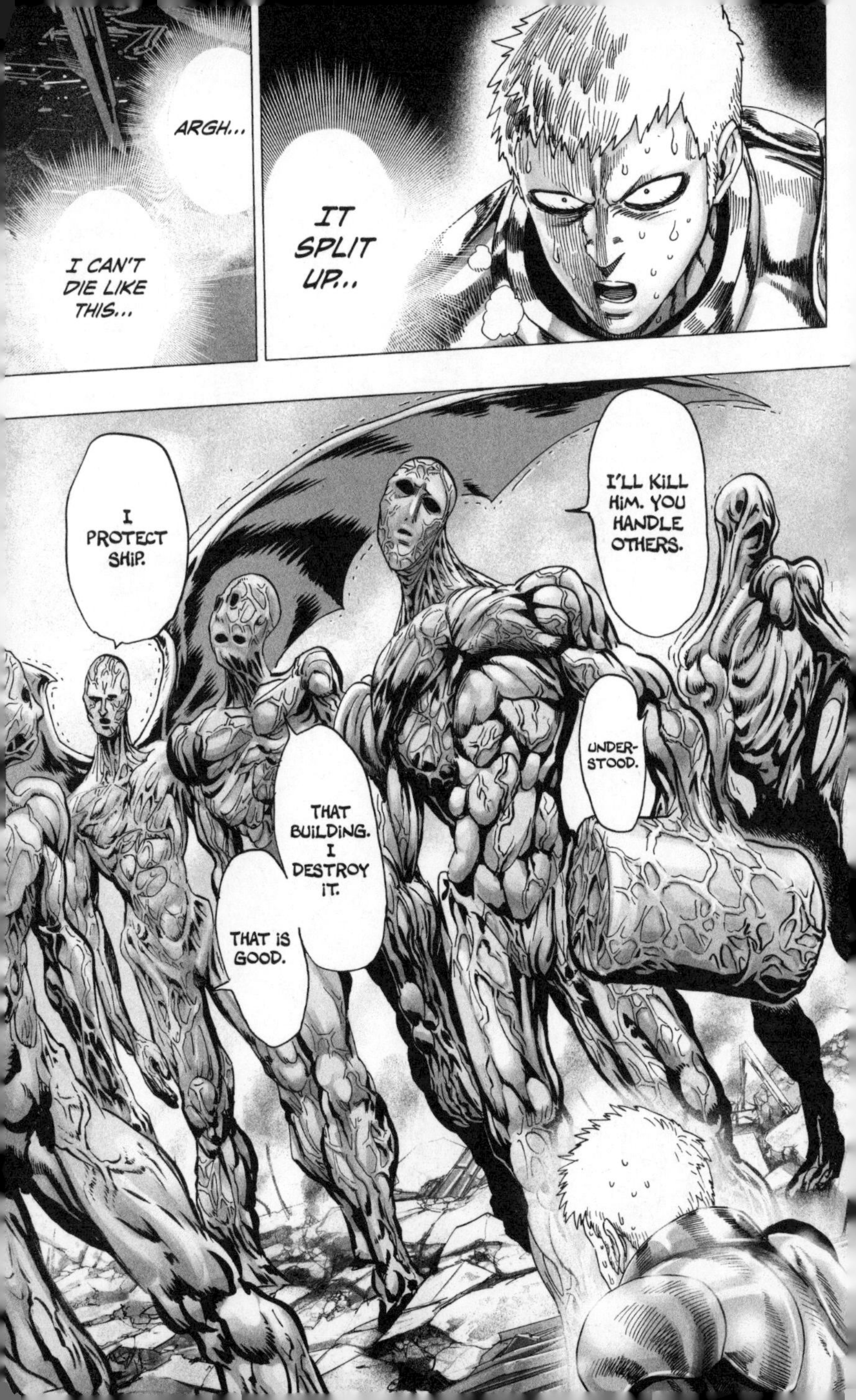
IT SPLIT UP...
ARGH...
I CAN'T DIE LIKE THIS...
I'LL KILL HIM. YOU HANDLE OTHERS.
UNDERSTOOD.
I PROTECT SHIP.
THAT BUILDING. I DESTROY IT.
THAT IS GOOD.

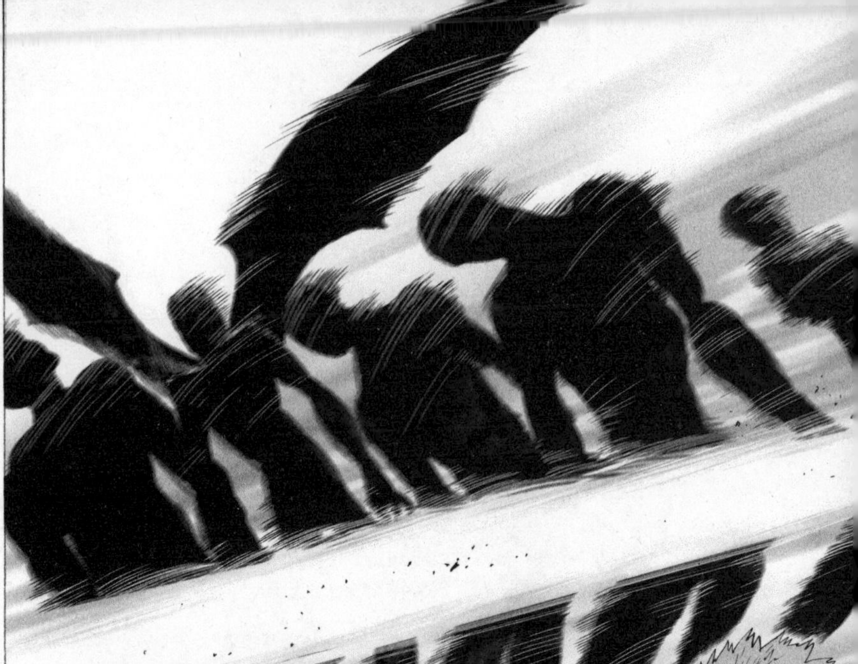

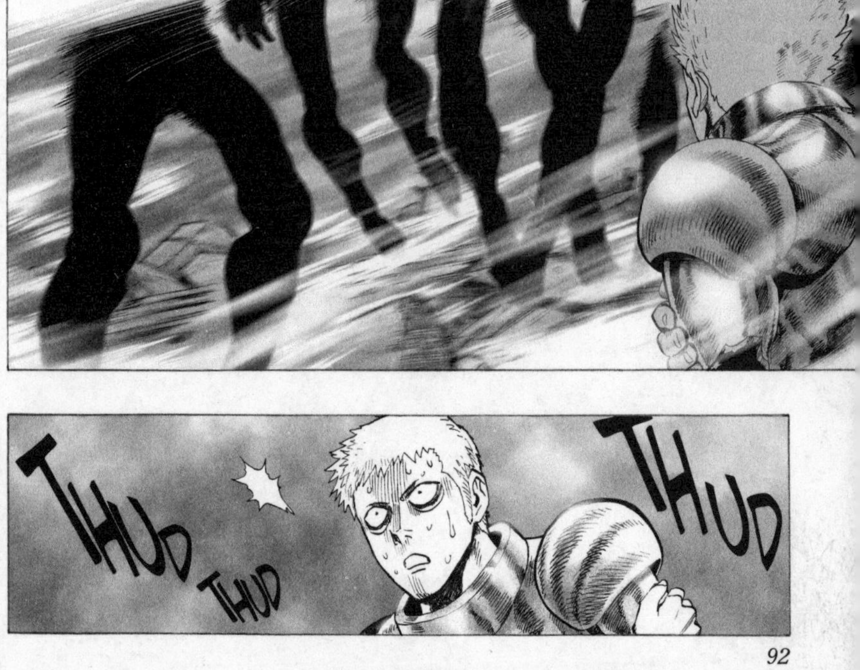
THUD
THUD
THUD

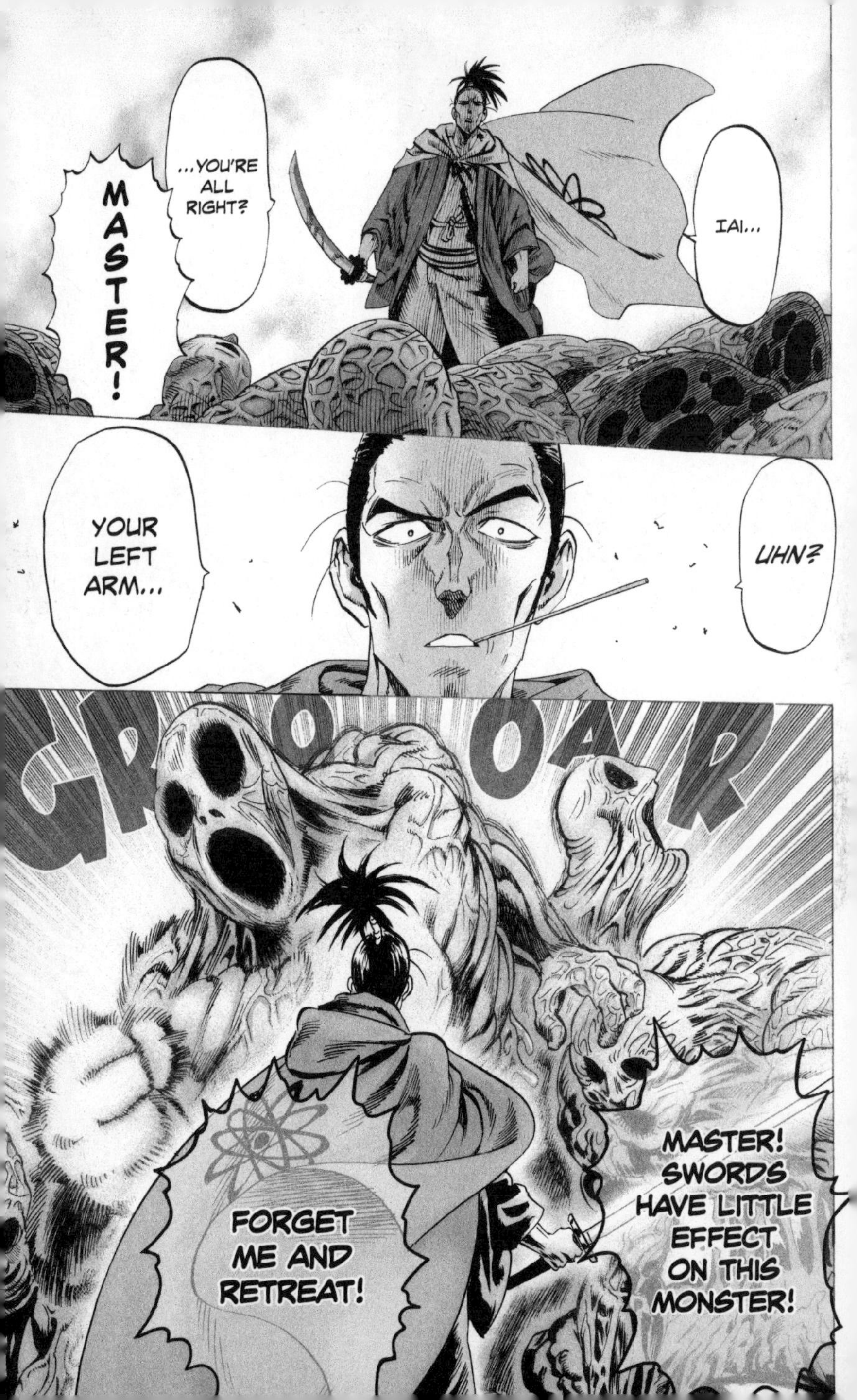
IAI...
...YOU'RE ALL RIGHT?
MASTER!
UHN?
YOUR LEFT ARM...
GROOOAR
MASTER! SWORDS HAVE LITTLE EFFECT ON THIS MONSTER!
FORGET ME AND RETREAT!

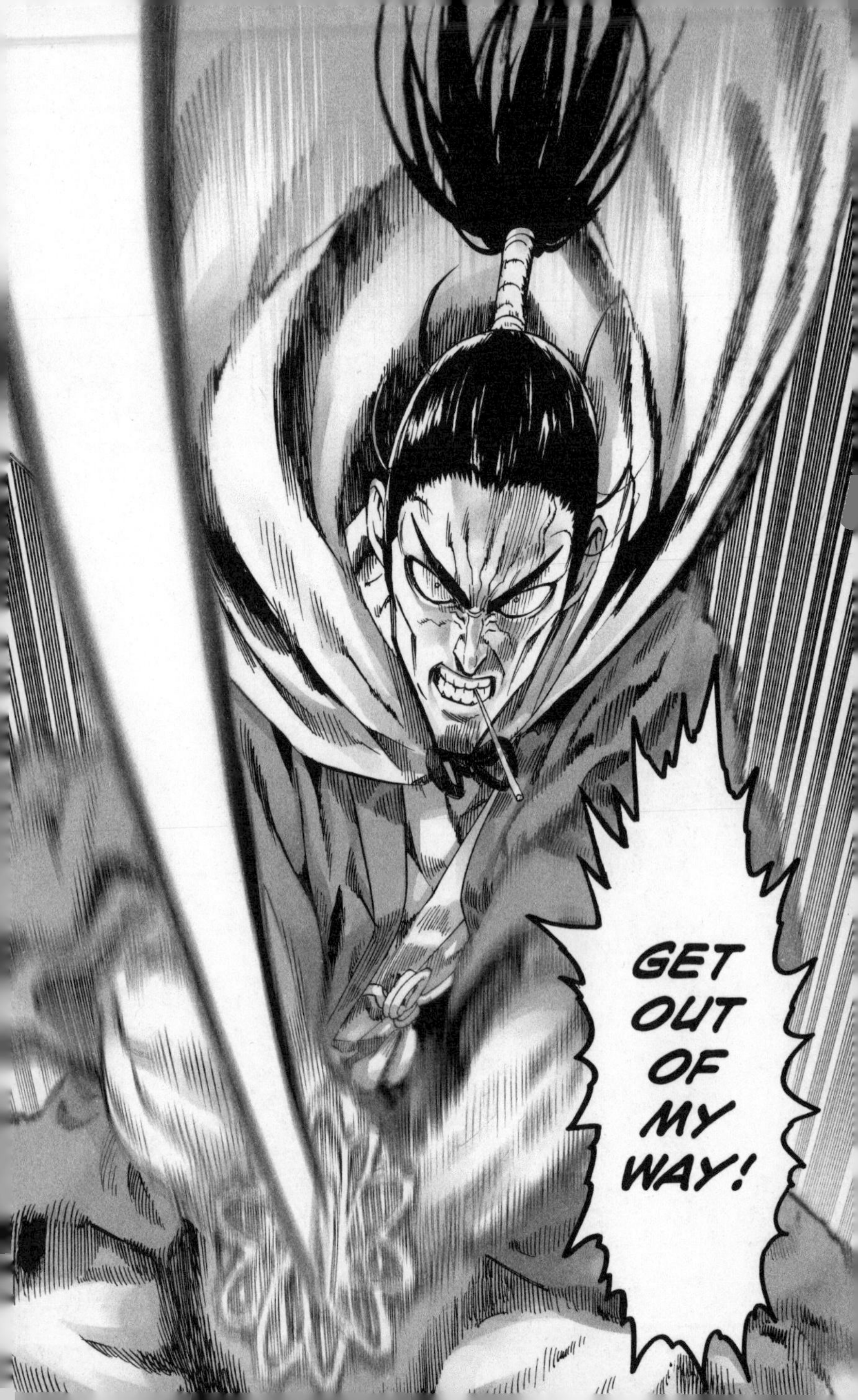
GET OUT OF MY WAY!

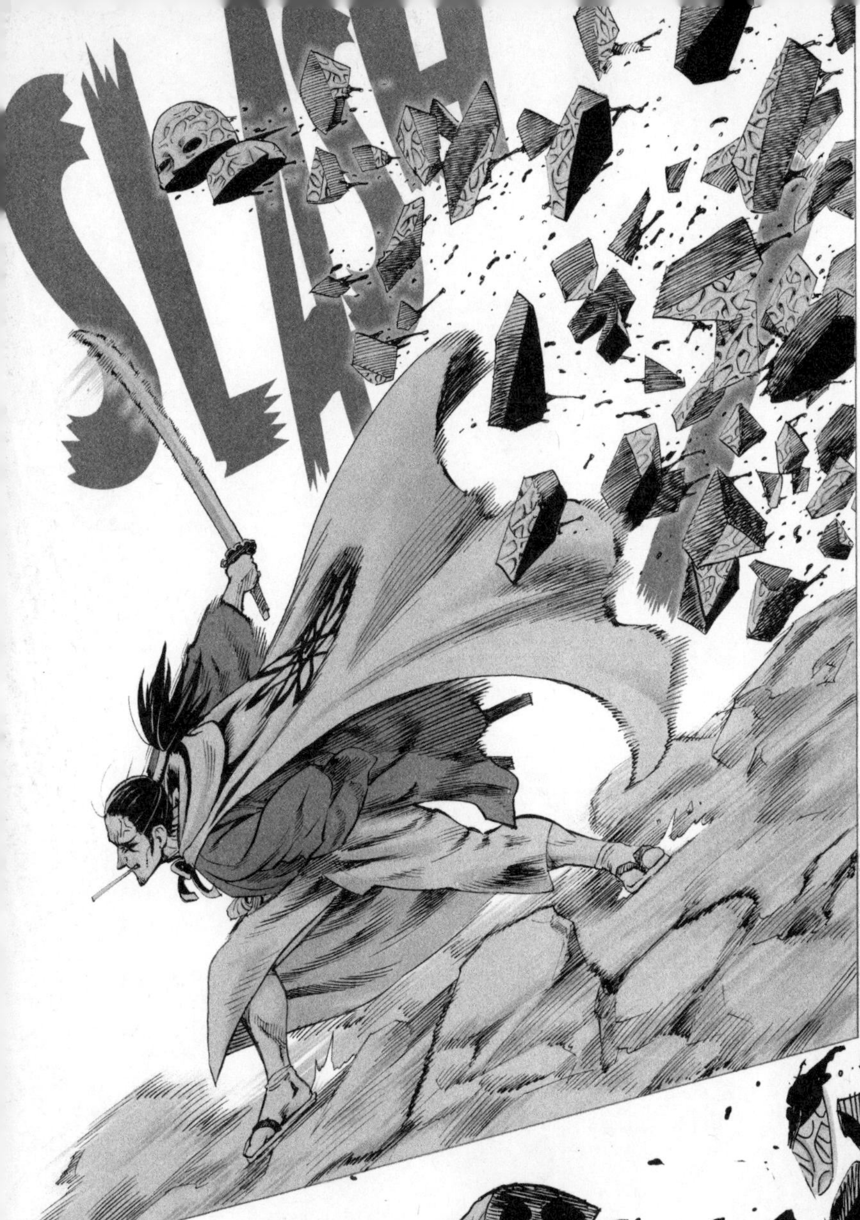
SLASH
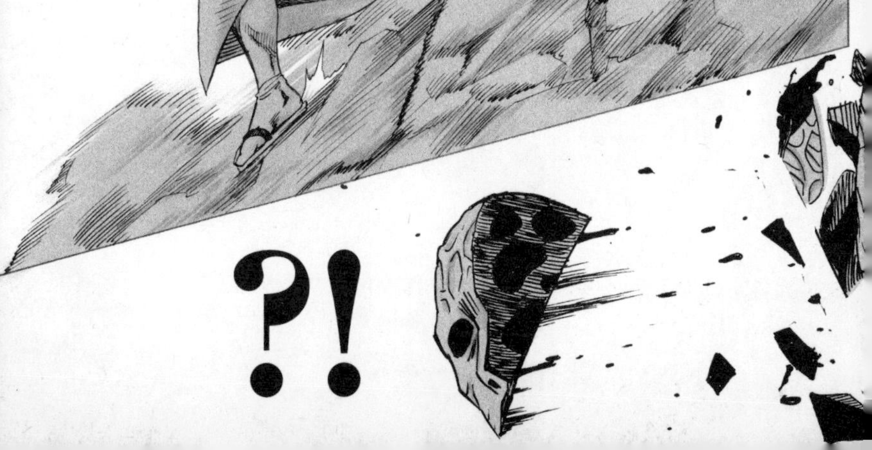
?!

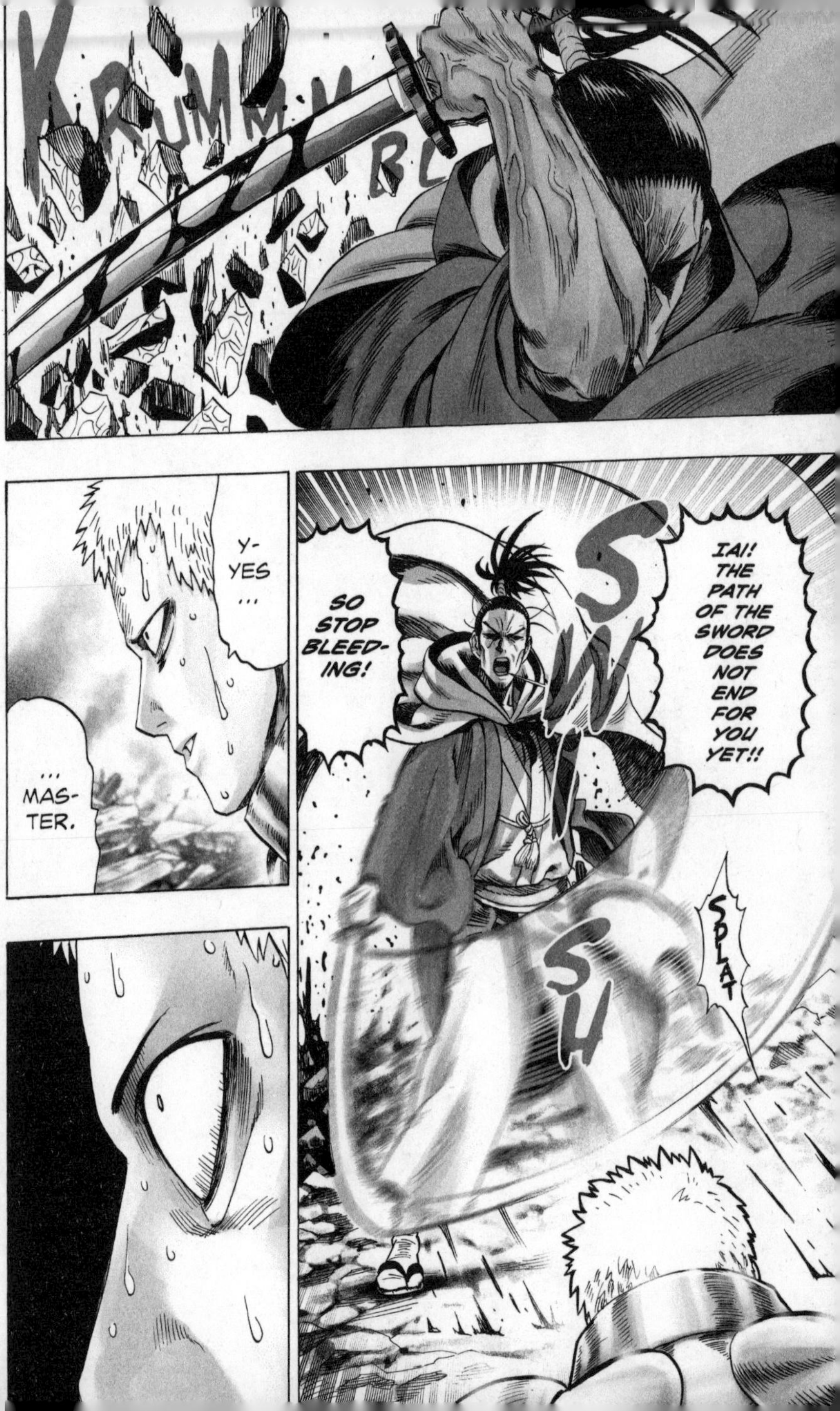
KRUMM
BL
IAI! THE PATH OF THE SWORD DOES NOT END FOR YOU YET!!
SW
SO STOP BLEEDING!
SPLAT
SH
Y-YES ...
... MASTER.

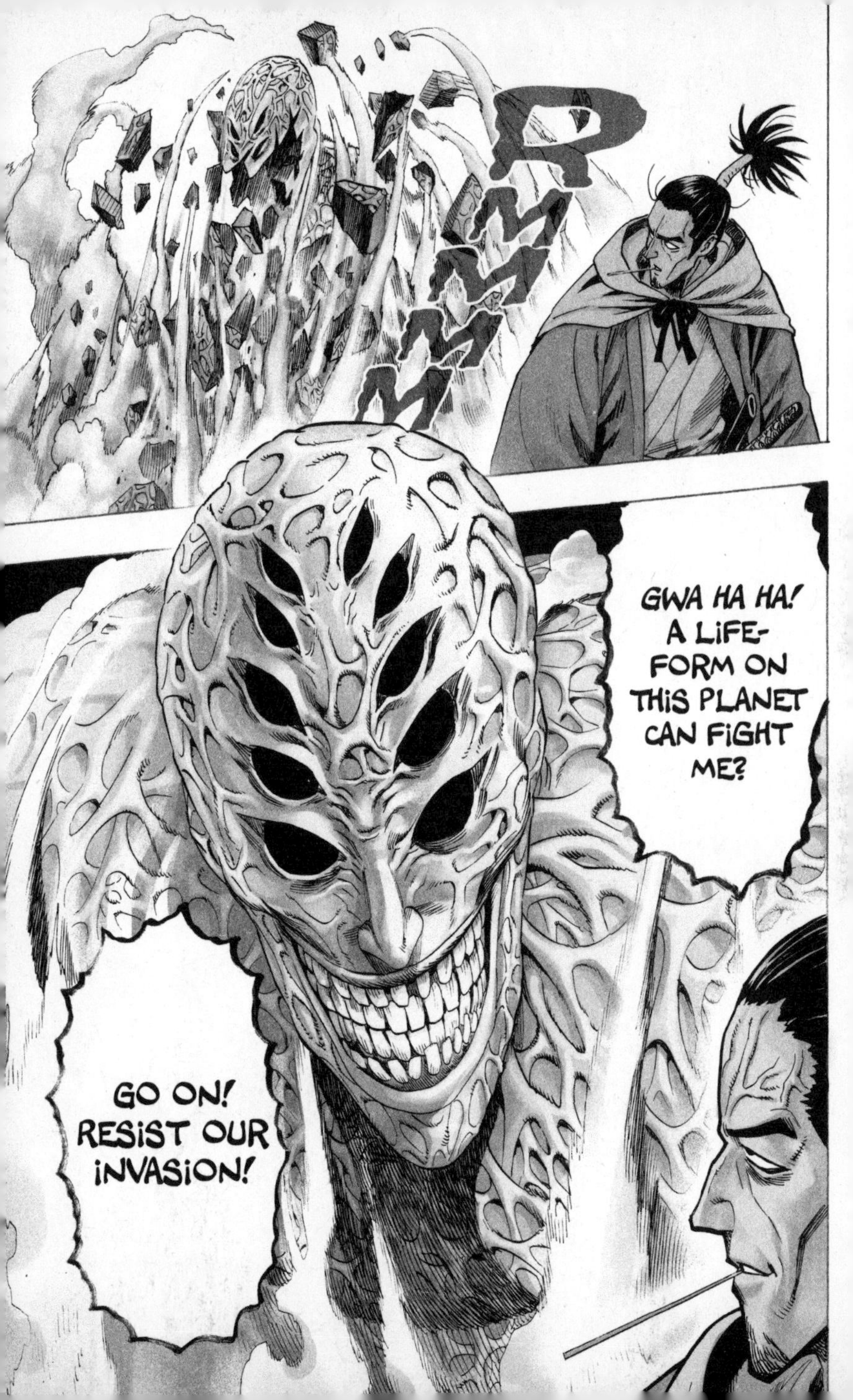
GWA HA HA! A LIFE-FORM ON THIS PLANET CAN FIGHT ME?
GO ON! RESIST OUR INVASION!

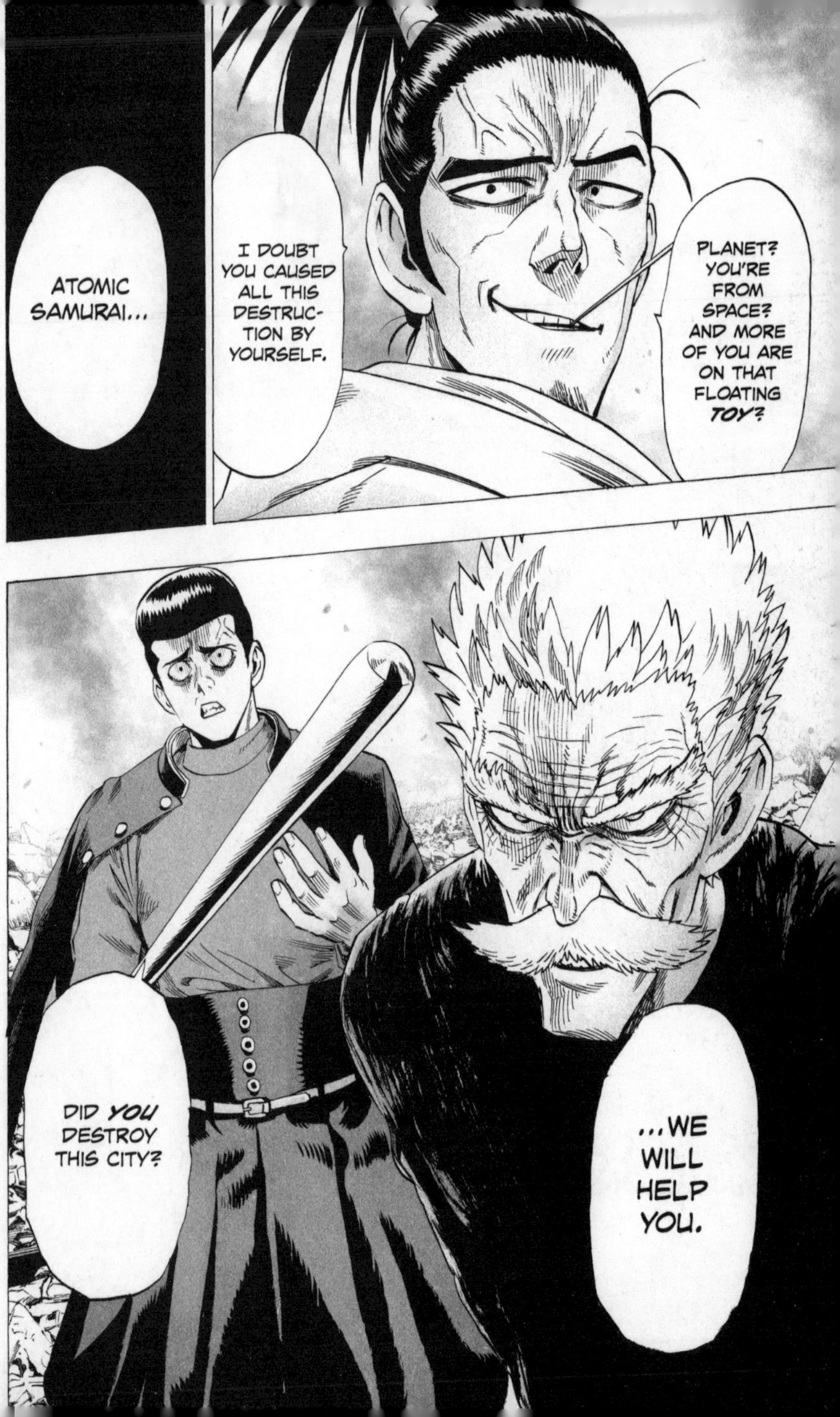
PLANET? YOU'RE FROM SPACE? AND MORE OF YOU ARE ON THAT FLOATING *TOY*?
I DOUBT YOU CAUSED ALL THIS DESTRUCTION BY YOURSELF.
ATOMIC SAMURAI...
...WE WILL HELP YOU.
DID *YOU* DESTROY THIS CITY?

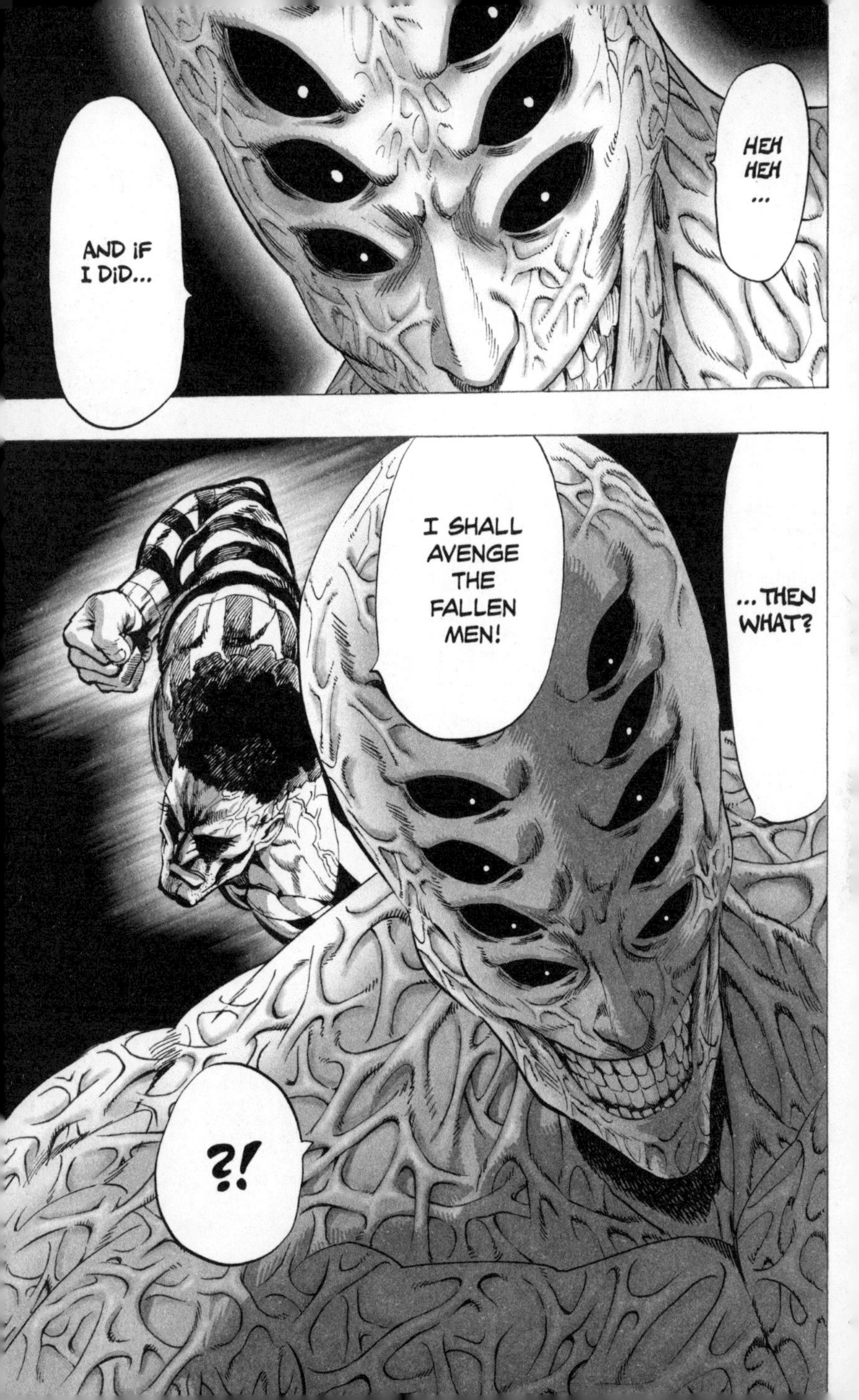
HEH HEH ...
AND IF I DID...
...THEN WHAT?
I SHALL AVENGE THE FALLEN MEN!
?!

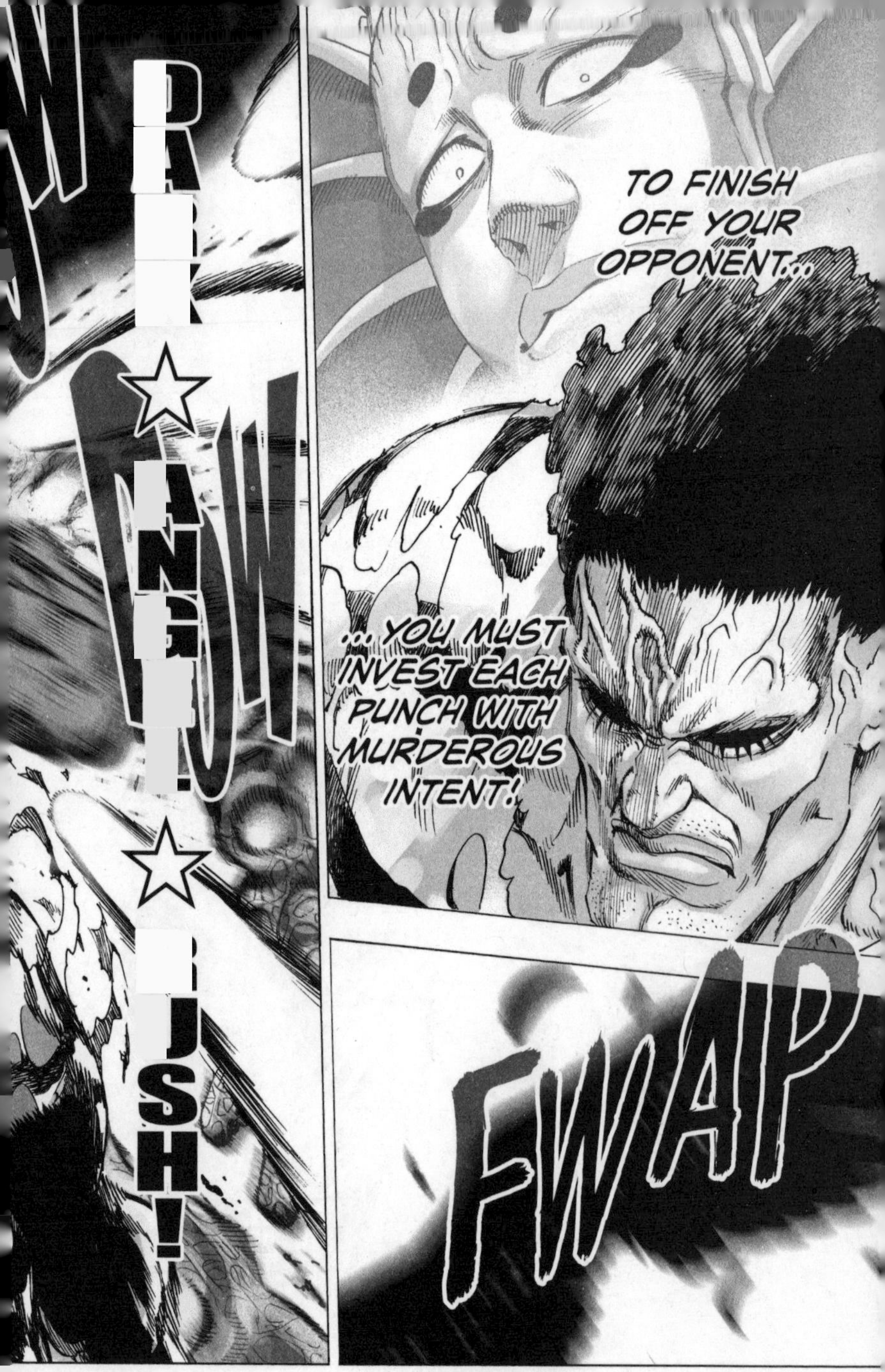
TO FINISH OFF YOUR OPPONENT...
...YOU MUST INVEST EACH PUNCH WITH MURDEROUS INTENT!
FWAP
DARK☆ANGEL☆RUSH!

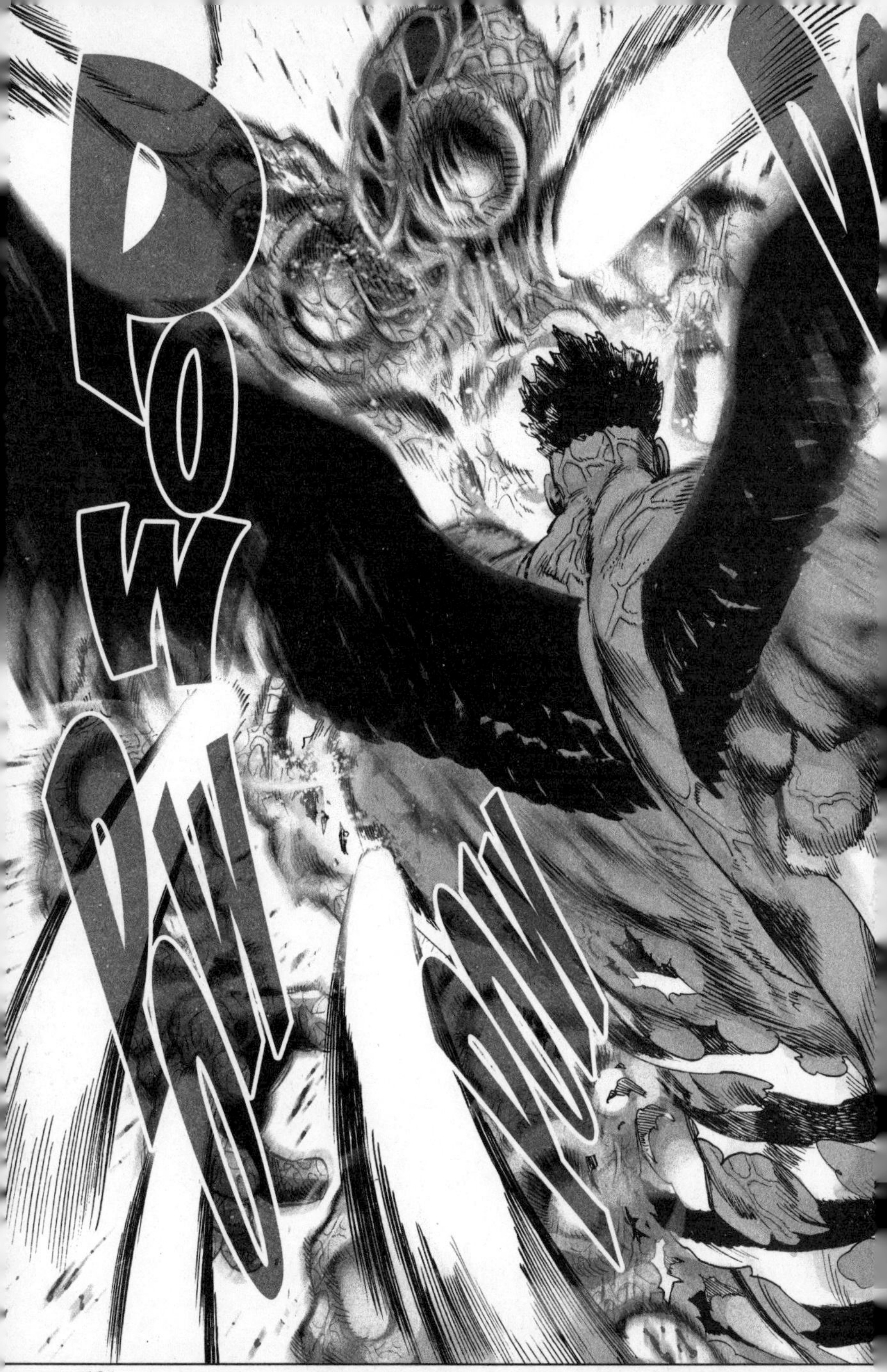

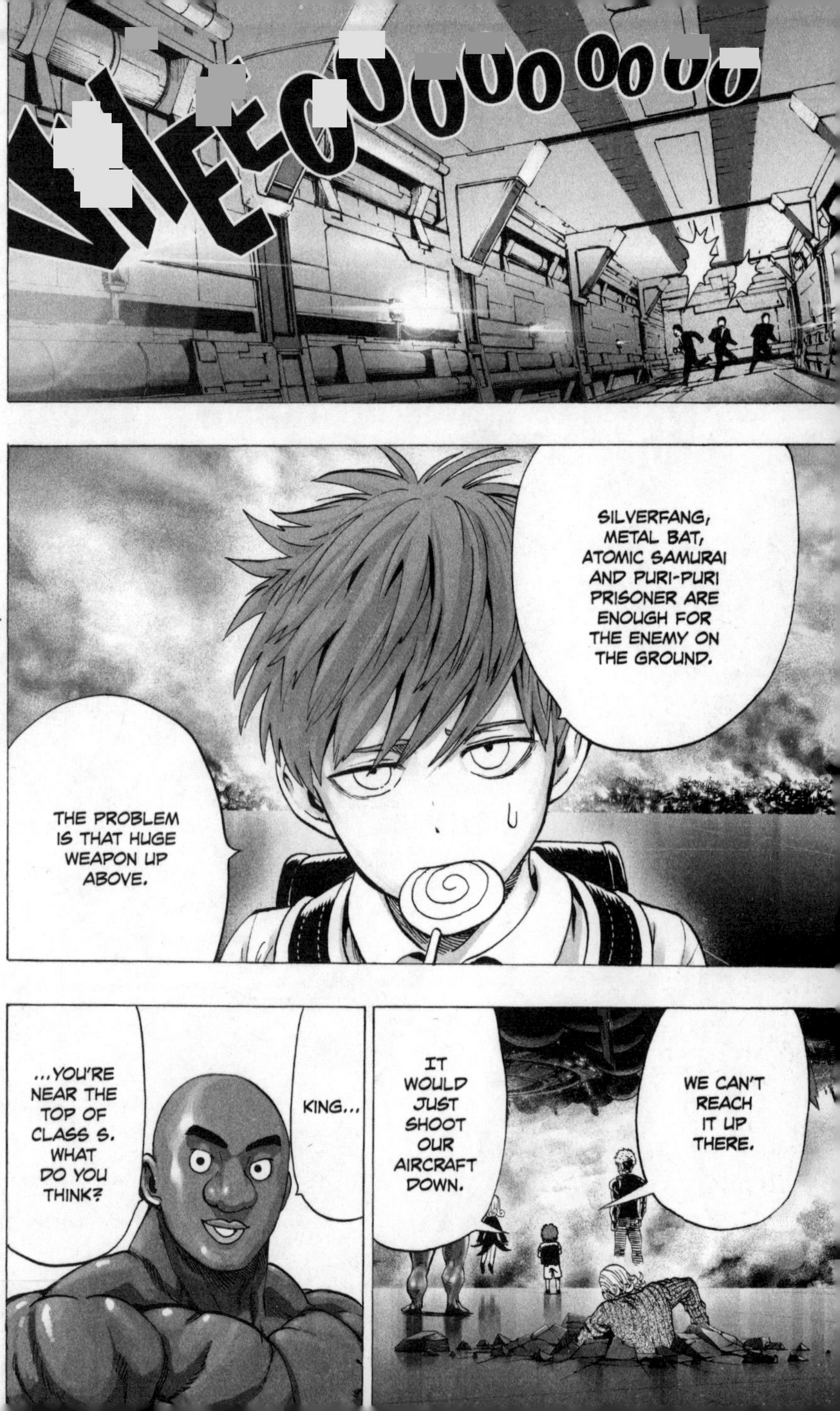
SILVERFANG, METAL BAT, ATOMIC SAMURAI AND PURI-PURI PRISONER ARE ENOUGH FOR THE ENEMY ON THE GROUND.
THE PROBLEM IS THAT HUGE WEAPON UP ABOVE.
WE CAN'T REACH IT UP THERE.
IT WOULD JUST SHOOT OUR AIRCRAFT DOWN.
KING...
...YOU'RE NEAR THE TOP OF CLASS S. WHAT DO YOU THINK?

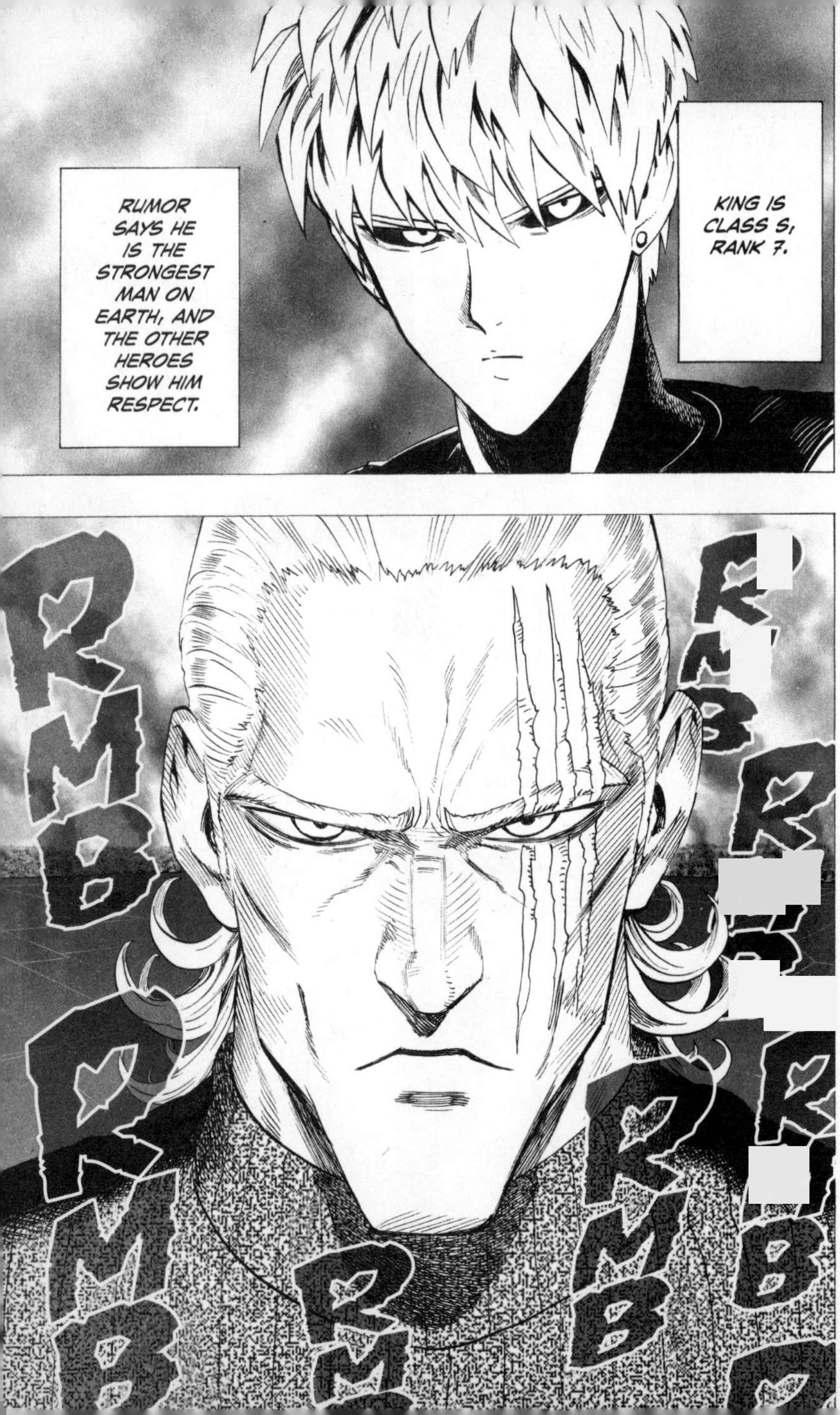
KING IS CLASS S, RANK 7.
RUMOR SAYS HE IS THE STRONGEST MAN ON EARTH, AND THE OTHER HEROES SHOW HIM RESPECT.
RMB
RMB
RMB
RMB
RMB
RMB

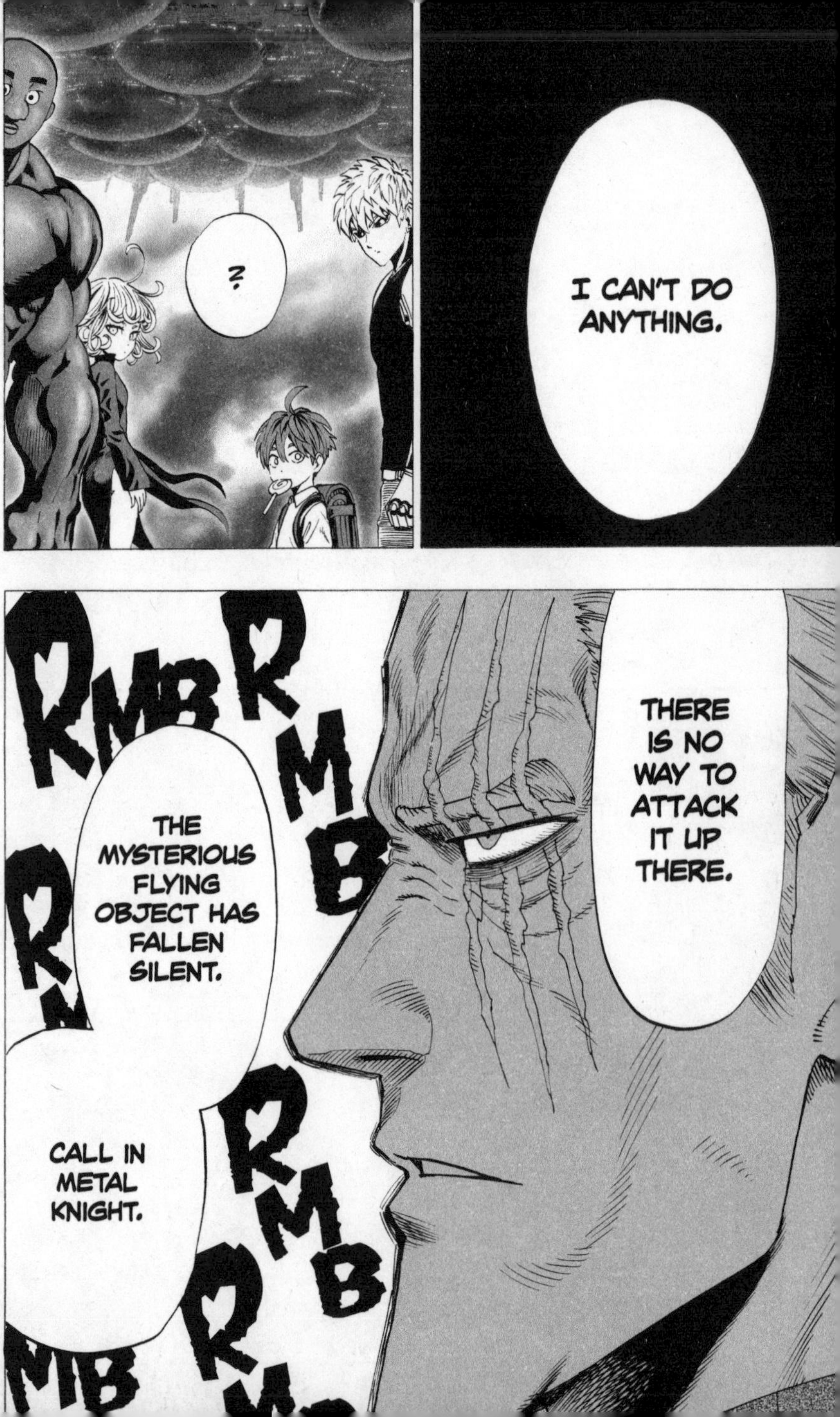
I CAN'T DO ANYTHING.
?
THERE IS NO WAY TO ATTACK IT UP THERE.
THE MYSTERIOUS FLYING OBJECT HAS FALLEN SILENT.
CALL IN METAL KNIGHT.

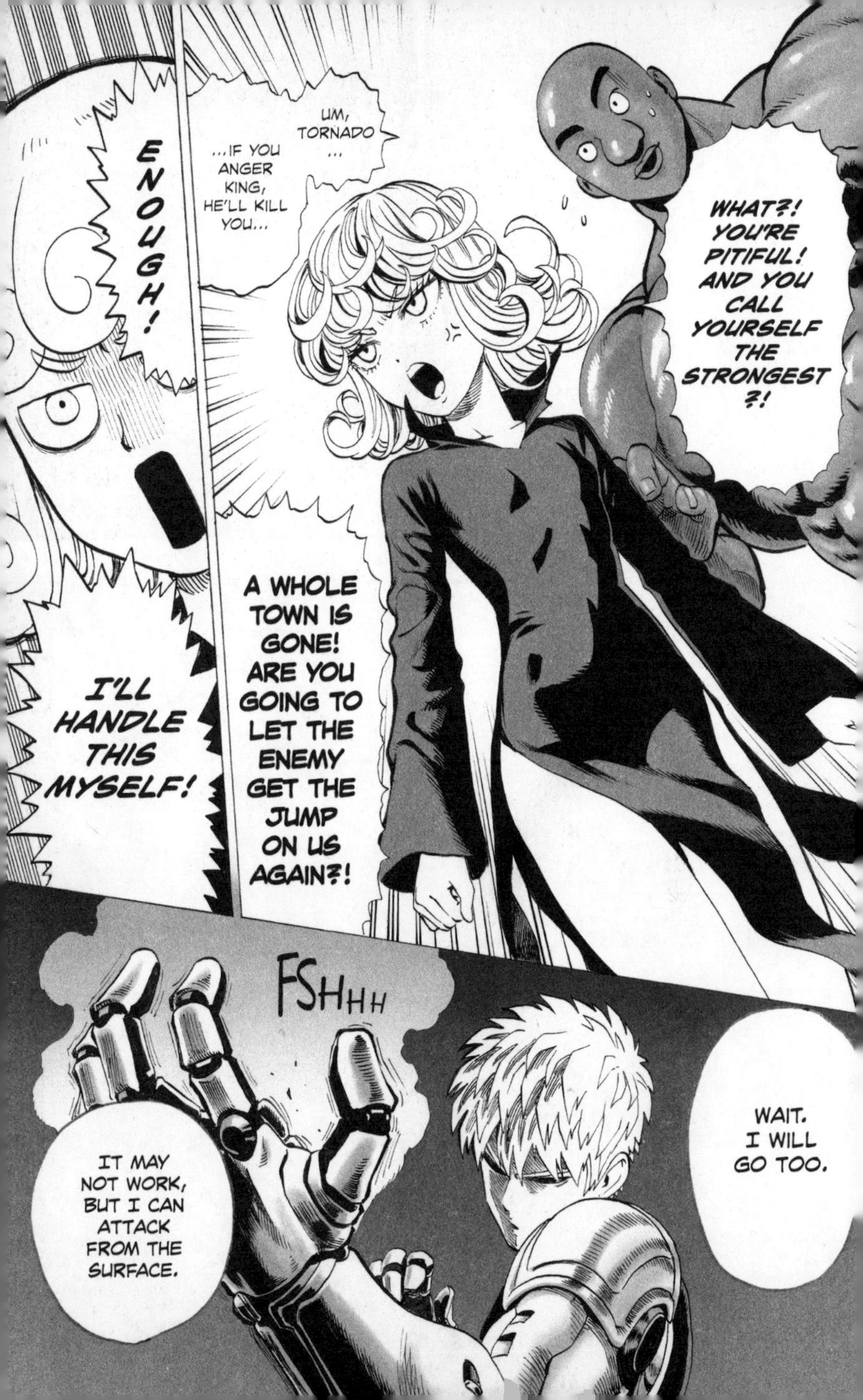
WHAT?! YOU'RE PITIFUL! AND YOU CALL YOURSELF THE STRONGEST?!
UM, TORNADO...
...IF YOU ANGER KING, HE'LL KILL YOU...
A WHOLE TOWN IS GONE! ARE YOU GOING TO LET THE ENEMY GET THE JUMP ON US AGAIN?!
ENOUGH!
I'LL HANDLE THIS MYSELF!
WAIT. I WILL GO TOO.
FSHHH
IT MAY NOT WORK, BUT I CAN ATTACK FROM THE SURFACE.

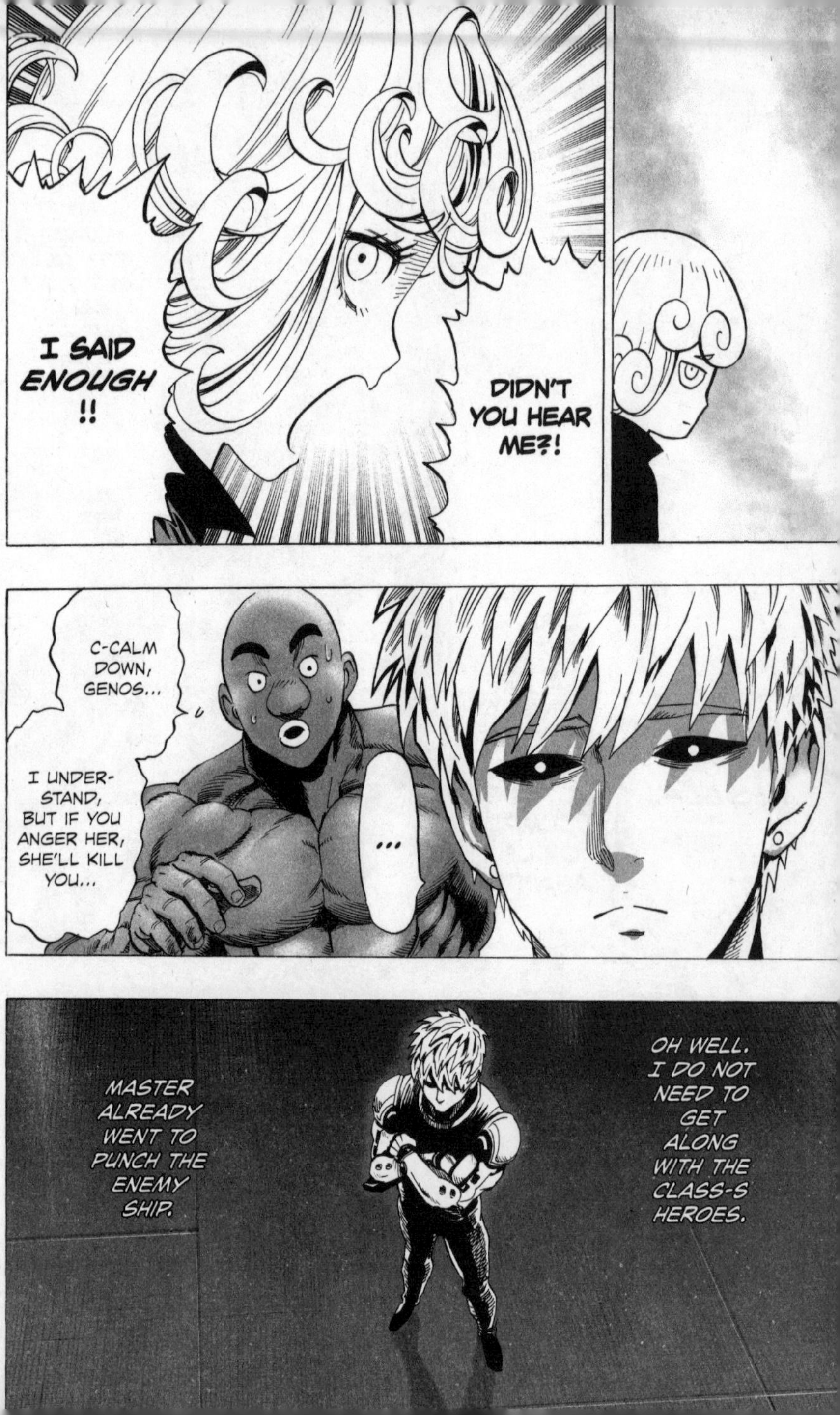
I SAID ENOUGH!!
DIDN'T YOU HEAR ME?!
C-CALM DOWN, GENOS...
I UNDERSTAND, BUT IF YOU ANGER HER, SHE'LL KILL YOU...
...
OH WELL. I DO NOT NEED TO GET ALONG WITH THE CLASS-S HEROES.
MASTER ALREADY WENT TO PUNCH THE ENEMY SHIP.

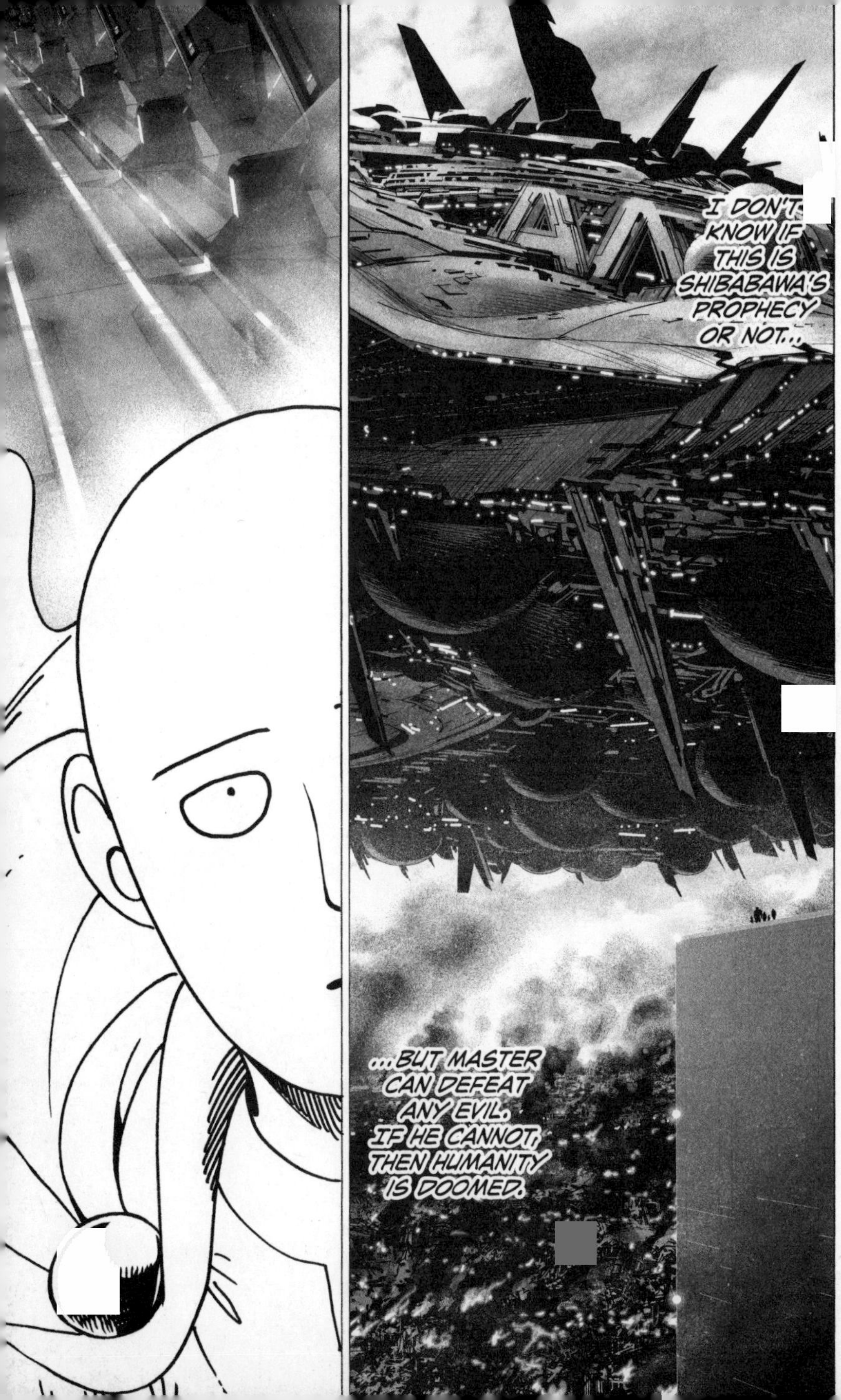
I DON'T KNOW IF THIS IS SHIBABAWA'S PROPHECY OR NOT...
...BUT MASTER CAN DEFEAT ANY EVIL. IF HE CANNOT, THEN HUMANITY IS DOOMED.

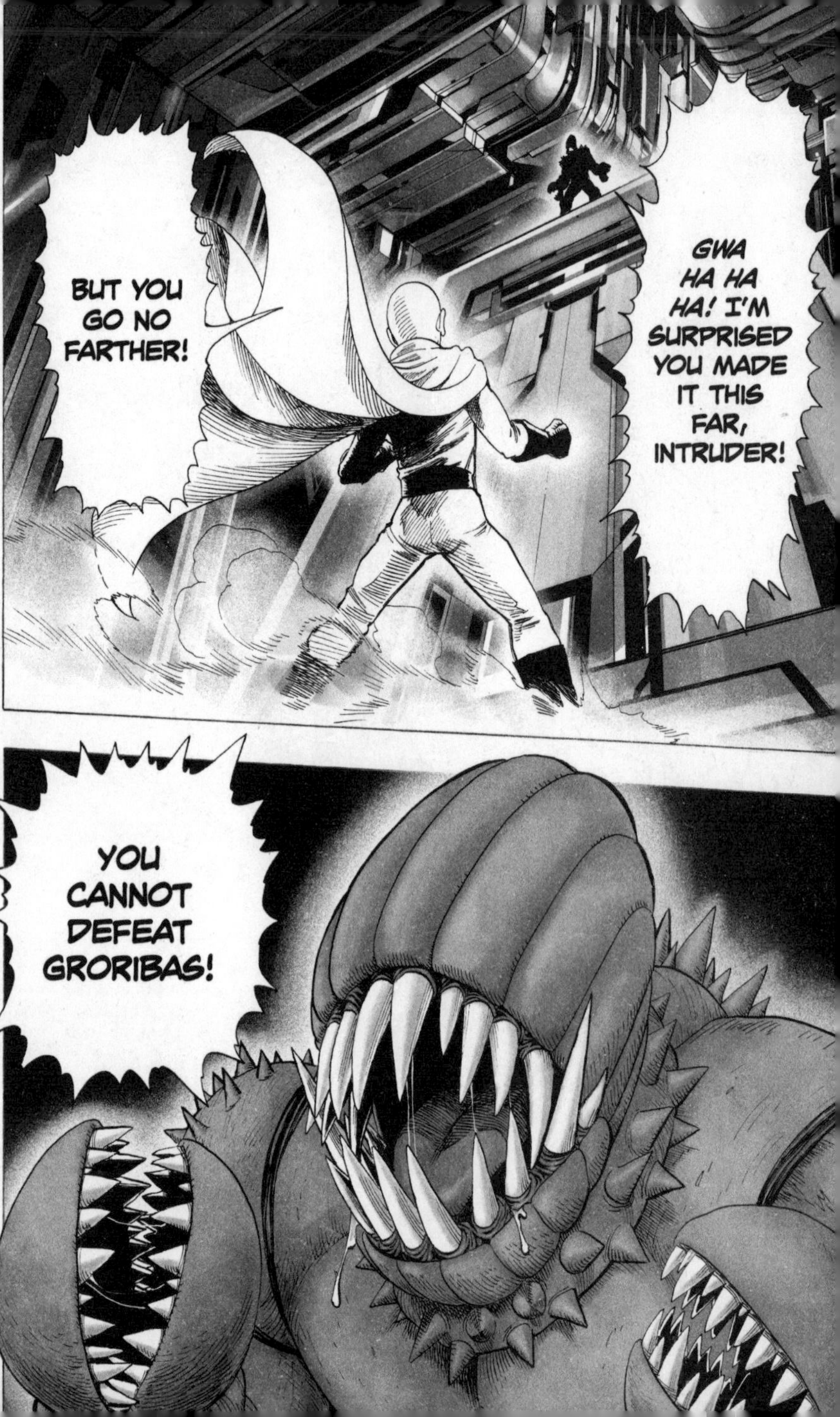
GWA HA HA HA! I'M SURPRISED YOU MADE IT THIS FAR, INTRUDER!
BUT YOU GO NO FARTHER!
YOU CANNOT DEFEAT GRORIBAS!

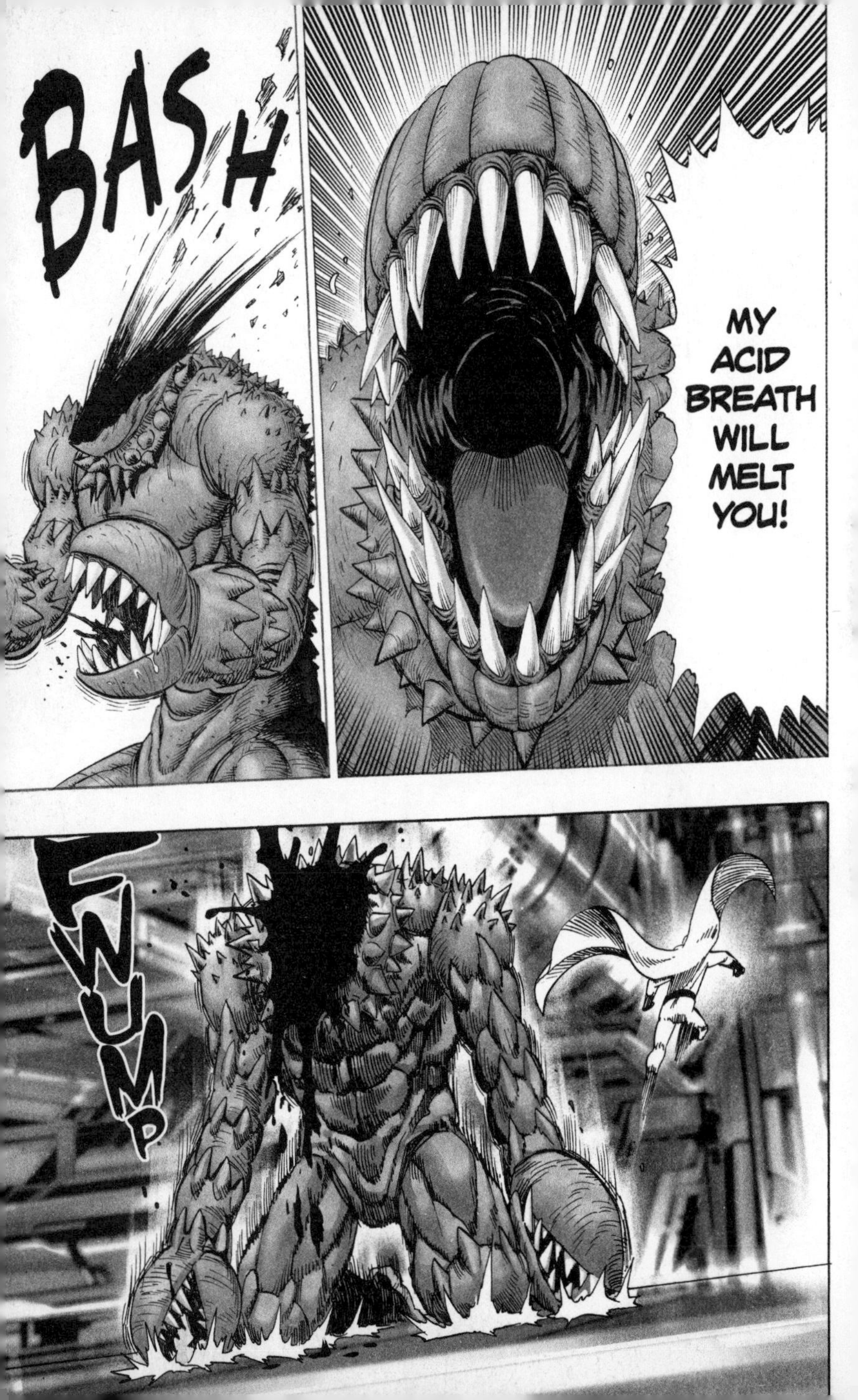
MY ACID BREATH WILL MELT YOU!
BASH
FWUMP

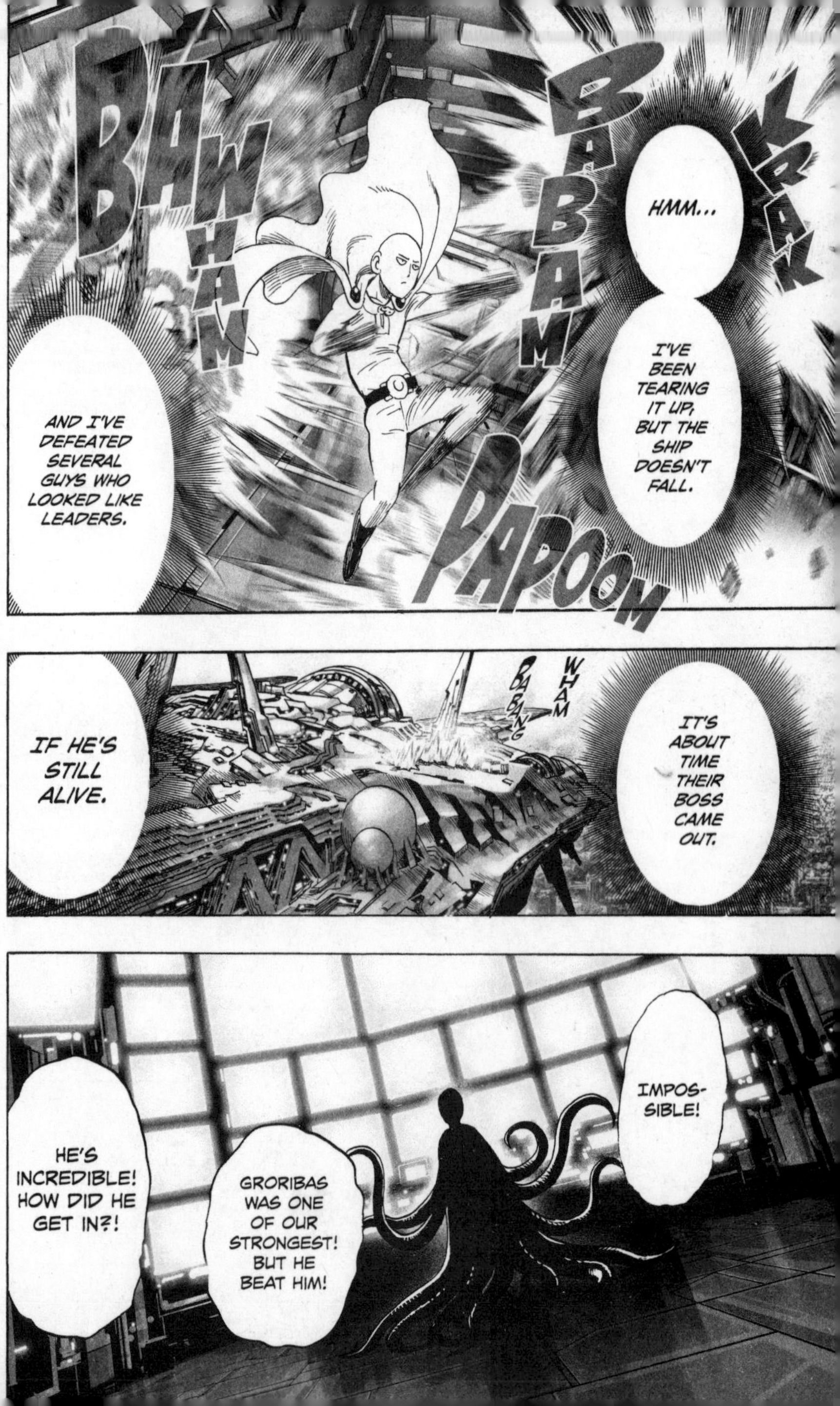
KRAK
HMM...
BABAM
I'VE BEEN TEARING IT UP, BUT THE SHIP DOESN'T FALL.
BAM
WHAM
PAPOOM
AND I'VE DEFEATED SEVERAL GUYS WHO LOOKED LIKE LEADERS.
IT'S ABOUT TIME THEIR BOSS CAME OUT.
WHAM
BABANG
IF HE'S STILL ALIVE.
IMPOS-SIBLE!
GRORIBAS WAS ONE OF OUR STRONGEST! BUT HE BEAT HIM!
HE'S INCREDIBLE! HOW DID HE GET IN?!

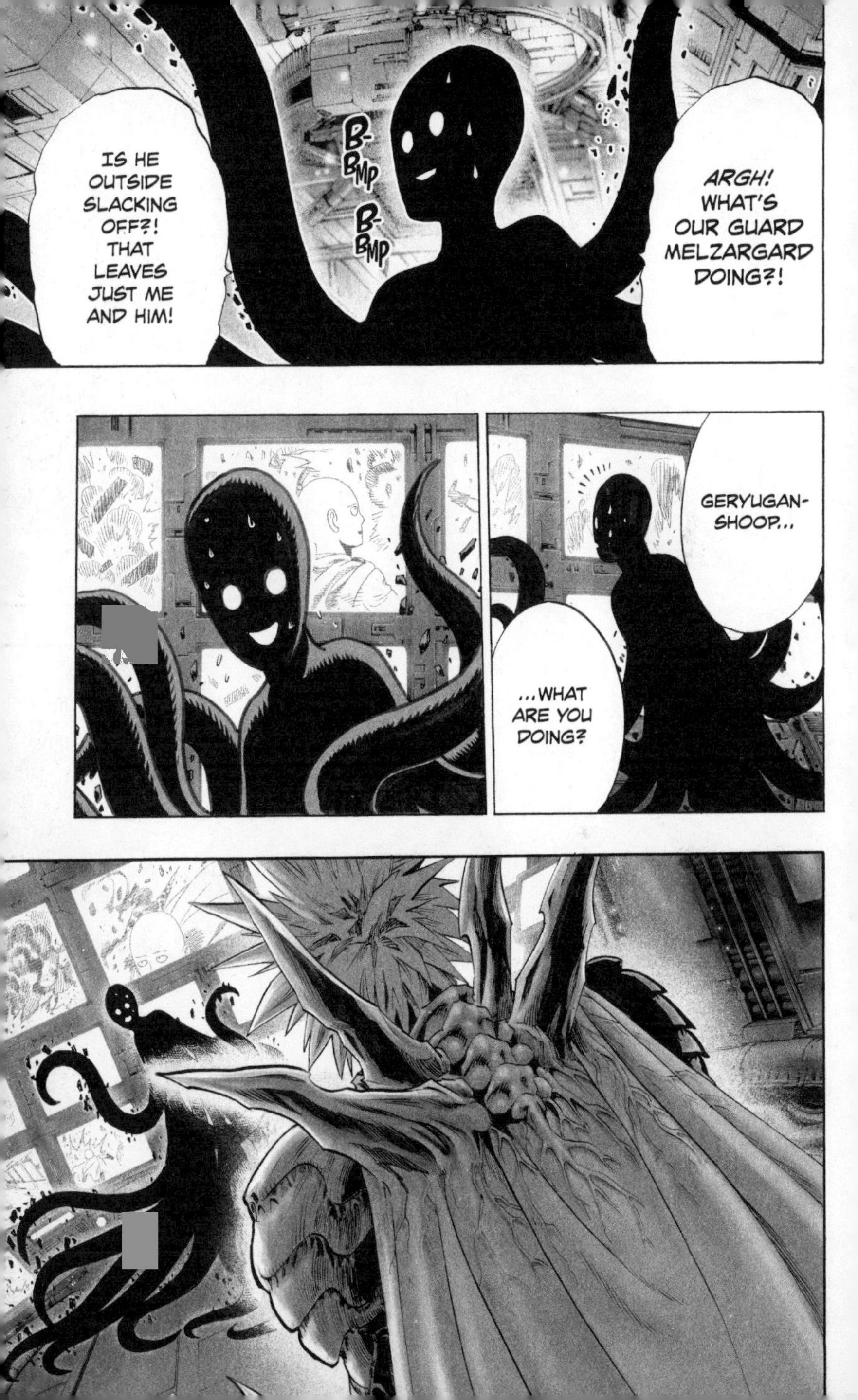
ARGH! WHAT'S OUR GUARD MELZARGARD DOING?!
B-BMP
B-BMP
IS HE OUTSIDE SLACKING OFF?! THAT LEAVES JUST ME AND HIM!
GERYUGAN-SHOOP...
...WHAT ARE YOU DOING?

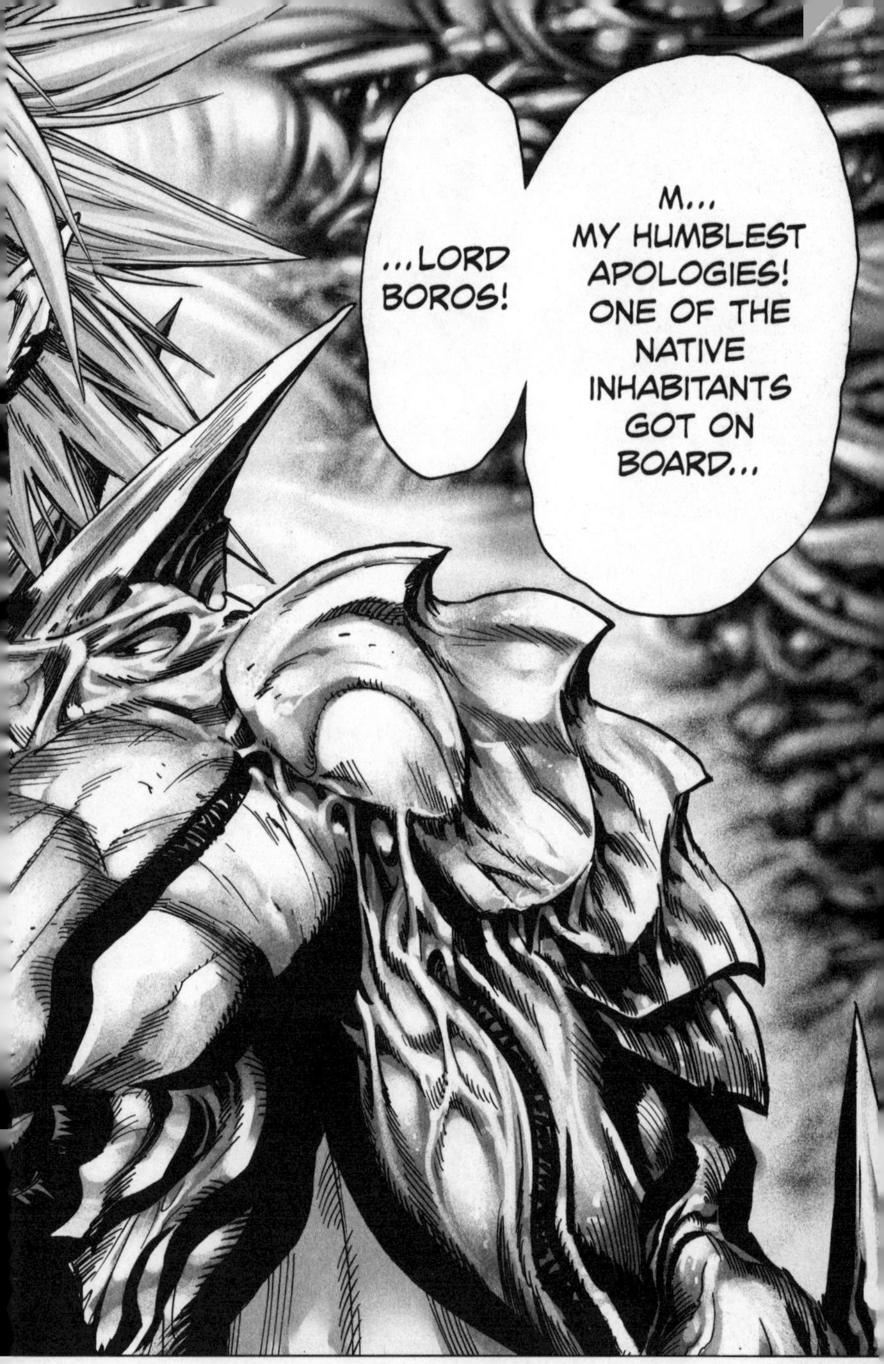
M... MY HUMBLEST APOLOGIES! ONE OF THE NATIVE INHABITANTS GOT ON BOARD...
...LORD BOROS!

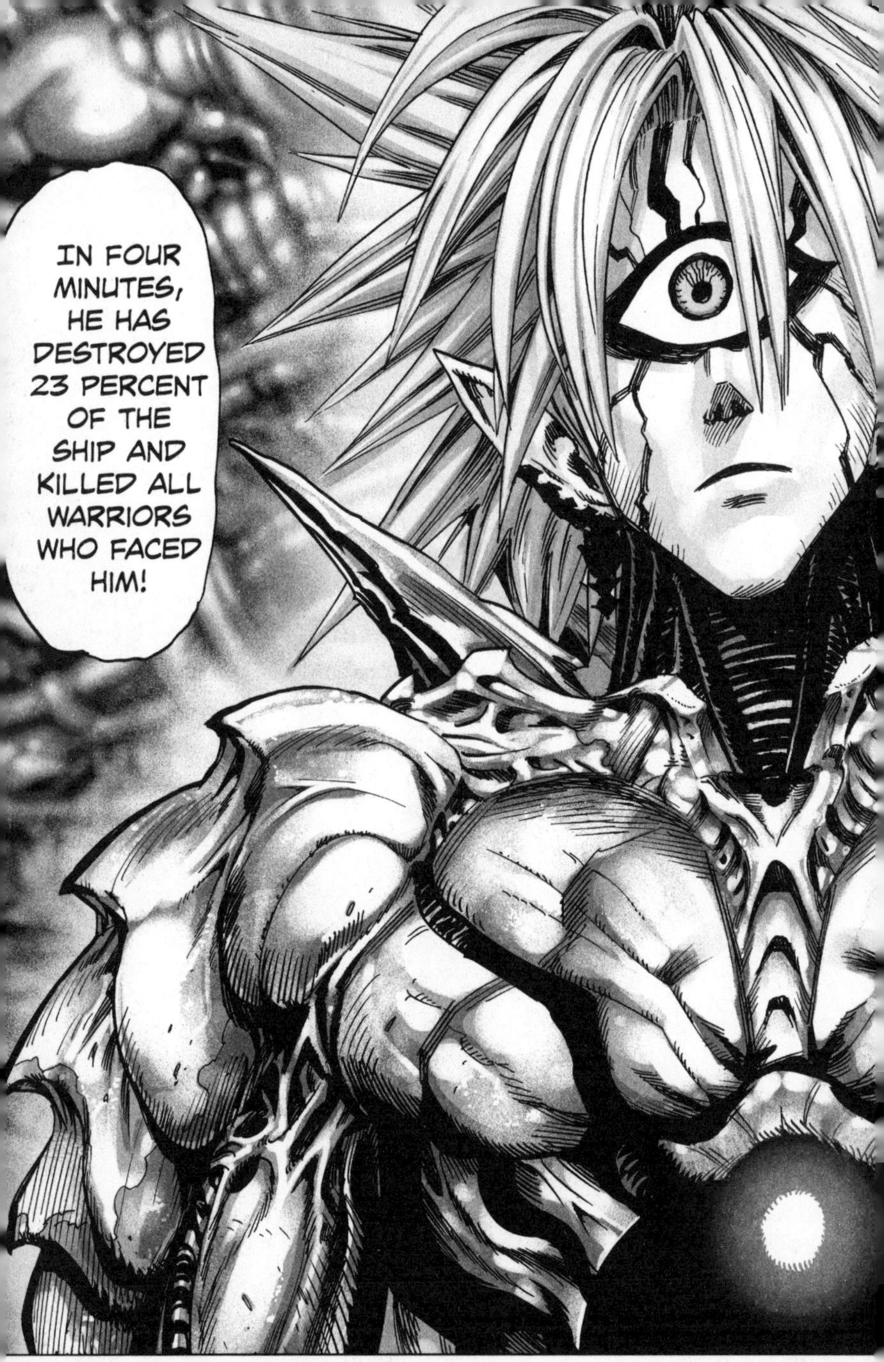
IN FOUR MINUTES, HE HAS DESTROYED 23 PERCENT OF THE SHIP AND KILLED ALL WARRIORS WHO FACED HIM!

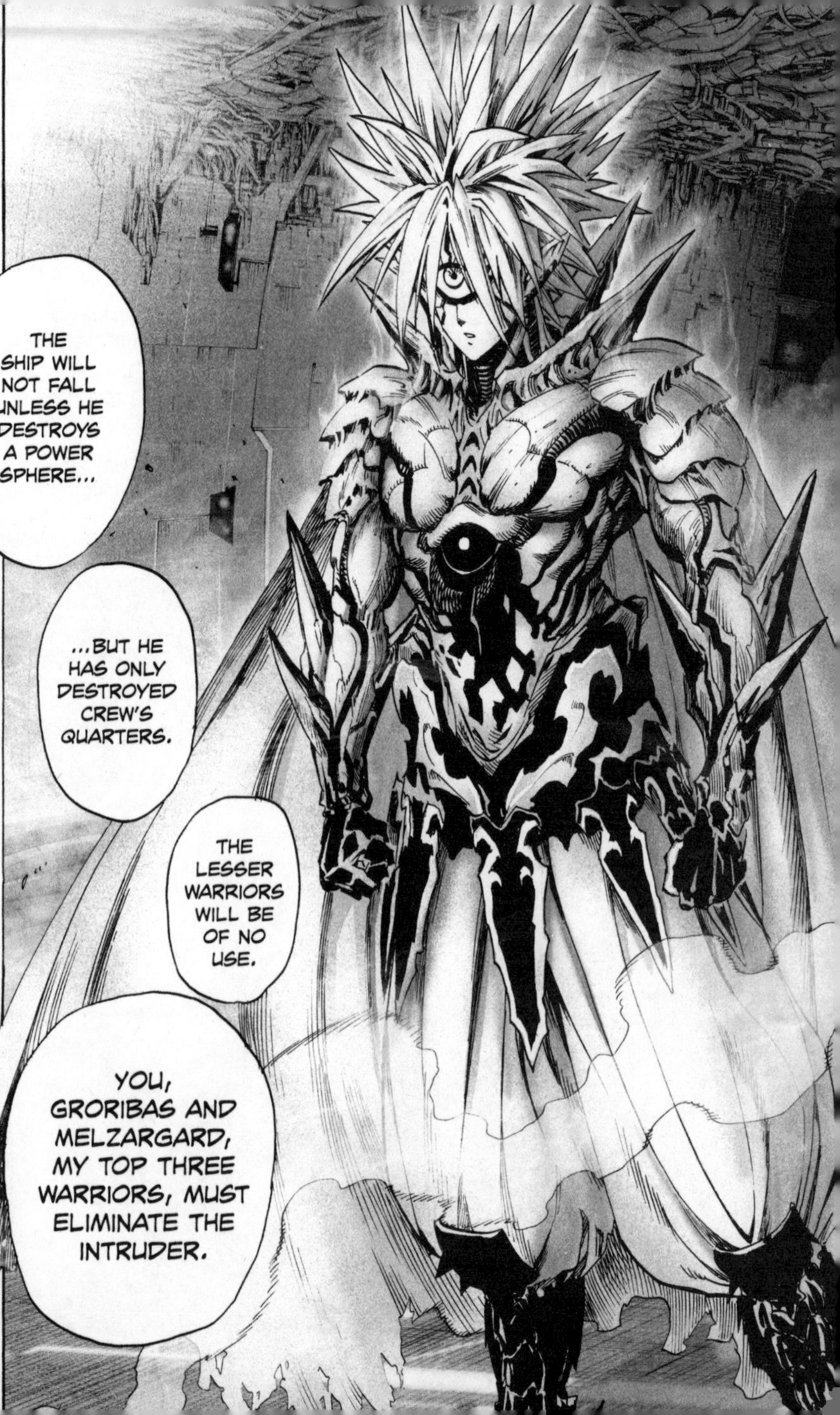
THE SHIP WILL NOT FALL UNLESS HE DESTROYS A POWER SPHERE...
...BUT HE HAS ONLY DESTROYED CREW'S QUARTERS.
THE LESSER WARRIORS WILL BE OF NO USE.
YOU, GRORIBAS AND MELZARGARD, MY TOP THREE WARRIORS, MUST ELIMINATE THE INTRUDER.

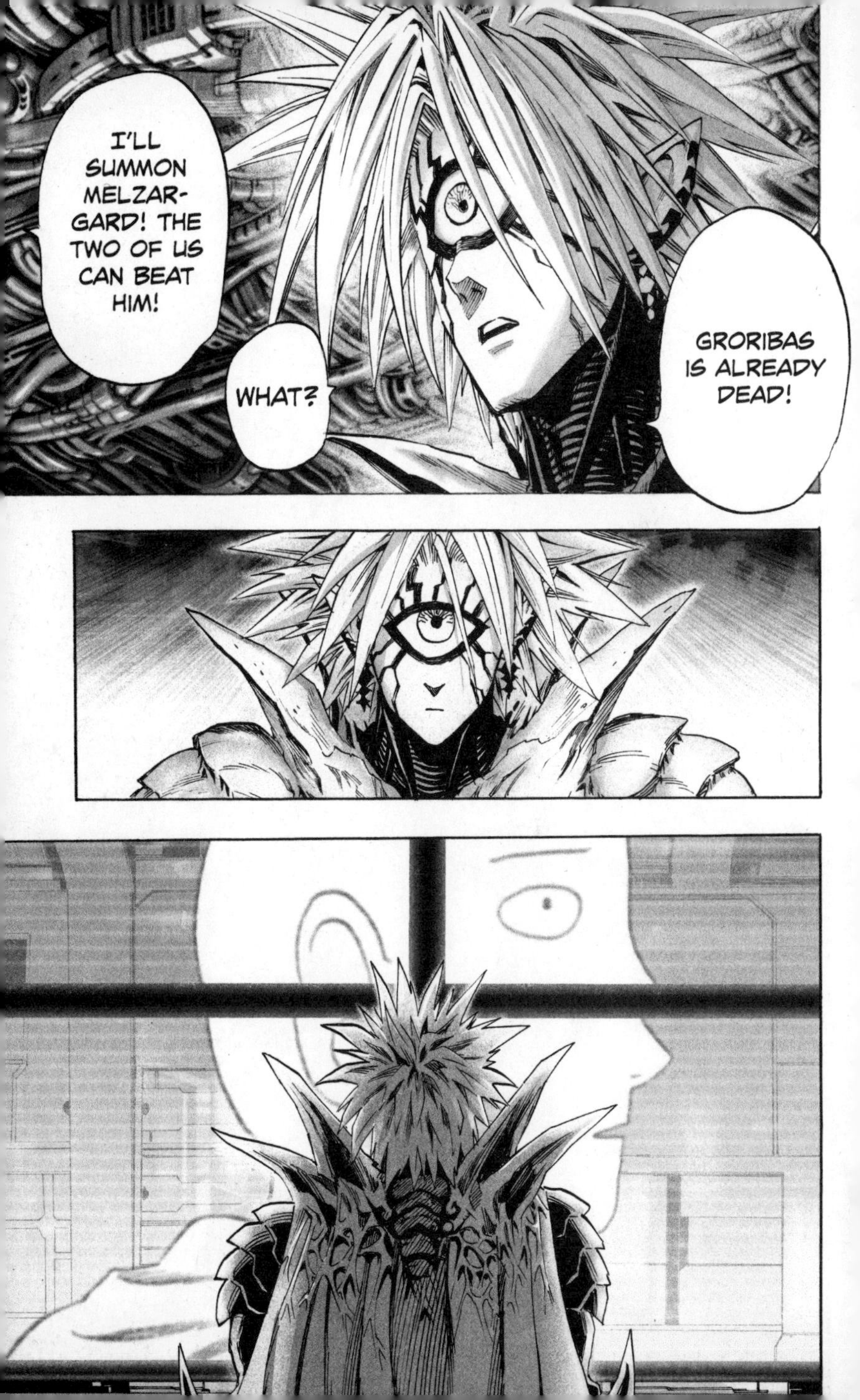
GRORIBAS IS ALREADY DEAD!
WHAT?
I'LL SUMMON MELZAR-GARD! THE TWO OF US CAN BEAT HIM!

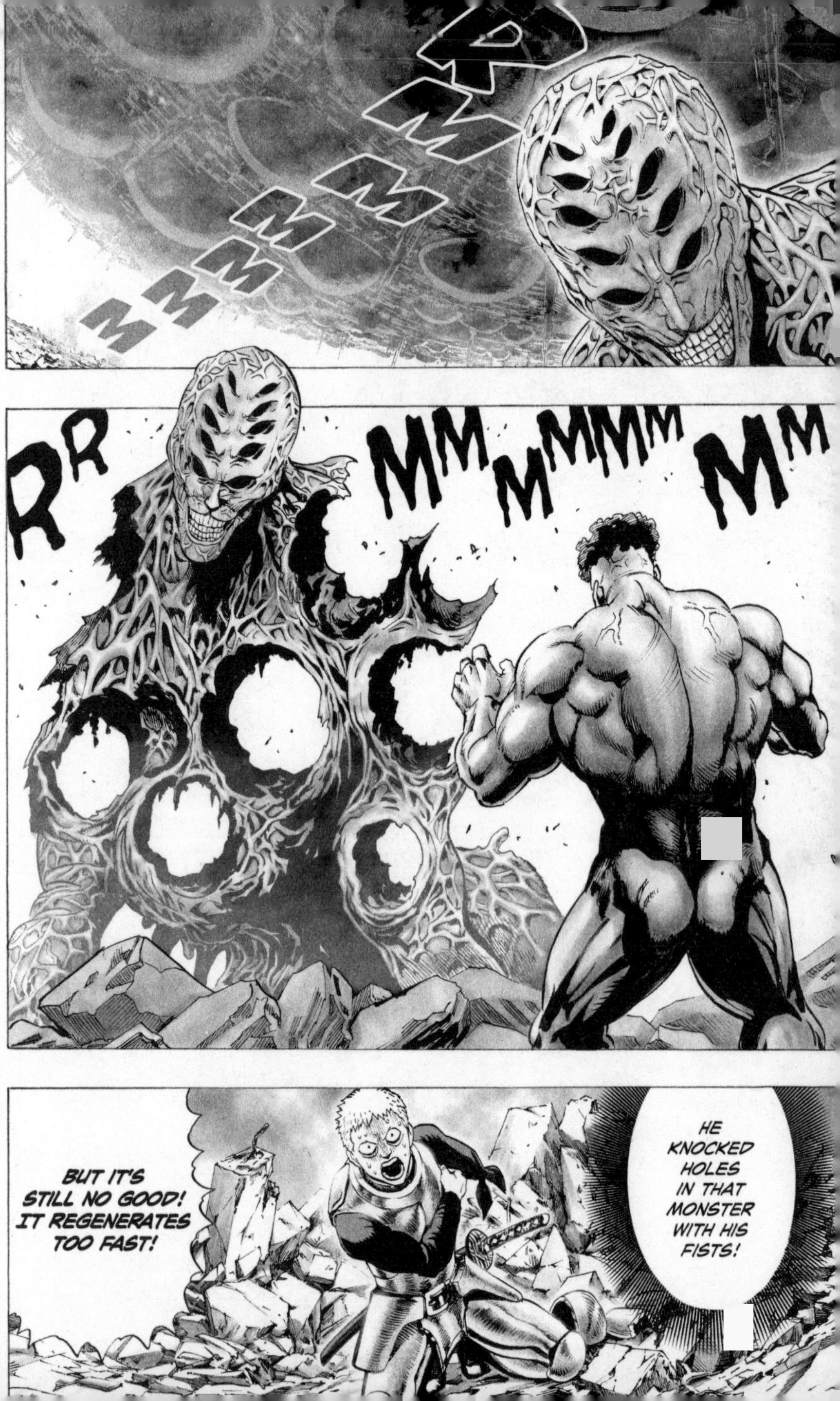
RRMMMMMMMMM
HE KNOCKED HOLES IN THAT MONSTER WITH HIS FISTS!
BUT IT'S STILL NO GOOD! IT REGENERATES TOO FAST!

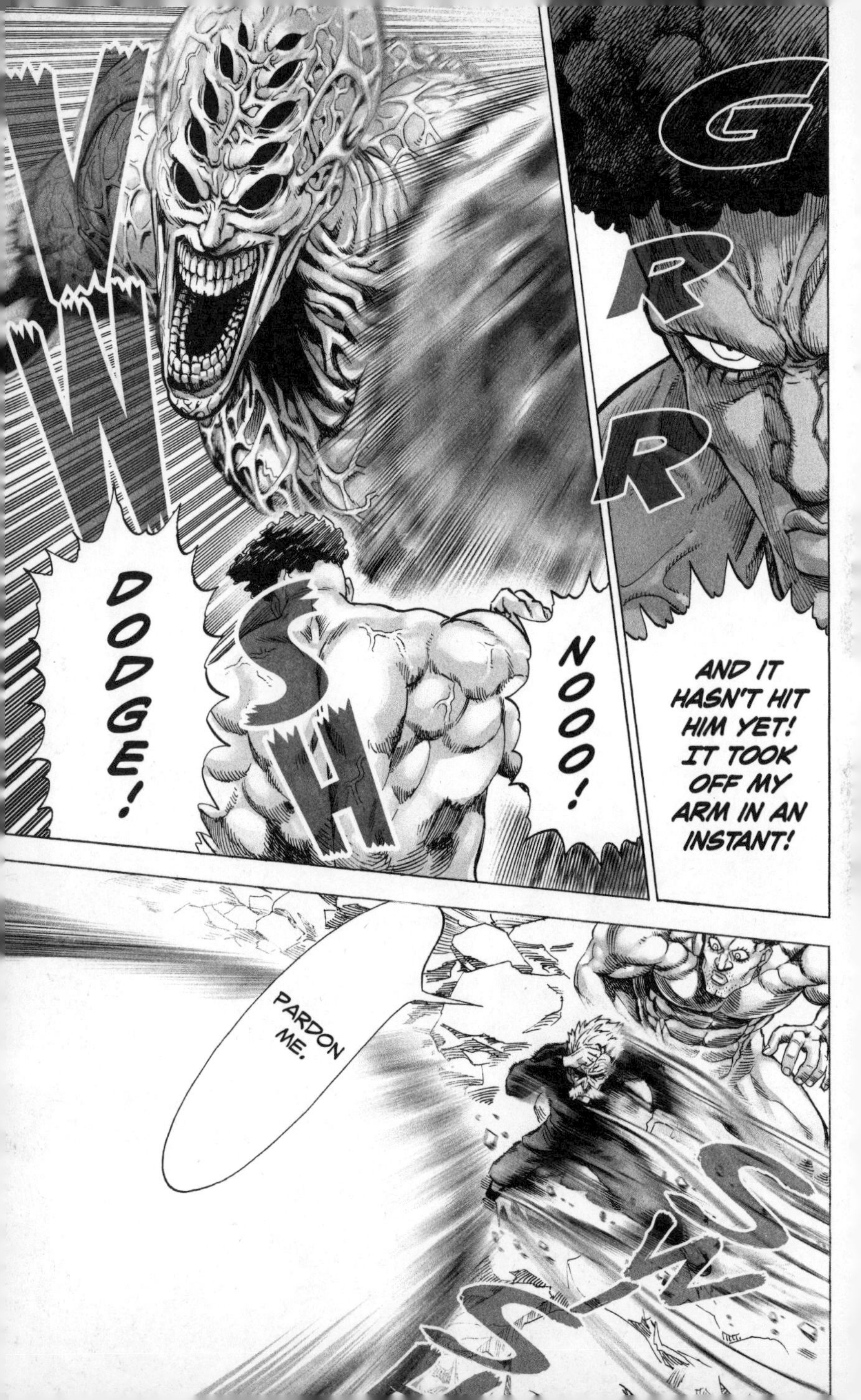
GRR
AND IT HASN'T HIT HIM YET! IT TOOK OFF MY ARM IN AN INSTANT!
NOOOO!
DODGE!
PARDON ME.

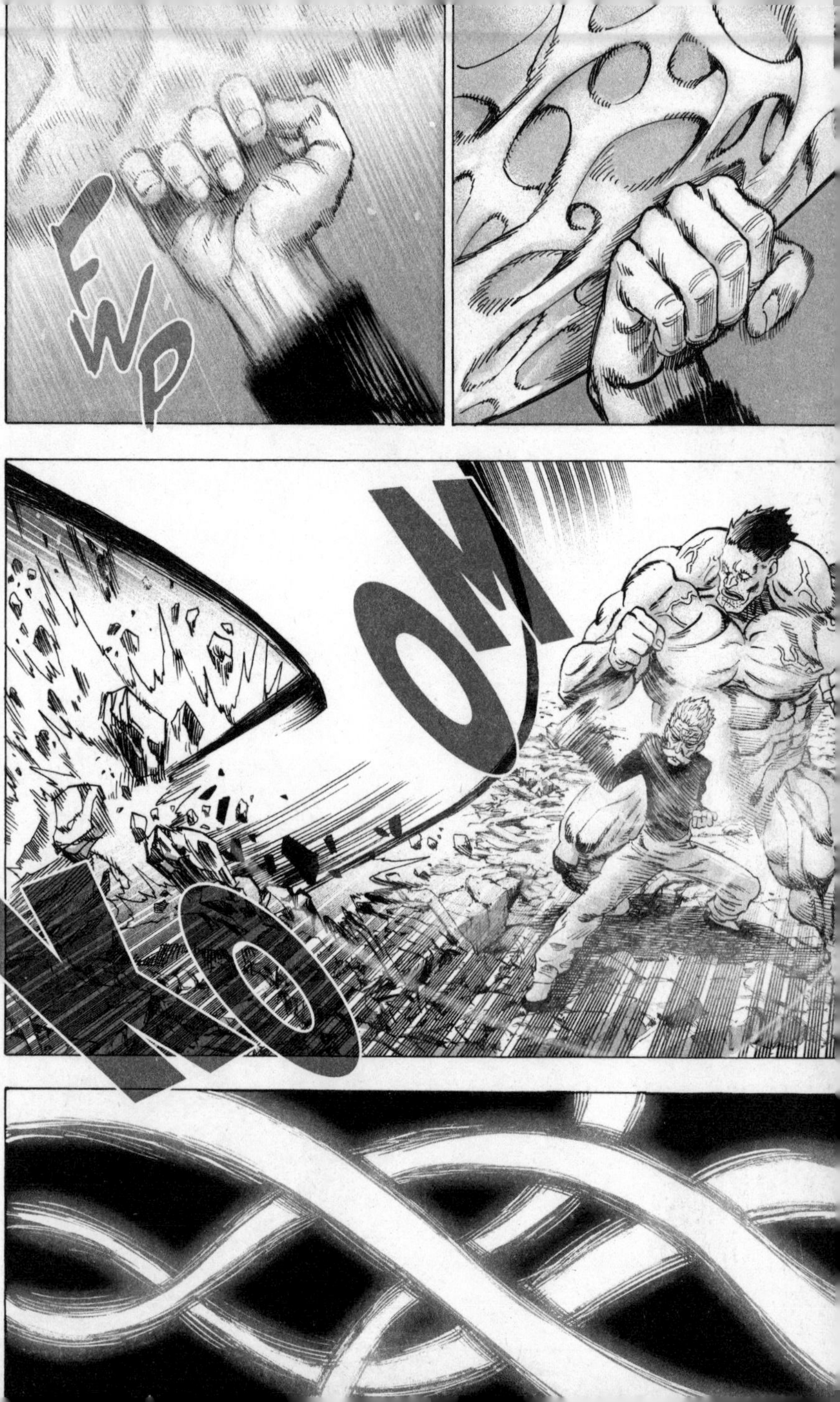
FWP
WOOM

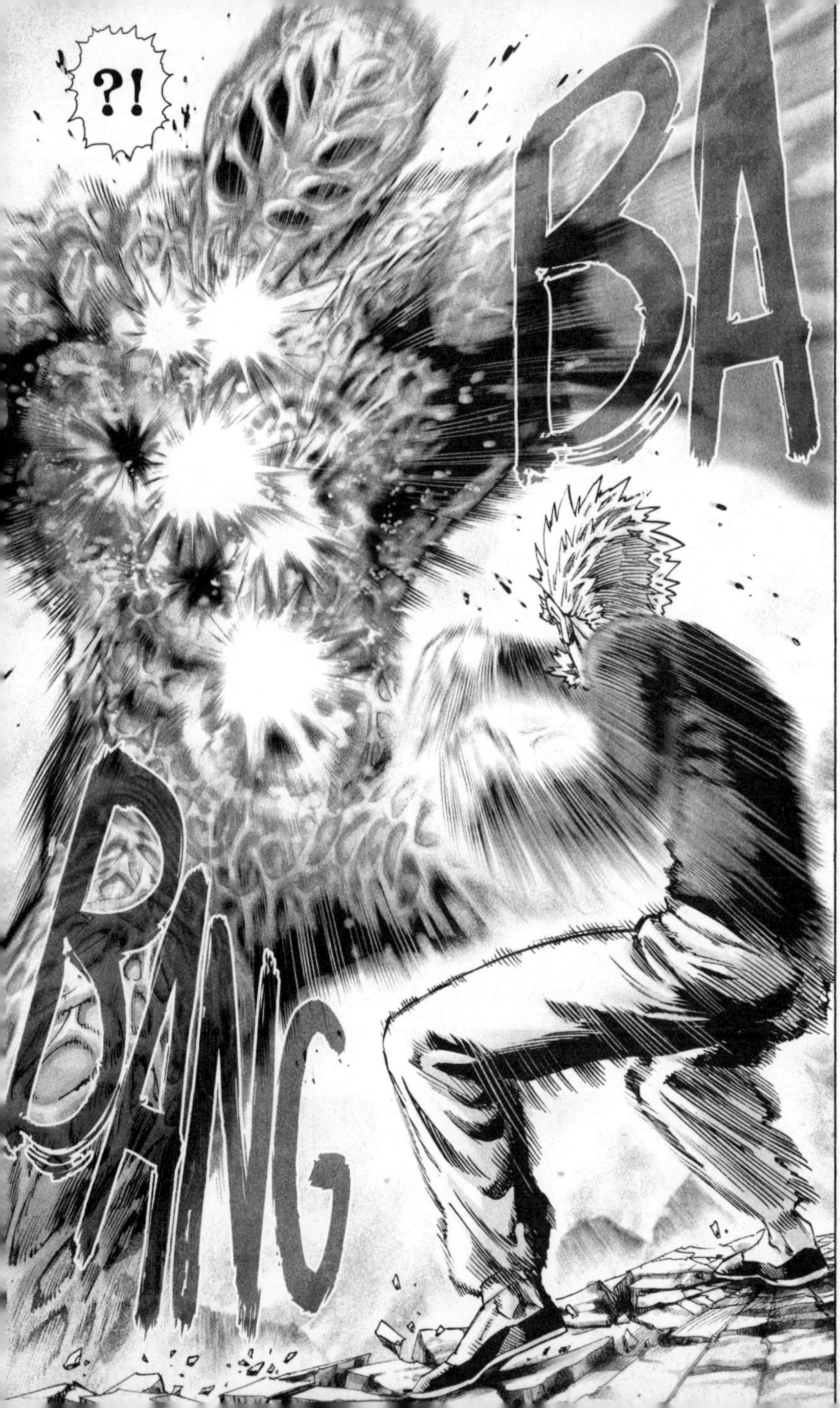
?!
BA
BANG

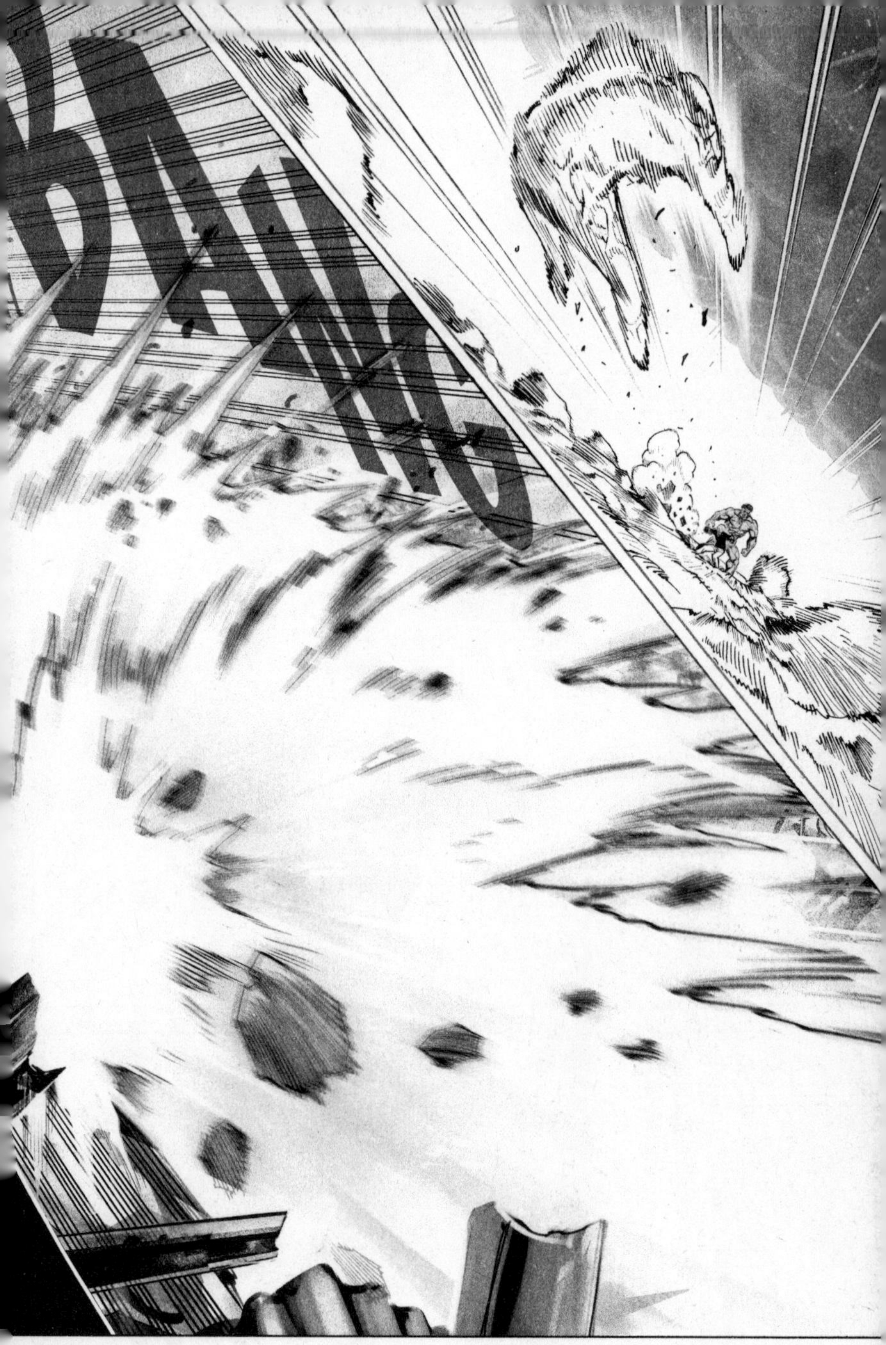
BANG

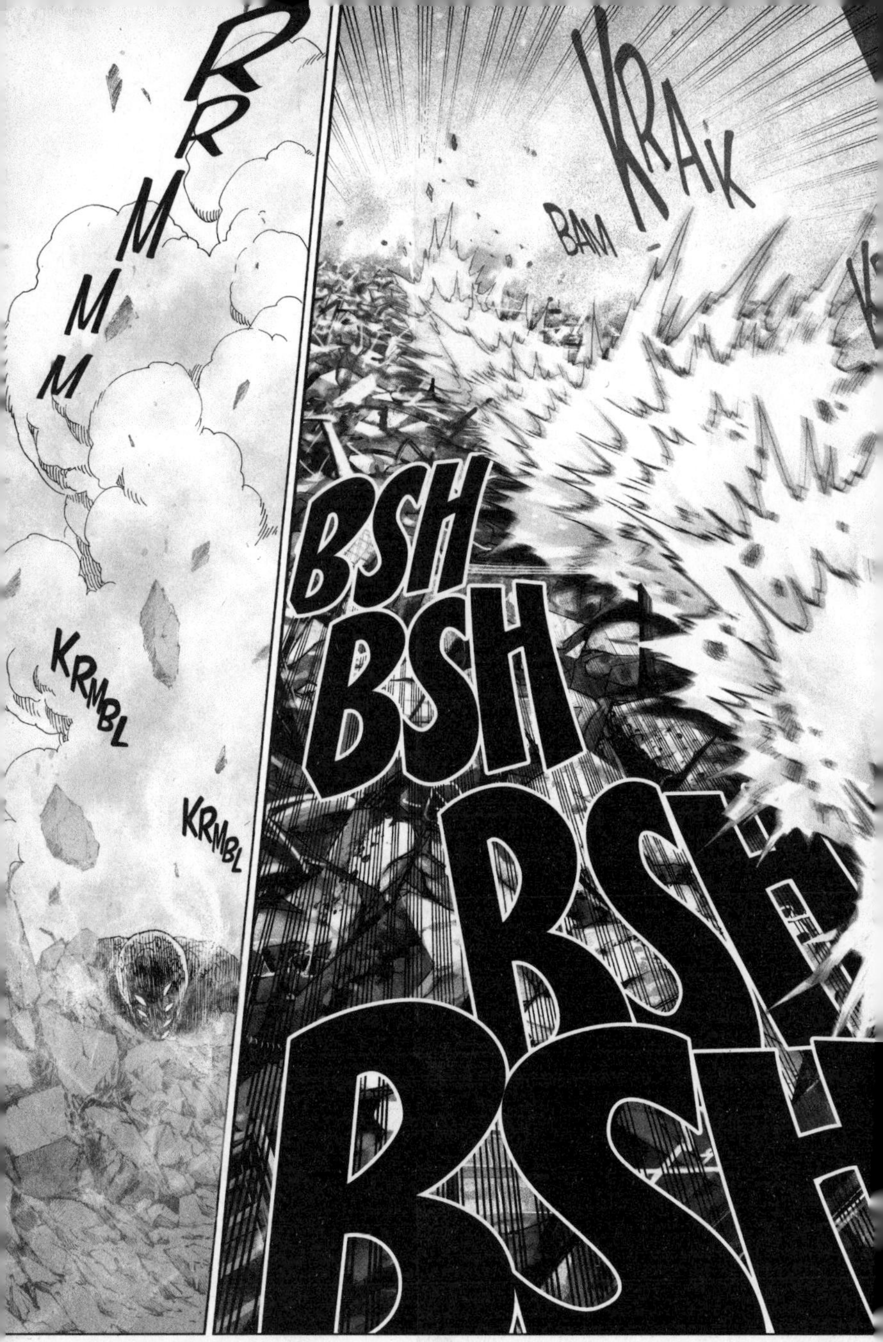
KRAiK
BAM
BSH
BSH
BSH
BSH
DRRMMMM
KRMBL
KRMBL

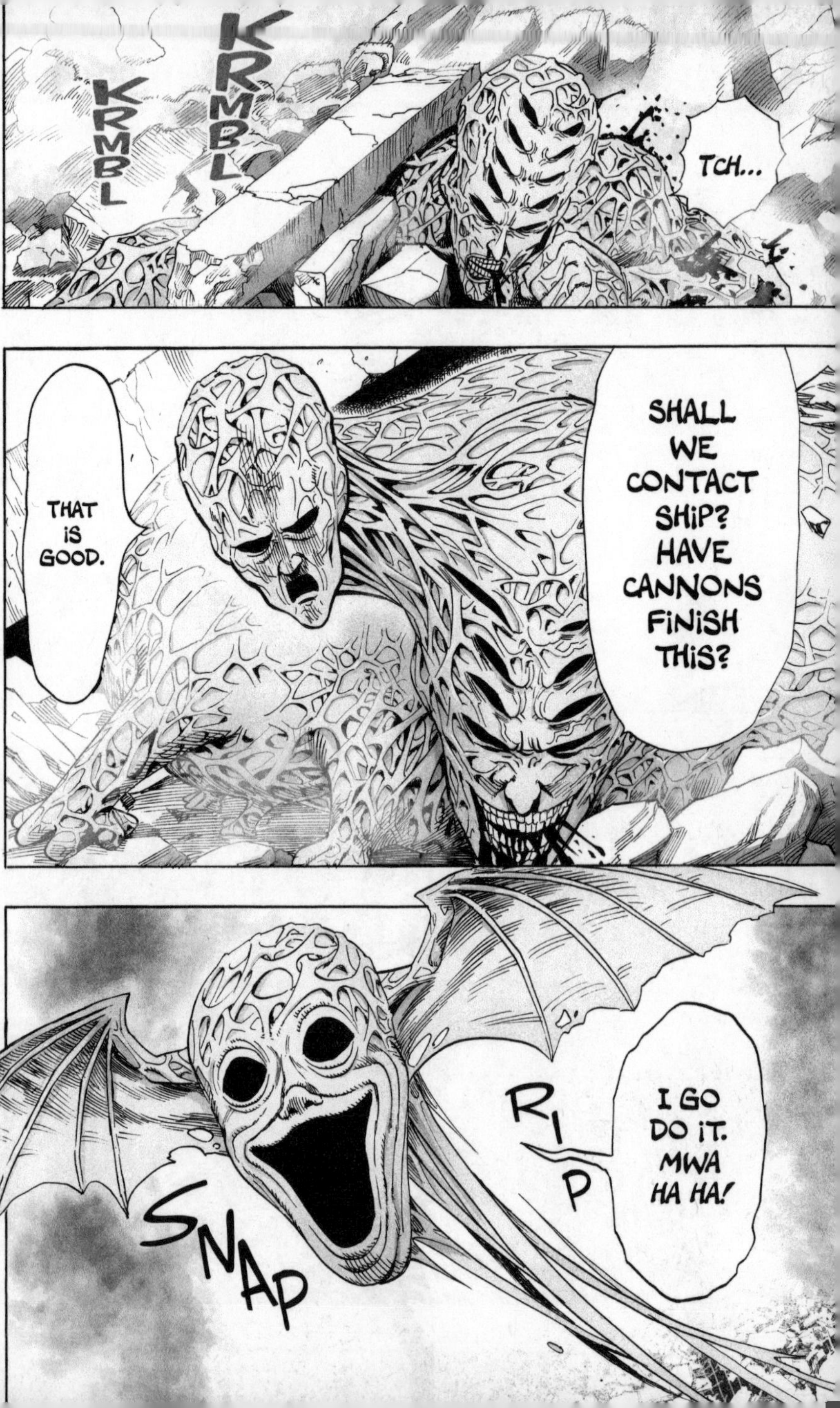
TCH...
KRMBL
KRMBL
SHALL WE CONTACT SHIP? HAVE CANNONS FINISH THIS?
THAT IS GOOD.
I GO DO IT. MWA HA HA!
RIP
SNAP

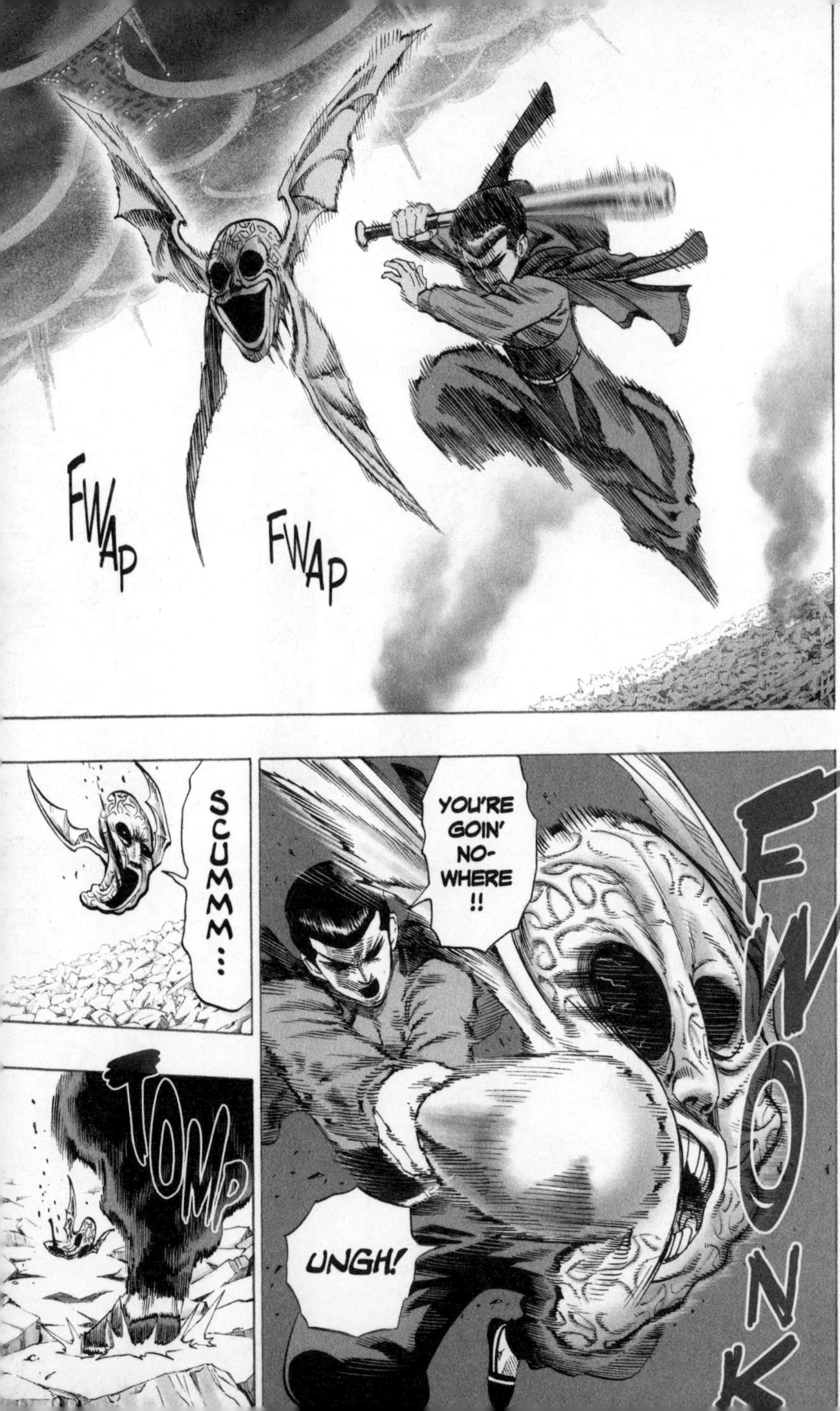
FWAP
FWAP
FWONK
YOU'RE GOIN' NO-WHERE!!
UNGH!
SCUMMM...
TOMP

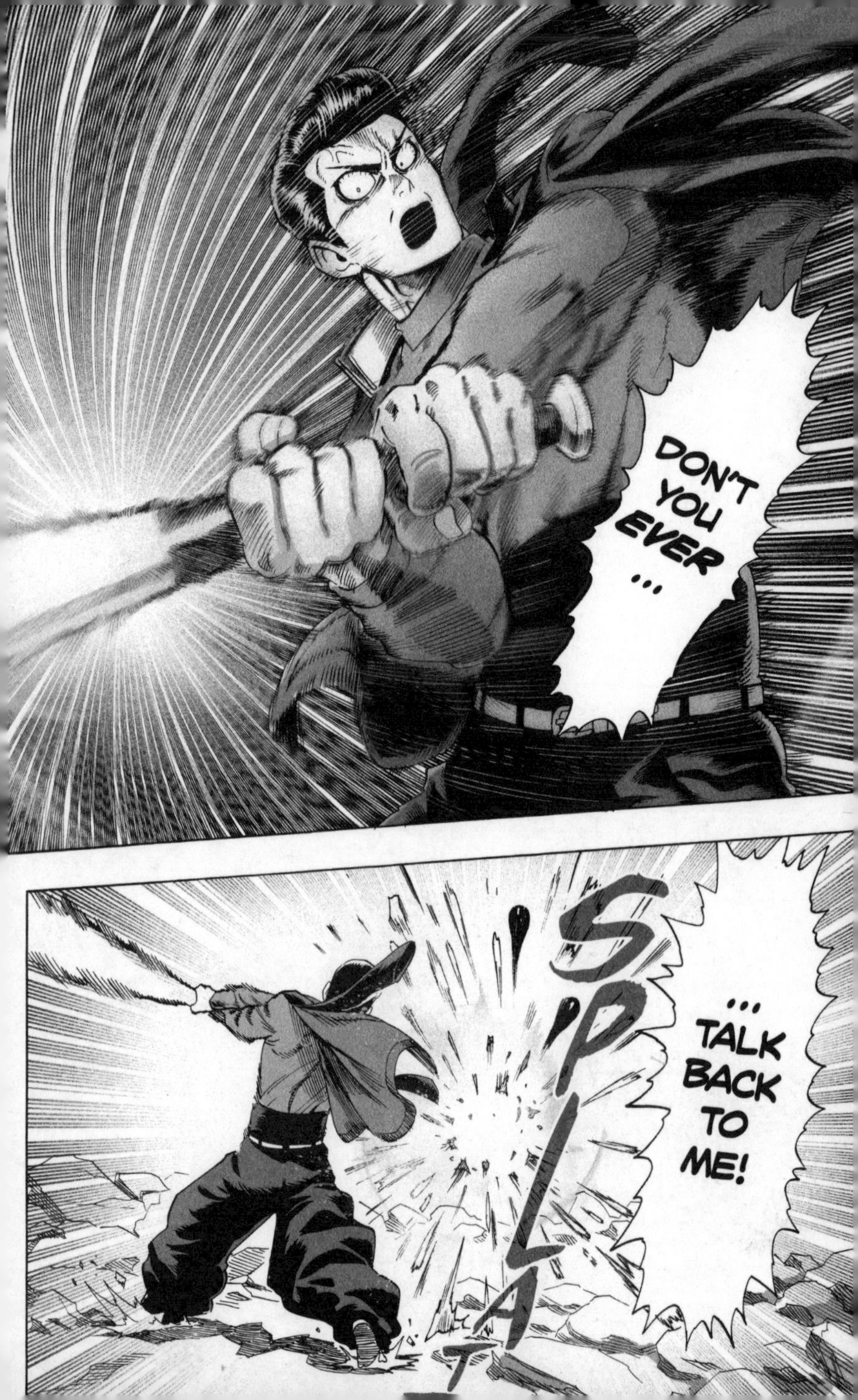
DON'T YOU EVER ...
SPLAT
... TALK BACK TO ME!

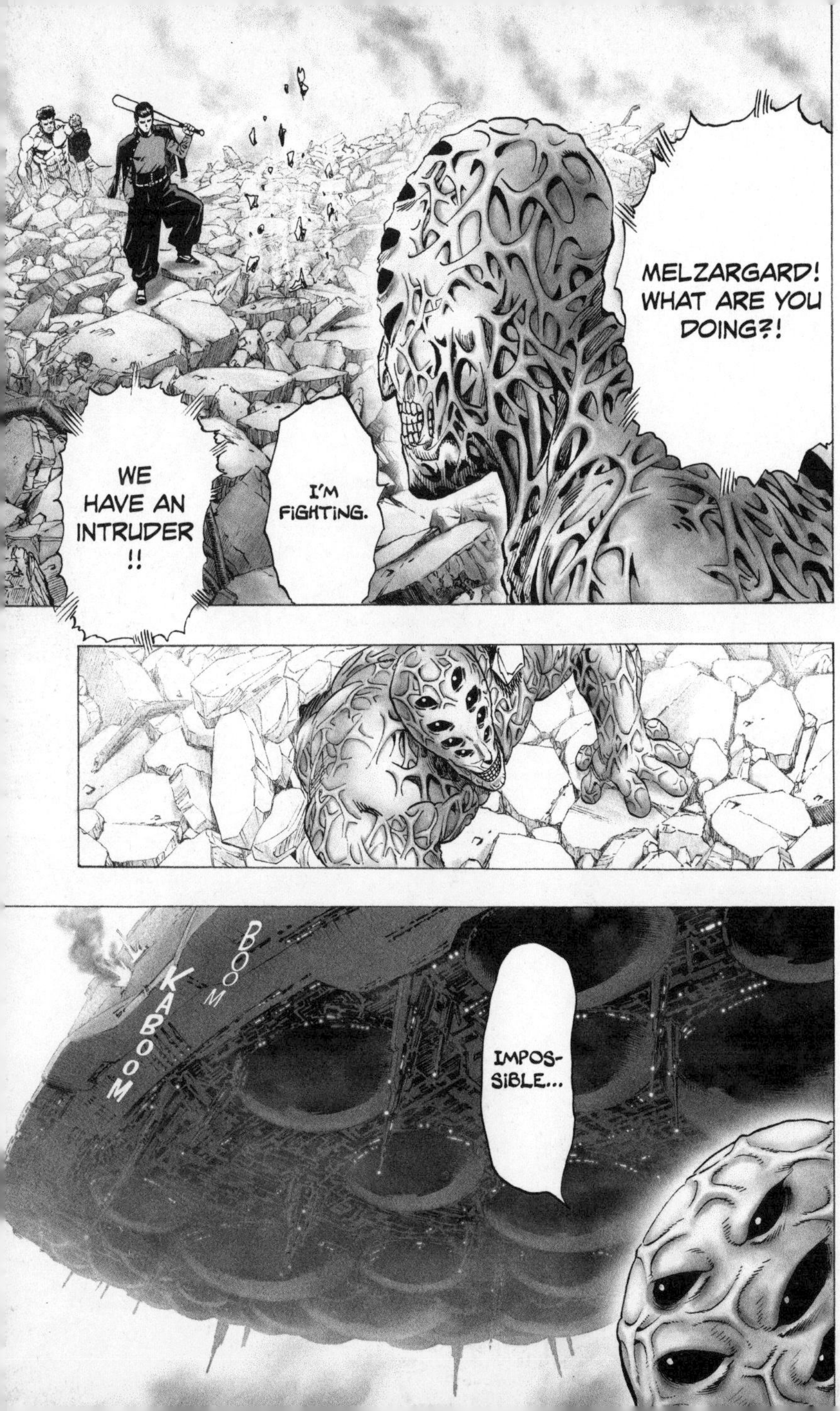
MELZARGARD! WHAT ARE YOU DOING?!
I'M FIGHTING.
WE HAVE AN INTRUDER !!
IMPOSSIBLE...
BOOM
KABOOM

BONUS

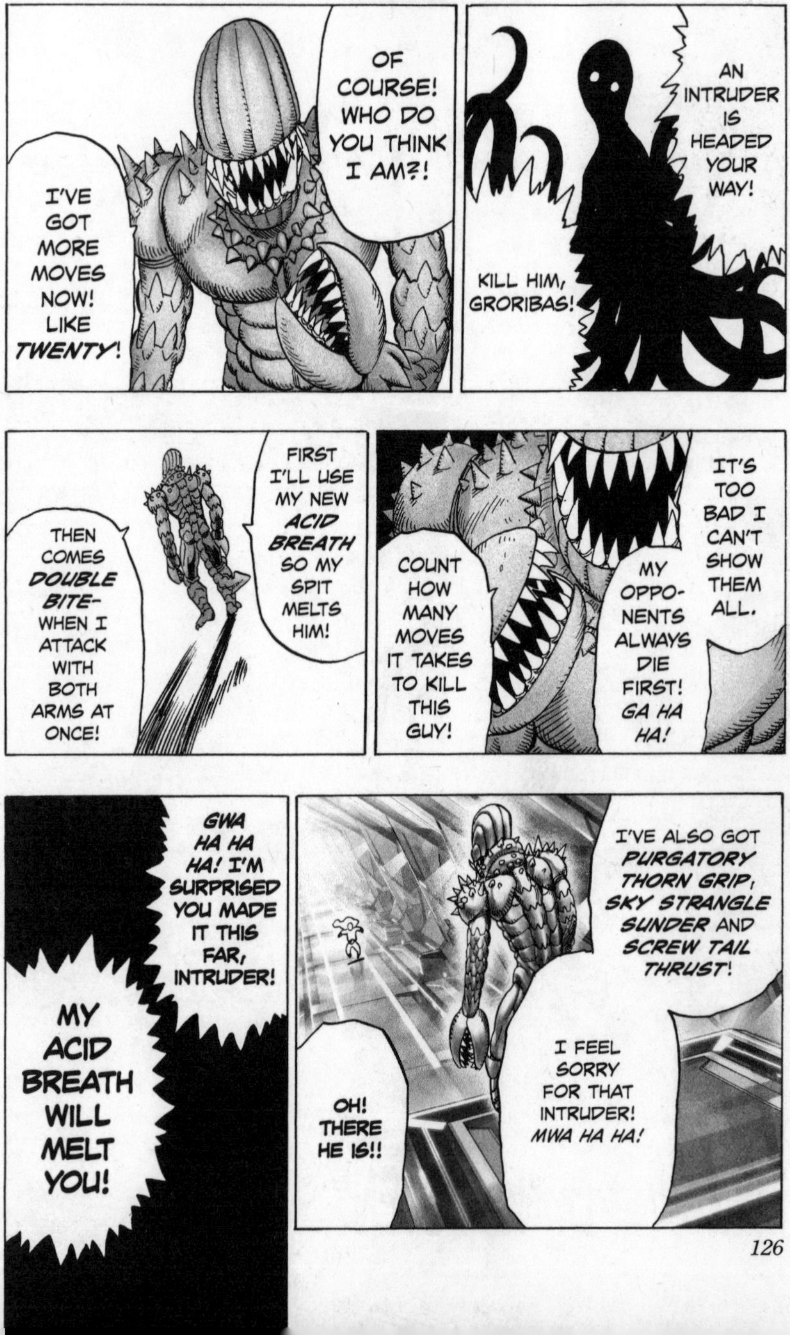
AN INTRUDER IS HEADED YOUR WAY!
KILL HIM, GRORIBAS!
OF COURSE! WHO DO YOU THINK I AM?!
I'VE GOT MORE MOVES NOW! LIKE *TWENTY*!
IT'S TOO BAD I CAN'T SHOW THEM ALL.
MY OPPONENTS ALWAYS DIE FIRST! *GA HA HA!*
COUNT HOW MANY MOVES IT TAKES TO KILL THIS GUY!
FIRST I'LL USE MY NEW *ACID BREATH* SO MY SPIT MELTS HIM!
THEN COMES *DOUBLE BITE*— WHEN I ATTACK WITH BOTH ARMS AT ONCE!
I'VE ALSO GOT *PURGATORY THORN GRIP*, *SKY STRANGLE SUNDER* AND *SCREW TAIL THRUST*!
I FEEL SORRY FOR THAT INTRUDER! *MWA HA HA!*
OH! THERE HE IS!!
GWA HA HA HA! I'M SURPRISED YOU MADE IT THIS FAR, INTRUDER!
MY ACID BREATH WILL MELT YOU!

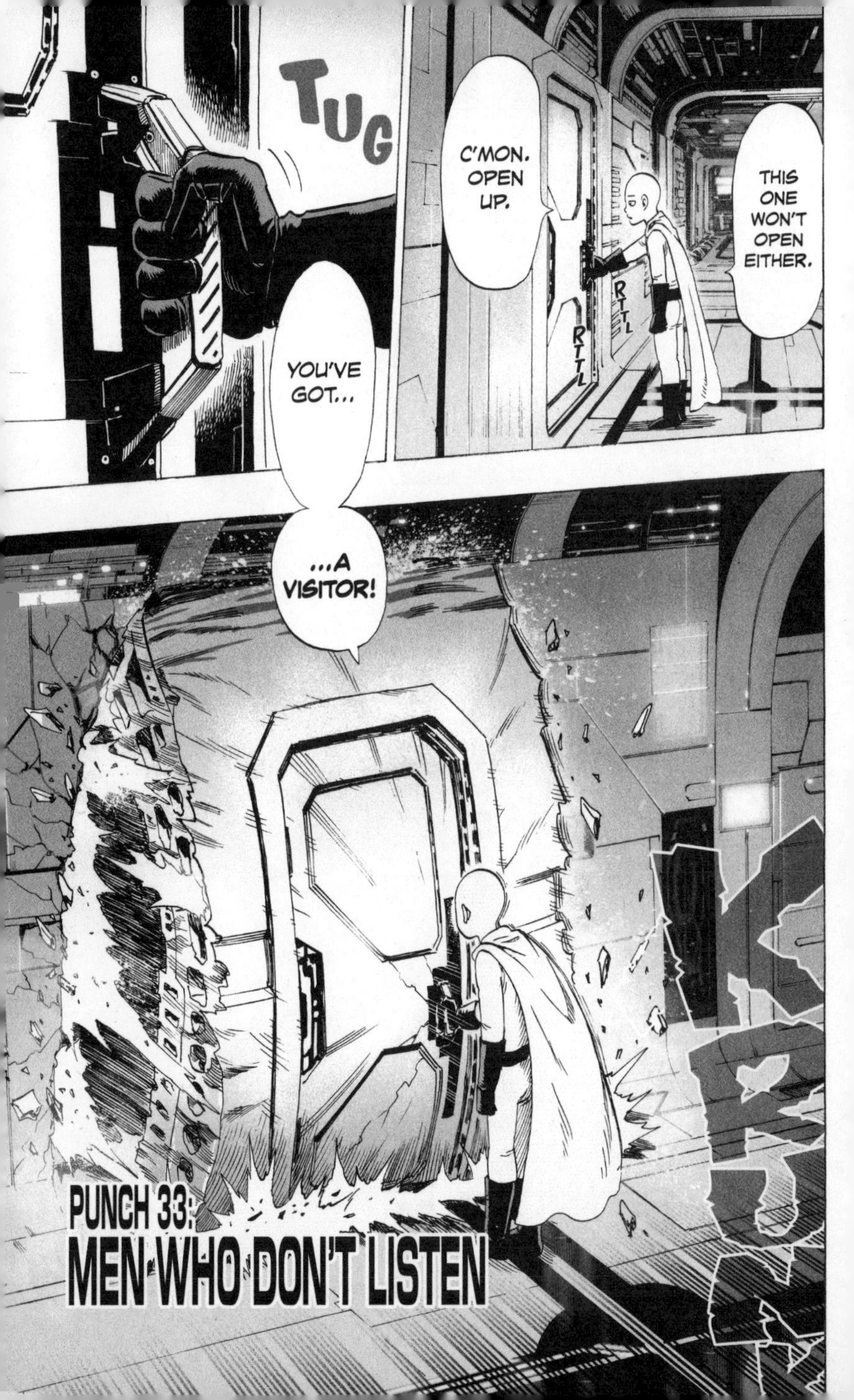
THIS ONE WON'T OPEN EITHER.
C'MON. OPEN UP.
RTTL
RTTL
TUG
YOU'VE GOT...
...A VISITOR!
PUNCH 33:
MEN WHO DON'T LISTEN

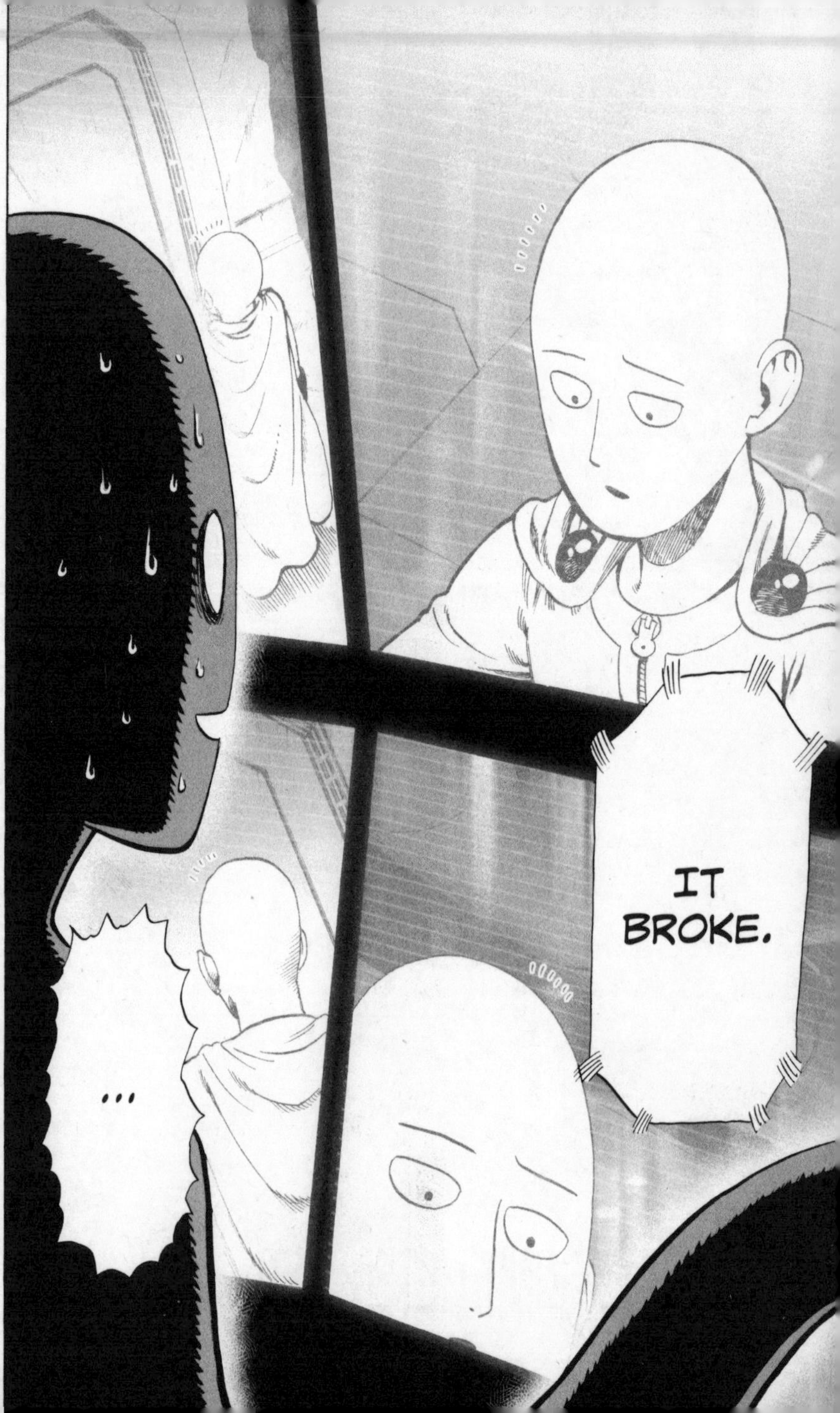
IT BROKE.
...

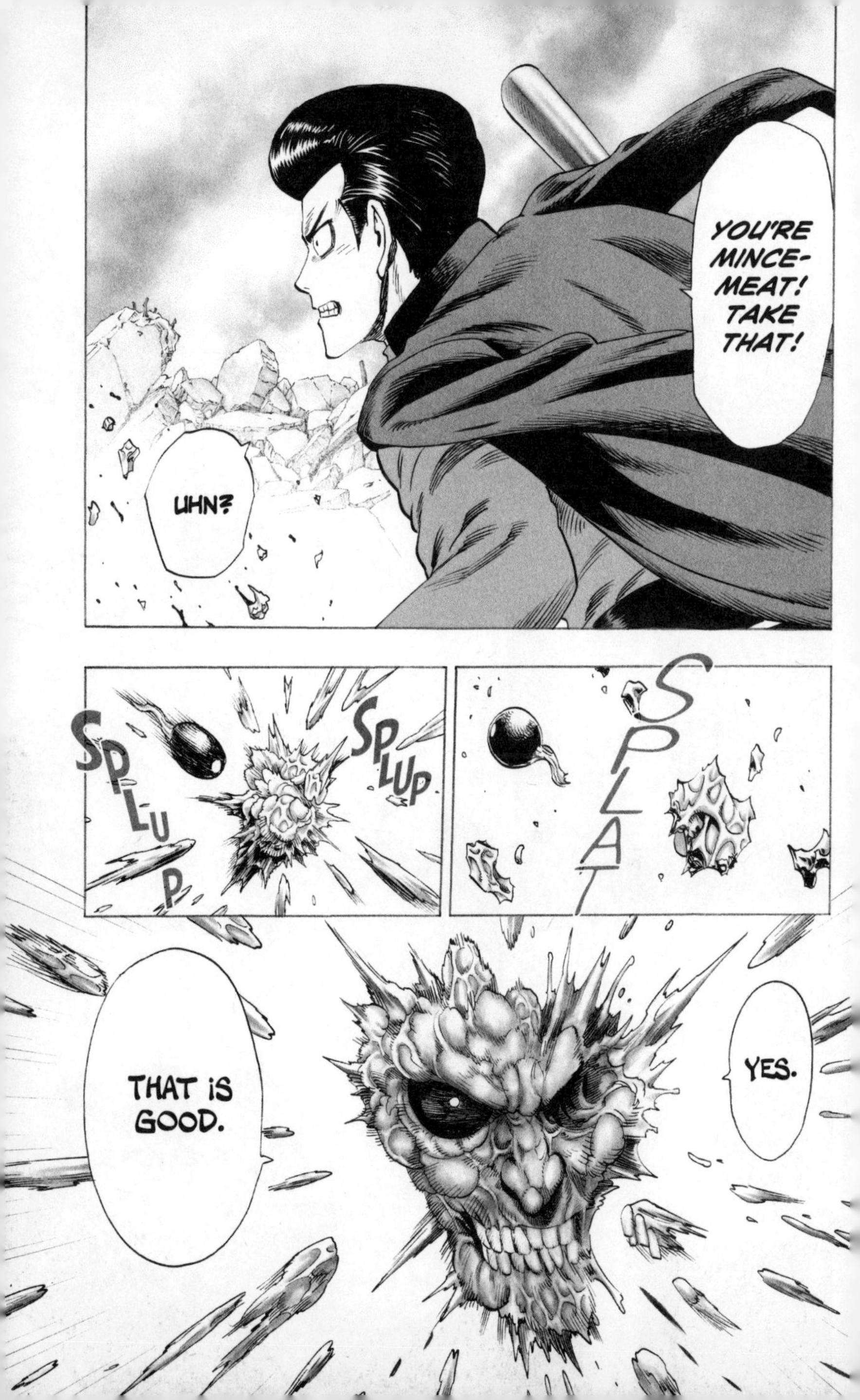
YOU'RE MINCE-MEAT! TAKE THAT!
UHN?
SPLAT
SPLUP
SPLUP
YES.
THAT IS GOOD.

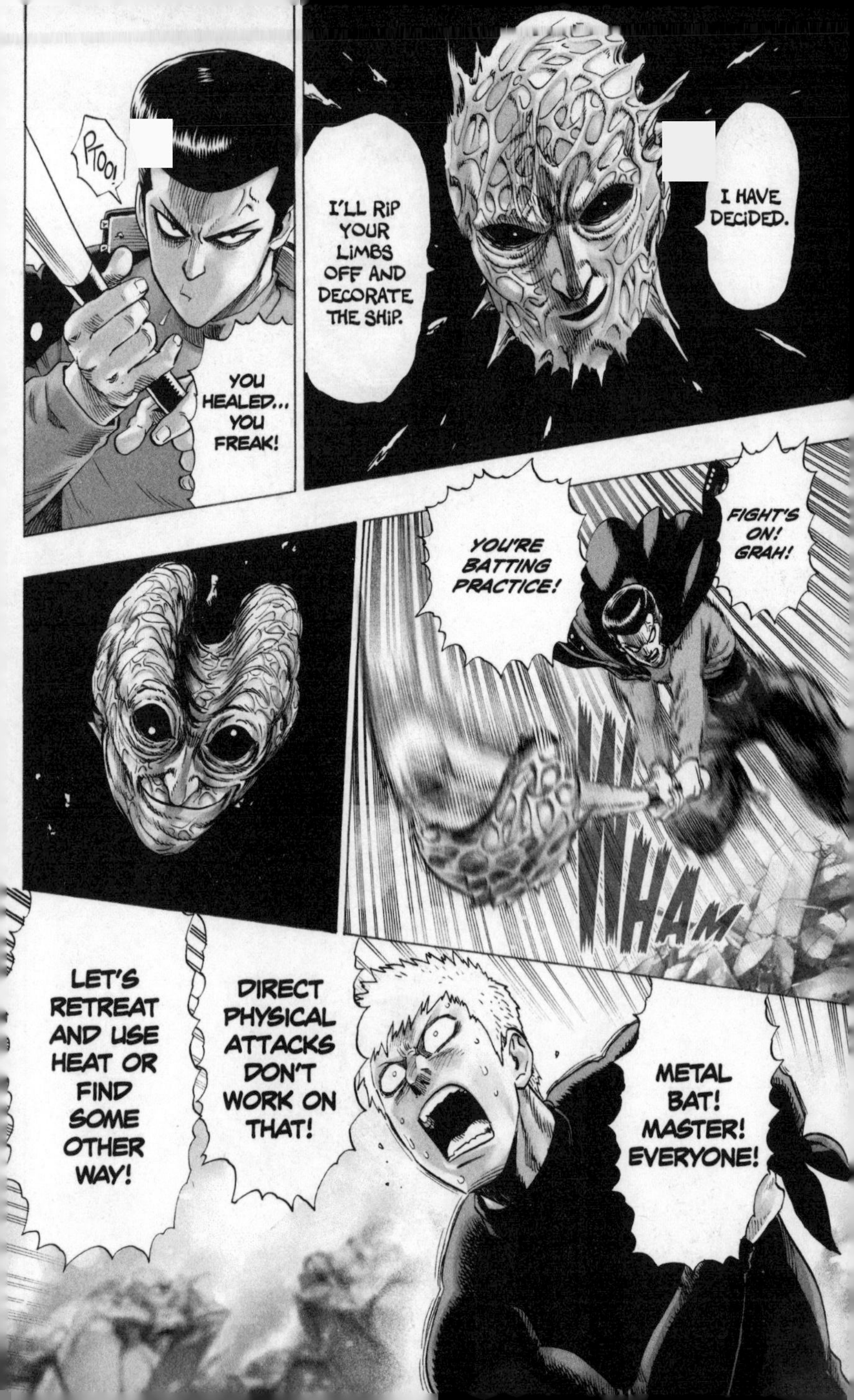
I HAVE DECIDED.
I'LL RIP YOUR LIMBS OFF AND DECORATE THE SHIP.
PTOO!
YOU HEALED... YOU FREAK!
FIGHT'S ON! GRAH!
YOU'RE BATTING PRACTICE!
WHAM
METAL BAT! MASTER! EVERYONE!
DIRECT PHYSICAL ATTACKS DON'T WORK ON THAT!
LET'S RETREAT AND USE HEAT OR FIND SOME OTHER WAY!

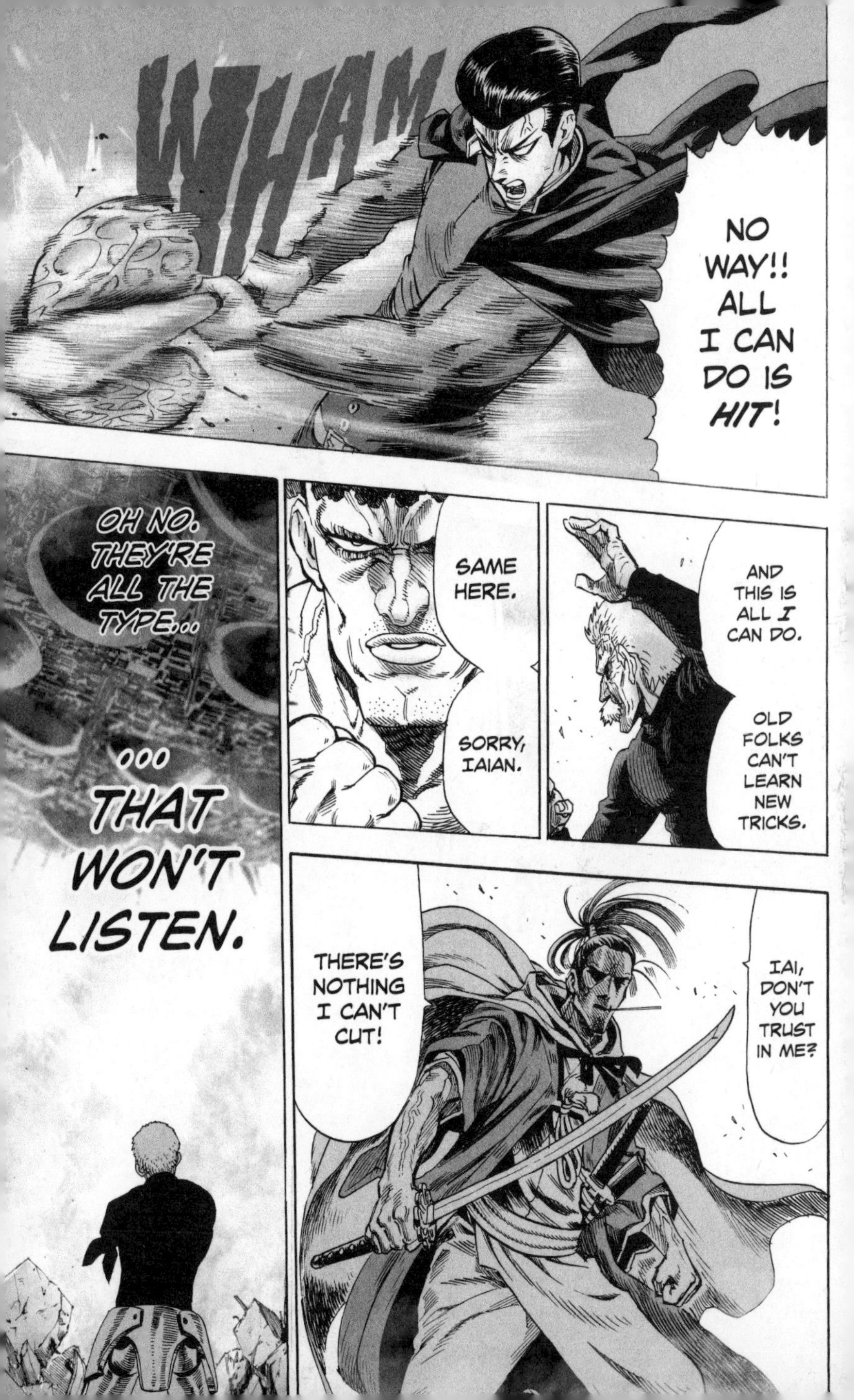
WHAM
NO WAY!! ALL I CAN DO IS *HIT*!
AND THIS IS ALL *I* CAN DO.
OLD FOLKS CAN'T LEARN NEW TRICKS.
SAME HERE.
SORRY, IAIAN.
IAI, DON'T YOU TRUST IN ME?
THERE'S NOTHING I CAN'T CUT!
OH NO. THEY'RE ALL THE TYPE...
...THAT WON'T LISTEN.

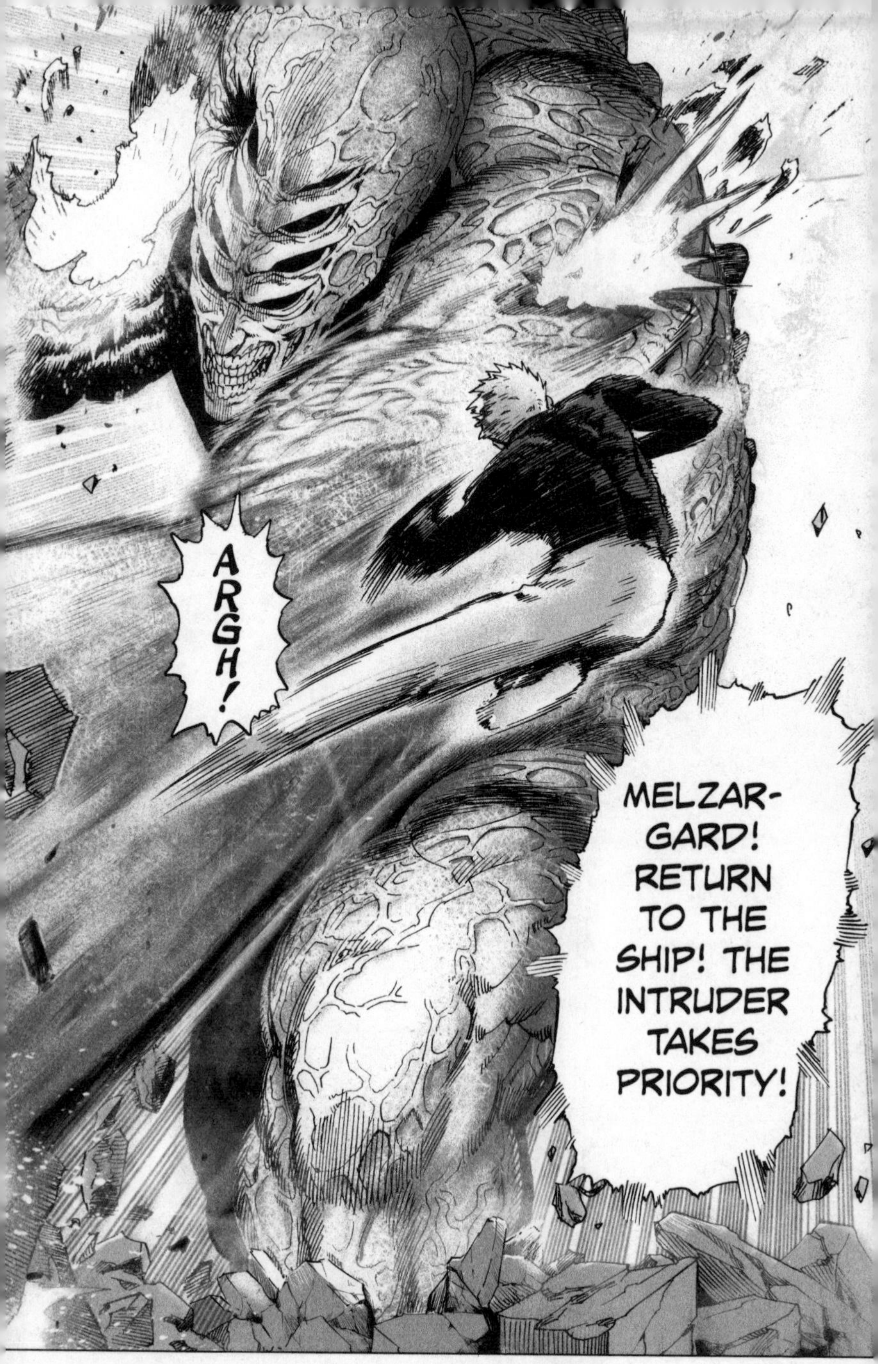
MELZARGARD! RETURN TO THE SHIP! THE INTRUDER TAKES PRIORITY!
ARGH!

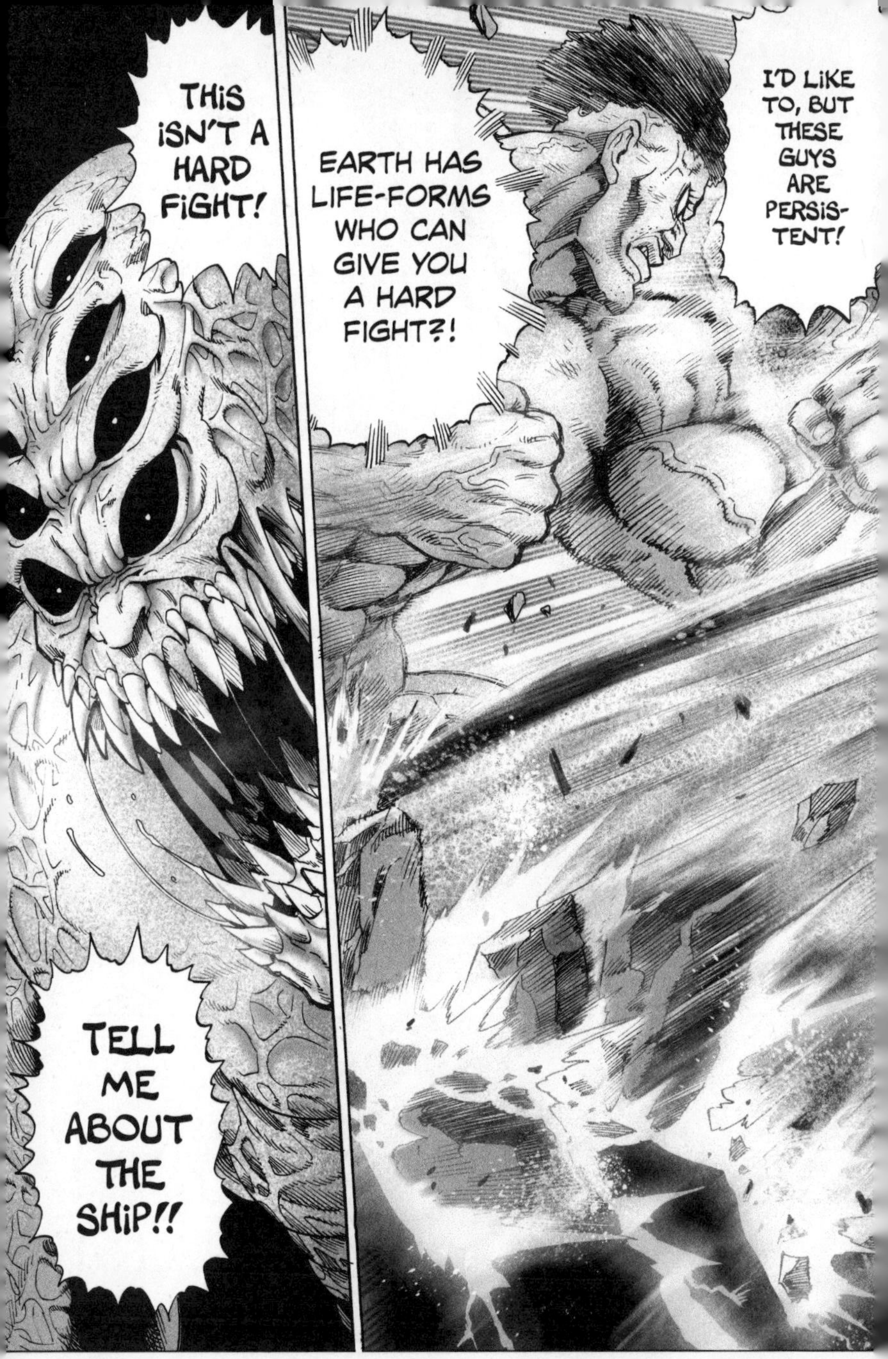
I'D LIKE TO, BUT THESE GUYS ARE PERSIS-TENT!
EARTH HAS LIFE-FORMS WHO CAN GIVE YOU A HARD FIGHT?!
THIS ISN'T A HARD FIGHT!
TELL ME ABOUT THE SHIP!!

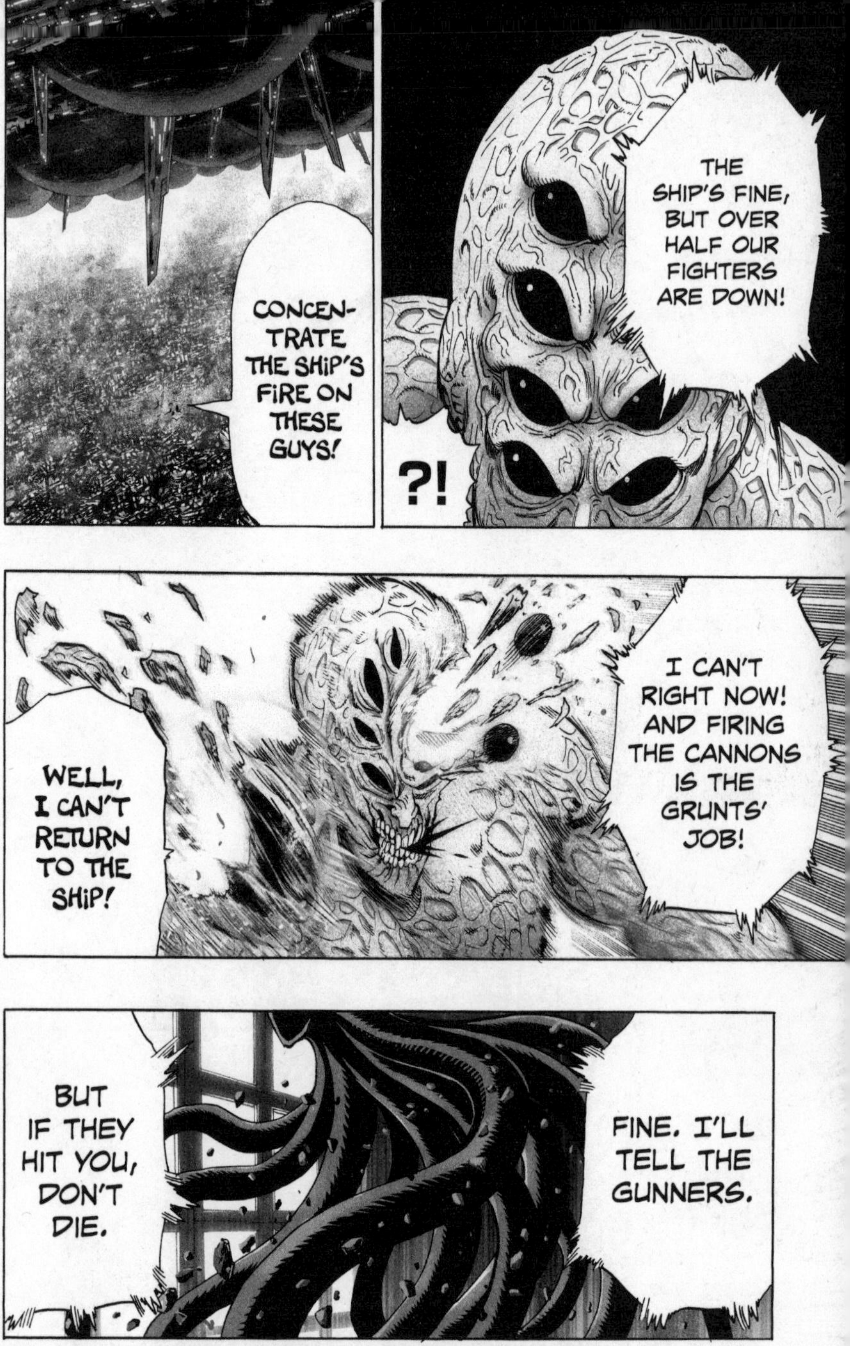
THE SHIP'S FINE, BUT OVER HALF OUR FIGHTERS ARE DOWN!
?!
CONCEN-TRATE THE SHIP'S FIRE ON THESE GUYS!
I CAN'T RIGHT NOW! AND FIRING THE CANNONS IS THE GRUNTS' JOB!
WELL, I CAN'T RETURN TO THE SHIP!
FINE. I'LL TELL THE GUNNERS.
BUT IF THEY HIT YOU, DON'T DIE.

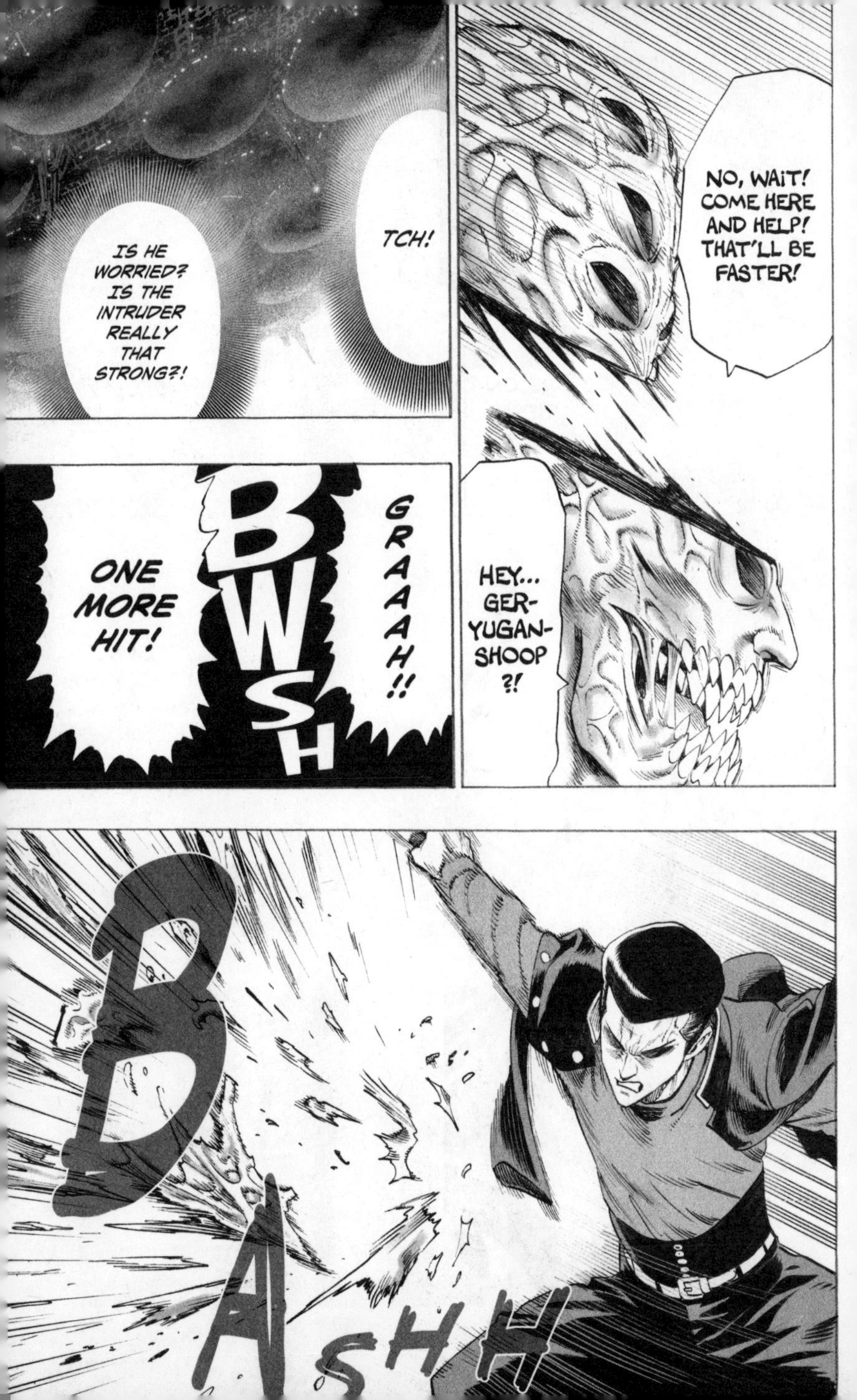
NO, WAIT! COME HERE AND HELP! THAT'LL BE FASTER!
TCH!
IS HE WORRIED? IS THE INTRUDER REALLY THAT STRONG?!
HEY... GER-YUGAN-SHOOP?!
GRAAAAH!!
BWSH
ONE MORE HIT!
BASHH

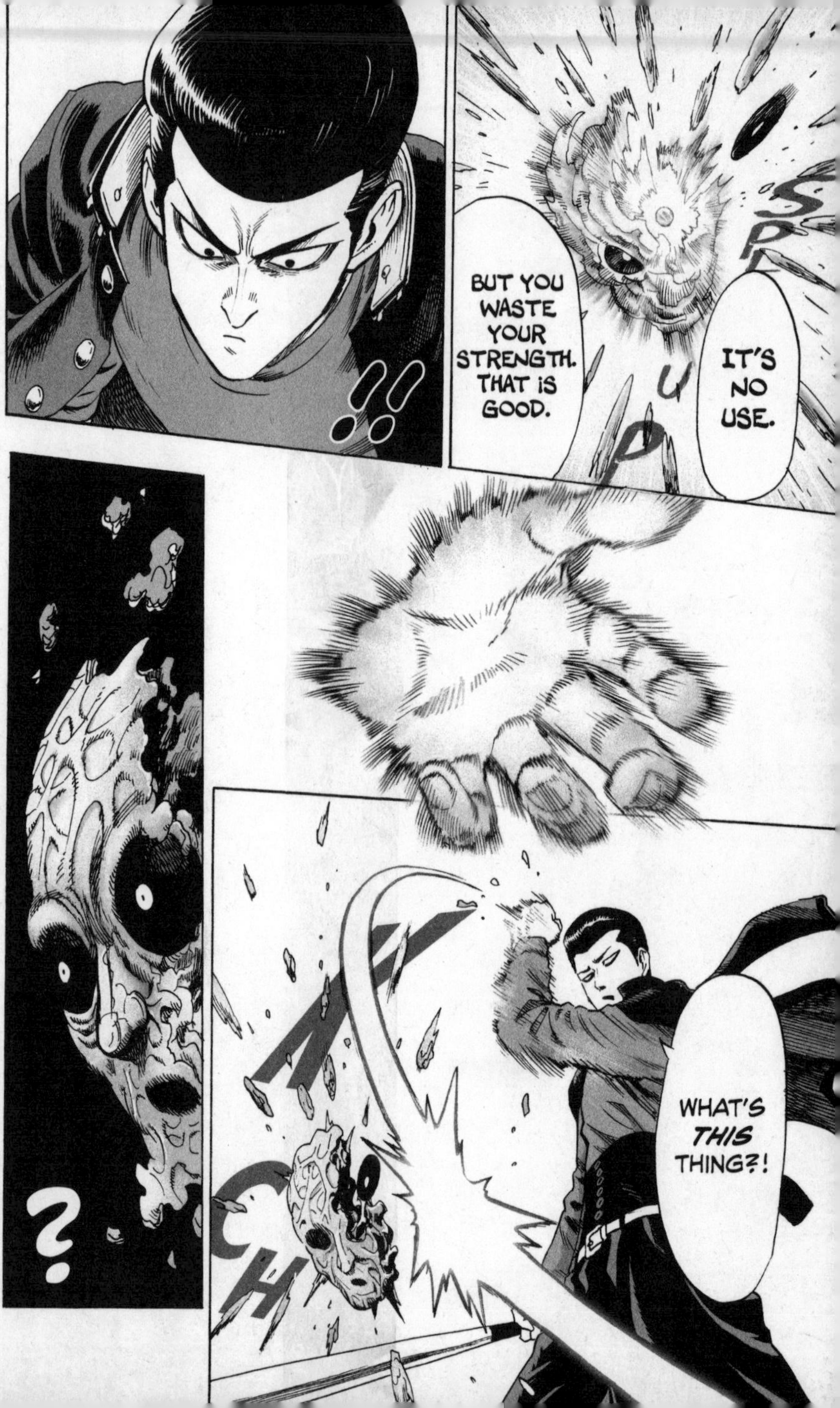
SPLUD
IT'S NO USE.
BUT YOU WASTE YOUR STRENGTH. THAT IS GOOD.
!!
WHAT'S *THIS* THING?!
?

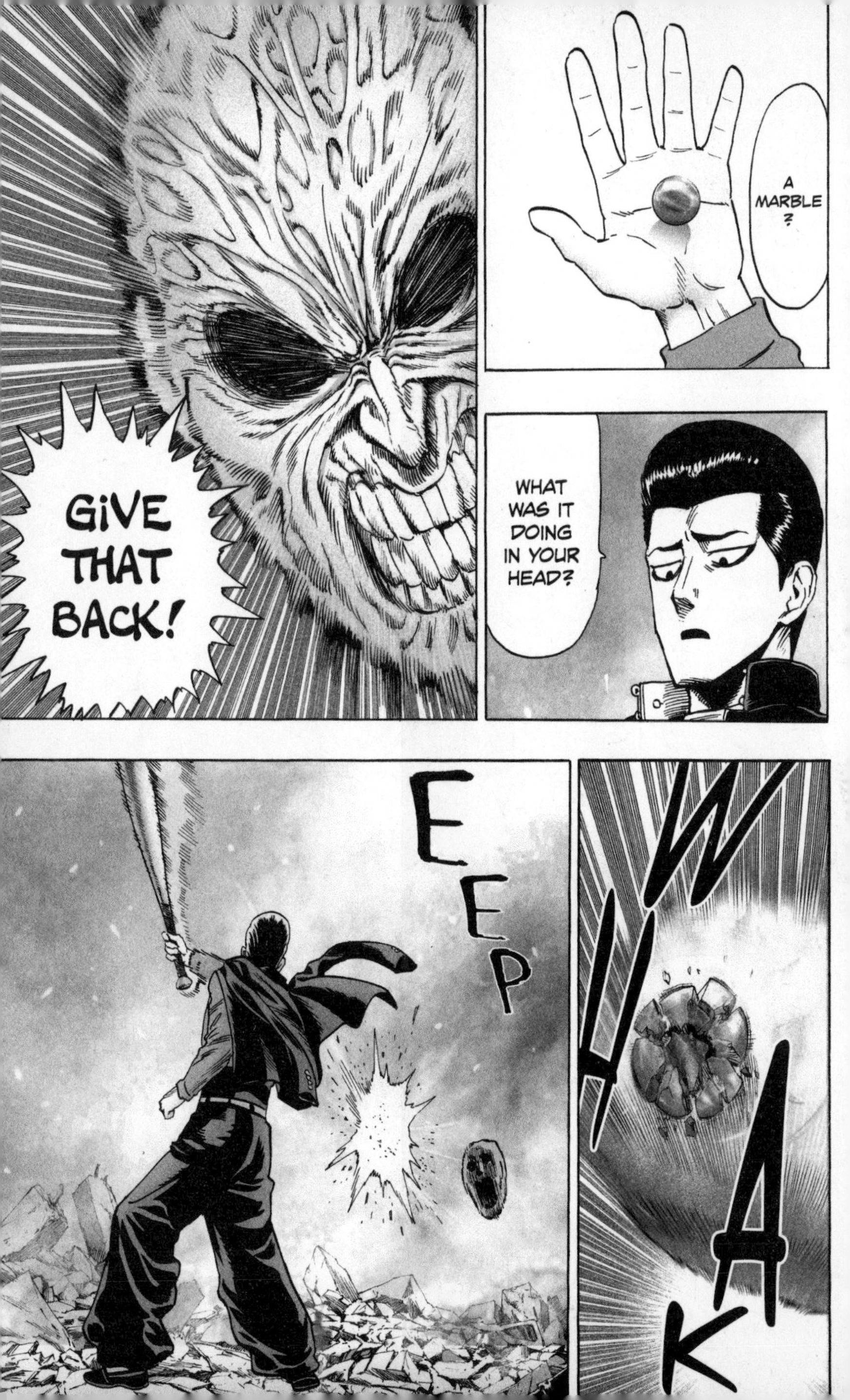
A MARBLE?
WHAT WAS IT DOING IN YOUR HEAD?
GIVE THAT BACK!
WHAK
EEP

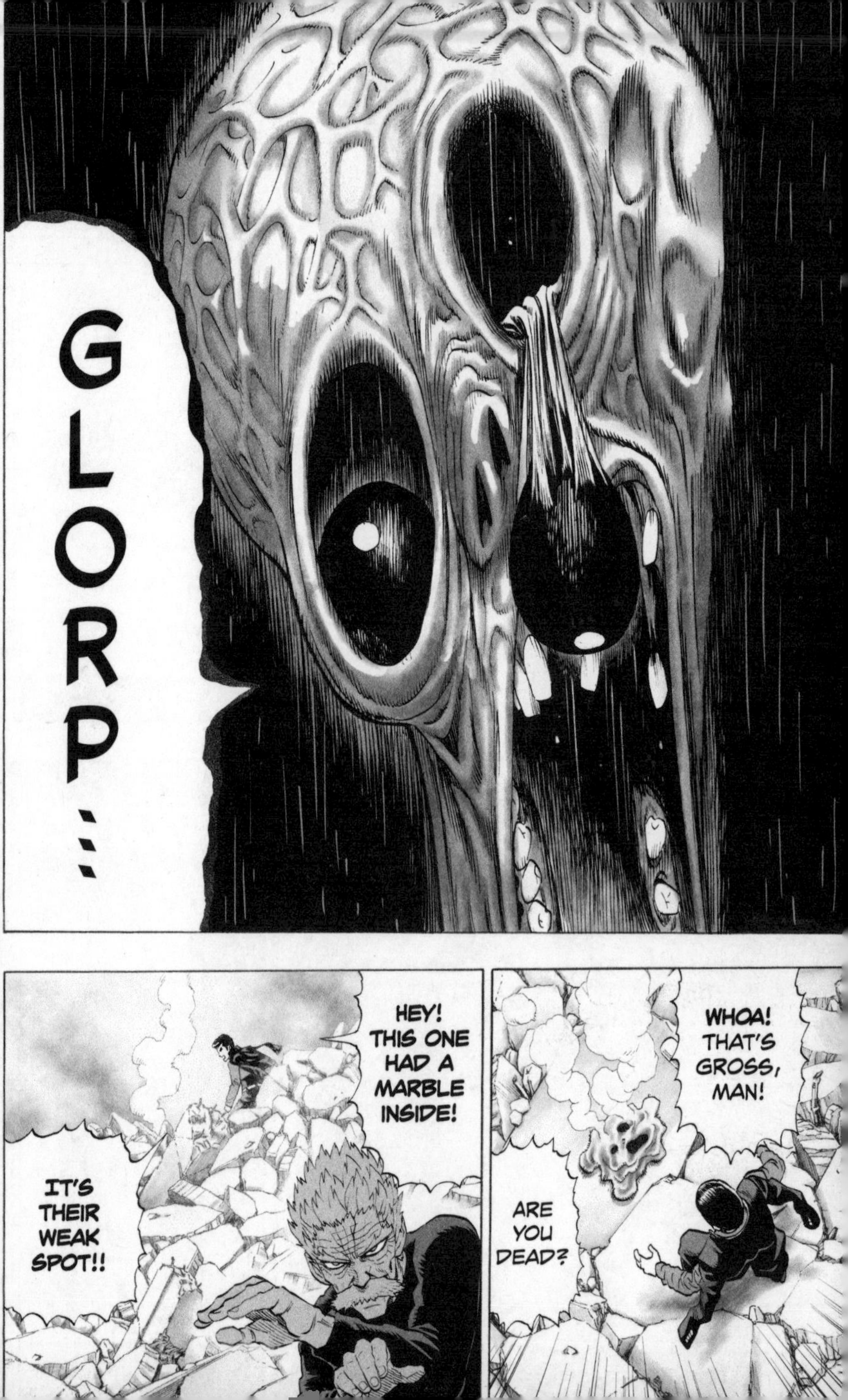
GLORP...
WHOA! THAT'S GROSS, MAN!
ARE YOU DEAD?
HEY! THIS ONE HAD A MARBLE INSIDE!
IT'S THEIR WEAK SPOT!!

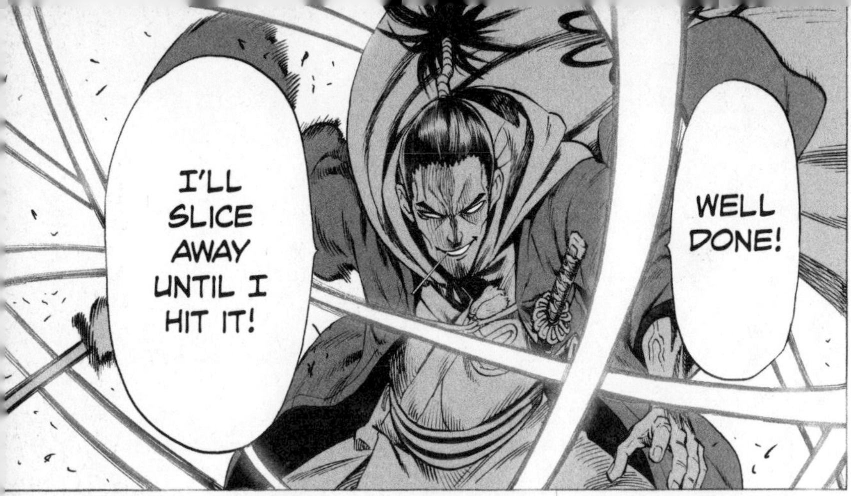
WELL DONE!
I'LL SLICE AWAY UNTIL I HIT IT!

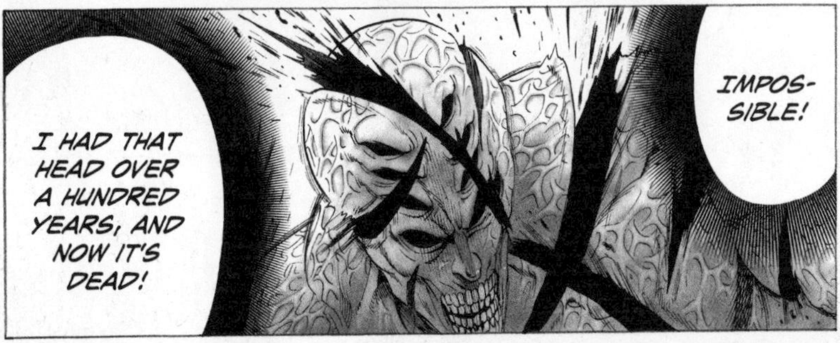
IMPOSSIBLE!
I HAD THAT HEAD OVER A HUNDRED YEARS, AND NOW IT'S DEAD!

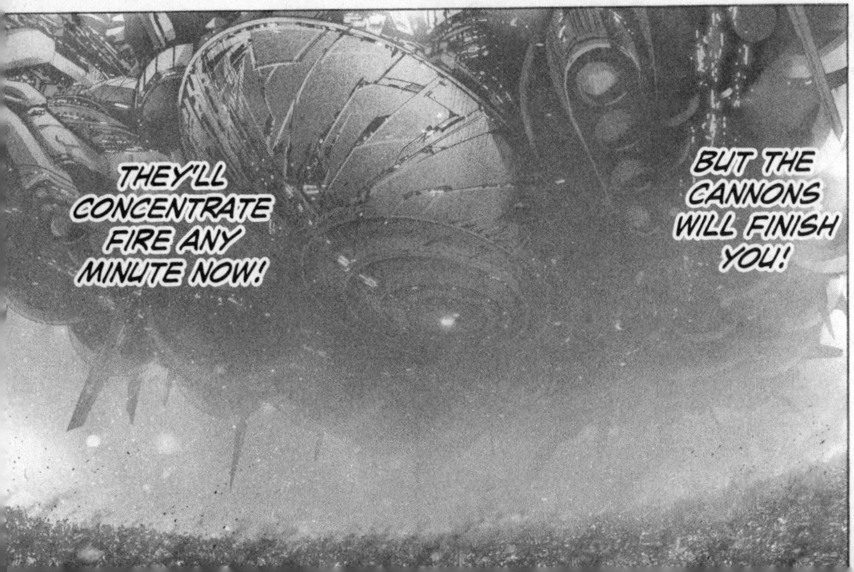
BUT THE CANNONS WILL FINISH YOU!
THEY'LL CONCENTRATE FIRE ANY MINUTE NOW!

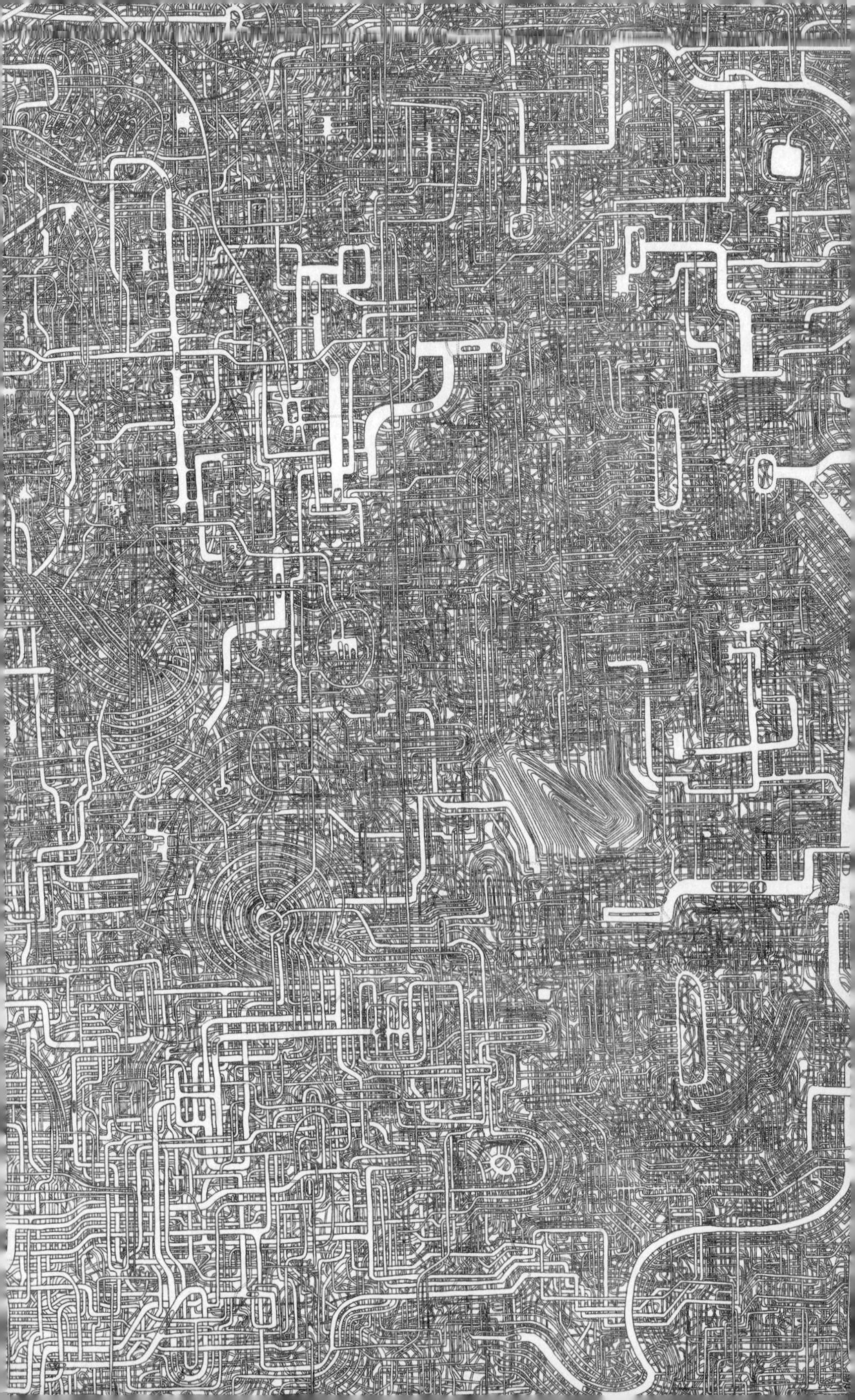

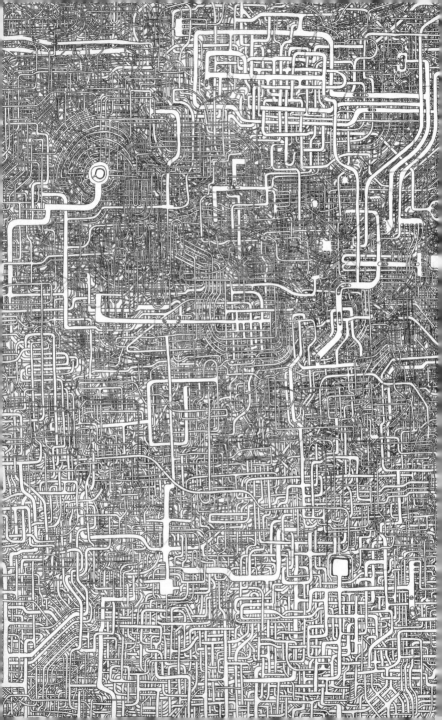

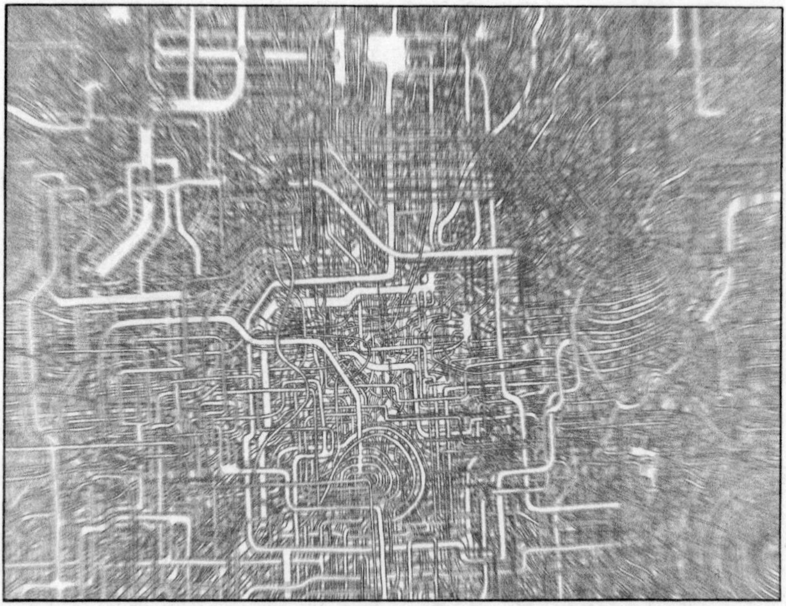
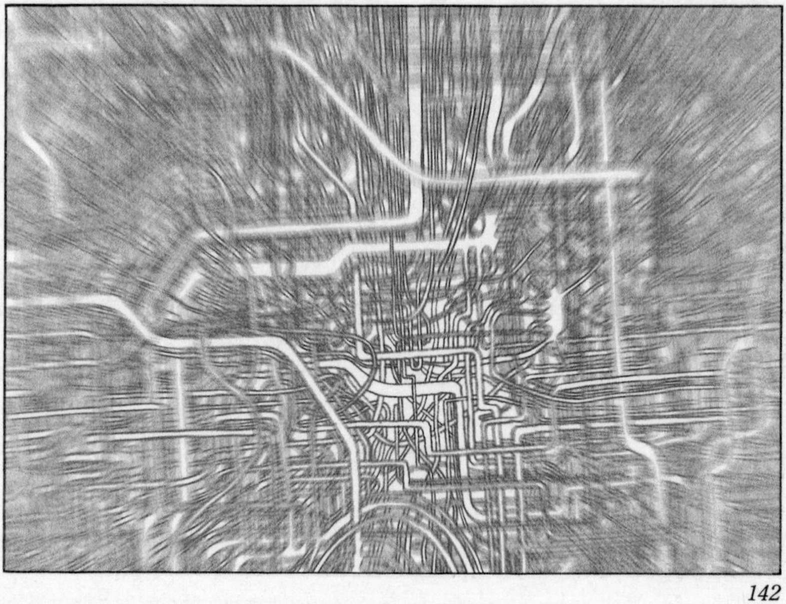

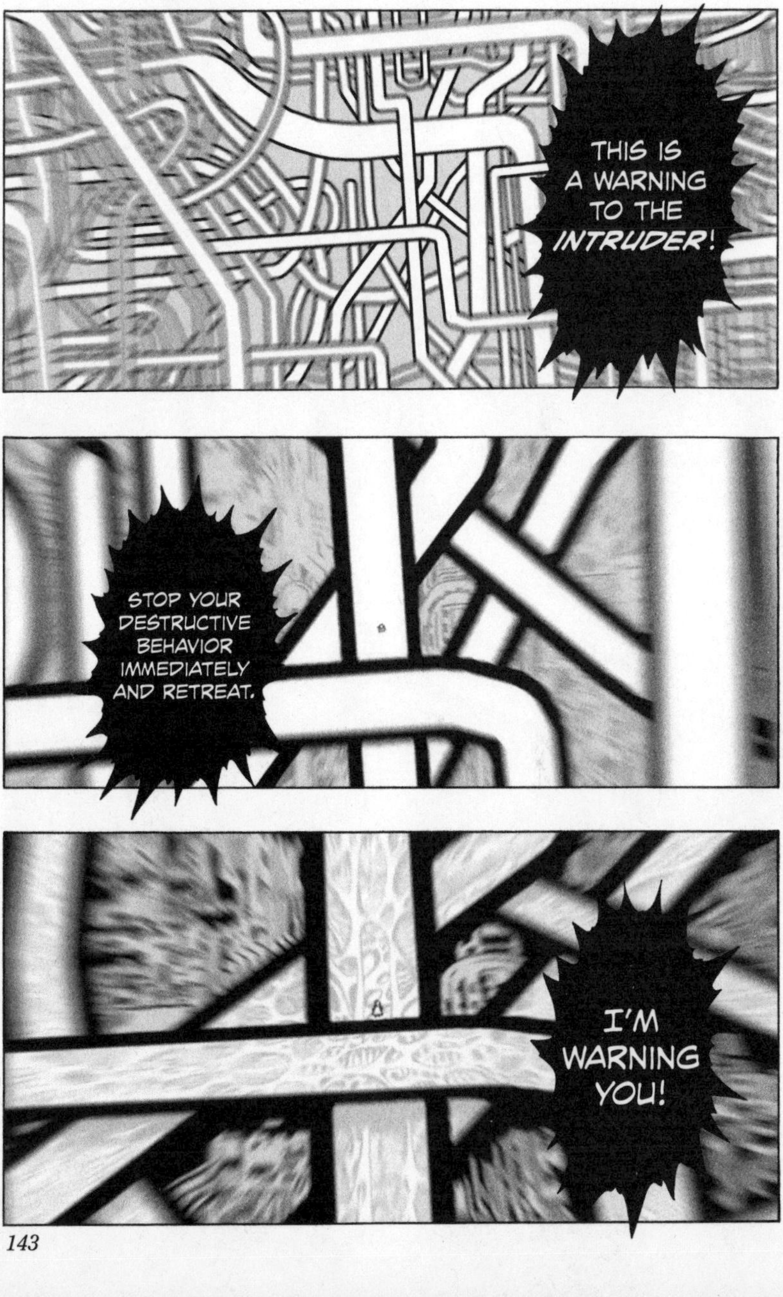
THIS IS A WARNING TO THE *INTRUDER*!
STOP YOUR DESTRUCTIVE BEHAVIOR IMMEDIATELY AND RETREAT.
I'M WARNING YOU!

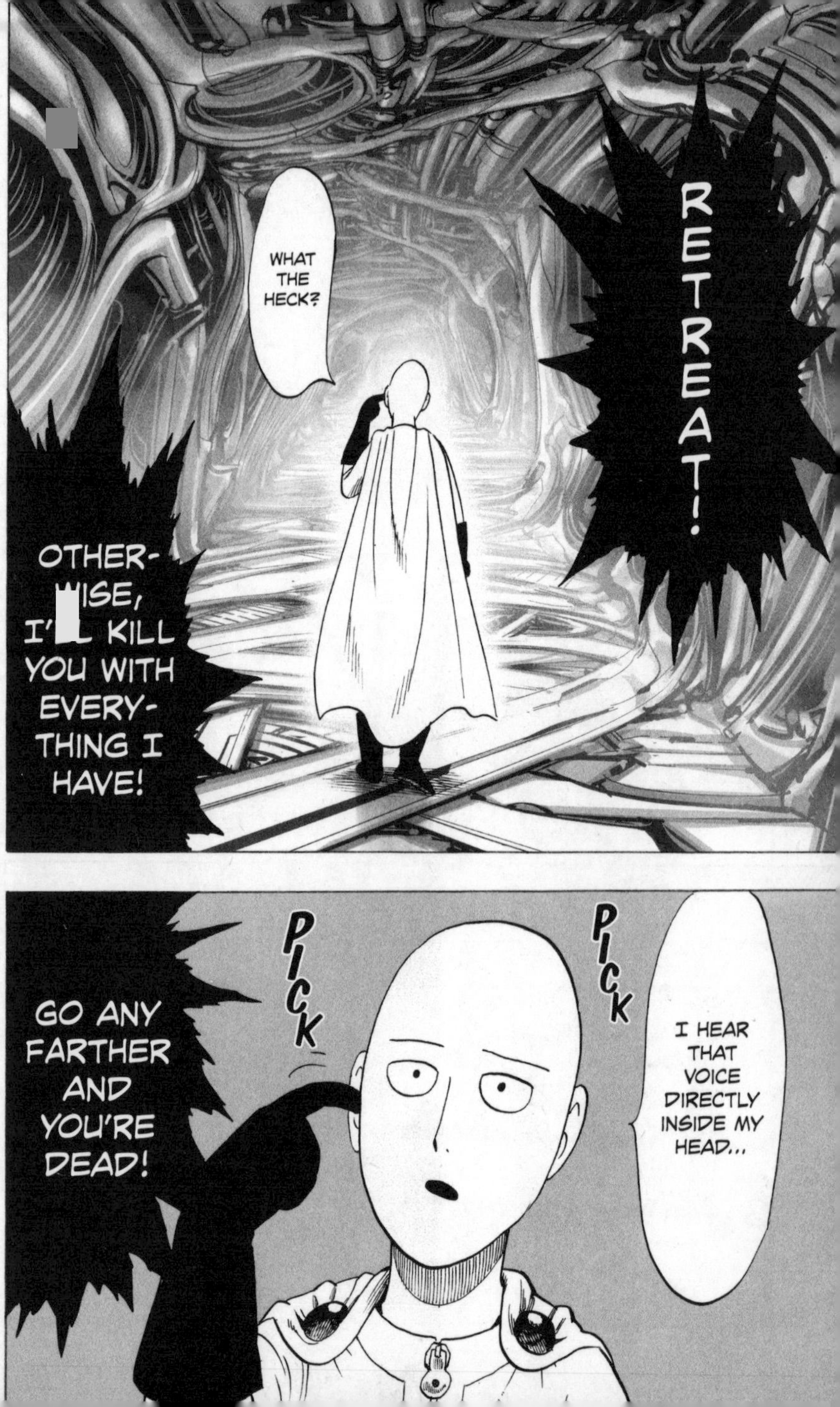
RETREAT!
WHAT THE HECK?
OTHERWISE, I'LL KILL YOU WITH EVERYTHING I HAVE!
I HEAR THAT VOICE DIRECTLY INSIDE MY HEAD...
PICK
PICK
GO ANY FARTHER AND YOU'RE DEAD!

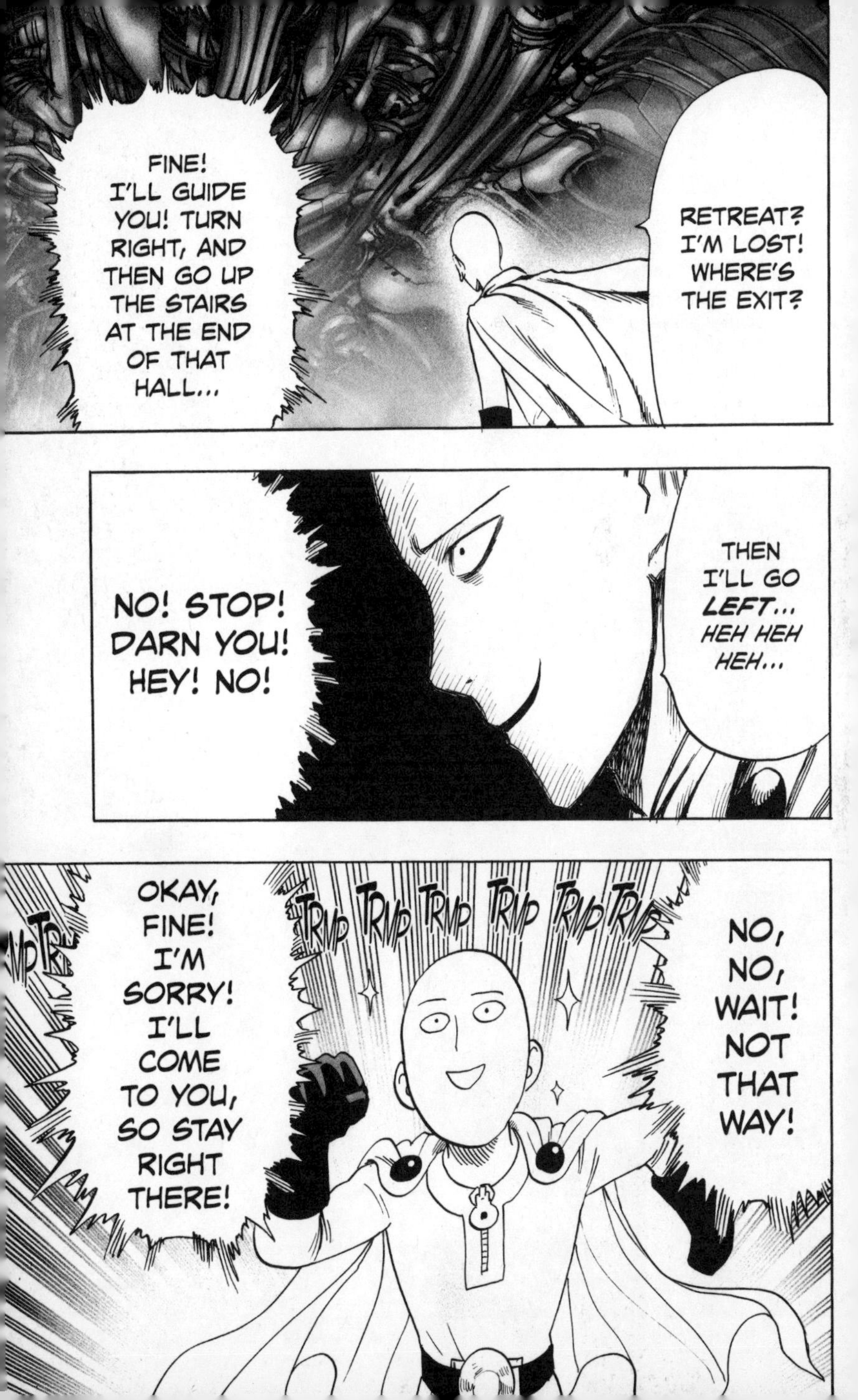
RETREAT? I'M LOST! WHERE'S THE EXIT?
FINE! I'LL GUIDE YOU! TURN RIGHT, AND THEN GO UP THE STAIRS AT THE END OF THAT HALL...
THEN I'LL GO *LEFT*... *HEH HEH HEH...*
NO! STOP! DARN YOU! HEY! NO!
NO, NO, WAIT! NOT THAT WAY!
TRMP TRMP TRMP TRMP TRMP TRMP
OKAY, FINE! I'M SORRY! I'LL COME TO YOU, SO STAY RIGHT THERE!

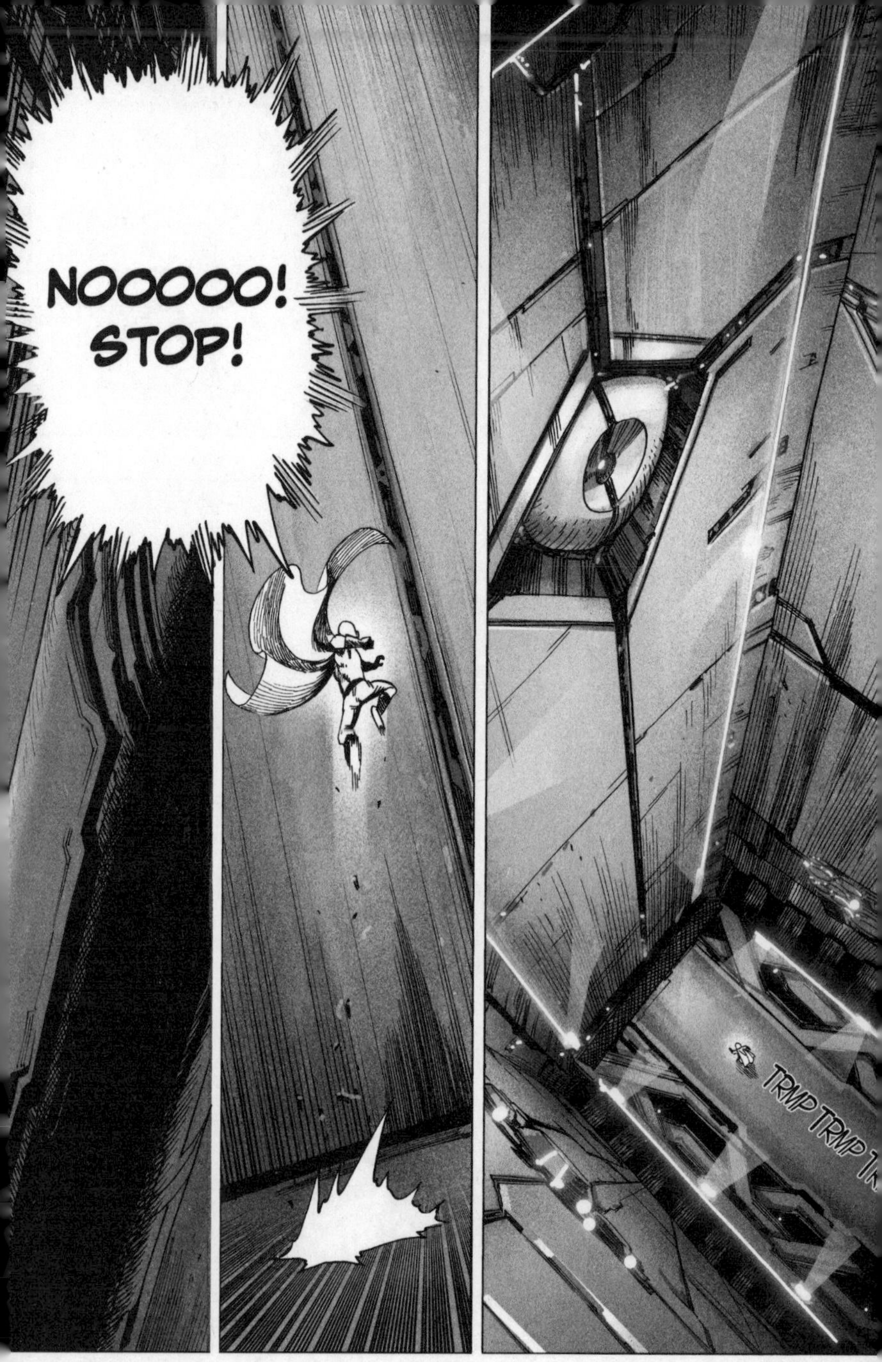
TRMP TRMP
NOOOOO! STOP!

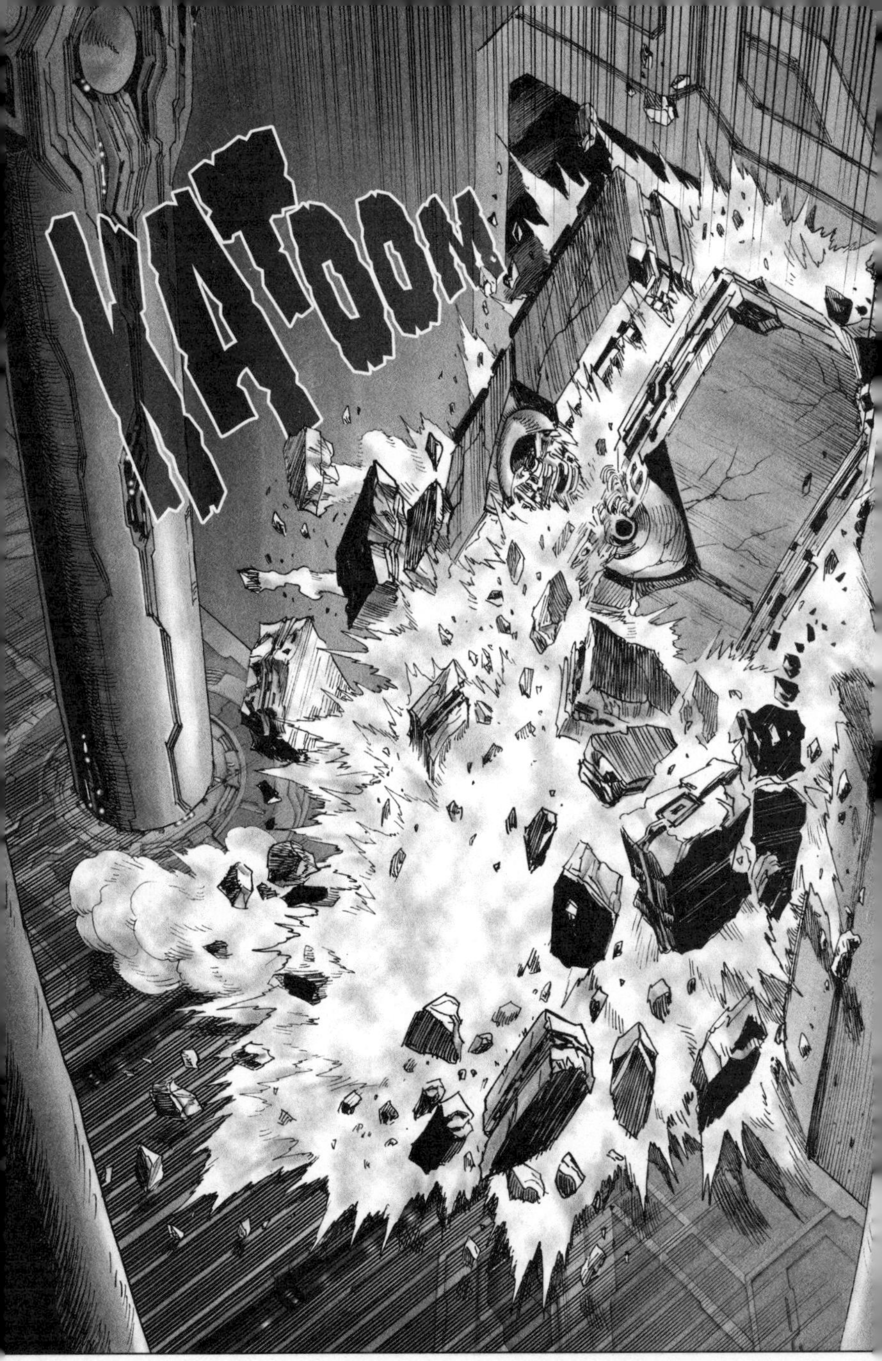
KATOOM

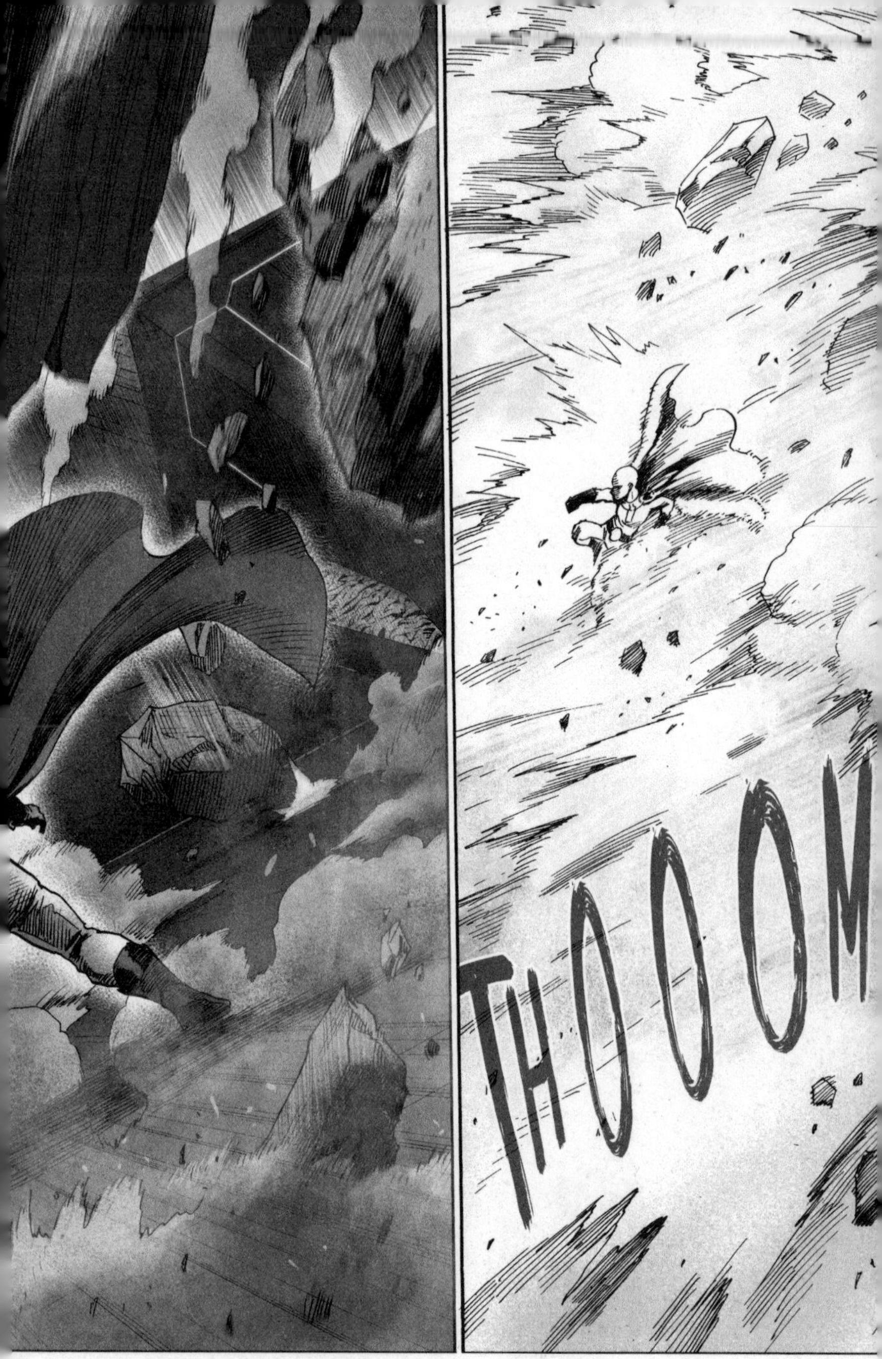
THOOOM

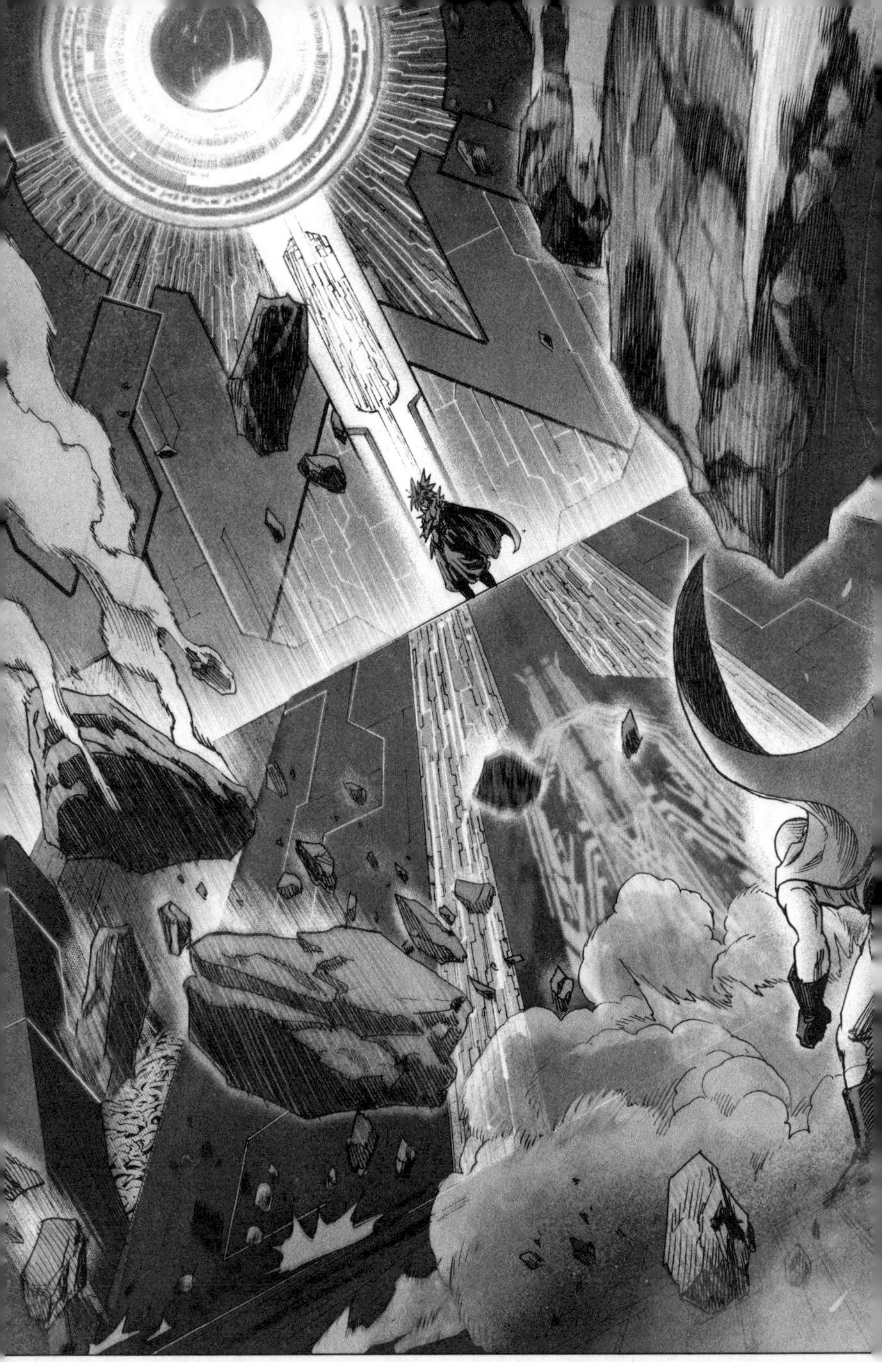

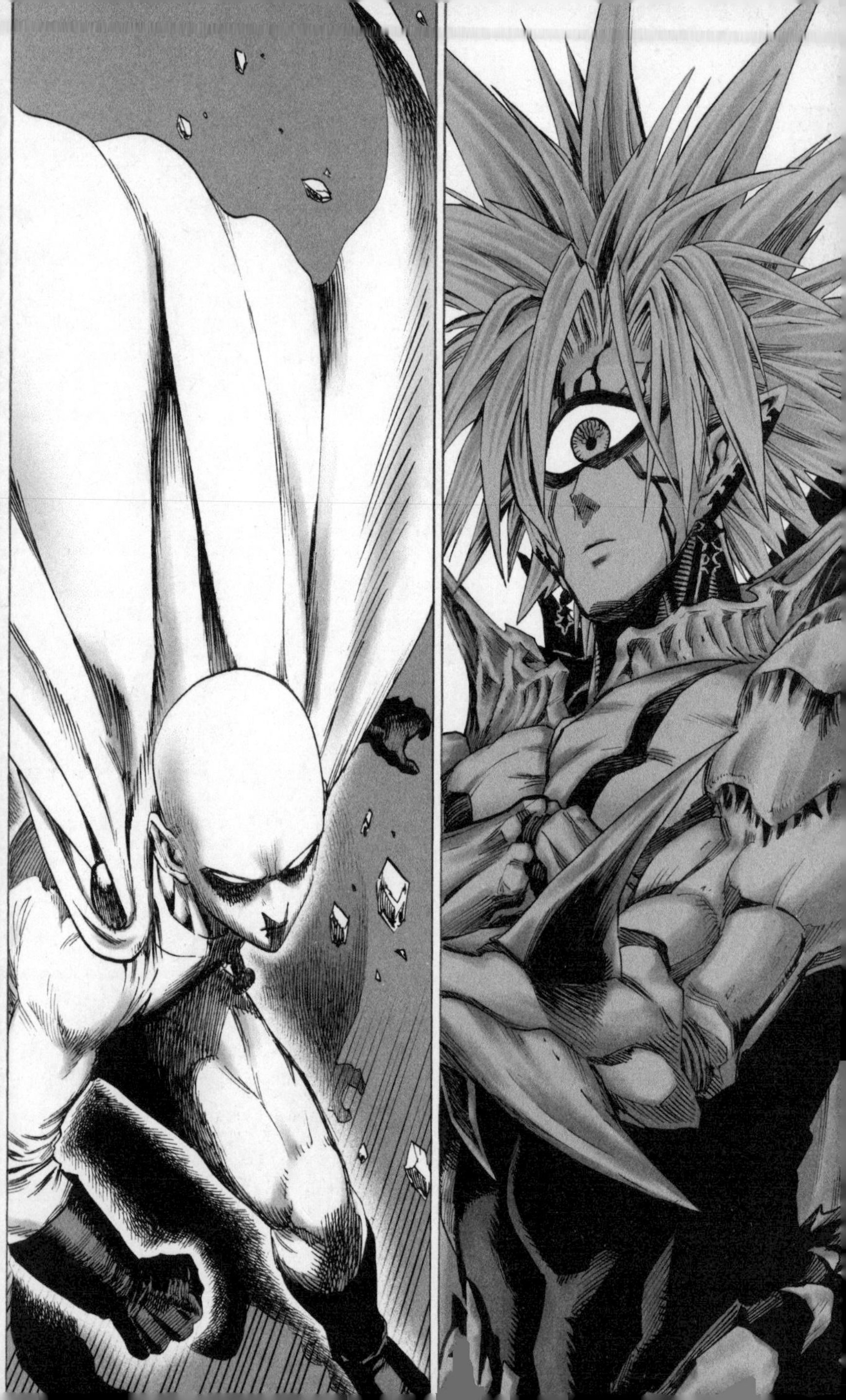

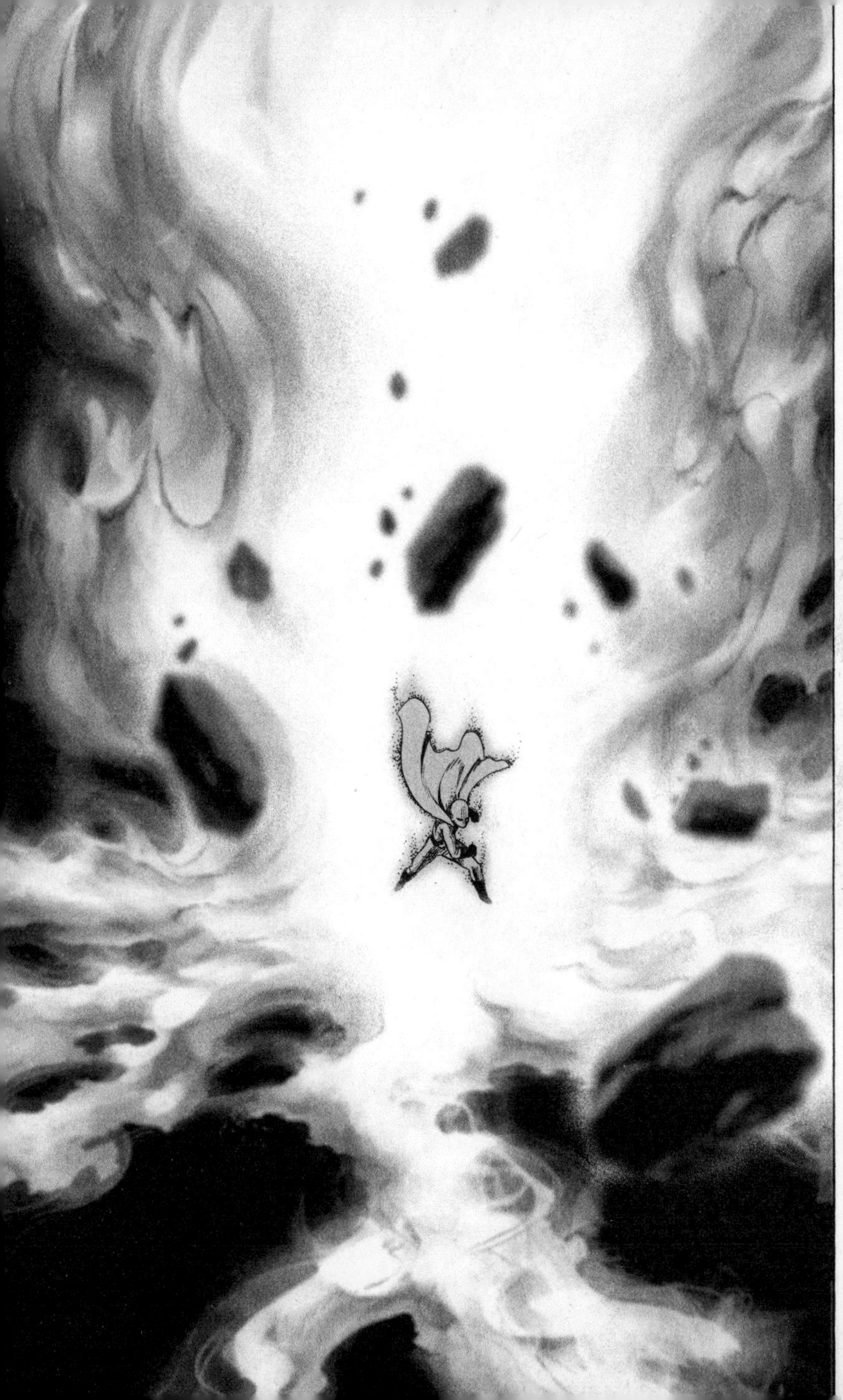

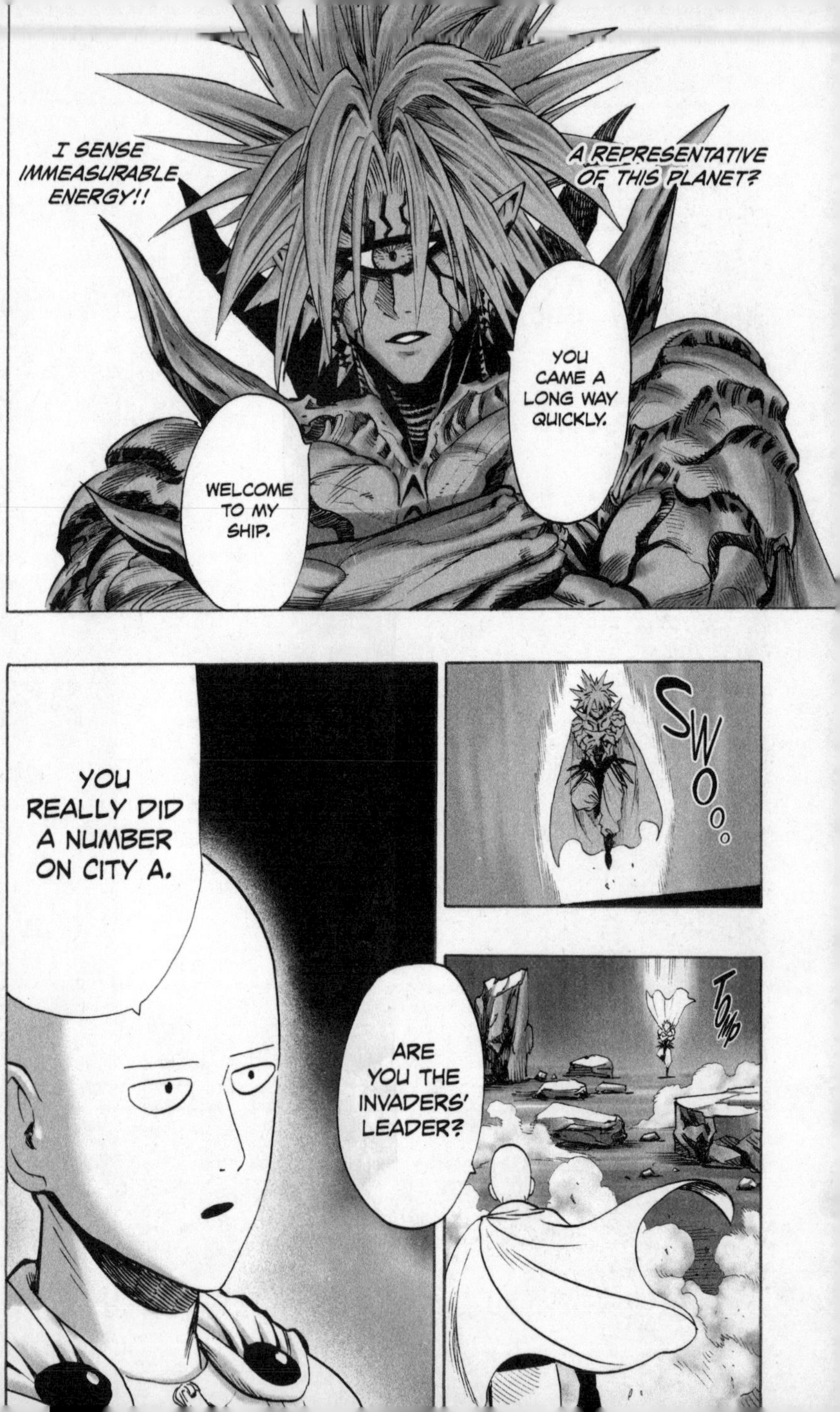
A REPRESENTATIVE OF THIS PLANET?
I SENSE IMMEASURABLE ENERGY!!
YOU CAME A LONG WAY QUICKLY.
WELCOME TO MY SHIP.
SWOOO
TOMP
YOU REALLY DID A NUMBER ON CITY A.
ARE YOU THE INVADERS' LEADER?

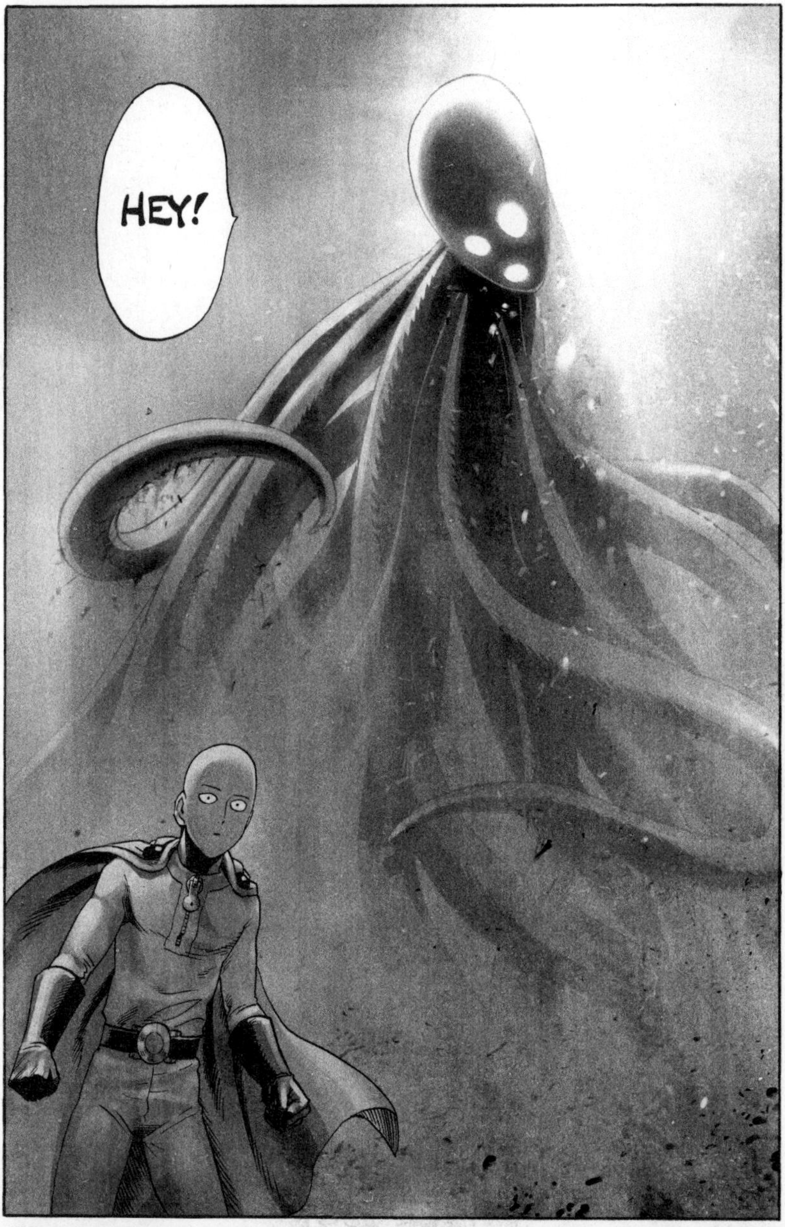
HEY!

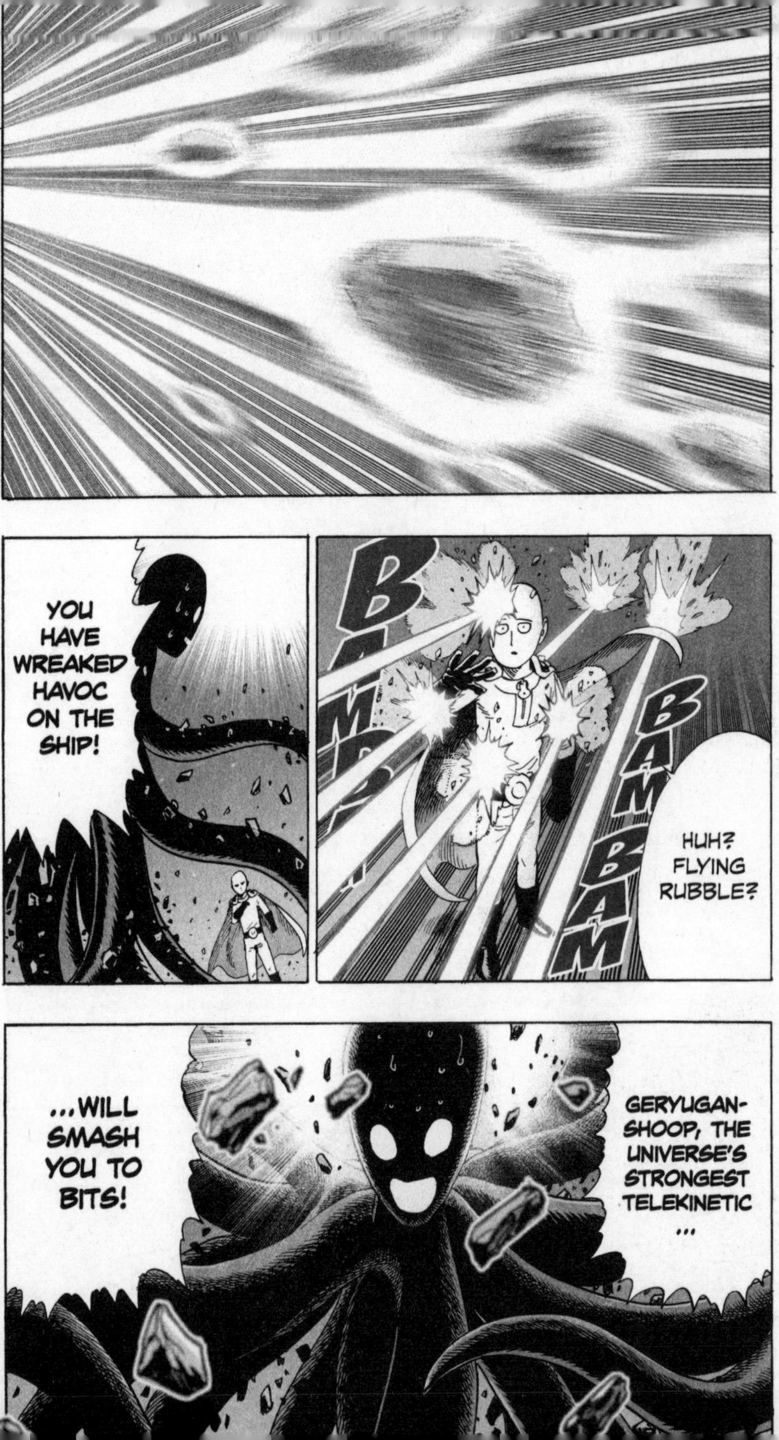
BAMBAM
HUH? FLYING RUBBLE?
YOU HAVE WREAKED HAVOC ON THE SHIP!
GERYUGANSHOOP, THE UNIVERSE'S STRONGEST TELEKINETIC...
...WILL SMASH YOU TO BITS!

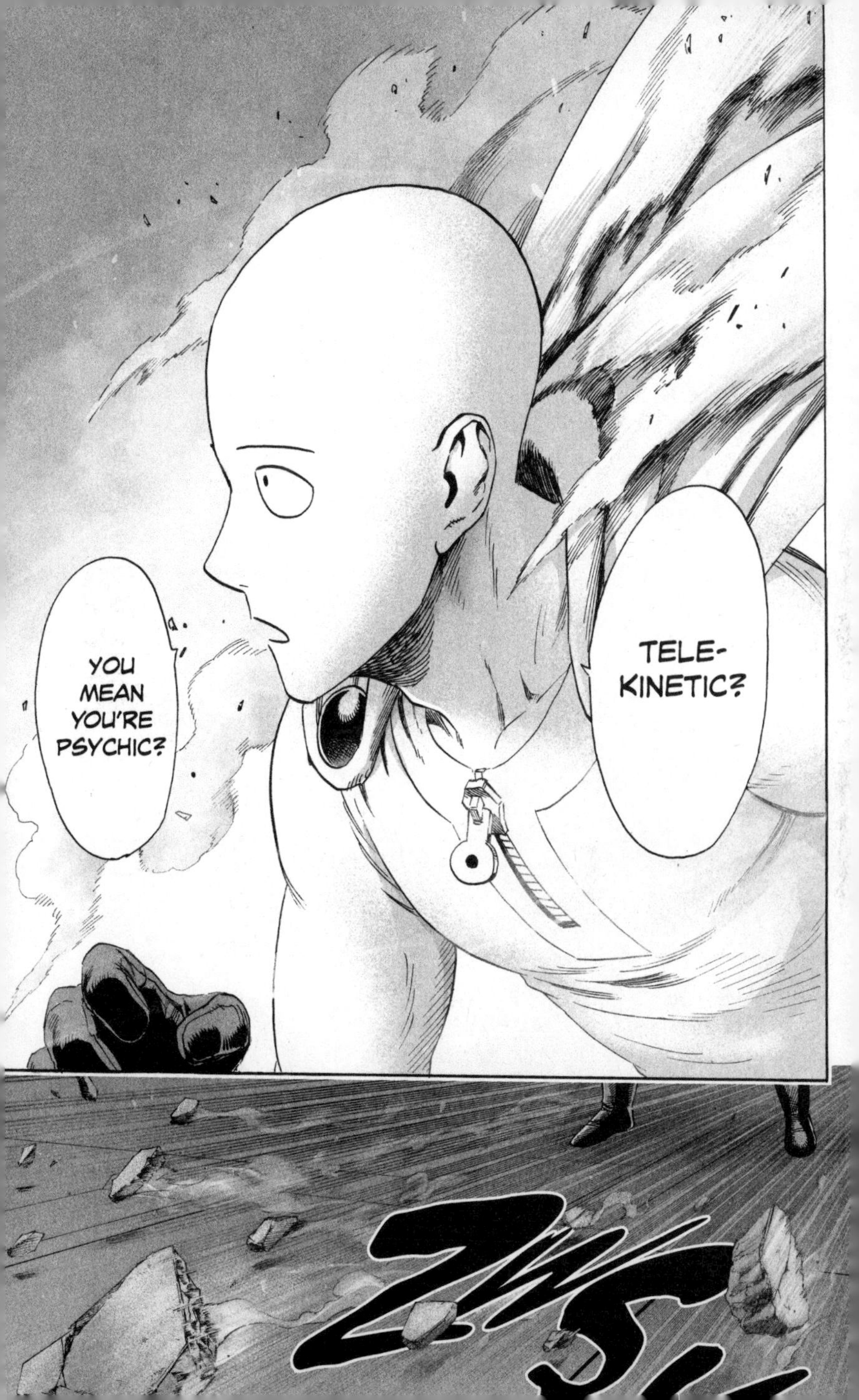
TELE-KINETIC?
YOU MEAN YOU'RE PSYCHIC?

The giant labyrinth in the spaceship appears with the consent of its creator, Kazuo Nomura.

Thank you very much.

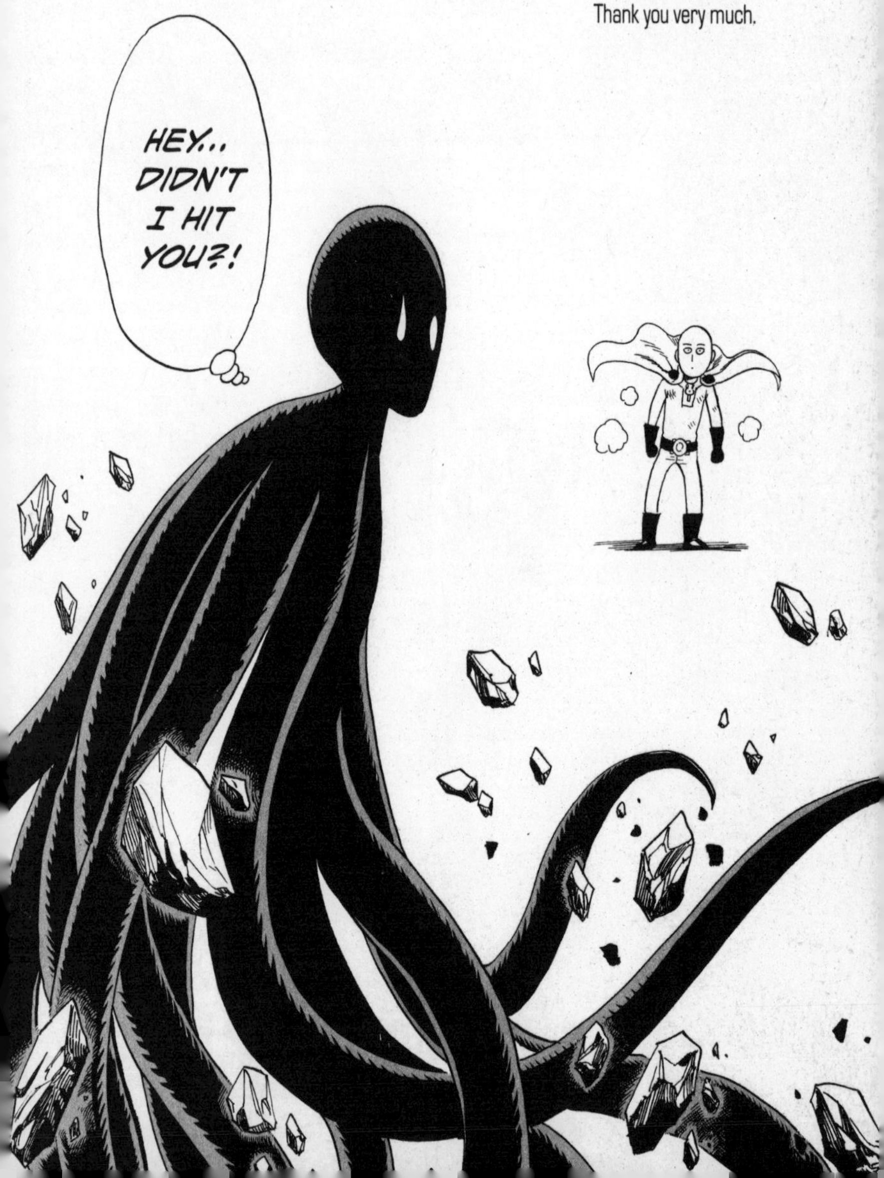
HEY... DIDN'T I HIT YOU?!

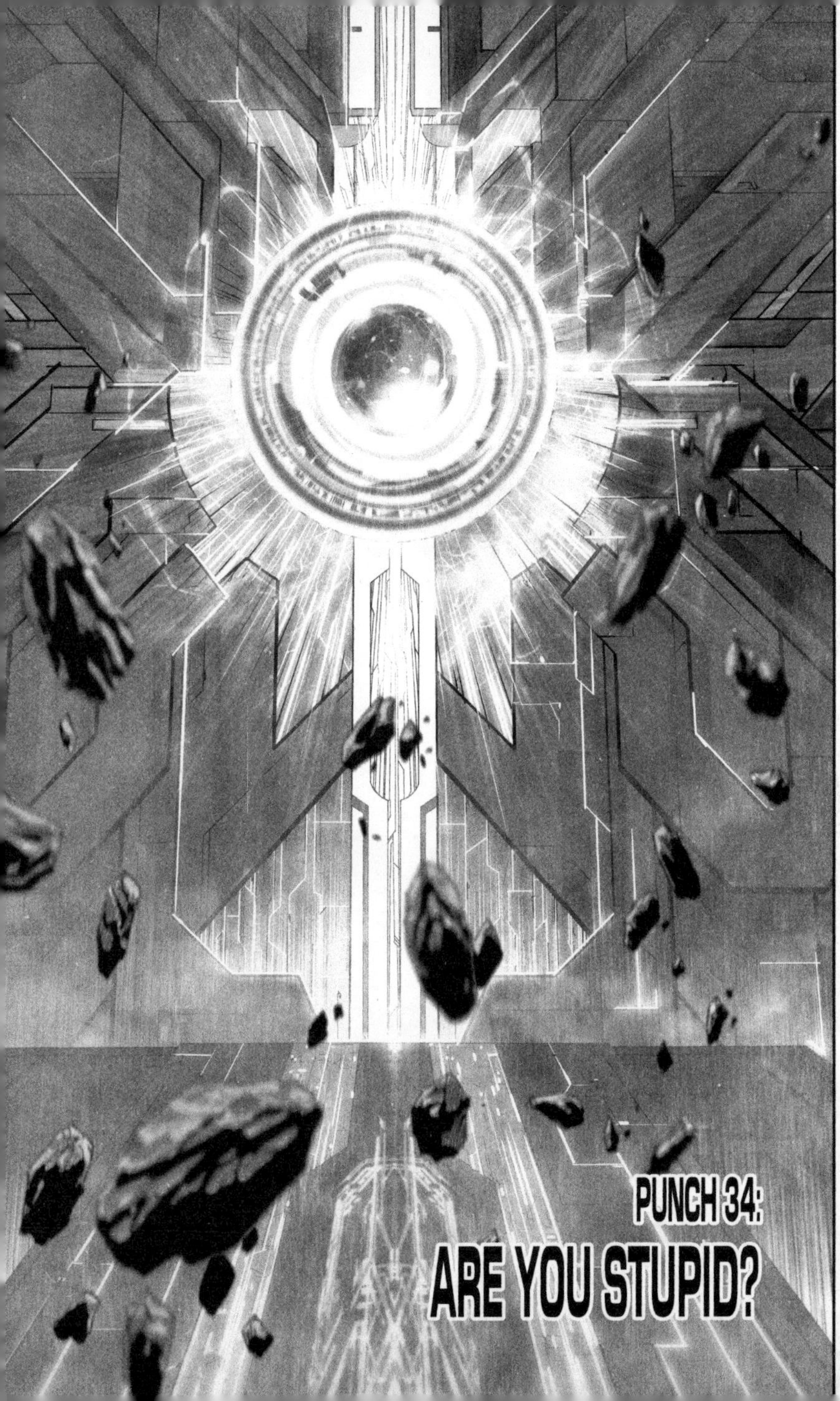
PUNCH 34:
ARE YOU STUPID?

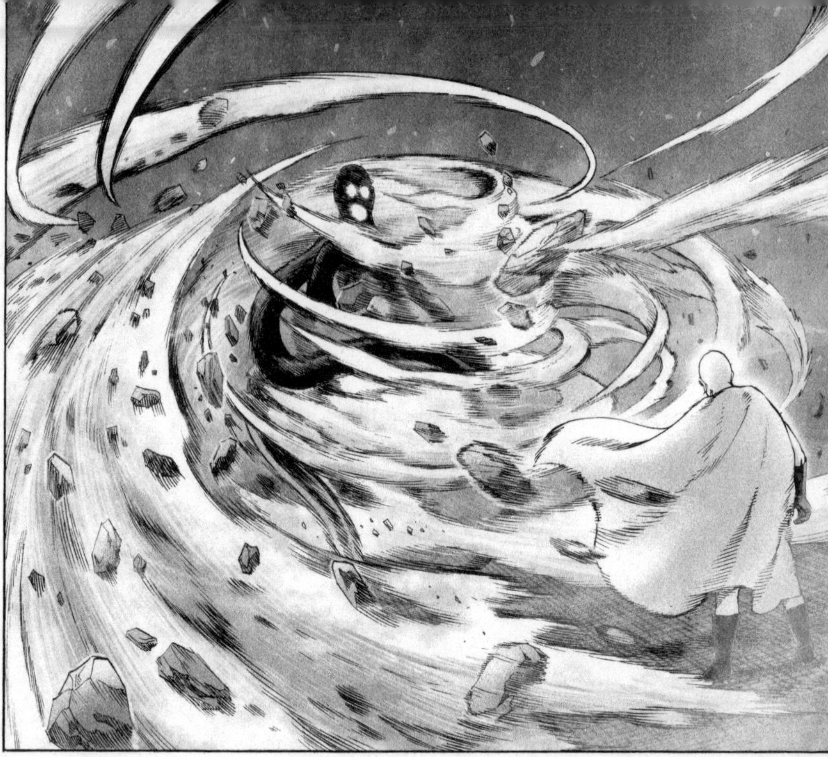

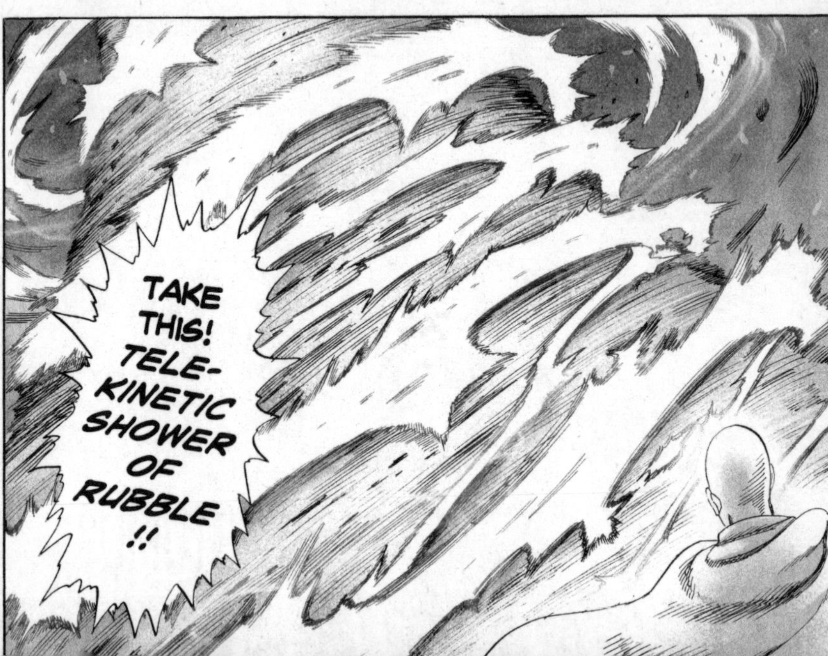
TAKE THIS! TELE-KINETIC SHOWER OF RUBBLE !!

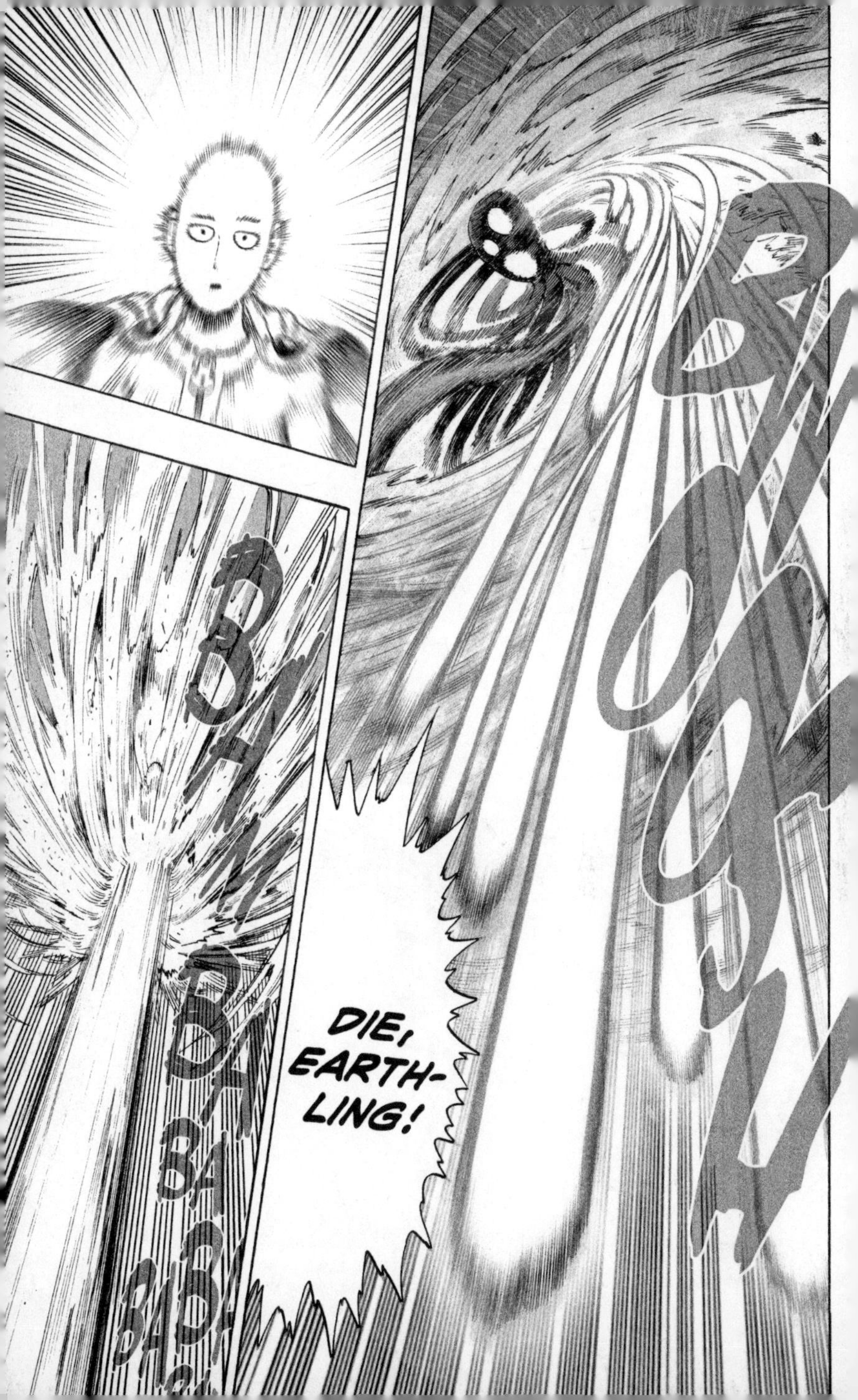
DIE, EARTH-LING!

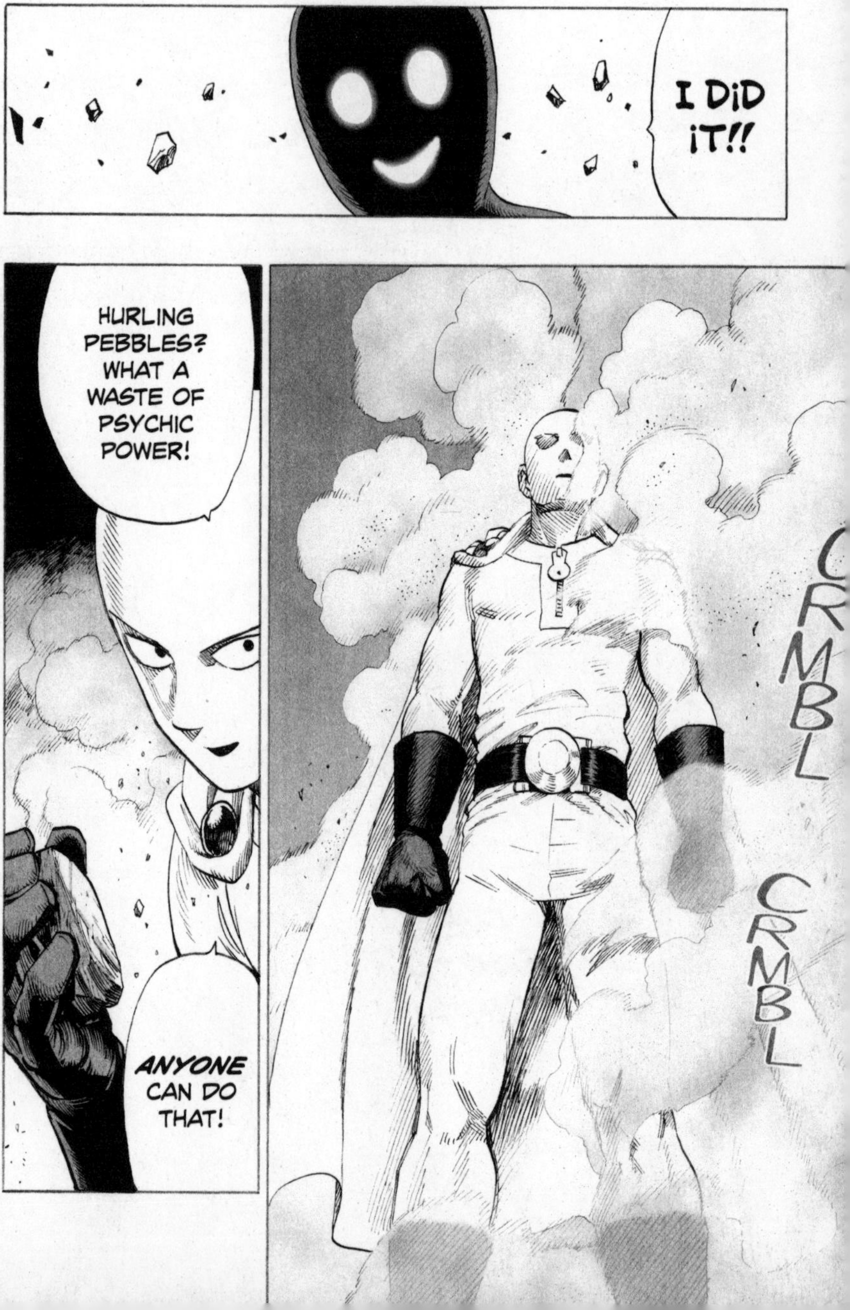
I DID IT!!
CRMBL
CRMBL
HURLING PEBBLES? WHAT A WASTE OF PSYCHIC POWER!
ANYONE CAN DO THAT!

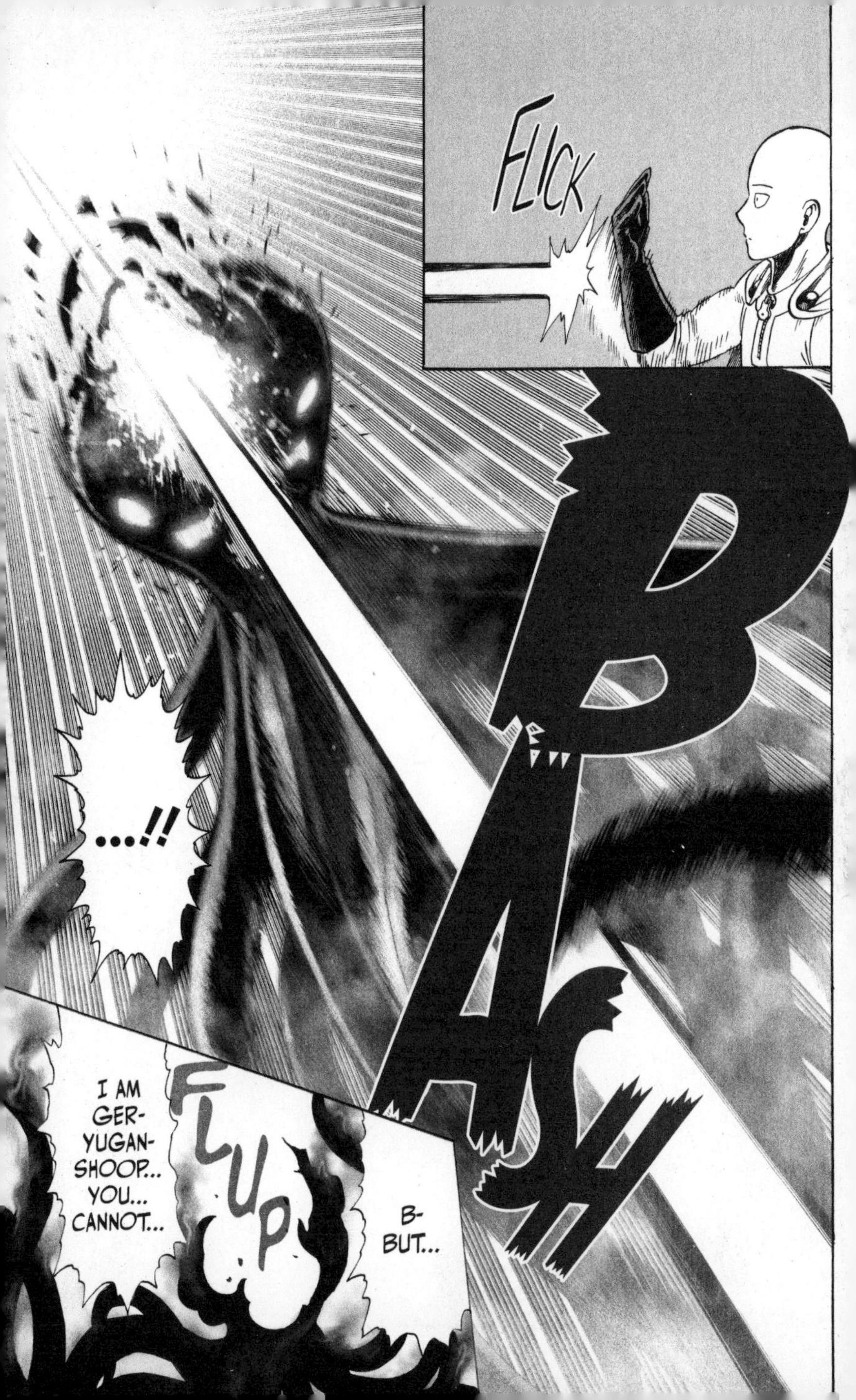
FLICK
BASH
...!!
B-
BUT...
FLUP
I AM
GER-
YUGAN-
SHOOP...
YOU...
CANNOT...

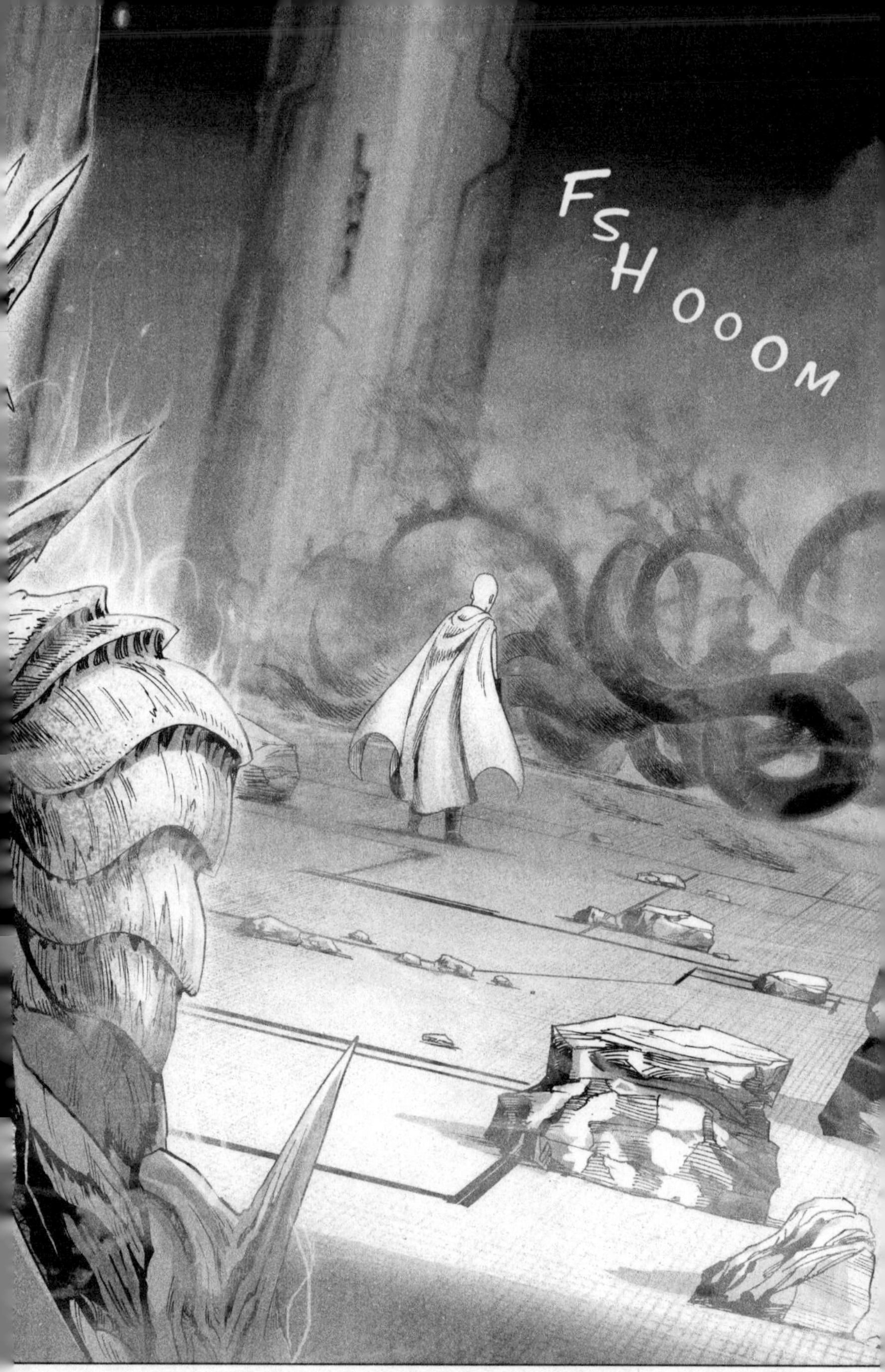
FSHOOOM

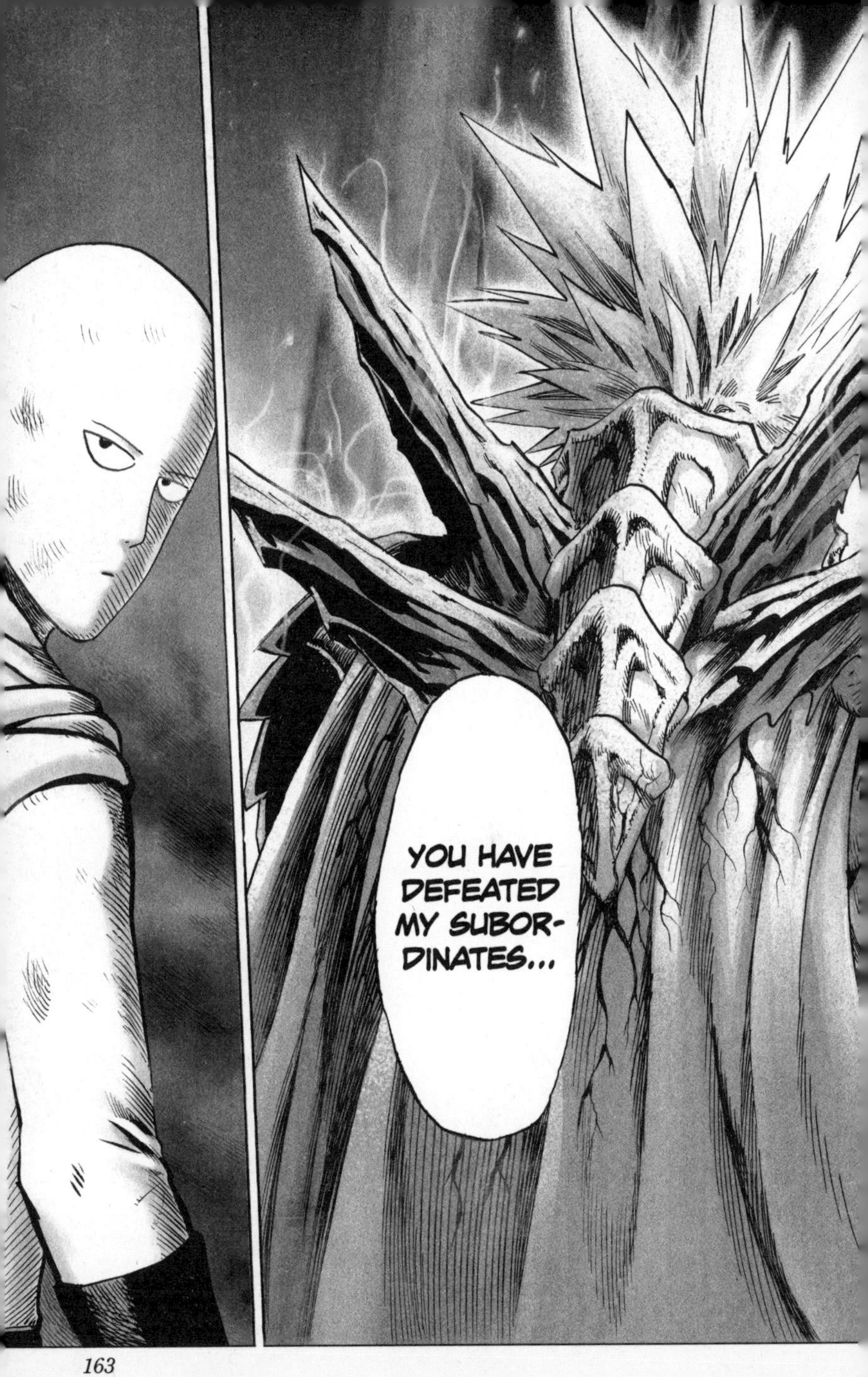
YOU HAVE DEFEATED MY SUBOR-DINATES...

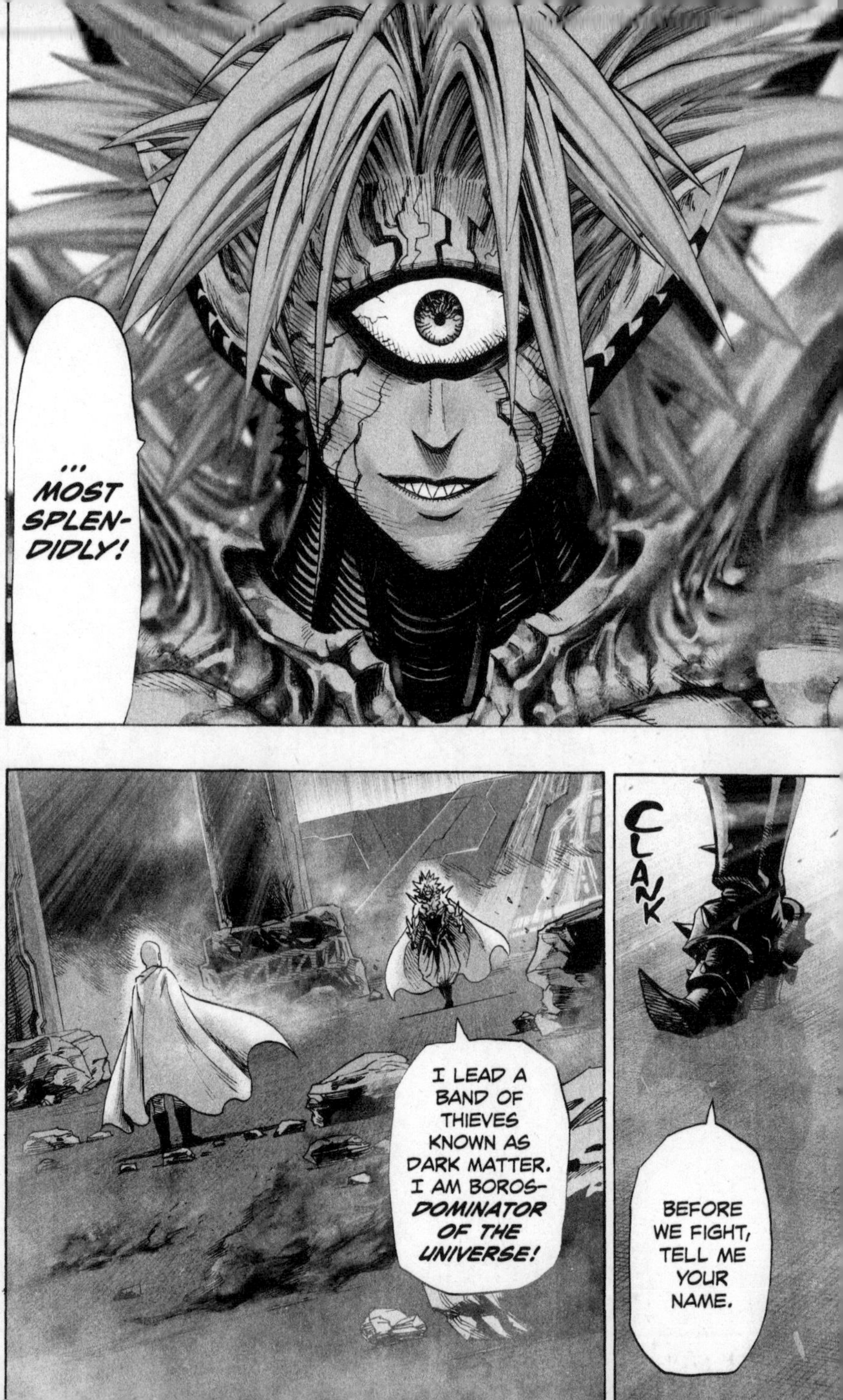
... MOST SPLEN-DIDLY!
CLANK
BEFORE WE FIGHT, TELL ME YOUR NAME.
I LEAD A BAND OF THIEVES KNOWN AS DARK MATTER. I AM BOROS-*DOMINATOR OF THE UNIVERSE!*

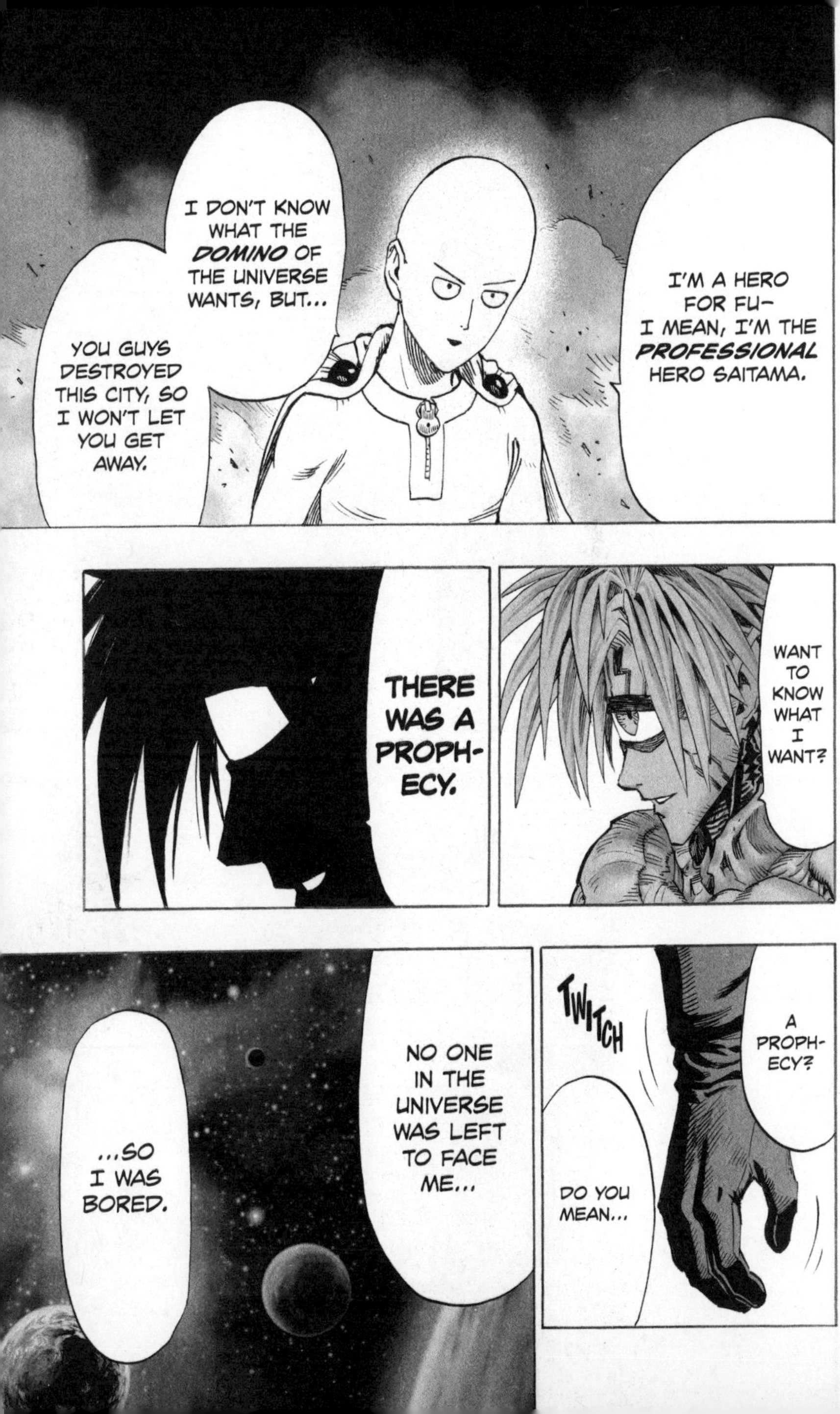
I'M A HERO FOR FU— I MEAN, I'M THE PROFESSIONAL HERO SAITAMA.
I DON'T KNOW WHAT THE DOMINO OF THE UNIVERSE WANTS, BUT...
YOU GUYS DESTROYED THIS CITY, SO I WON'T LET YOU GET AWAY.
WANT TO KNOW WHAT I WANT?
THERE WAS A PROPHECY.
A PROPHECY?
TWITCH
DO YOU MEAN...
NO ONE IN THE UNIVERSE WAS LEFT TO FACE ME...
...SO I WAS BORED.

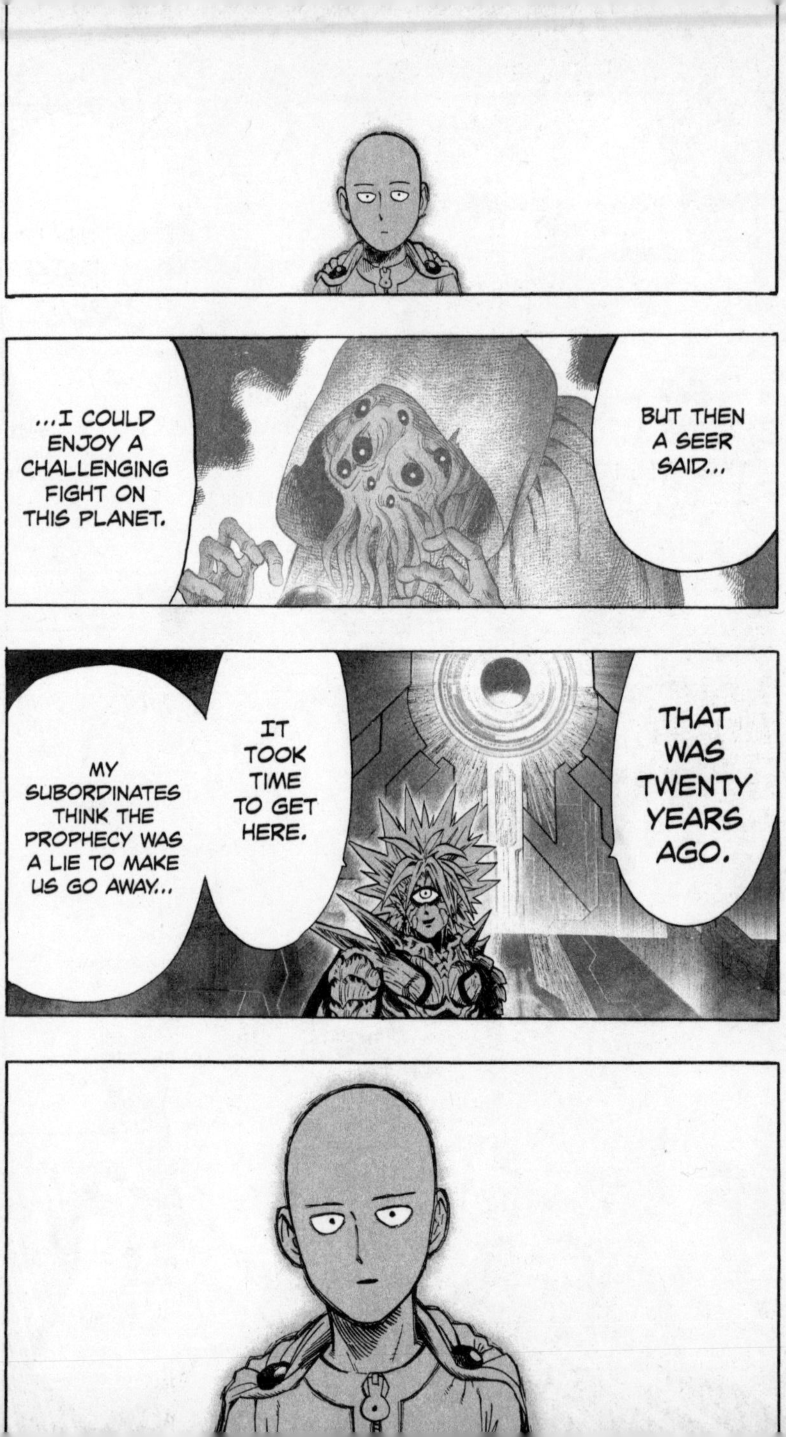
BUT THEN A SEER SAID...
...I COULD ENJOY A CHALLENGING FIGHT ON THIS PLANET.
THAT WAS TWENTY YEARS AGO.
IT TOOK TIME TO GET HERE.
MY SUBORDINATES THINK THE PROPHECY WAS A LIE TO MAKE US GO AWAY...

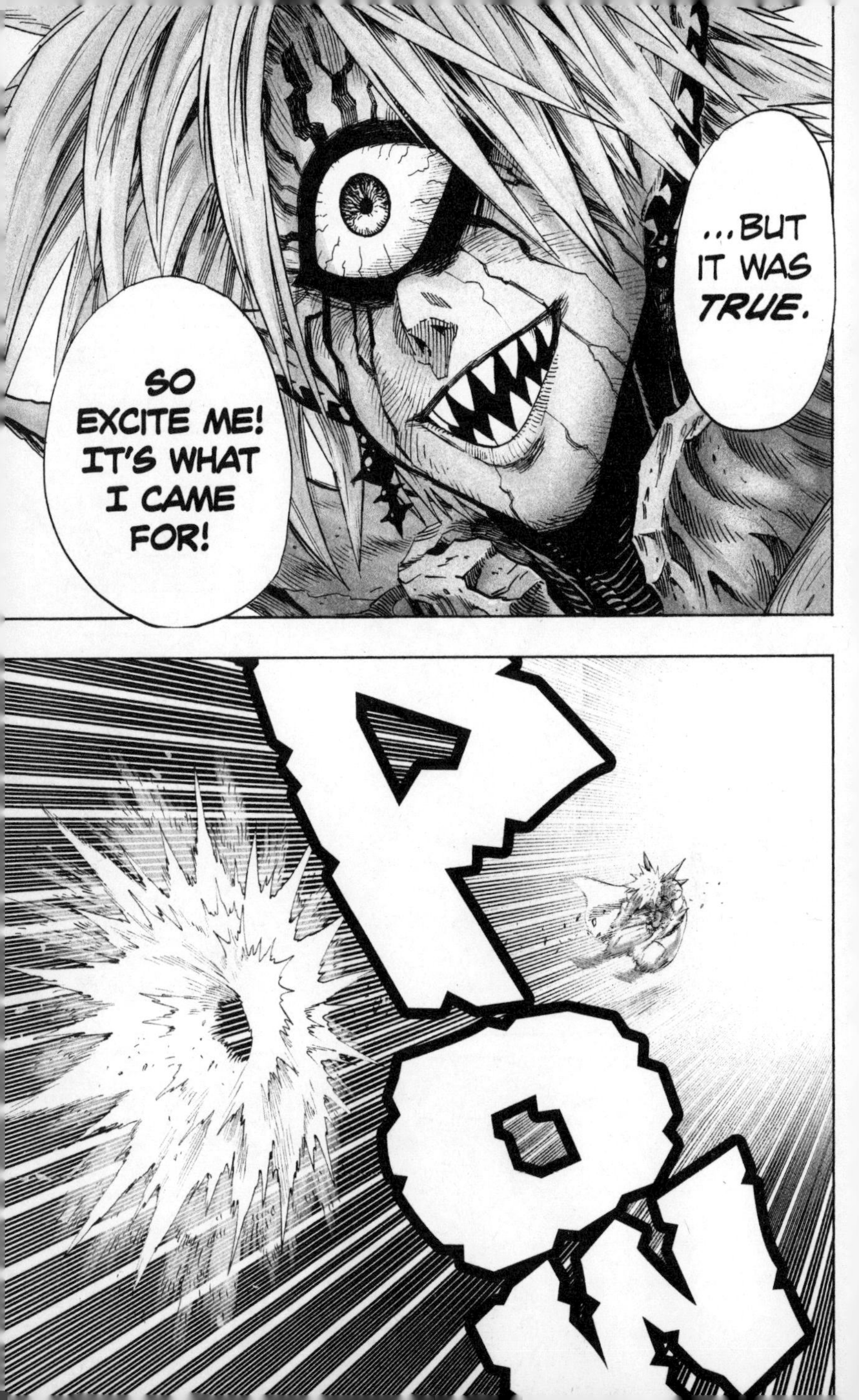
...BUT IT WAS TRUE.
SO EXCITE ME! IT'S WHAT I CAME FOR!

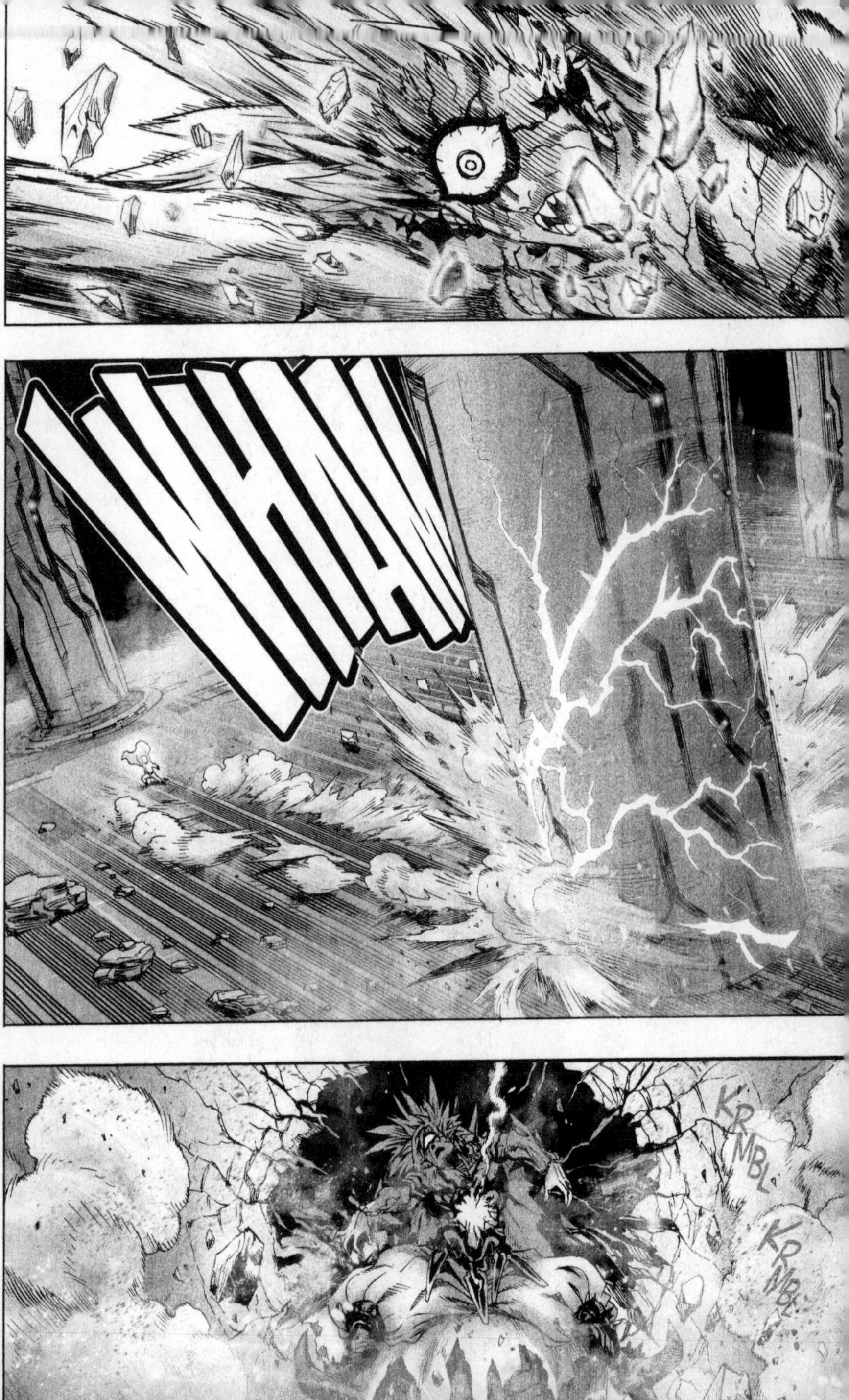
WHAM
KRMBL
KRMBL

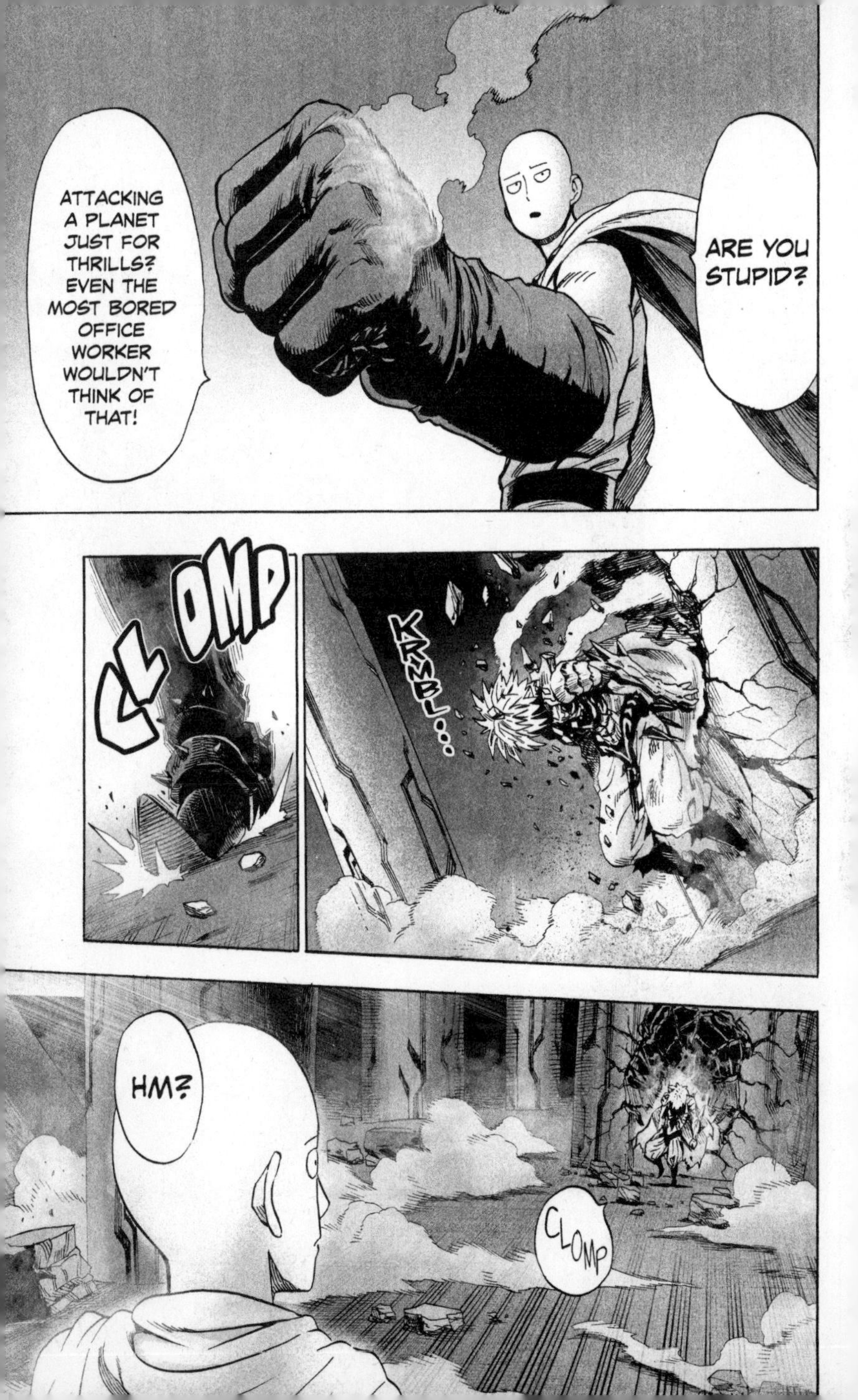
ARE YOU STUPID?
ATTACKING A PLANET JUST FOR THRILLS? EVEN THE MOST BORED OFFICE WORKER WOULDN'T THINK OF THAT!
KRMBL...
CLOMP
CLOMP
HM?

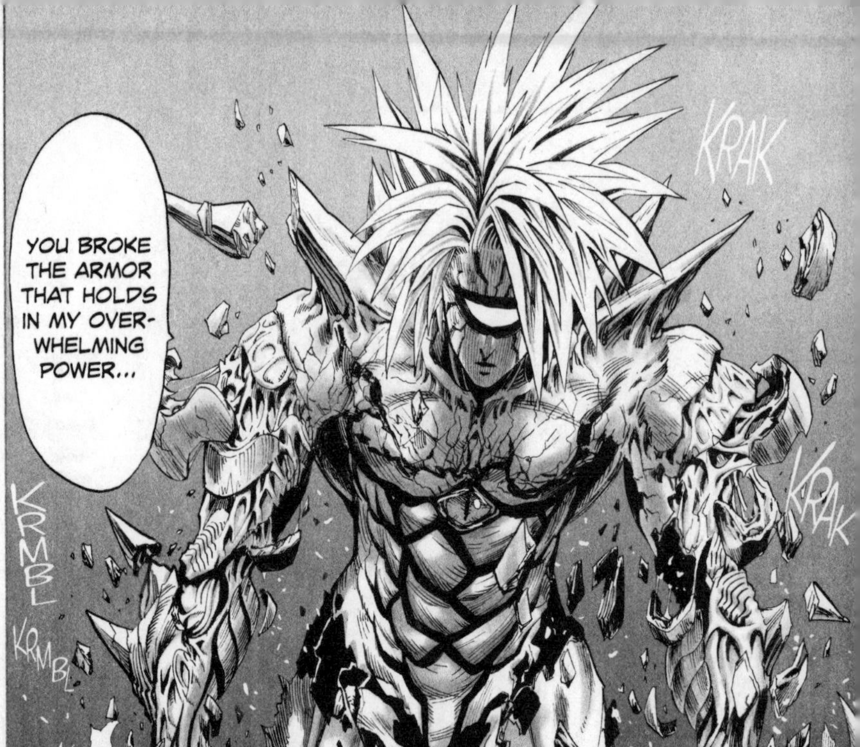
KRAK
YOU BROKE THE ARMOR THAT HOLDS IN MY OVER-WHELMING POWER...
KRAK
KRMBL
KRMBL

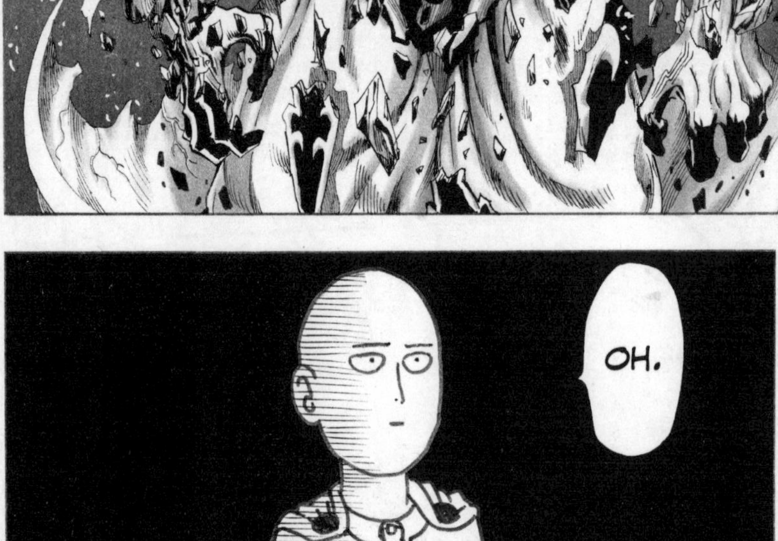
OH.

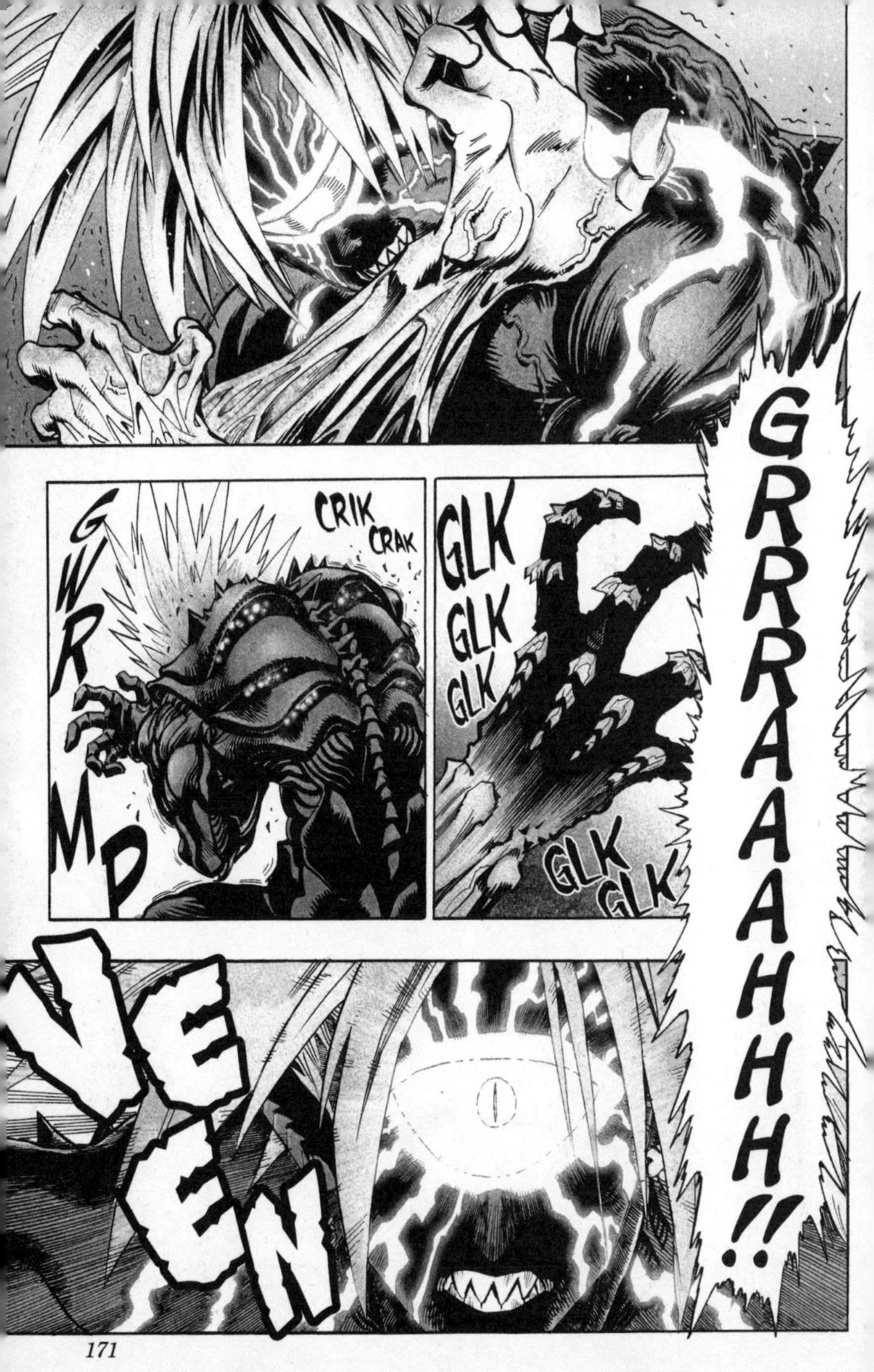
GRRRAAAHHH!!
GLK GLK GLK
GLK GLK
CRIK CRAK
GWRMP
VEEN

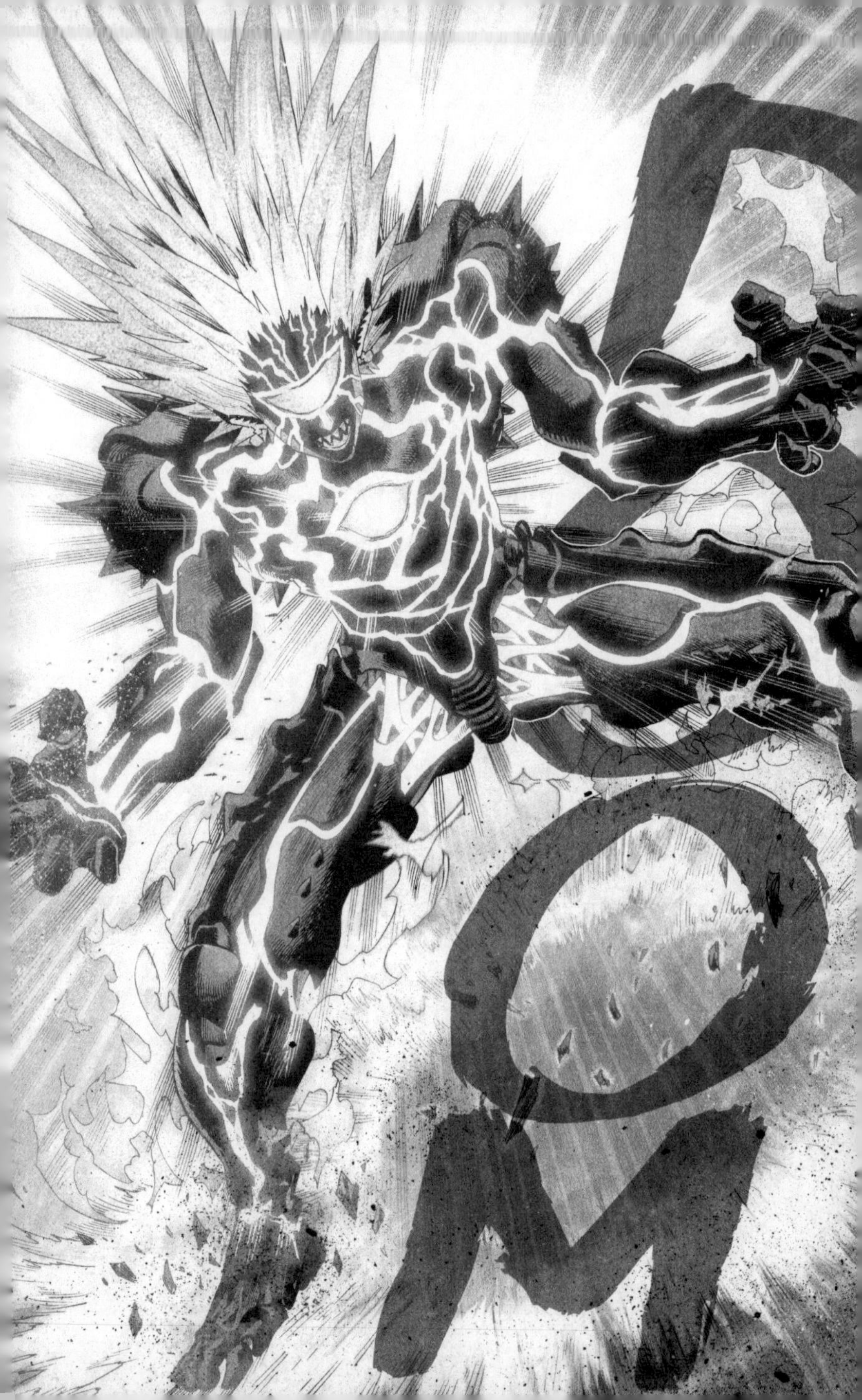

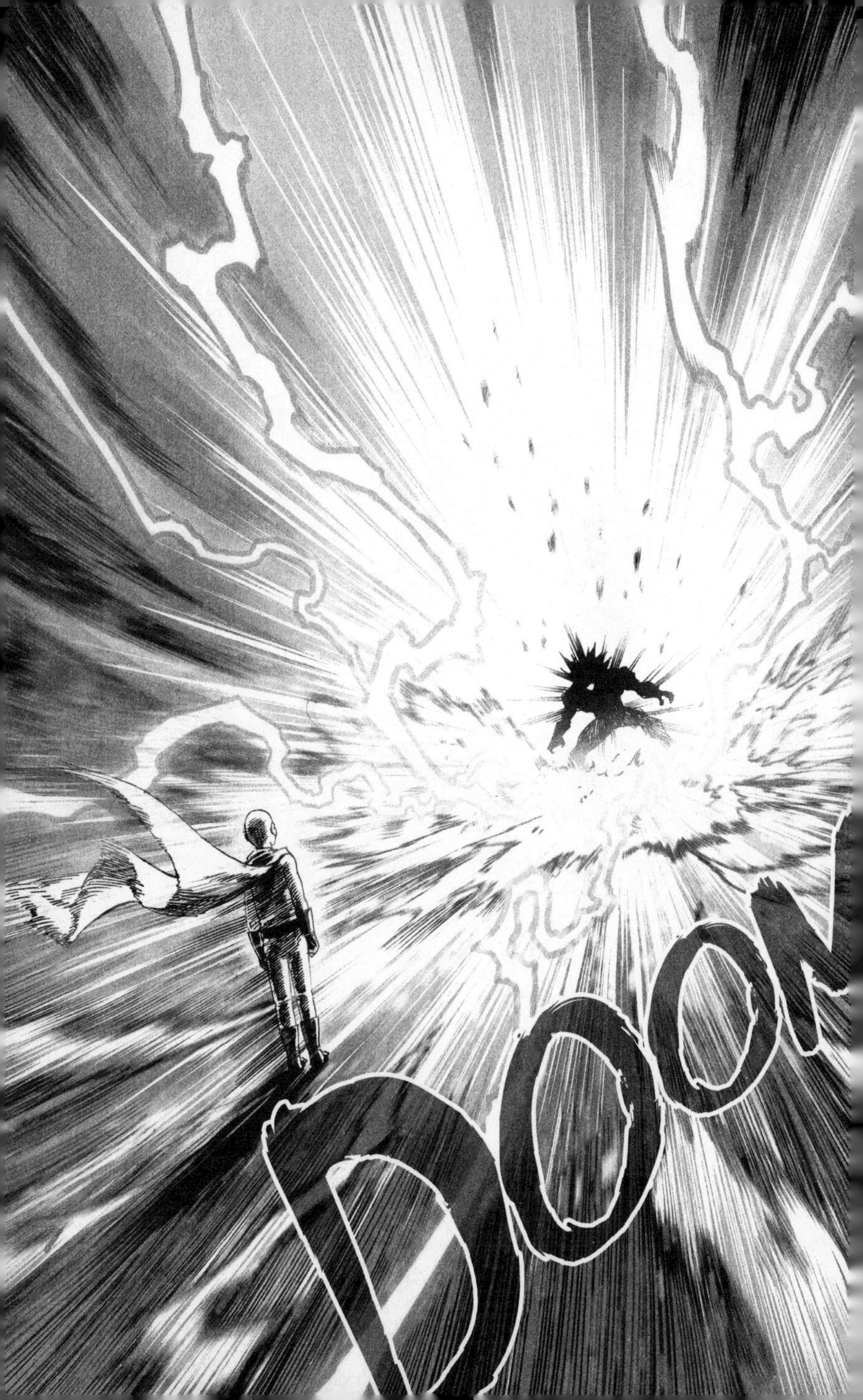
DOOM

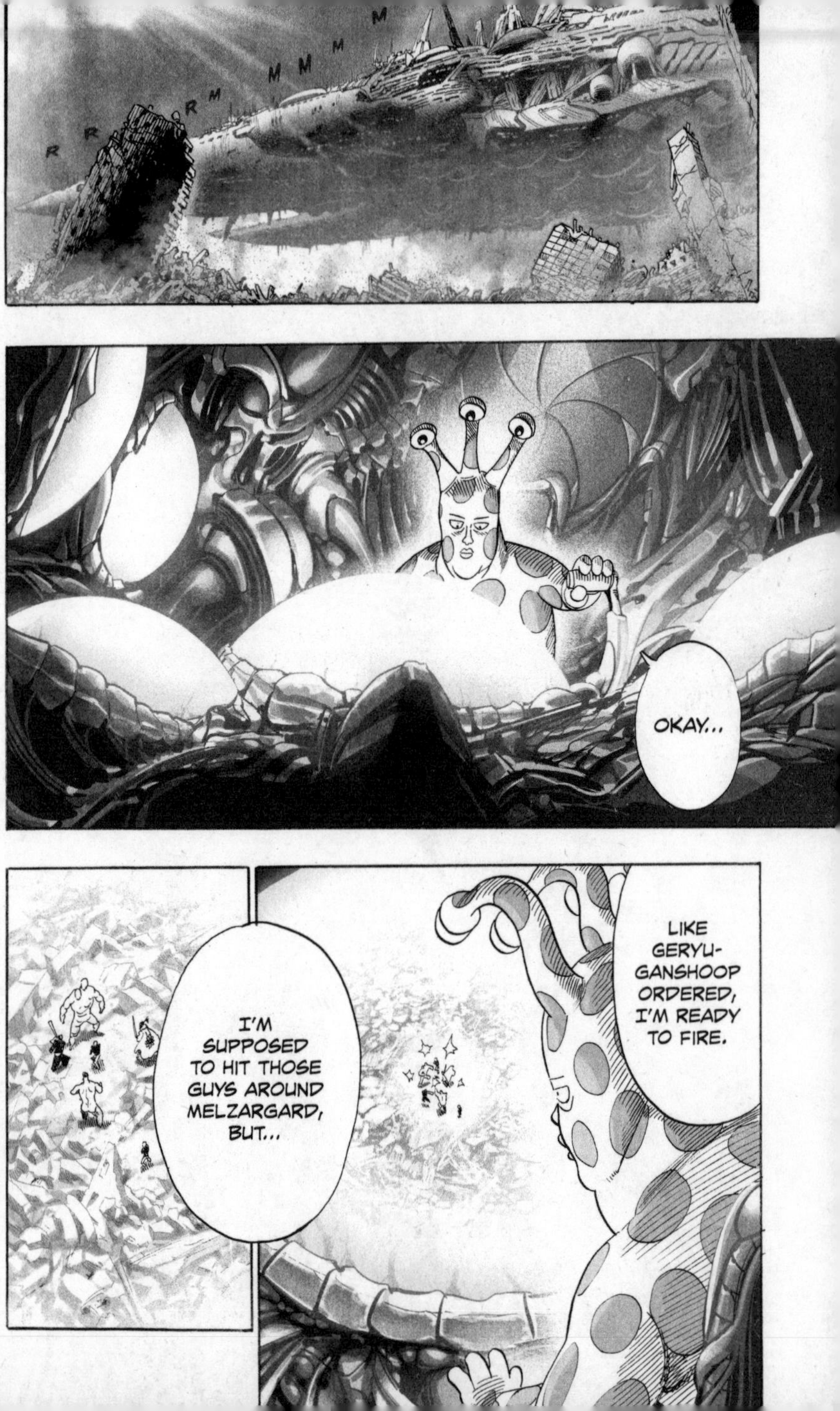
RRRMMMMM
OKAY...
LIKE GERYUGANSHOOP ORDERED, I'M READY TO FIRE.
I'M SUPPOSED TO HIT THOSE GUYS AROUND MELZARGARD, BUT...

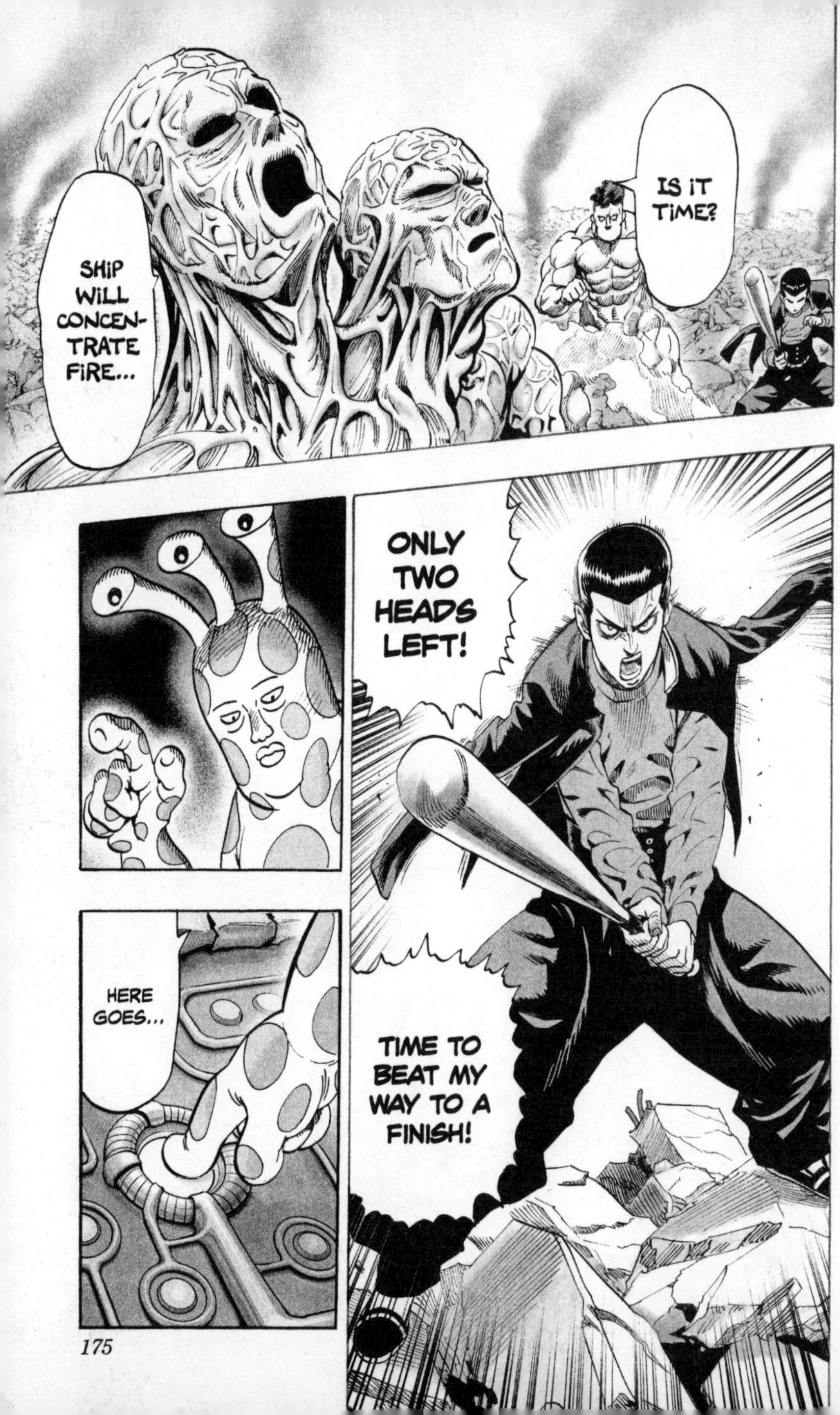
IS IT TIME?
SHIP WILL CONCENTRATE FIRE...
ONLY TWO HEADS LEFT!
TIME TO BEAT MY WAY TO A FINISH!
HERE GOES...

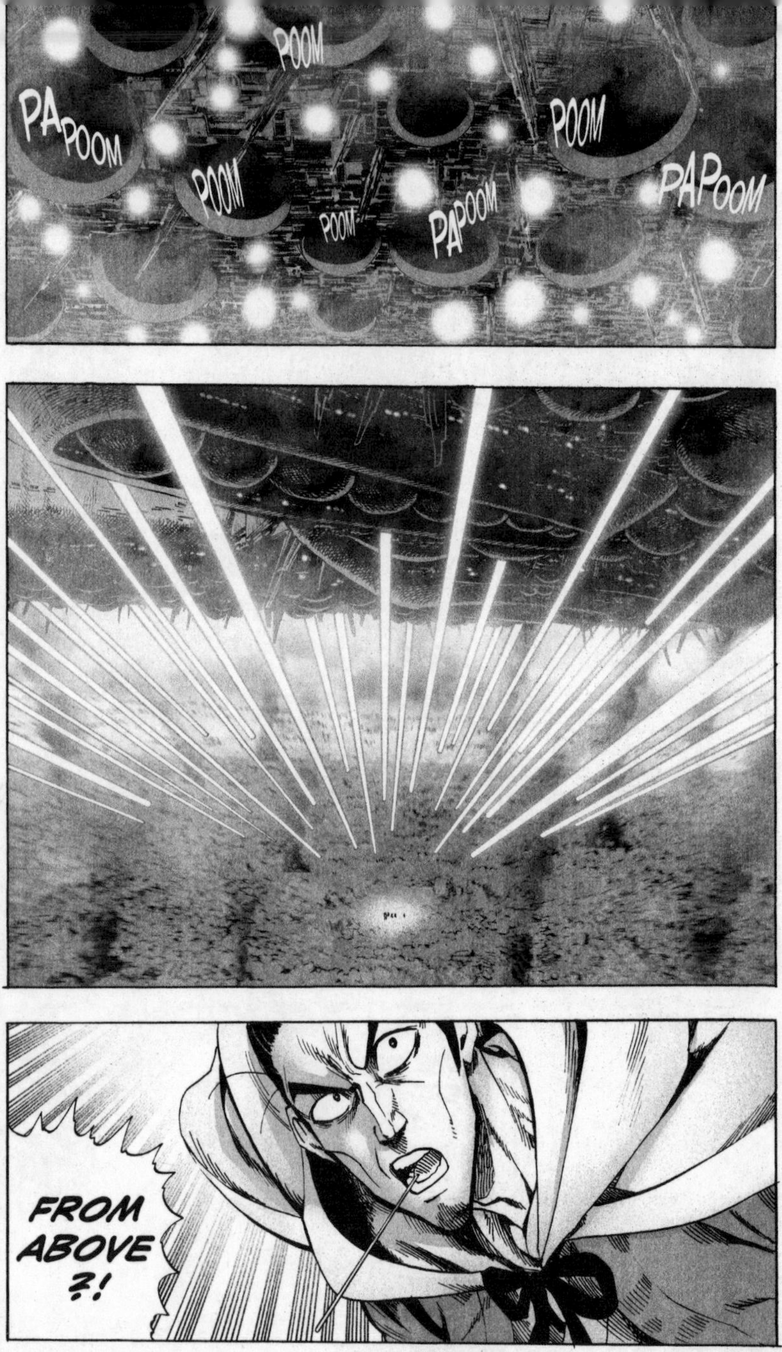
POOM
POOM
PAPOOM
PAPOOM
POOM
POOM
PAPOOM
FROM ABOVE ?!

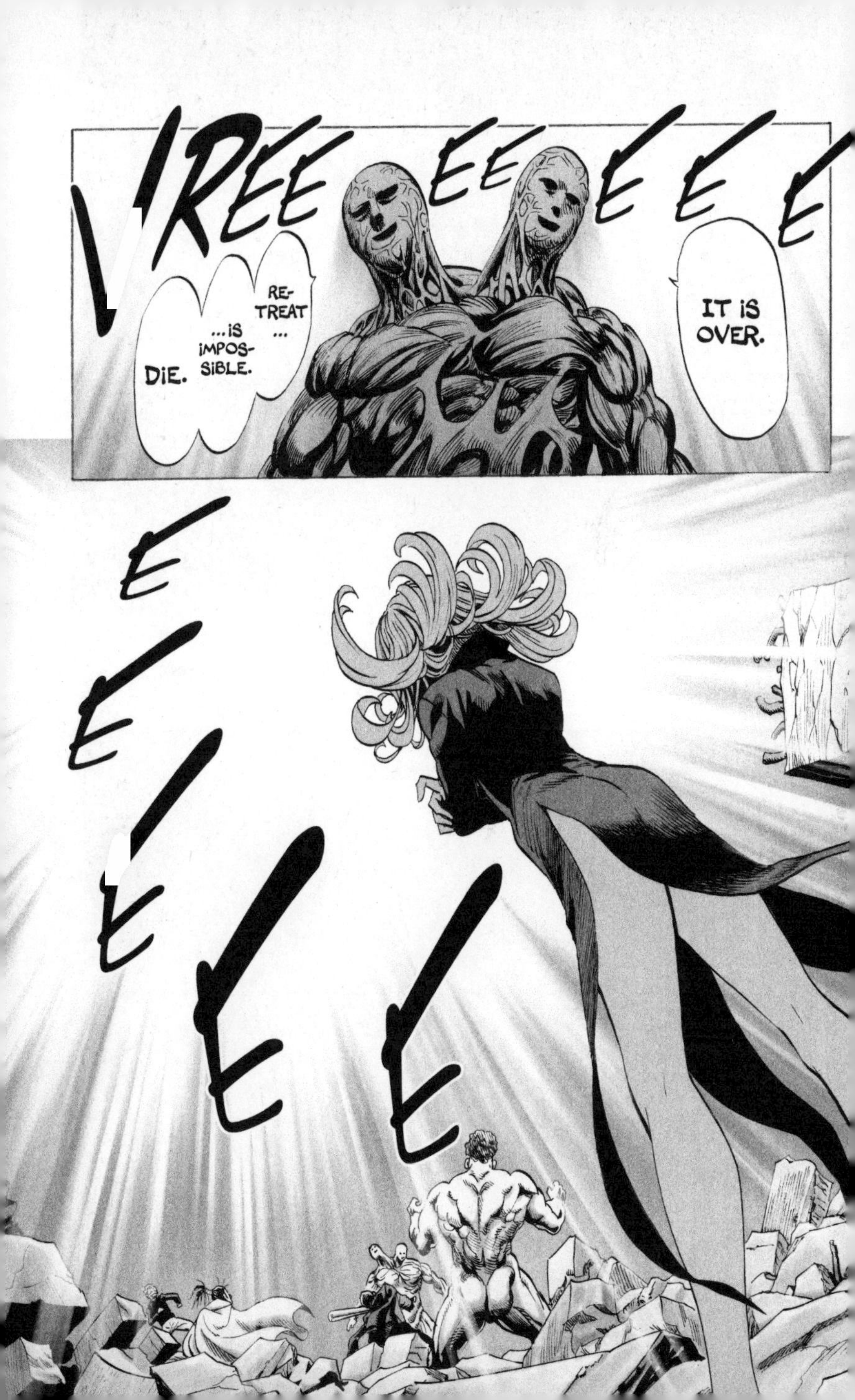
IT IS OVER.
RETREAT ...
...IS IMPOSSIBLE.
DIE.

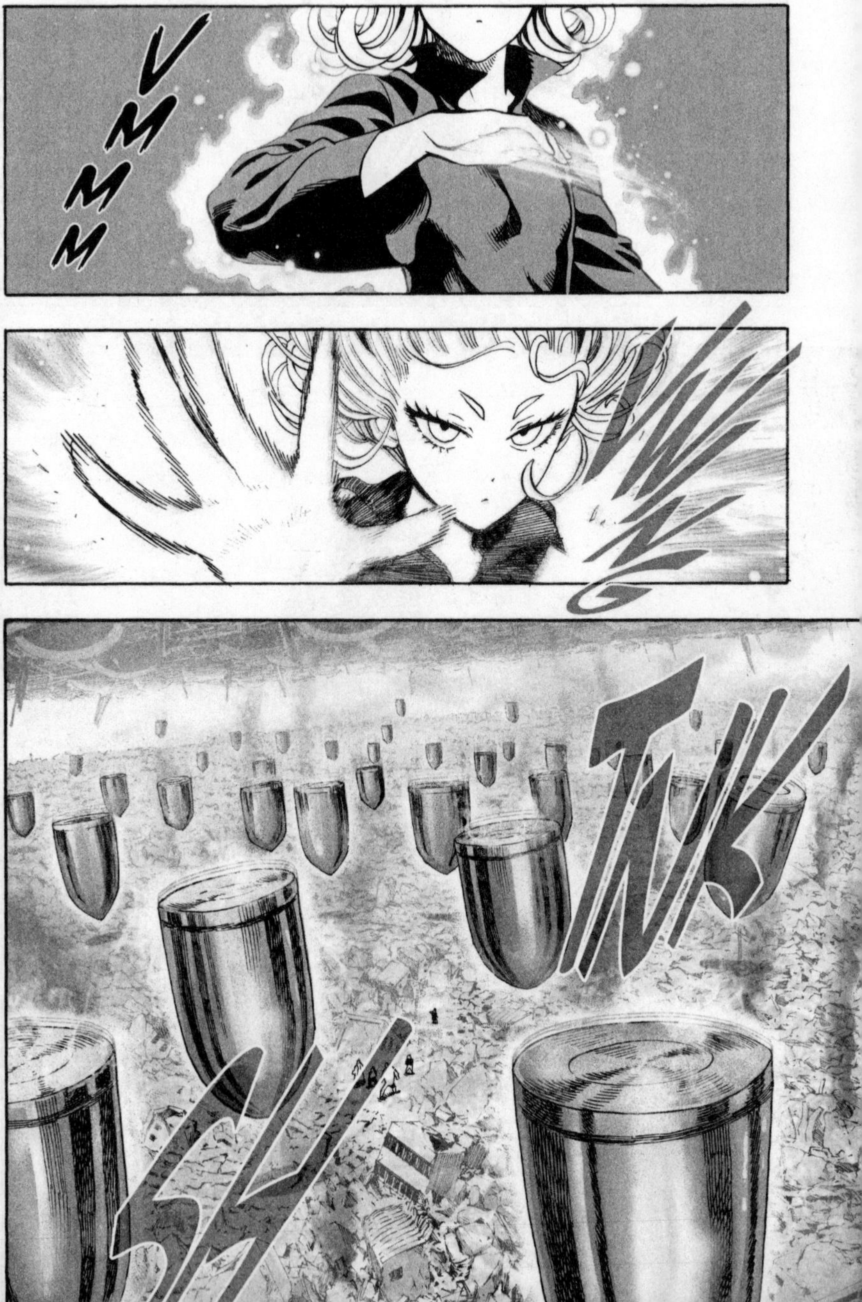
VMMMM
TNK

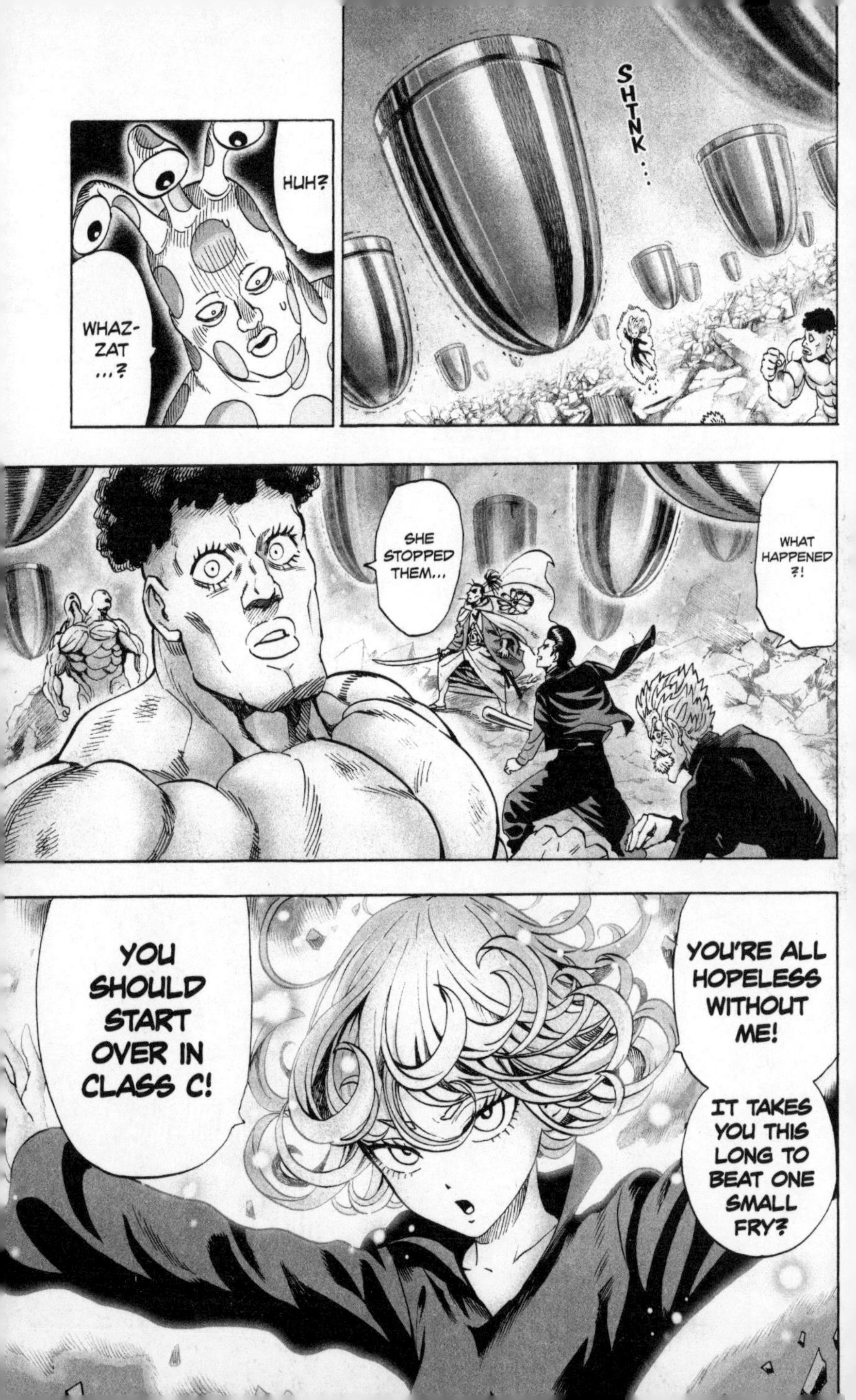
SHTNK...
HUH?
WHAZ-ZAT ...?
WHAT HAPPENED ?!
SHE STOPPED THEM...
YOU'RE ALL HOPELESS WITHOUT ME!
IT TAKES YOU THIS LONG TO BEAT ONE SMALL FRY?
YOU SHOULD START OVER IN CLASS C!

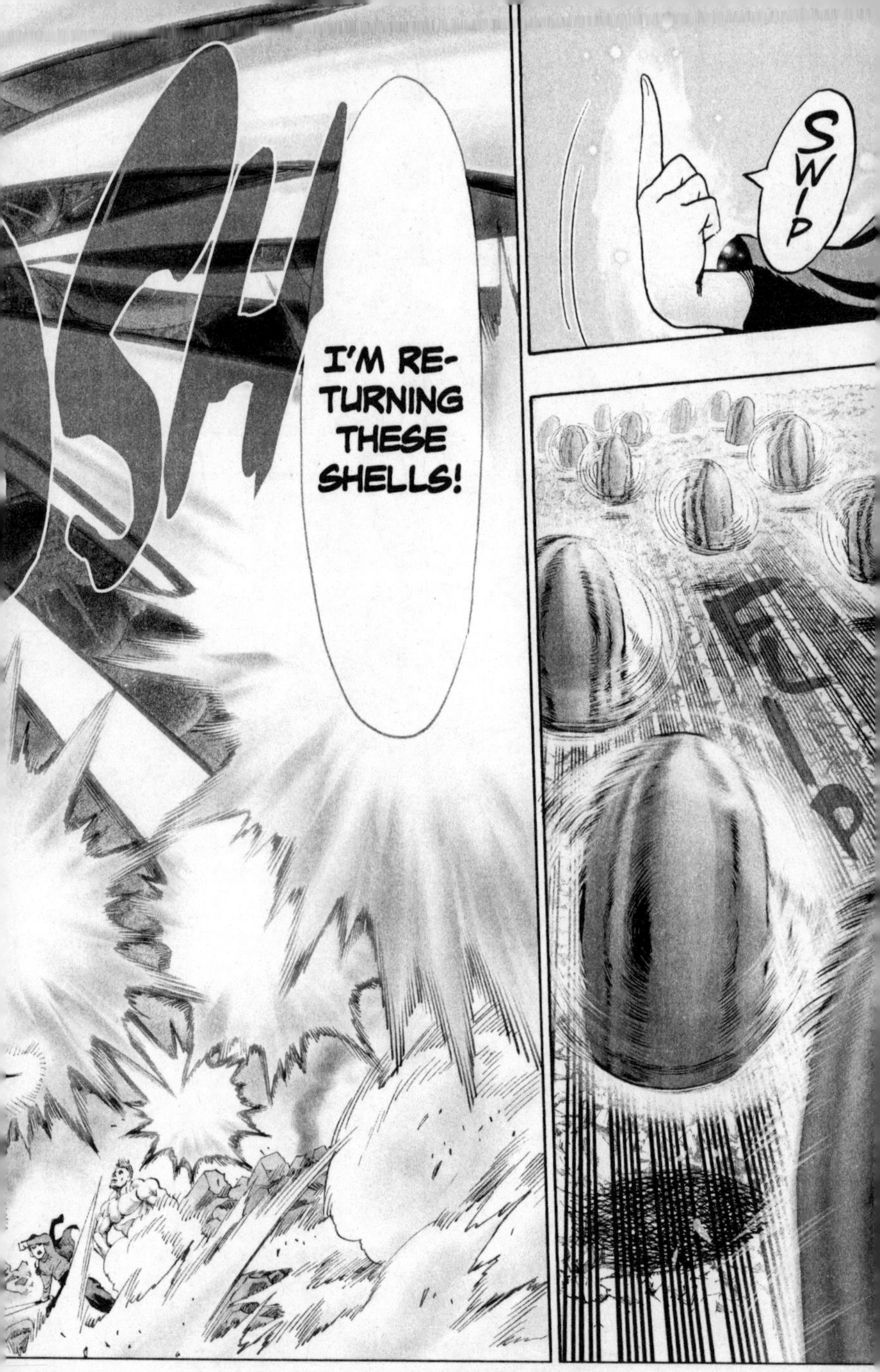
SWIP
FLIP
I'M RE-TURNING THESE SHELLS!

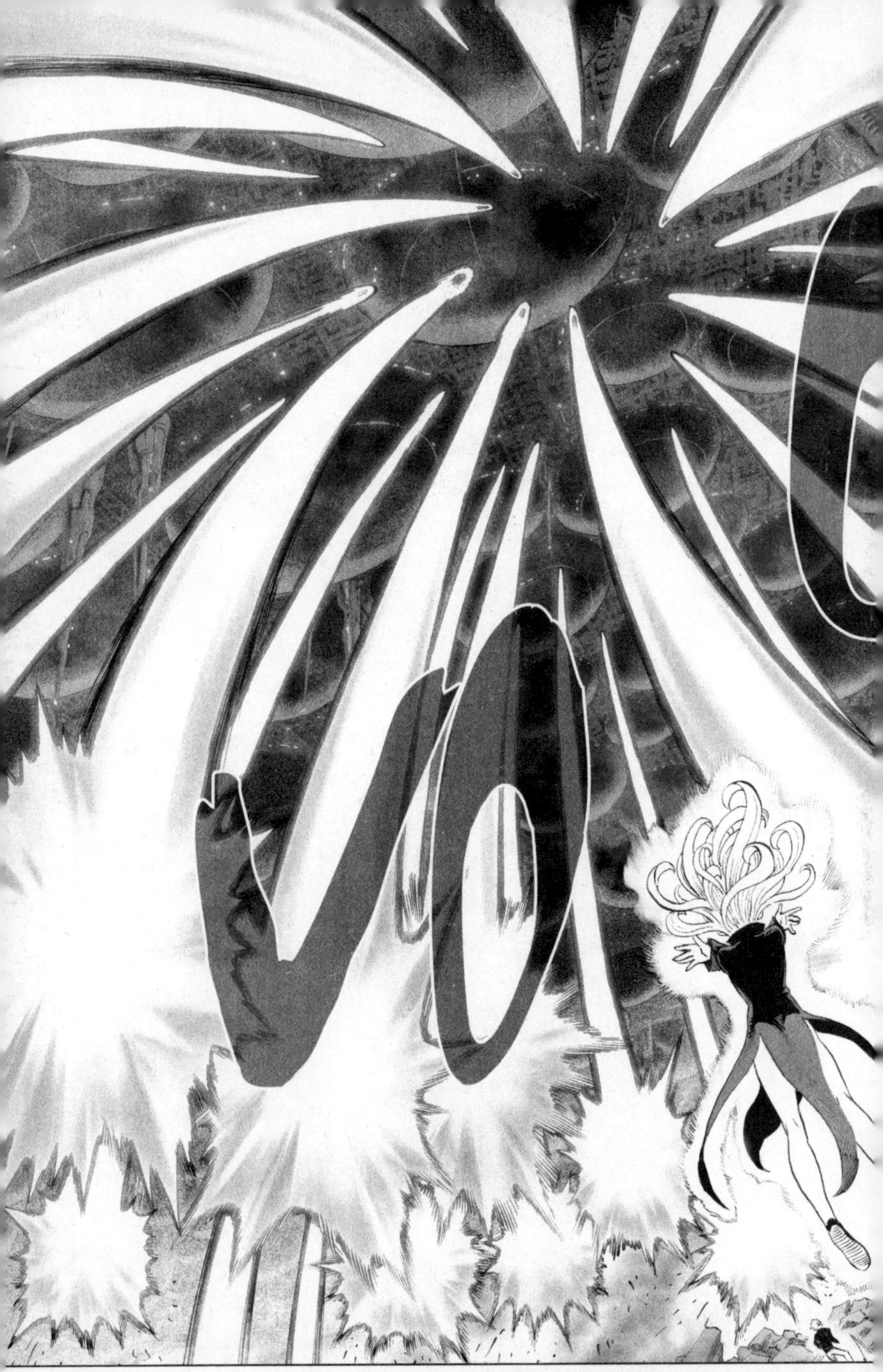

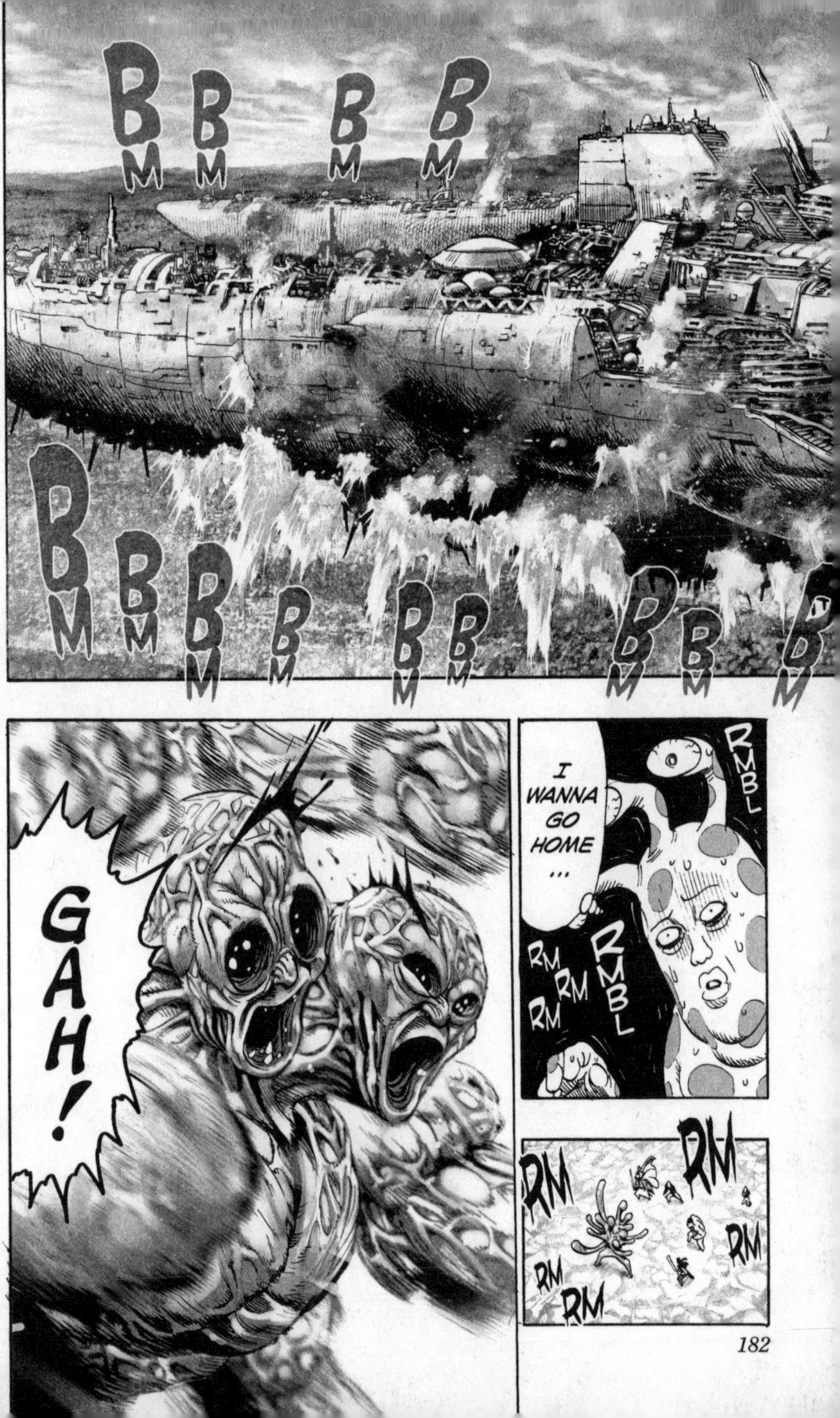
BM BM BM BM
BM BM BM BM BM BM BM BM BM BM
RMBL
I WANNA GO HOME ...
RMBL
RM RM RM
RM RM
RM RM RM
GAH!

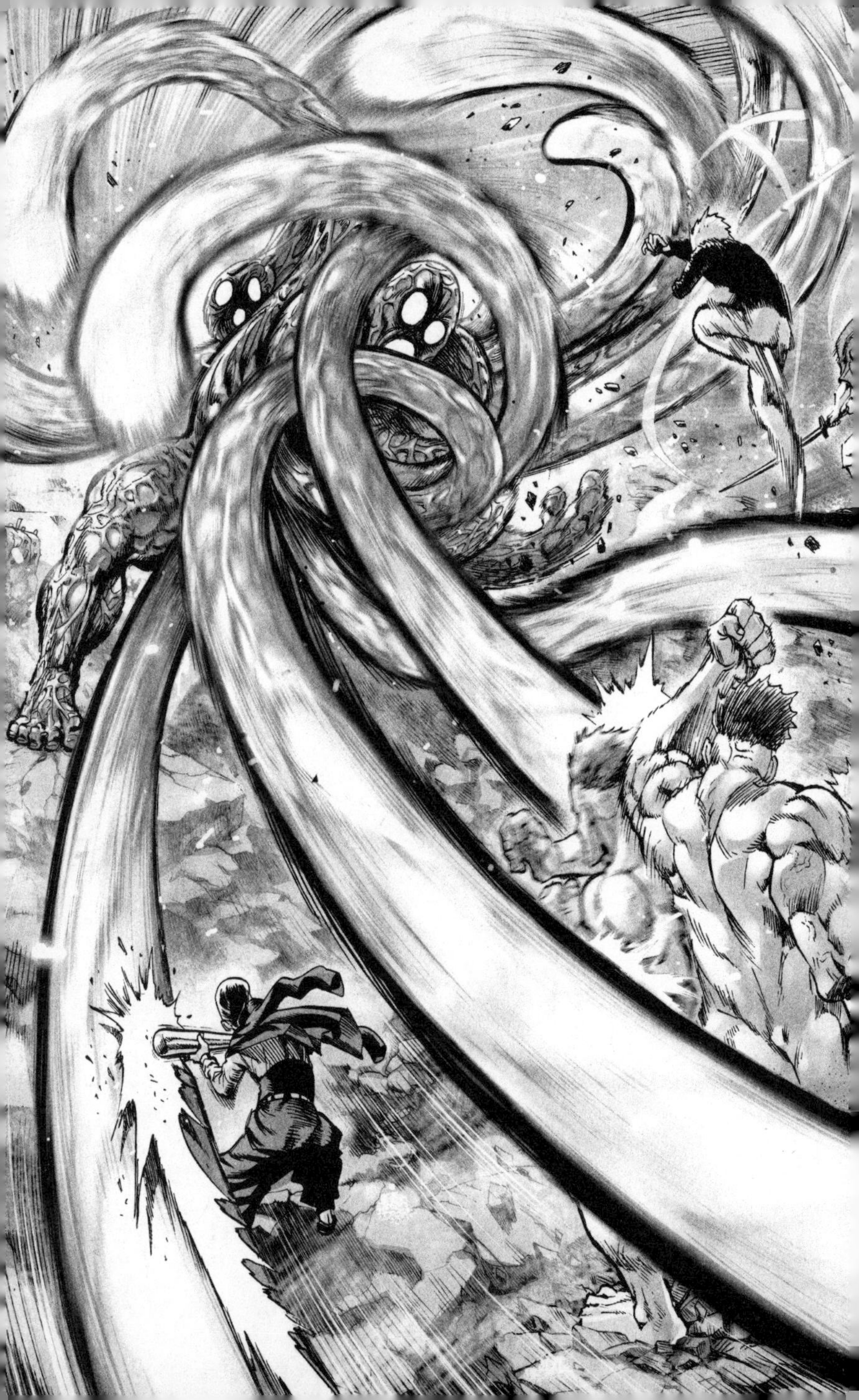

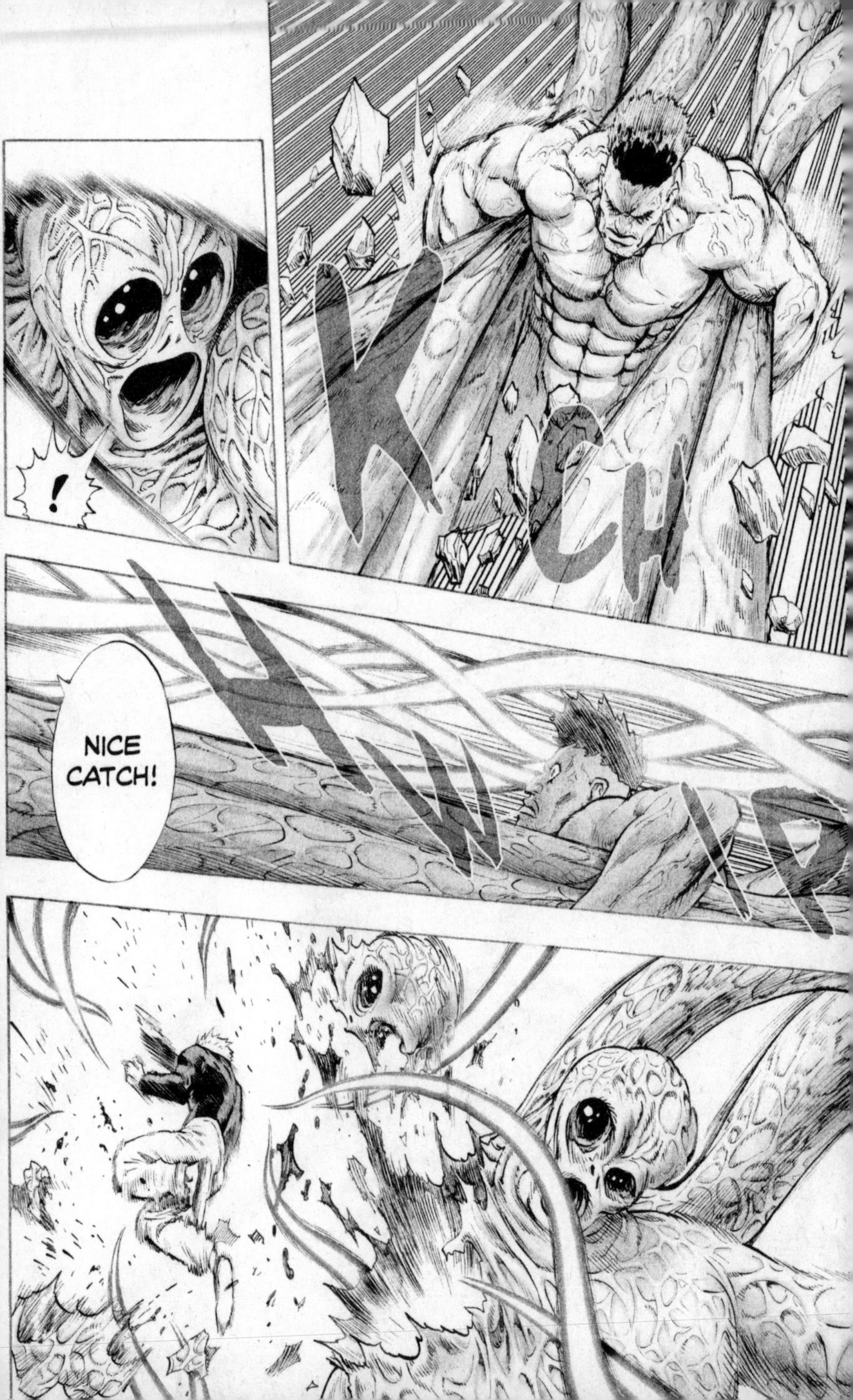
!
NICE CATCH!

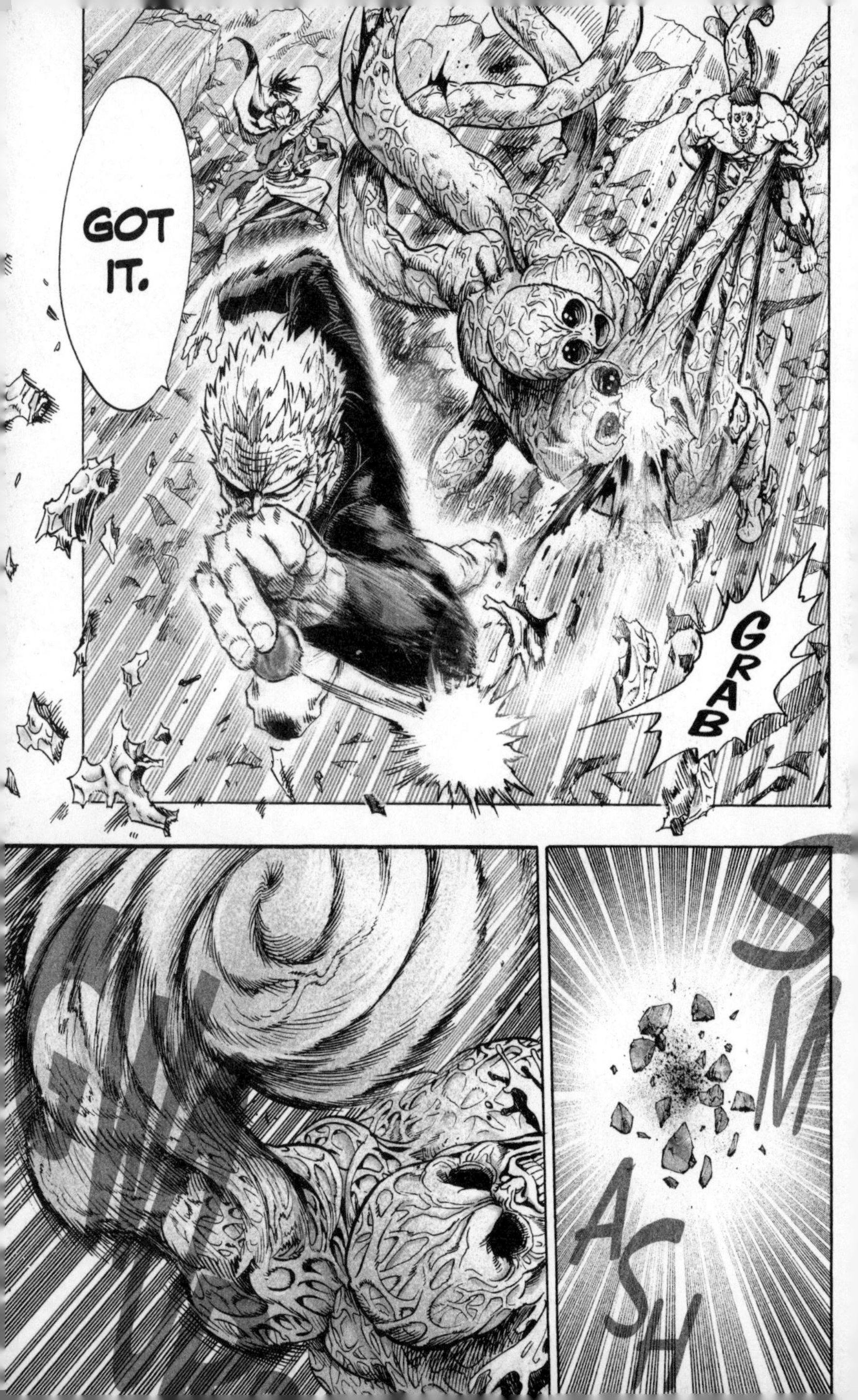
GOT IT.
GRAB
SMASH

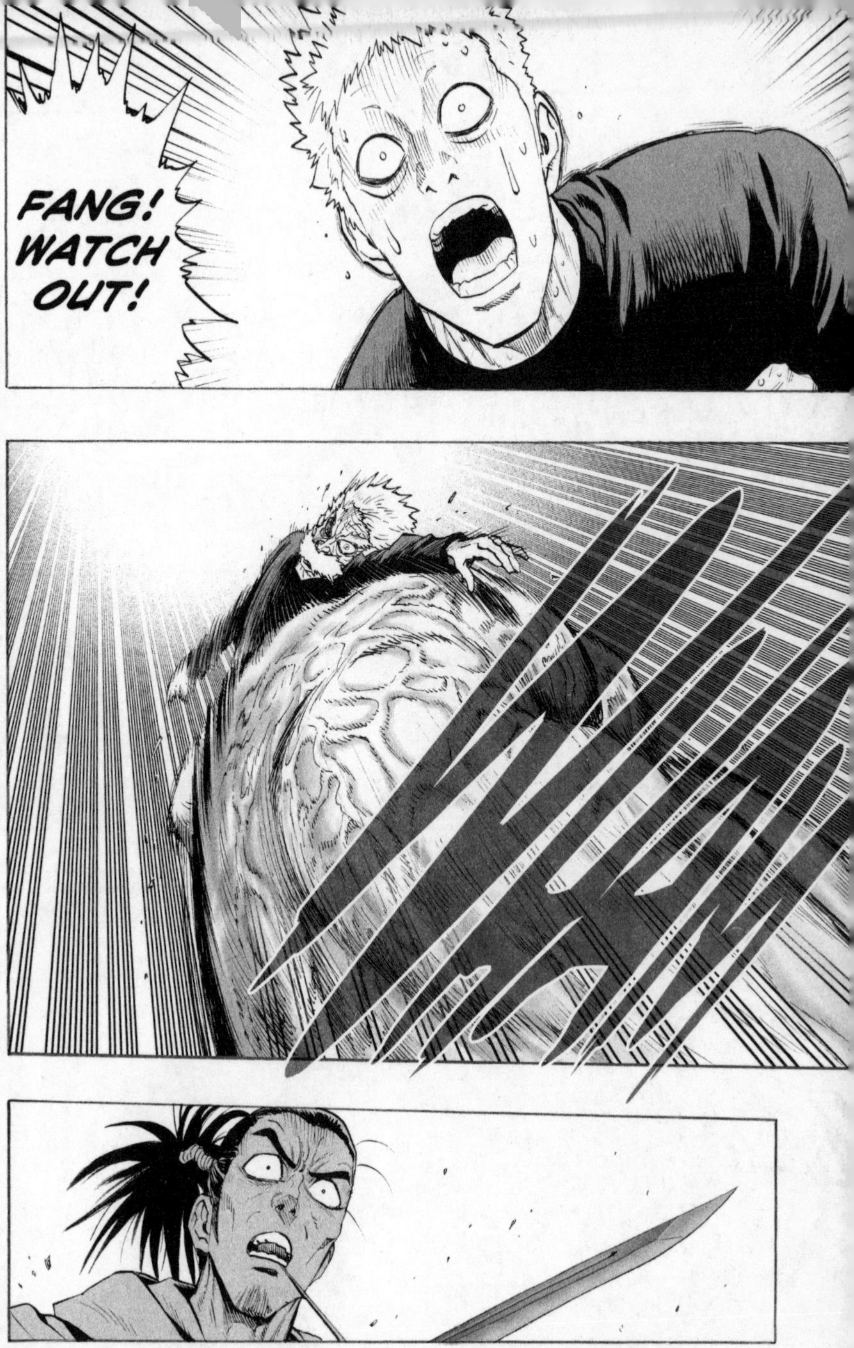
FANG! WATCH OUT!

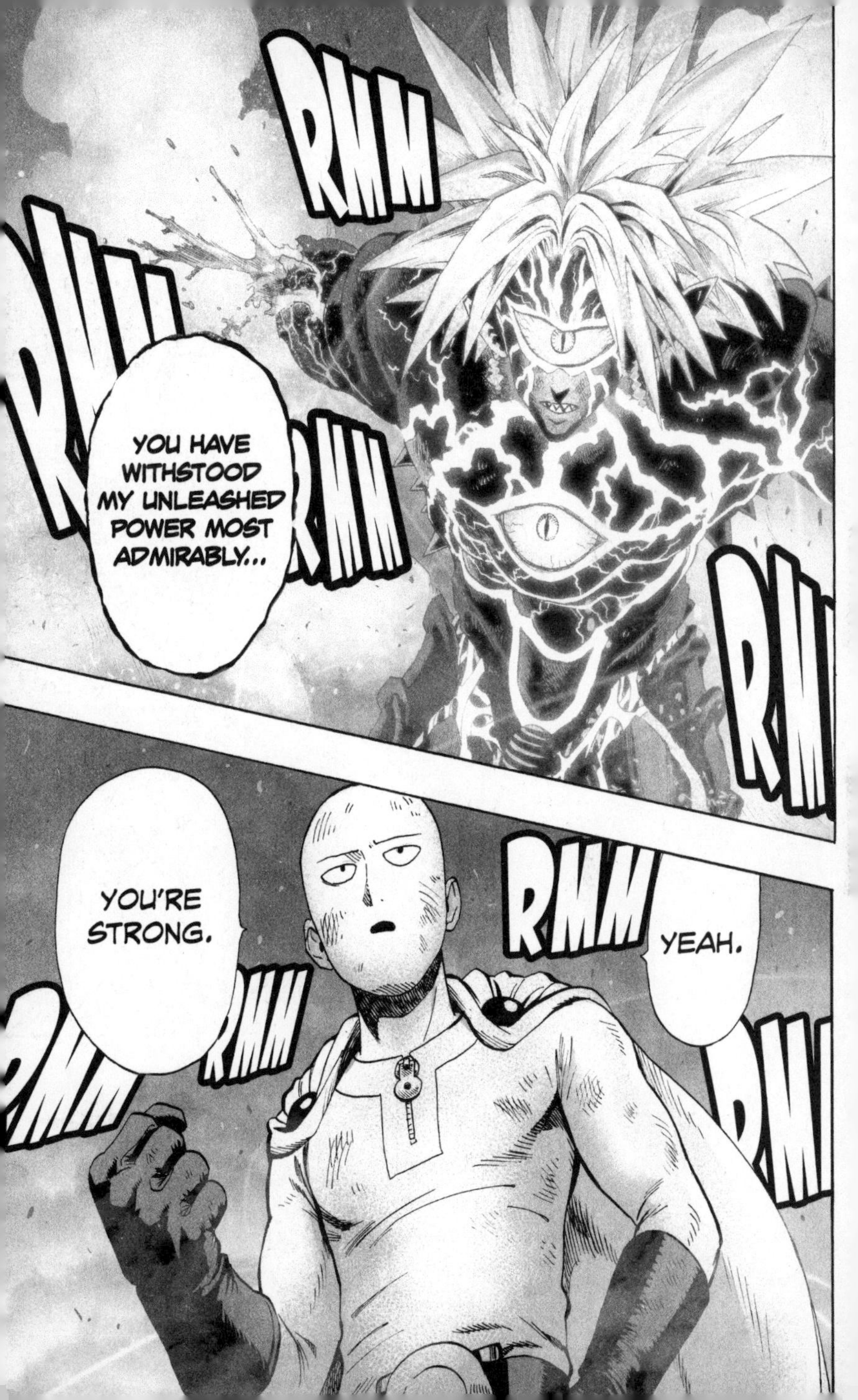
RMM
RMM
RMM
YOU HAVE WITHSTOOD MY UNLEASHED POWER MOST ADMIRABLY...
RMM
YOU'RE STRONG.
YEAH.
RMM
RMM

BONUS

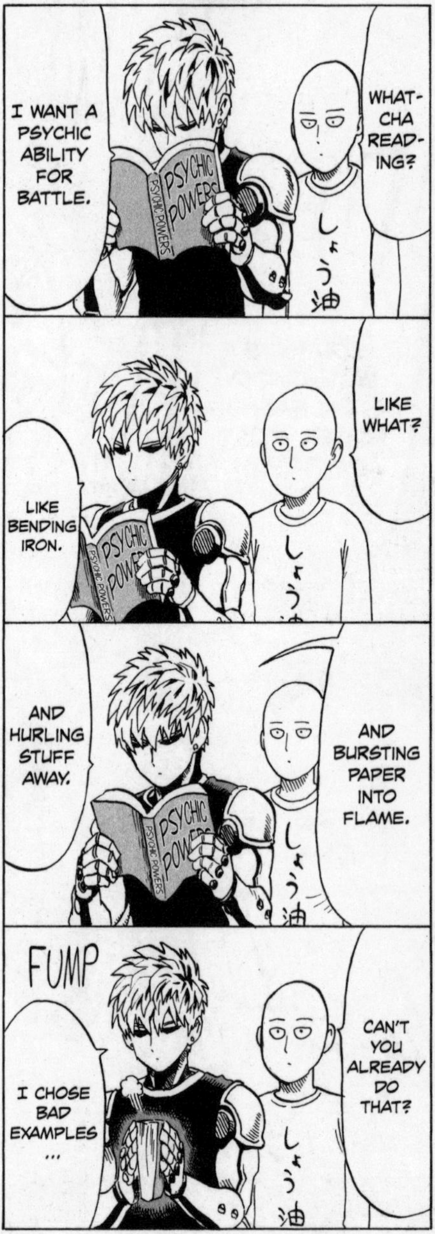
WHATCHA READING?
I WANT A PSYCHIC ABILITY FOR BATTLE.
PSYCHIC POWERS
しょう油
LIKE WHAT?
LIKE BENDING IRON.
PSYCHIC POWERS
AND BURSTING PAPER INTO FLAME.
AND HURLING STUFF AWAY.
PSYCHIC POWERS
しょう油
CAN'T YOU ALREADY DO THAT?
FUMP
I CHOSE BAD EXAMPLES ...
しょう油

BONUS MANGA: SALMON

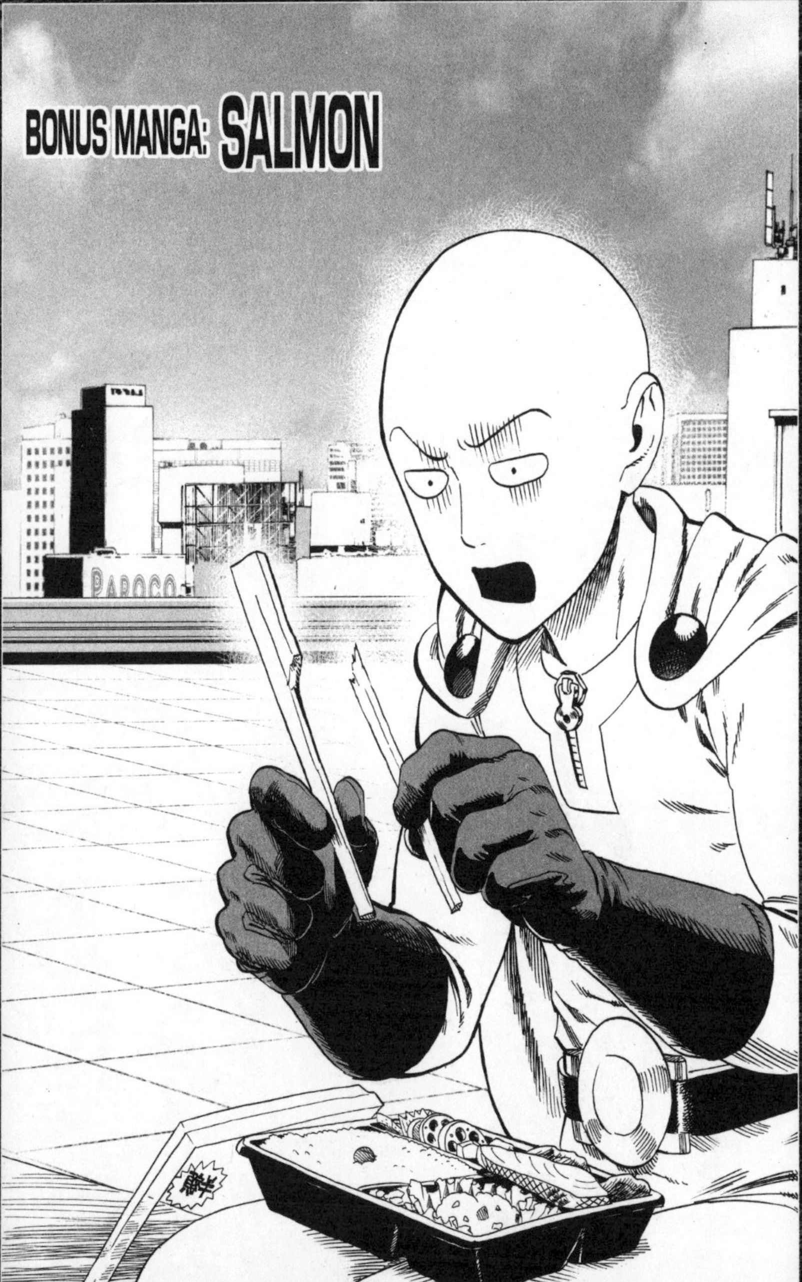
PAROCO
鮭

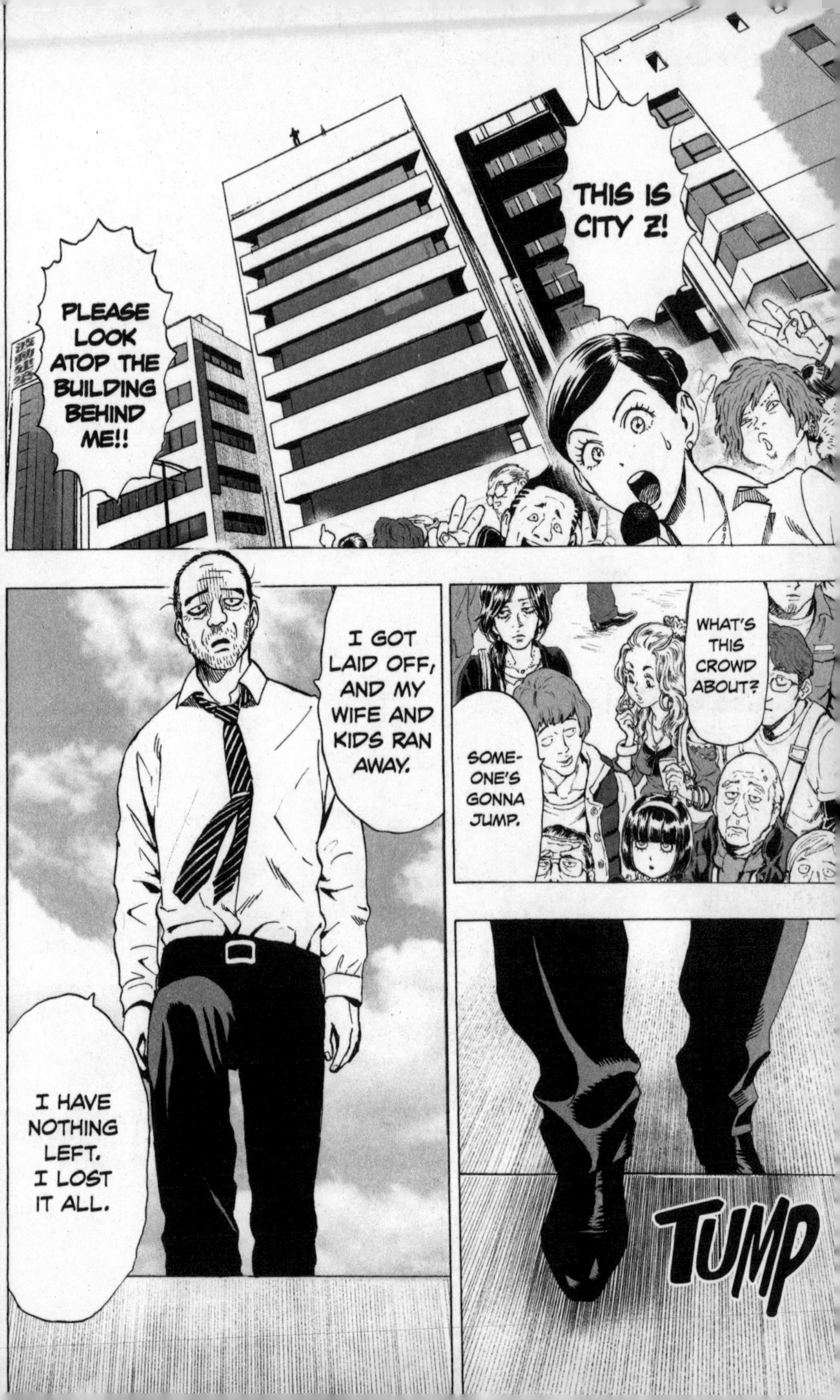
THIS IS CITY Z!
PLEASE LOOK ATOP THE BUILDING BEHIND ME!!
WHAT'S THIS CROWD ABOUT?
SOME-ONE'S GONNA JUMP.
TUMP
I GOT LAID OFF, AND MY WIFE AND KIDS RAN AWAY.
I HAVE NOTHING LEFT. I LOST IT ALL.

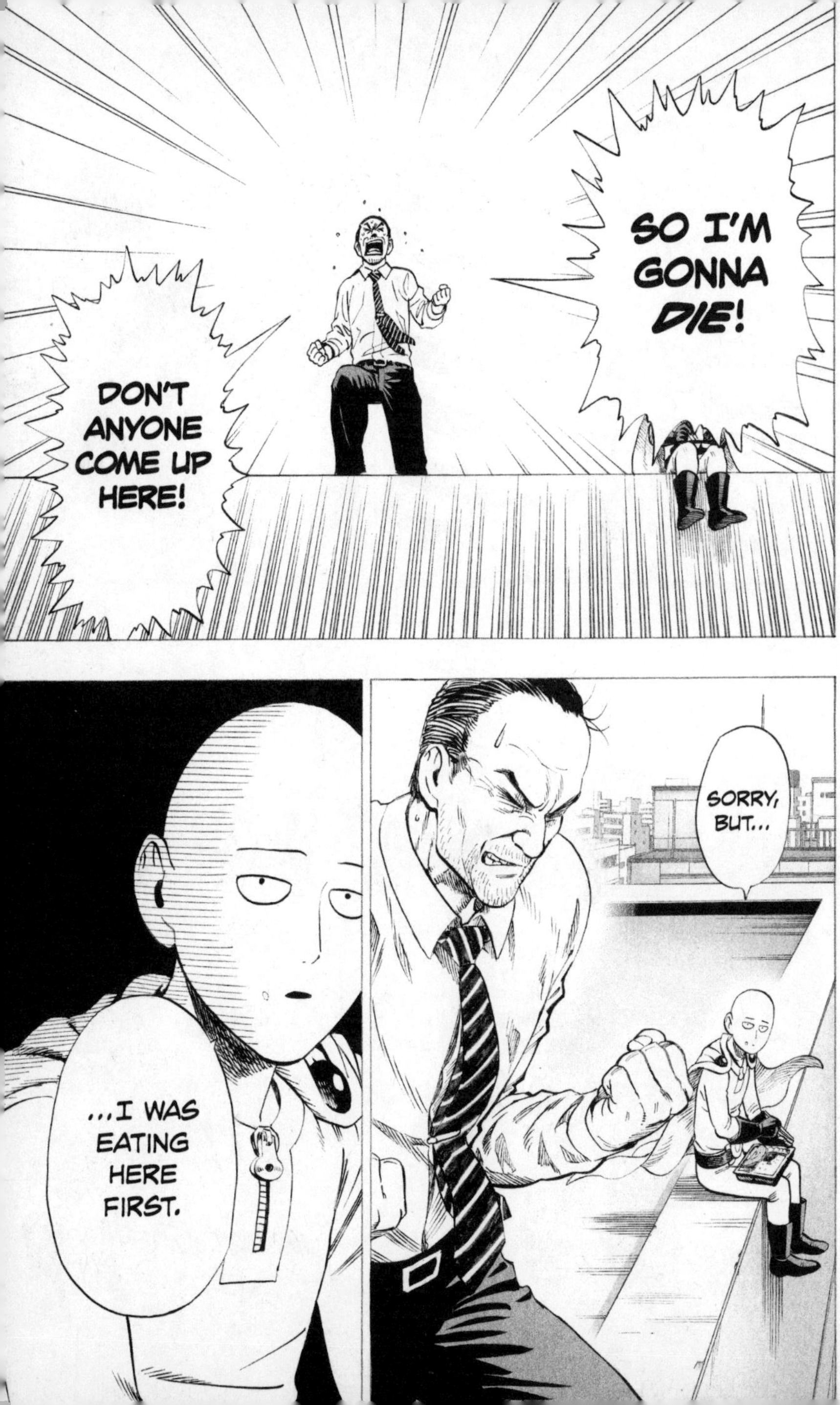
SO I'M GONNA DIE!
DON'T ANYONE COME UP HERE!
SORRY, BUT...
...I WAS EATING HERE FIRST.

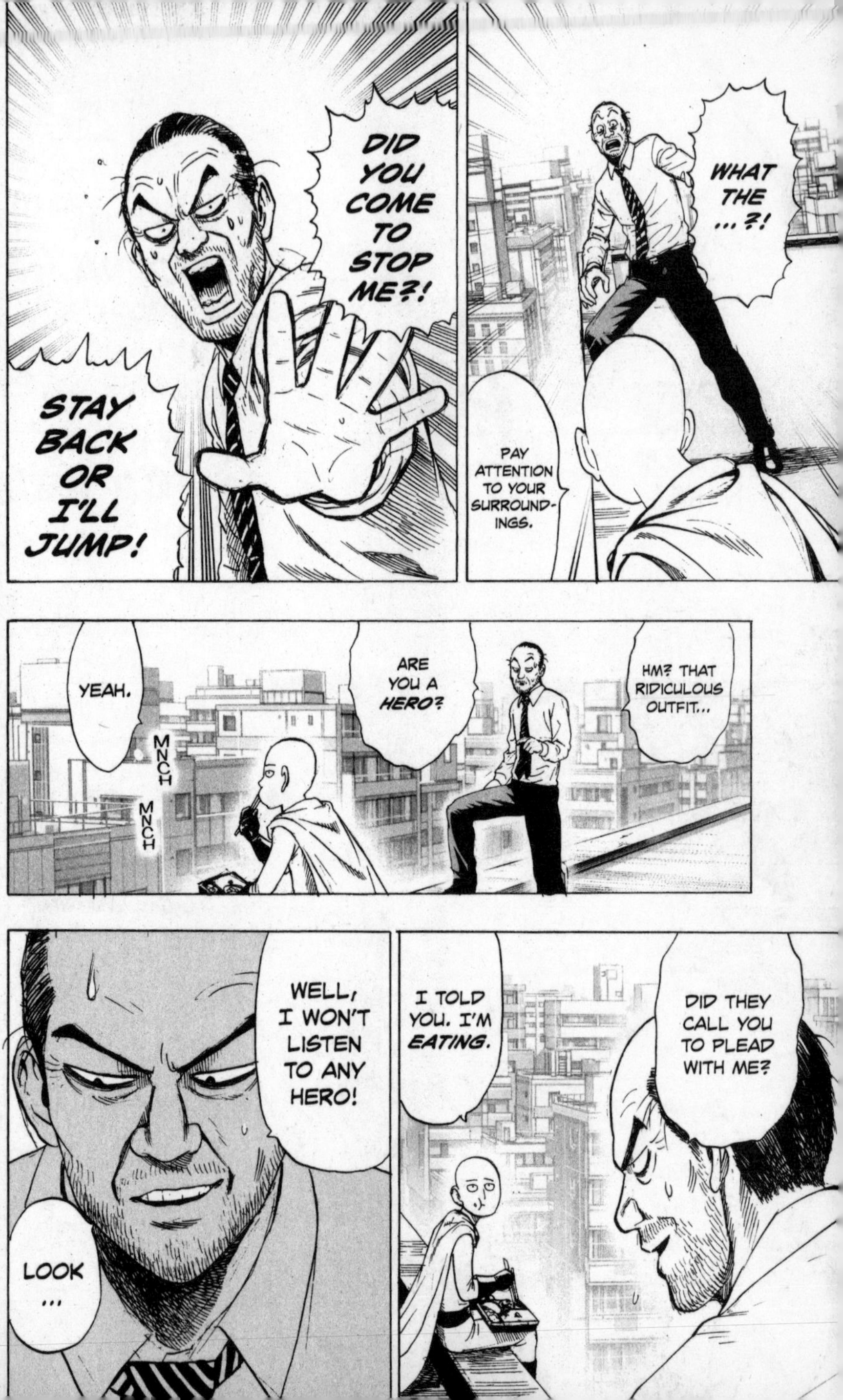
WHAT THE ...?!
PAY ATTENTION TO YOUR SURROUND-INGS.
DID YOU COME TO STOP ME?!
STAY BACK OR I'LL JUMP!
HM? THAT RIDICULOUS OUTFIT...
ARE YOU A *HERO*?
YEAH.
MNCH
MNCH
DID THEY CALL YOU TO PLEAD WITH ME?
I TOLD YOU. I'M *EATING*.
WELL, I WON'T LISTEN TO ANY HERO!
LOOK ...

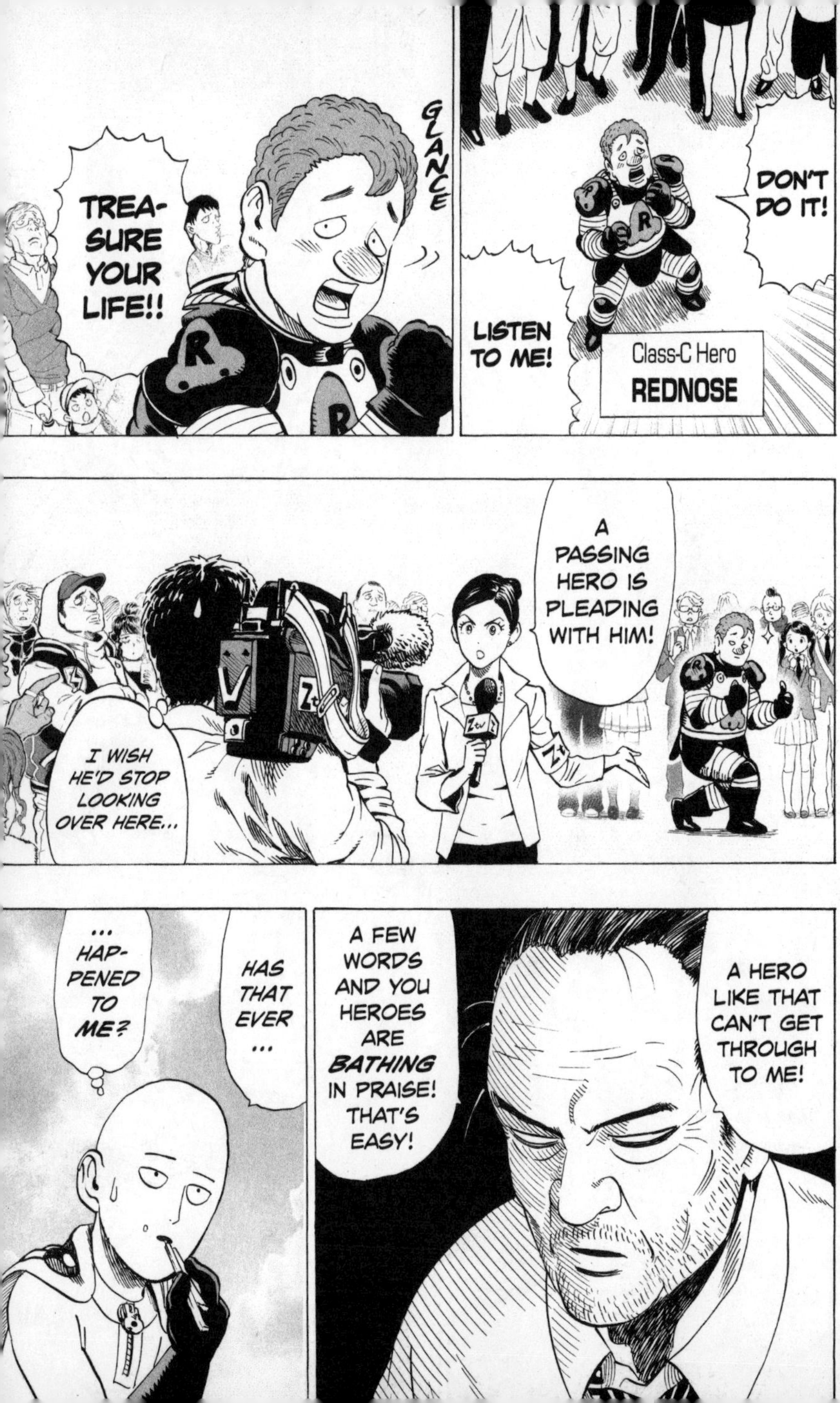
DON'T DO IT!
LISTEN TO ME!
Class-C Hero
REDNOSE
GLANCE
TREA-SURE YOUR LIFE!!
A PASSING HERO IS PLEADING WITH HIM!
I WISH HE'D STOP LOOKING OVER HERE...
A HERO LIKE THAT CAN'T GET THROUGH TO ME!
A FEW WORDS AND YOU HEROES ARE BATHING IN PRAISE! THAT'S EASY!
HAS THAT EVER ...
... HAP-PENED TO ME?

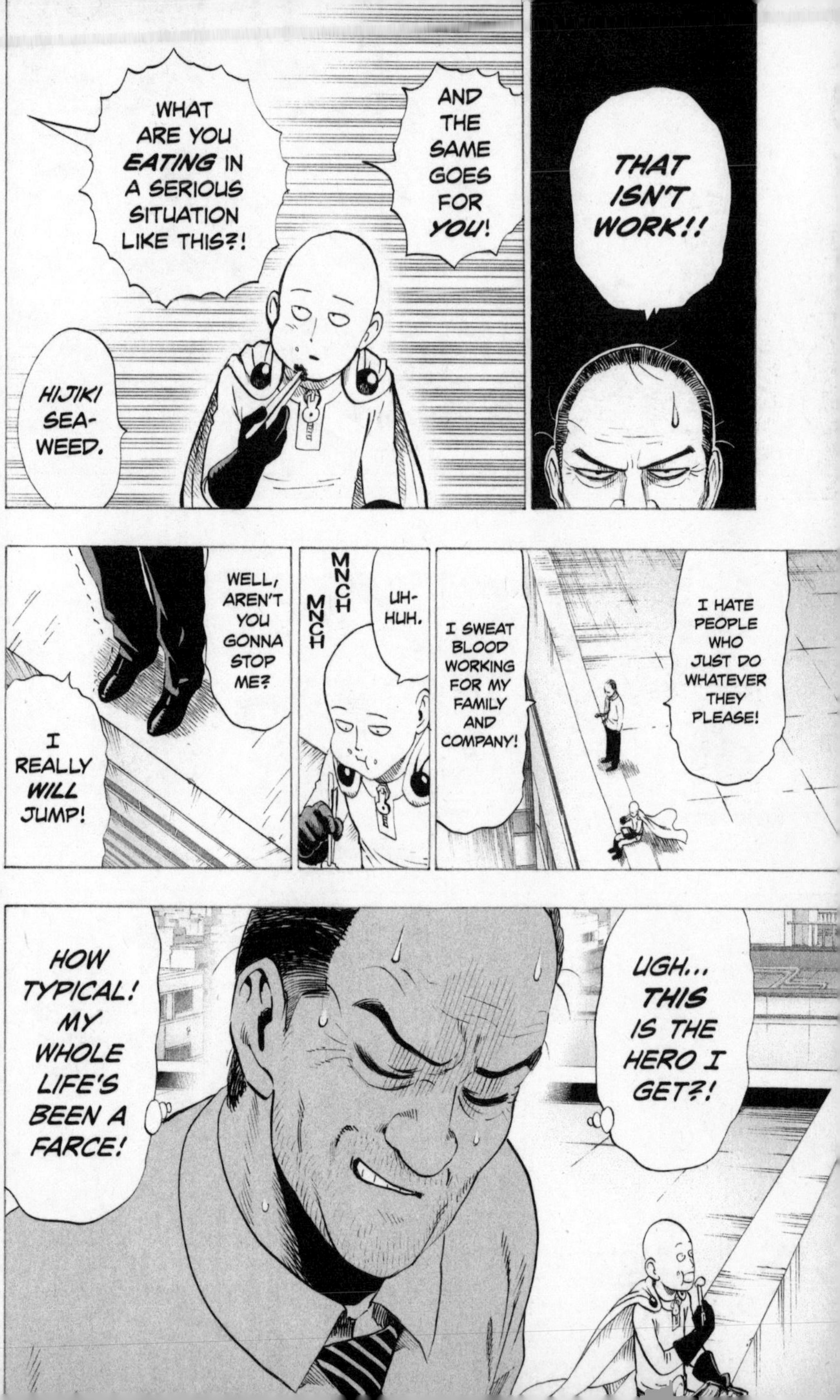
THAT ISN'T WORK!!
AND THE SAME GOES FOR YOU!
WHAT ARE YOU EATING IN A SERIOUS SITUATION LIKE THIS?!
HIJIKI SEAWEED.
I HATE PEOPLE WHO JUST DO WHATEVER THEY PLEASE!
I SWEAT BLOOD WORKING FOR MY FAMILY AND COMPANY!
UH-HUH.
MNCH
MNCH
WELL, AREN'T YOU GONNA STOP ME?
I REALLY WILL JUMP!
UGH... THIS IS THE HERO I GET?!
HOW TYPICAL! MY WHOLE LIFE'S BEEN A FARCE!

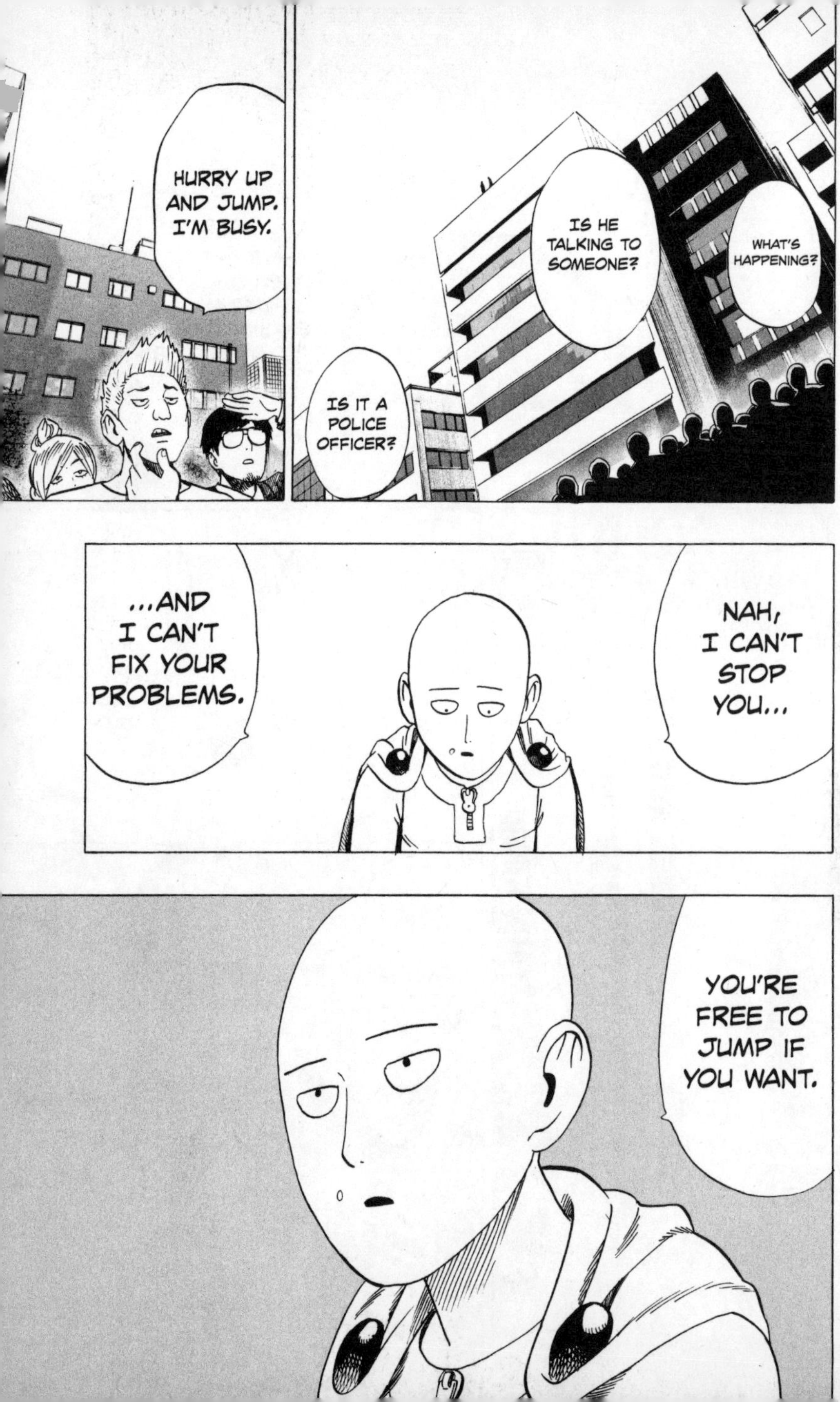
WHAT'S HAPPENING?
IS HE TALKING TO SOMEONE?
IS IT A POLICE OFFICER?
HURRY UP AND JUMP. I'M BUSY.
NAH, I CAN'T STOP YOU...
...AND I CAN'T FIX YOUR PROBLEMS.
YOU'RE FREE TO JUMP IF YOU WANT.

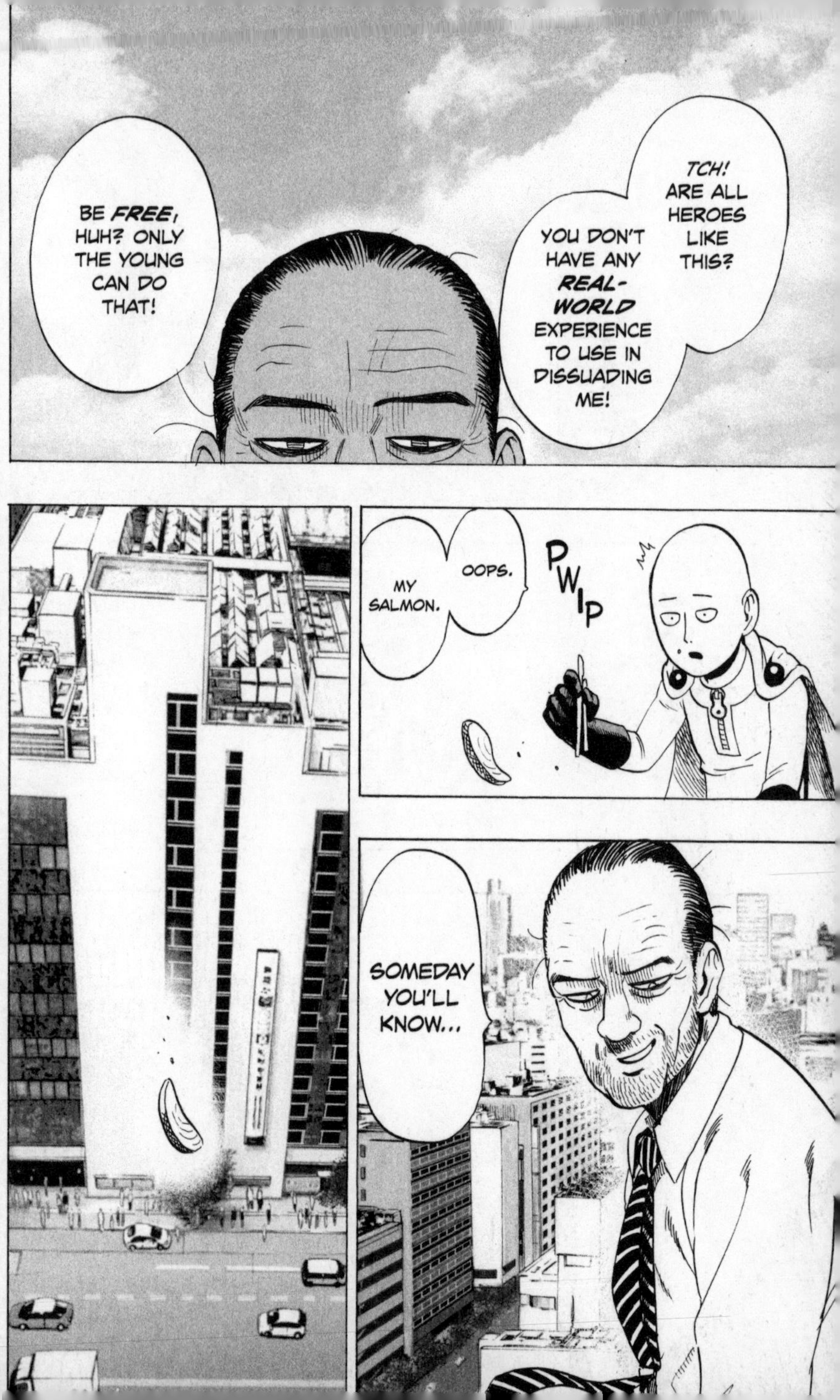
TCH! ARE ALL HEROES LIKE THIS?
YOU DON'T HAVE ANY *REAL-WORLD* EXPERIENCE TO USE IN DISSUADING ME!
BE *FREE*, HUH? ONLY THE YOUNG CAN DO THAT!
PWIP
OOPS.
MY SALMON.
SOMEDAY YOU'LL KNOW...

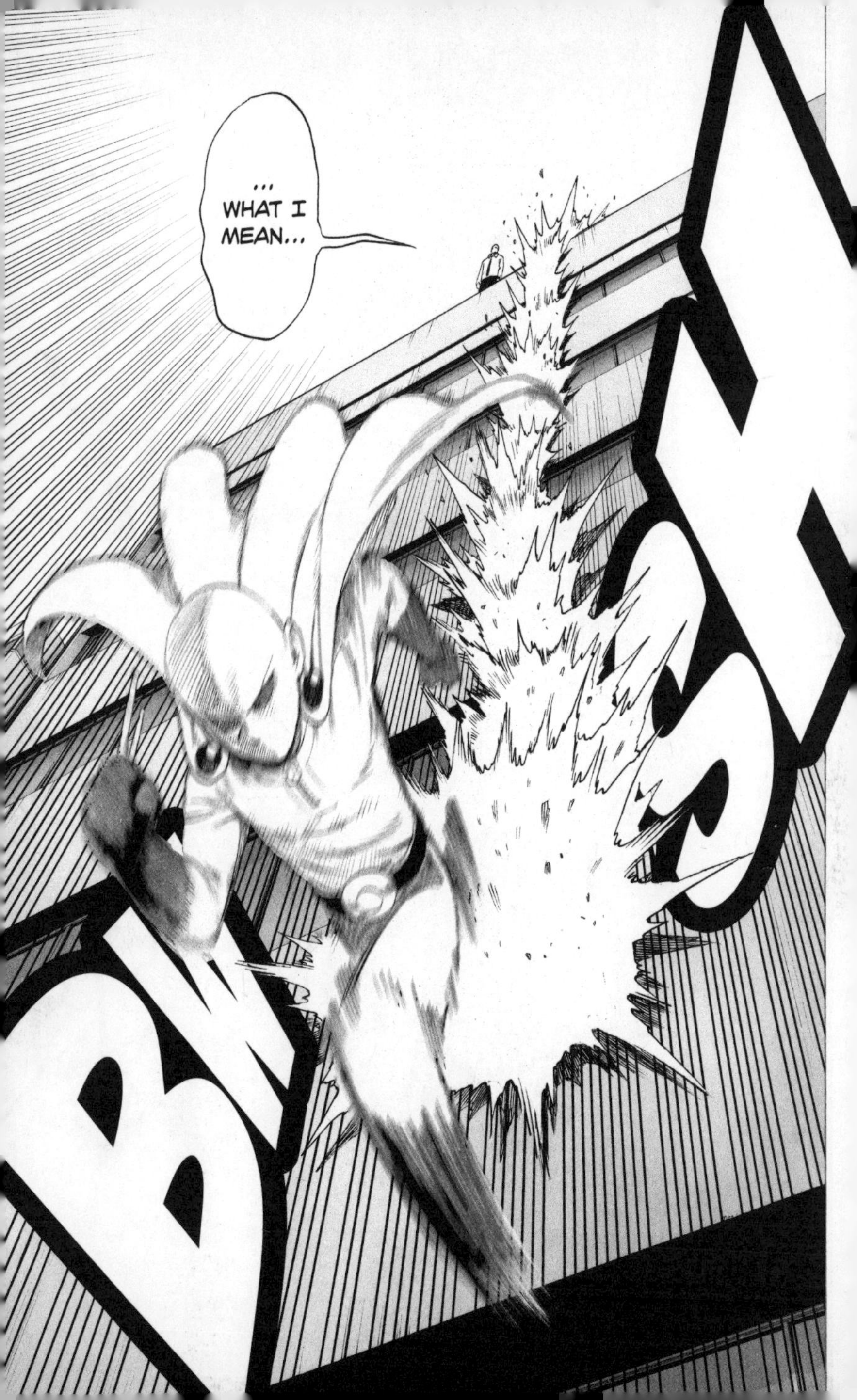
... WHAT I MEAN...

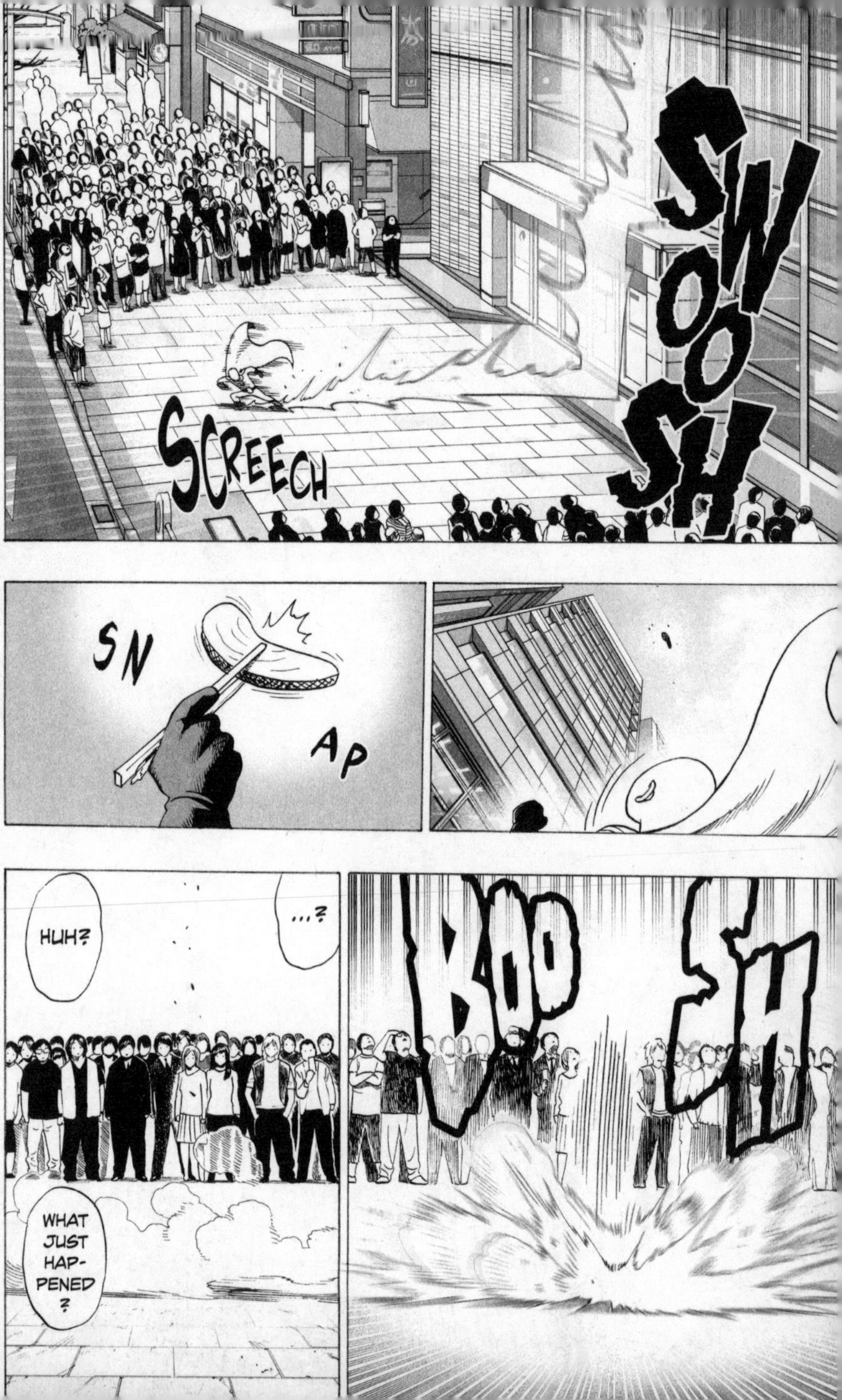
SWOOSH
SCREECH
SNAP
BOOSH
...?
HUH?
WHAT JUST HAP-PENED?

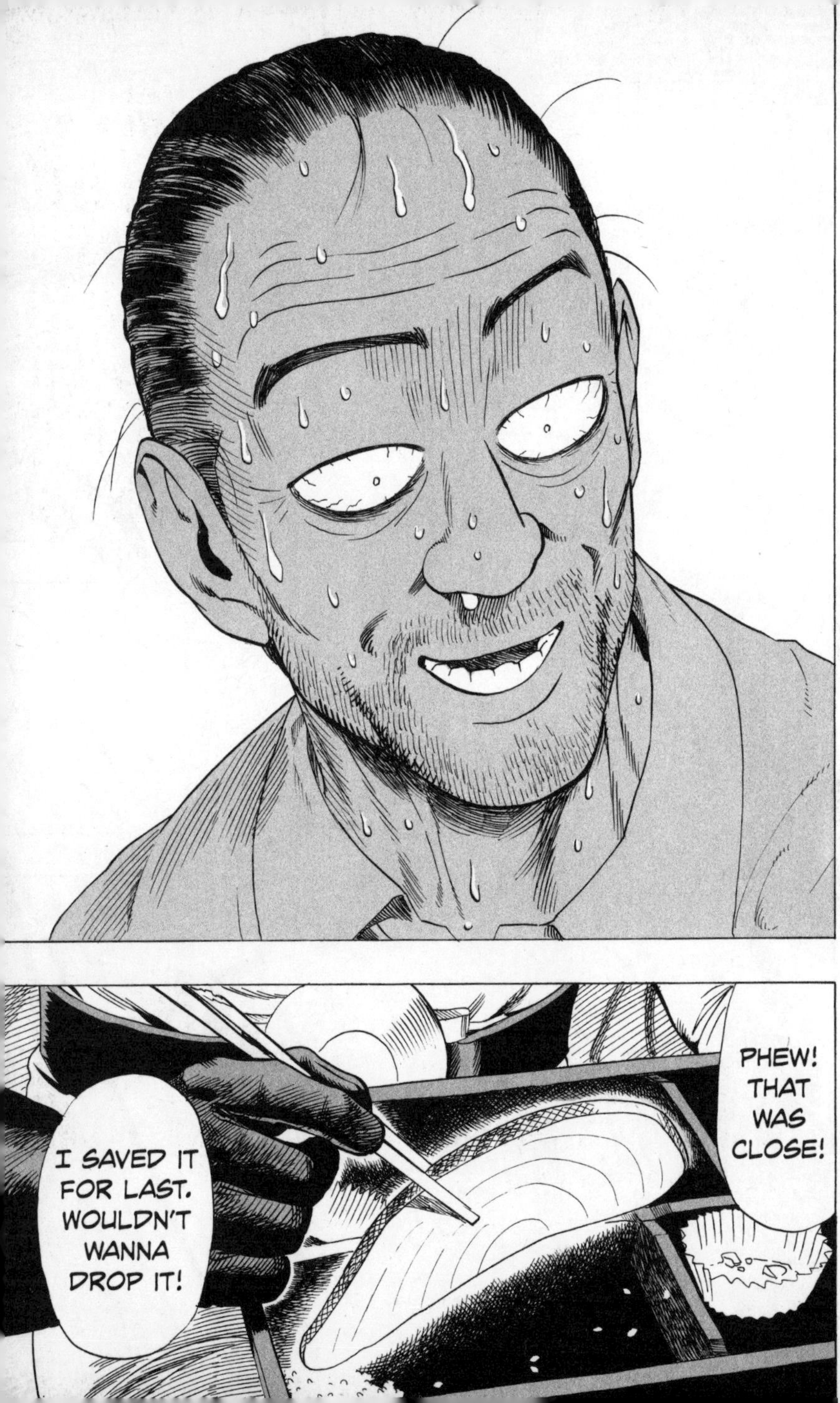
PHEW! THAT WAS CLOSE!
I SAVED IT FOR LAST. WOULDN'T WANNA DROP IT!

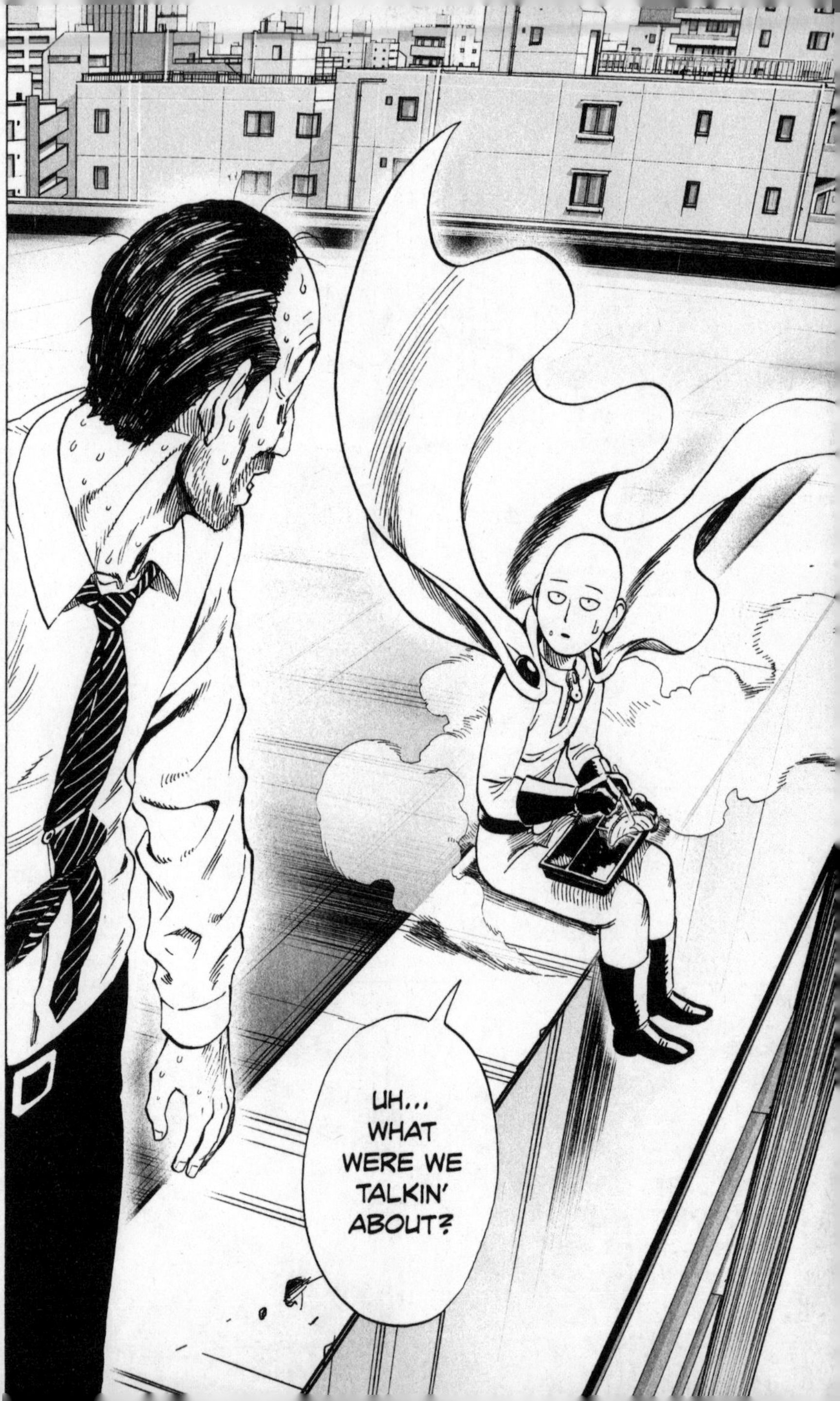
UH... WHAT WERE WE TALKIN' ABOUT?

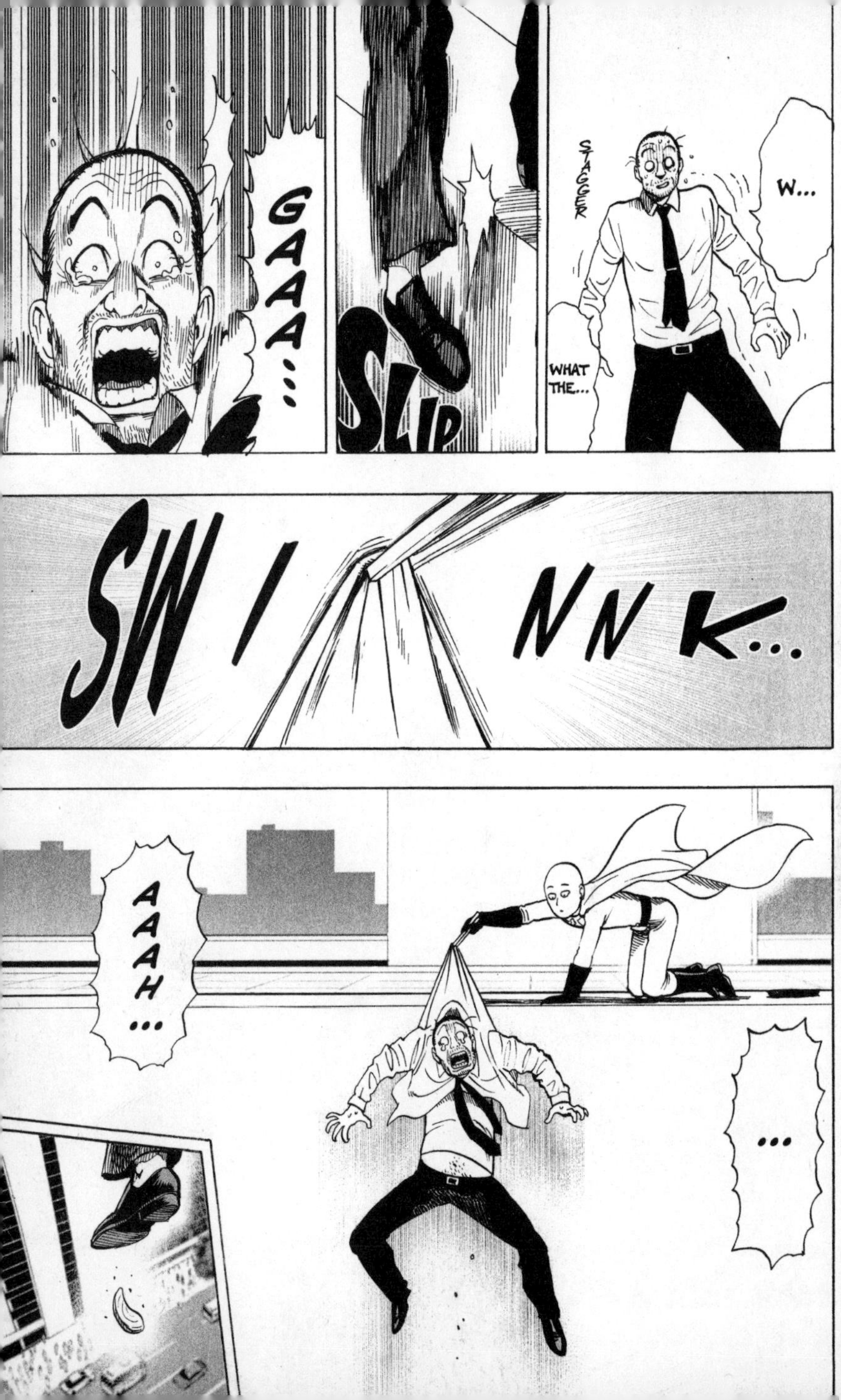

W...
STAGGER
WHAT THE...
SLIP
GAAAA...
SWINNNK...
AAAH...
...

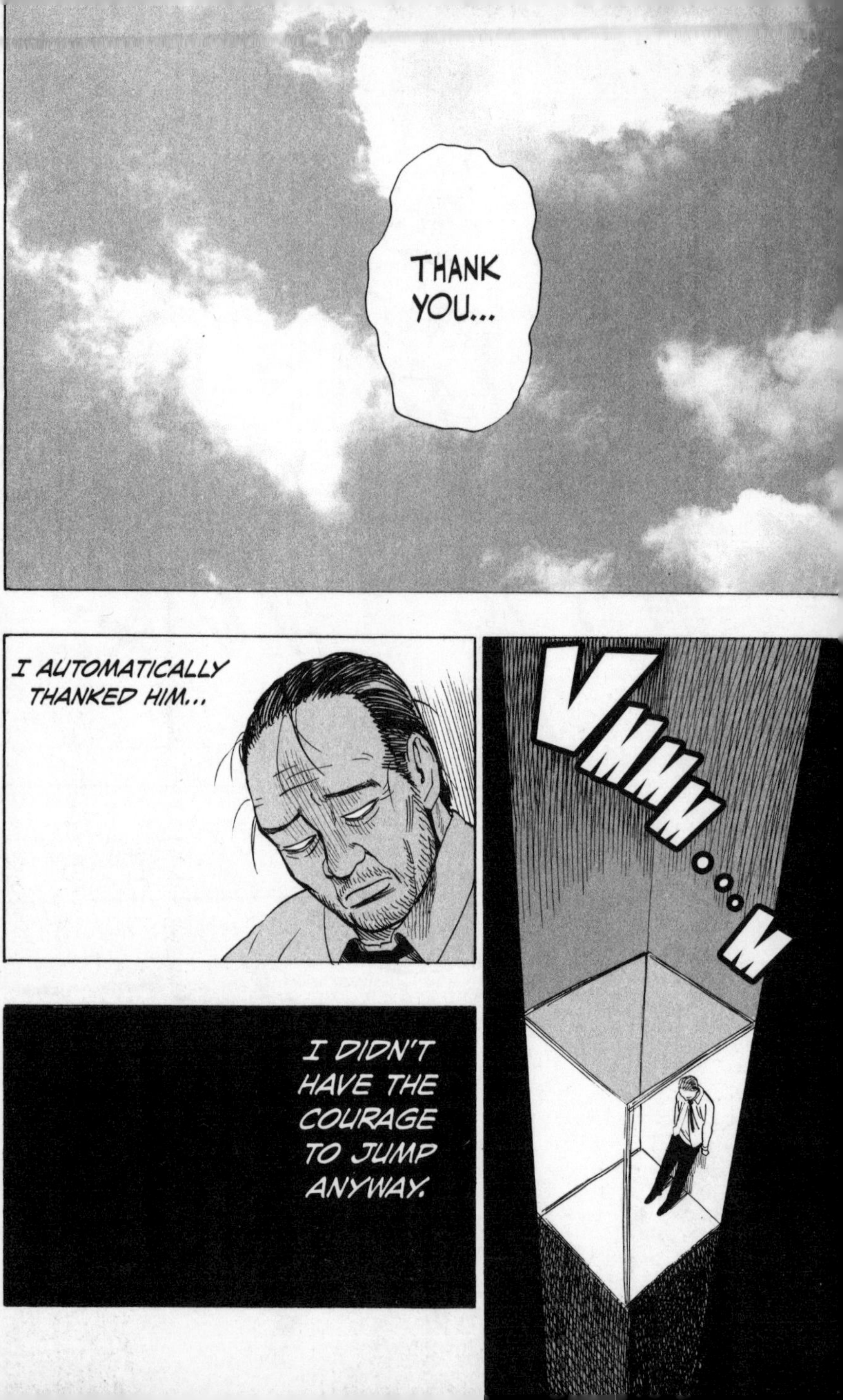
THANK YOU...
VMMM...M
I AUTOMATICALLY THANKED HIM...
I DIDN'T HAVE THE COURAGE TO JUMP ANYWAY.

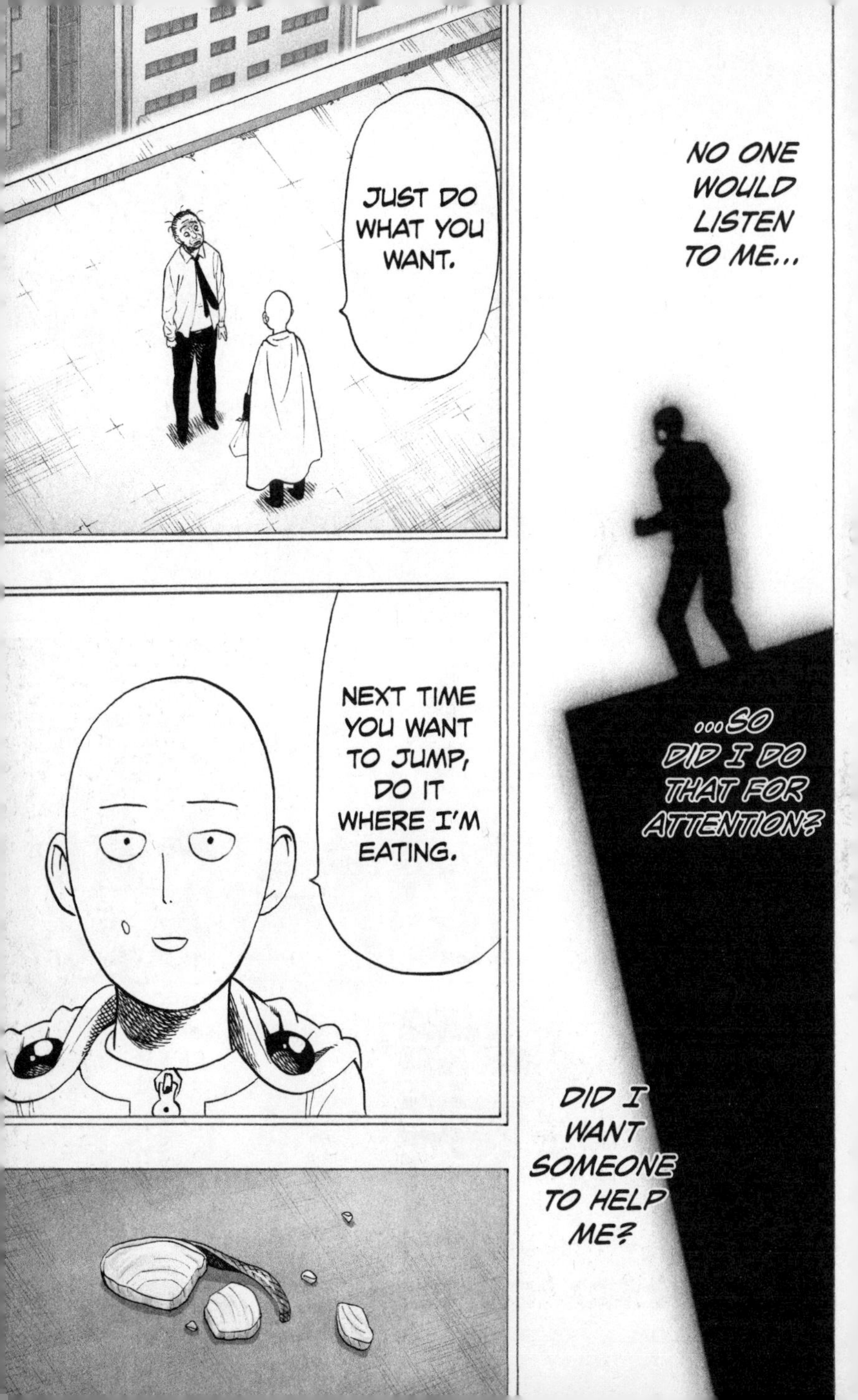
NO ONE WOULD LISTEN TO ME...
...SO DID I DO THAT FOR ATTENTION?
DID I WANT SOMEONE TO HELP ME?
JUST DO WHAT YOU WANT.
NEXT TIME YOU WANT TO JUMP, DO IT WHERE I'M EATING.

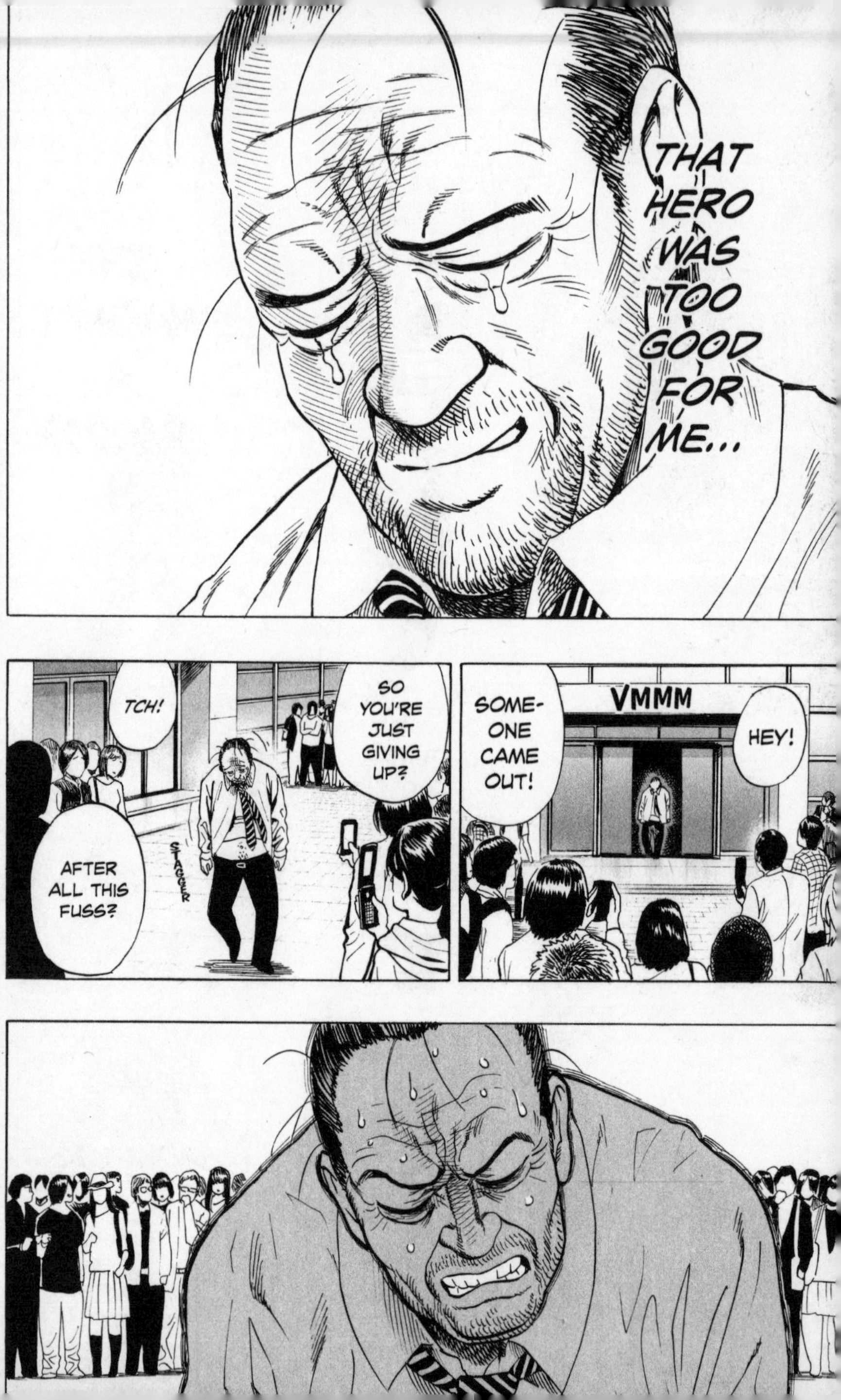
THAT HERO WAS TOO GOOD FOR ME...
HEY!
VMMM
SOME-ONE CAME OUT!
SO YOU'RE JUST GIVING UP?
TCH!
STAGGER
AFTER ALL THIS FUSS?

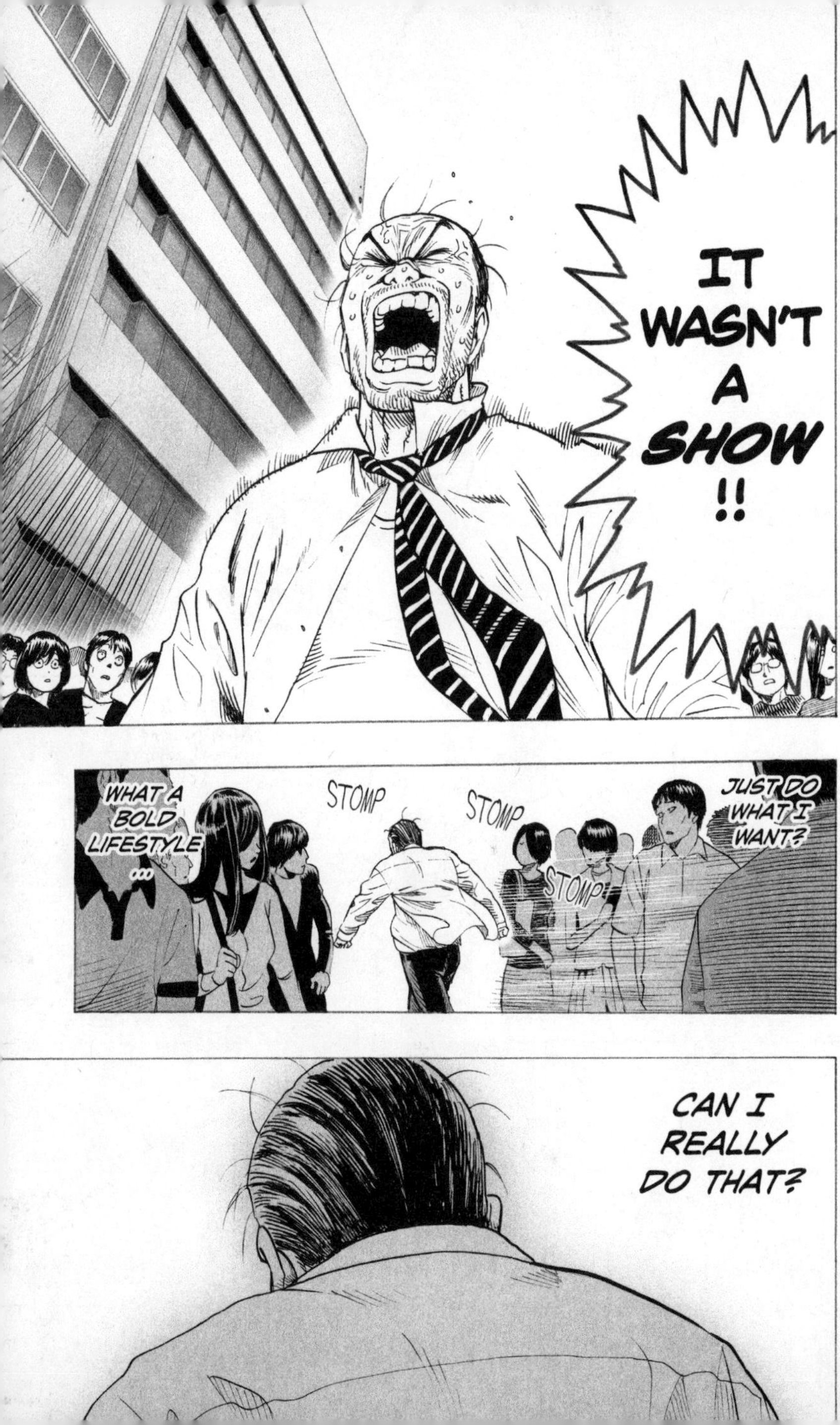
IT WASN'T A SHOW!!
JUST DO WHAT I WANT?
STOMP
STOMP
STOMP
WHAT A BOLD LIFESTYLE...
CAN I REALLY DO THAT?

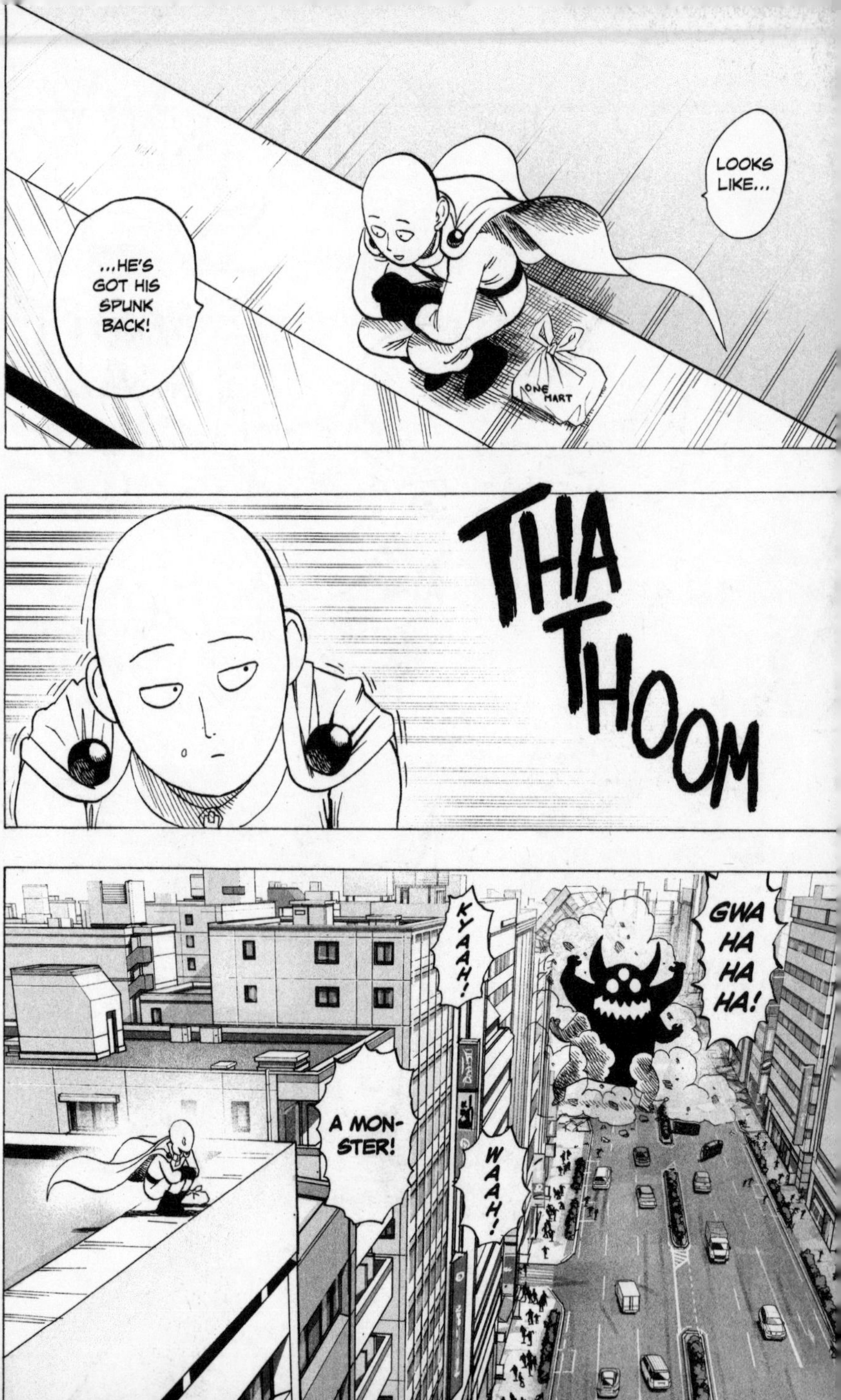
LOOKS LIKE...
...HE'S GOT HIS SPUNK BACK!
ONE MART
THA THOOM
GWA HA HA HA HA!
KYAAH!
A MON-STER!
WAAH!

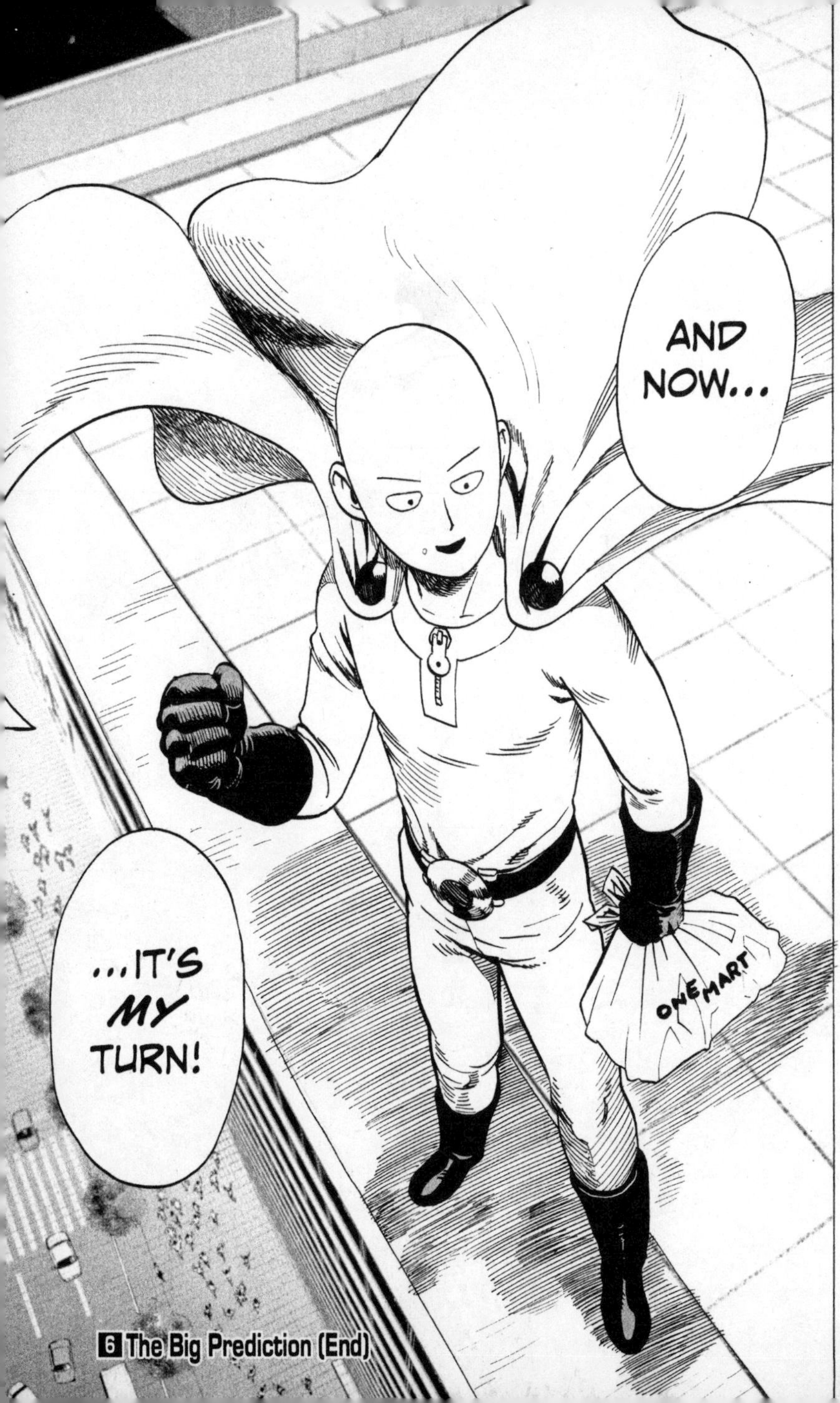
AND NOW...
...IT'S MY TURN!
ONEMART

6 The Big Prediction (End)

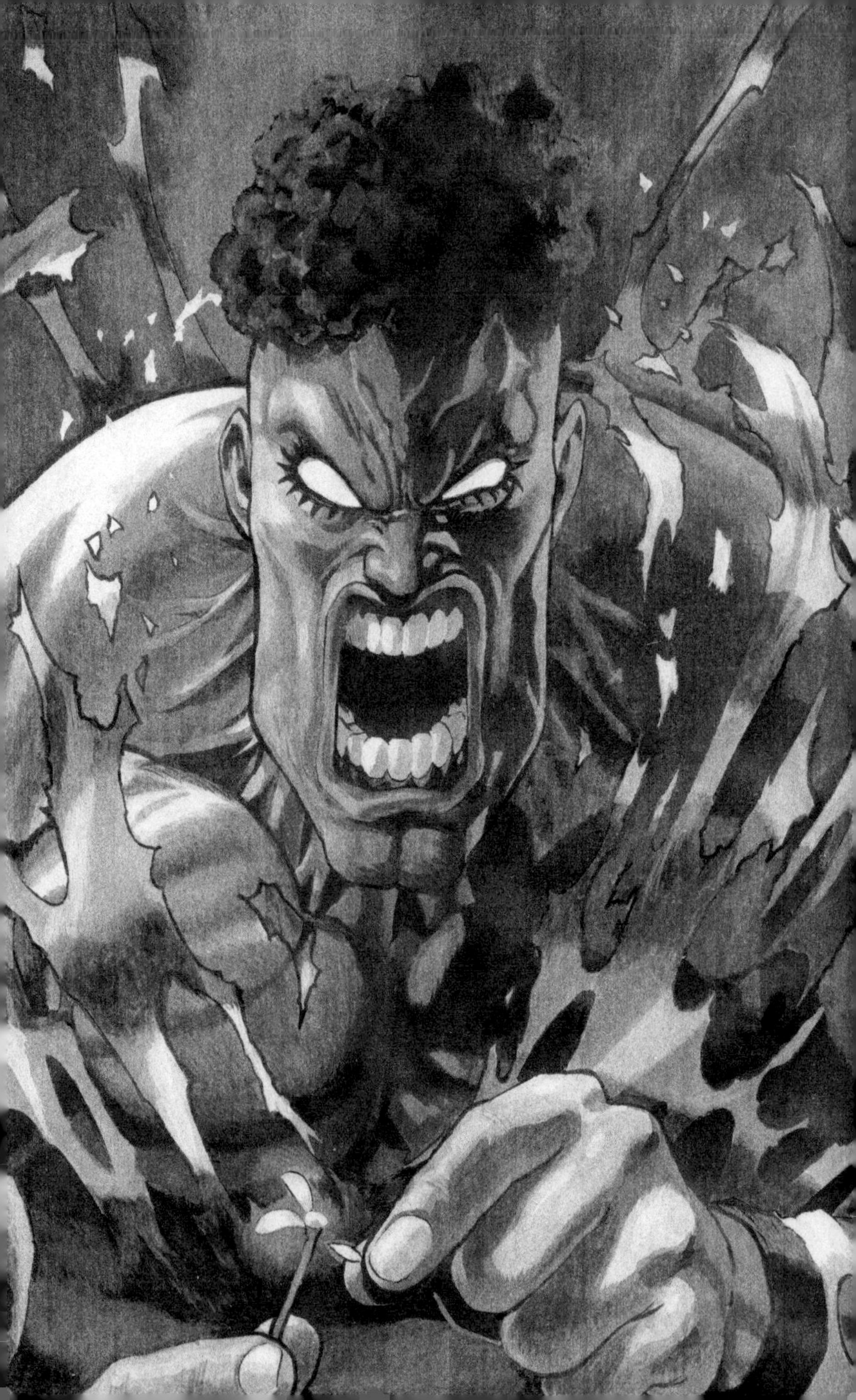

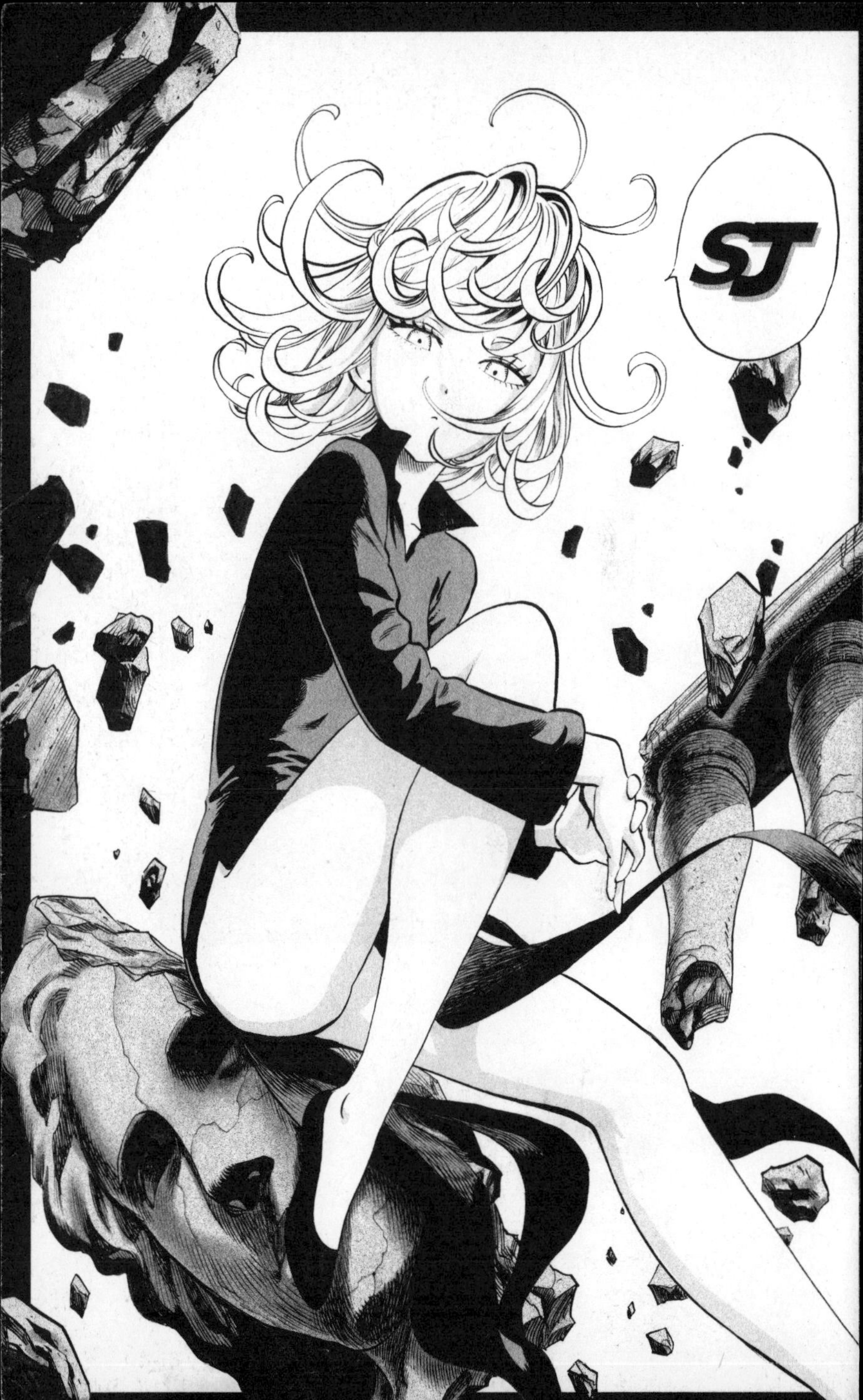
SJ

END NOTES

PAGE 188:

Saitama's shirt says "soy sauce."

ONE-PUNCH MAN
VOLUME 6
SHONEN JUMP MANGA EDITION

STORY BY | ONE
ART BY | YUSUKE MURATA

TRANSLATION | JOHN WERRY
TOUCH-UP ART AND LETTERING | JAMES GAUBATZ
DESIGN | FAWN LAU
SHONEN JUMP SERIES EDITOR | JOHN BAE
GRAPHIC NOVEL EDITOR | JENNIFER LEBLANC

ONE-PUNCH MAN © 2012 by ONE, Yusuke Murata
All rights reserved
First published in Japan in 2012 by SHUEISHA Inc., Tokyo.
English translation rights arranged by SHUEISHA Inc.

The stories, characters and incidents mentioned in this
publication are entirely fictional.

Printed in the U.S.A.

Published by VIZ Media, LLC
P.O. Box 77010
San Francisco, CA 94107

10 9 8 7 6 5 4 3 2 1
First printing, May 2016

www.viz.com

www.shonenjump.com

★EYESHIELD 21

STORY BY RIICHIRO INAGAKI
ART BY YUSUKE MURATA

From the artist of *One-Punch Man!*

Wimpy Sena Kobayakawa has been running away from bullies all his life. But when the football gear comes on, things change—Sena's speed and uncanny ability to elude big bullies just might give him what it takes to become a great high school football hero! Catch all the bone-crushing action and slapstick comedy of Japan's hottest football manga!

DEATH NOTE
デスノート

How to Use It

1. The human whose name is written in this note shall die.

Light Yagami is an ace student with great prospects—and he's bored out of his mind. But all that changes when he finds the Death Note, a notebook dropped by a rogue Shinigami death god. Any human whose name is written in the notebook dies, and now Light has vowed to use the power of the Death Note to rid the world of evil. But when criminals begin dropping dead, the authorities send the legendary detective L to track down the killer. With L hot on his heels, will Light lose sight of his noble goal...or his life?

All **12 volumes** of the legendary manga series are available now wherever manga is sold.

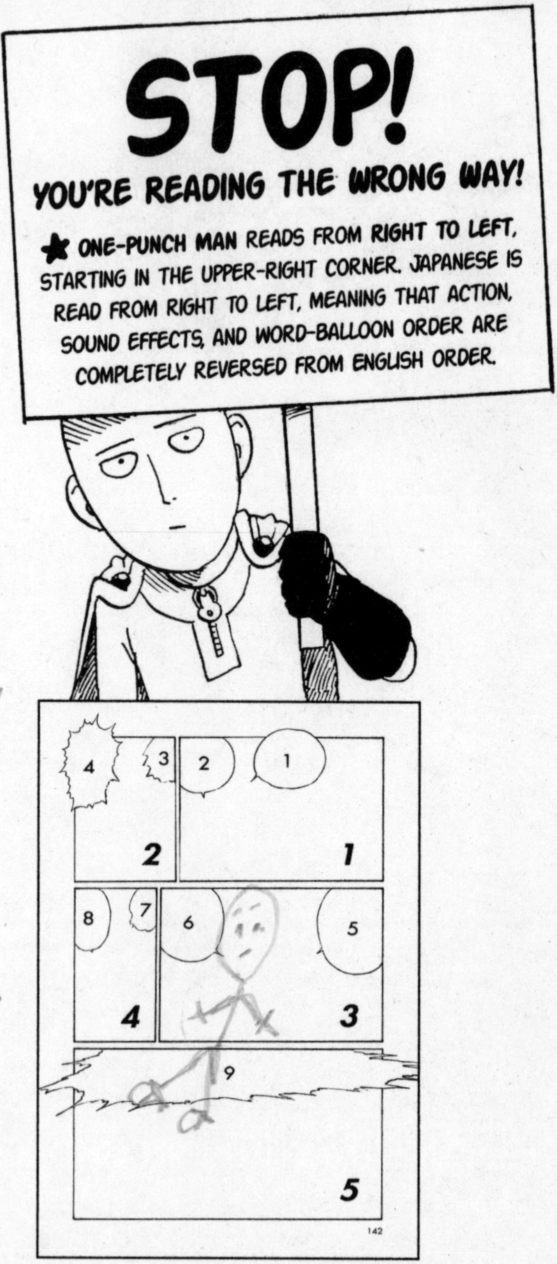
STOP!
YOU'RE READING THE WRONG WAY!
★ ONE-PUNCH MAN READS FROM RIGHT TO LEFT, STARTING IN THE UPPER-RIGHT CORNER. JAPANESE IS READ FROM RIGHT TO LEFT, MEANING THAT ACTION, SOUND EFFECTS, AND WORD-BALLOON ORDER ARE COMPLETELY REVERSED FROM ENGLISH ORDER.

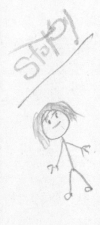